NEW FRENCH SELF TAUGHT

THE LANGUAGE SERIES

New French Self Taught
New German Self Taught
New Italian Self Taught
New Russian Self Taught
New Spanish Self Taught

THE QUICK, PRACTICAL WAY TO

READING • WRITING • SPEAKING • UNDERSTANDING

NEW FRENCH SELF TAUGHT

Revised by

FRÉDÉRIC ERNST, Emeritus Professor

New York University

With Pronunciation and Phonetics by

PROFESSOR DORA BASHOUR

Hunter College

A Funk & Wagnalls Book

Published by Thomas Y. Crowell

New York

NEW FRENCH SELF TAUGHT
Revised

Based on The Language Phone Method of Practical Linguistry. The French Language, copyright, 1945. *New French Self Taught,* copyright, 1952, by Funk & Wagnalls Company.

Library of Congress Catalog Card No. 58-9846

81 10 9 8 7 6 5 4

Printed in the United States of America

CONTENTS

FOREWORD

In the present revision, corrections and changes have been made throughout. The grammatical section has been simplified and adapted to present American methods; outmoded expressions have been brought up to date. A completely new introduction to French pronunciation makes use of the International Phonetic Alphabet which is now found in practically all standard French-English dictionaries. These phonetic symbols are also used throughout the new edition to indicate the pronunciation of many words and expressions. This important innovation is the work of a phonetics specialist, Professor Dora Bashour of Hunter College of the City of New York.

This new approach to pronunciation, together with the careful study of the revised text, should give excellent results. The use of the set of Language Phone Method recordings, made by native-born speakers, will impart to the learner the authentic sounds of the French language.

Frédéric Ernst

Emeritus Professor of French
New York University

The Method Explained

EVERY man and woman of intelligence realizes the imperative need of having command of a foreign language. The realization becomes more acute day by day as the fact is borne in on us that what once were known, in the old-fashioned phrase, as the "ends of the earth" are now, so to speak, practically our front lawn. Traveling by airplane we reach the remotest regions in flashes of time. By radio we know hour by hour what farthest distant peoples have on their minds and on their tongues. So it becomes increasingly necessary that we be able to tell them in their own language what we think and what we want to do.

Whether in professional, diplomatic, social, or commercial life, a sound and sure knowledge of our fellow man's language is the great essential of understanding among men and nations of the world.

The method used in this book, which is labeled "The Language Phone Method," is not new and has been successfully followed by thousands of students. By experiment and research, it was discovered many years ago that a thorough and workable command of a foreign language is not learned by long and arduous memorization of the grammatical rules of a language. Modern educational science now follows the far more efficient method that is presented in these pages. It is the most rational and simple method ever devised for learning a foreign language.

THE PRACTICAL MASTERY OF FOREIGN LANGUAGES

To think in a language not your mother tongue means that you will express yourself with sympathetic understanding of the people who speak that language. It means that you can converse easily and naturally as a good neighbor and a good friend. It is the great achievement of the method in this book that it enables its users easily and speedily to speak a foreign language just as fluently as their own. In doing this the student becomes accustomed to thinking in that language as well.

LANGUAGE AND GRAMMAR

are in no sense synonymous, although some school methods might lead us to suppose so.

Grammar is the science of language and, while necessary and desirable, is not so important as the ability to speak the language itself. Can anyone doubt this? Consider the majority of people you meet. Listen to their speech and examine it. Do they know the rules of English grammar? Do not even the very young children of educated persons express themselves correctly without ever having studied a single line of grammatical definitions? Yet,

THE STUDY OF GRAMMAR IS MADE EASY

"but it must be taught," as was said long ago by the great Erasmus, "at the proper time and kept within proper limits."

Colloquial mastery must precede it. Grammar will not then confuse, but will assist the pupil. It will cease to be a drudgery and will become a plain and simple explanation of forms and idioms already learned. It will no longer be an uncertain foundation, but will cap the edifice that has been reared by practical linguistic exercises. This is the true purpose of grammar, and in this sense it is taught throughout this book. A celebrated explorer and the master of many languages once wrote: "The only correct and scientific method by which a foreign language can be learned is to adopt

NATURE'S OWN WAY

by which all persons, whether children or adults, educated or otherwise, rapidly and correctly acquire the language which they constantly hear and which they are instinctively impelled to imitate when living in a foreign country."

It has often been observed that foreigners in the United States learn English seemingly with ease and surely with rapidity. Many of them know nothing of the principles of grammar. Some of them may be too young or may lack sufficient education to be able to read or write their native language. Despite such handicaps they master English sufficiently well within a few months to be able to make themselves understood. The quality of the English they acquire depends greatly on the kind of people they associate with. Judging by the facility with which foreigners in this country acquire English, it becomes obvious that when Americans live in a foreign country they must find some system which will enable them to obtain command of the language of that country in this same manner.

WHAT IS THE SYSTEM WHICH WE INSTINCTIVELY FOLLOW WHEN LIVING IN A FOREIGN COUNTRY?

At first the mind is confused by the multiplicity of foreign sounds heard. We try to grasp the ideas expressed in the strange tongue, and failing to do so we naturally are bewildered.

This state of mental confusion generally passes in about three or four weeks. The ear has become accustomed to some of these sounds and instinctively we begin to imitate the PHRASES we have heard most frequently pronounced by the persons surrounding us, and which, at the same time, are most necessary to our wants.

Now, what is our greatest necessity? Which of the needs of humanity is of paramount importance to young and old alike? It is nourishment—eating and drinking.

Consequently, the first sentences usually mastered are such as these: "*Please give me something to eat,*" or "*Please bring me the menu,*" or "*Please let me have a steak and some potatoes.*"

Such sentences are necessary to everyone; and it may be remarked that nature, through the mastery of these first simple sentences, points out

THE TRUE AND ONLY WAY

in which languages can be learned.

It is THROUGH SENTENCES, *and never through single, isolated words.* The verbs are the soul and backbone of all speech, and it is only by and through the proper study of verbs that mastery of a language can be attained.

To return to the sentence: "*Please bring me the menu.*" Not knowing any other expression, you cling to these words and use them again and again for your various needs.

For instance, when you want matches, or an umbrella, or some towels, instead of saying to the attendant: "*Please bring me the menu,*" you will point to the object and say to him: "*Please bring me* —— ."

Consider here the simplicity of this mode of teaching. By mastering this first little phrase, you have been furnished with a "sentence-mold" by the use of which hundreds of correct sentences may be composed.

The attendant, understanding your abbreviated phrase and gesture, "*Please bring me* ——," will give you the words "*matches,*" "*umbrella,*" or "*some towels*" in the language of the country in which you are living. You repeat these new words over and over again until they come quite naturally to you. In this way you go on from day to day, in fact from hour to hour, until after a few months you are able to express yourself readily and fluently. This is the process by which sounds become language. This is the mode in which any foreign language is learned when we live in a foreign country.

For those studying a foreign language here at home, it is necessary to use a text book containing practical idiomatic speech.

AN INDISPENSABLE VADE-MECUM

Language is divided into the Language of Literature and the Language of Every-day Life.

What part of English is used by the majority of people? The language of literature or the expressions of common life? What do our children speak when they enter school and receive their first lessons in spelling and reading? *The language of every-day life.* They understand and MUST be able to understand and follow their teachers before they can proceed to the study of English grammar. They MUST know common, every-day English before they can comprehend and appreciate the beauties of Shakespeare, Milton, and Tennyson.

Throughout this book the aim has been to give nothing but practical phrases and sentences which are used in the ordinary transactions of life. The proper selection of the vocabulary of practical life is the first distinguishing feature of the method according to which the lessons that follow have been prepared. Highly important as this part of the method is, it is a mere detail of the whole plan. The student must not overlook the fact that

DISCONNECTED, ISOLATED WORDS ARE NOT LANGUAGE

A person might learn a whole dictionary by heart and yet not be able to converse. As long as a child can use single words only, he cannot carry on a conversation. This book is based on the well tested theory that instead of beginning studies with little bits of baby sentences that no adult was ever known to use, the start should be made with connected, rational sentences, such as are employed in every-day language. Also, instead of learning phrases—the construction of which is the same as that of our native tongue—the student, from the beginning, should learn idiomatic sentences, the formation of which is utterly different from our mode of speaking. We must learn

TO THINK IN THE FOREIGN LANGUAGE ITSELF

No one can speak a foreign tongue properly who does not think in it. This is so old a maxim no one can doubt it. Yet the difficulty of learning to think in a foreign language seems at first insurmountable.

Is it possible to learn to think in a foreign language without actually living in the country of that language? Of course when we live in a foreign country and hear nothing but the foreign vernacular, it is easy to understand how we acquire the power of thinking in that foreign language.

But how can we hope to obtain the same results here in the United States where we cannot always associate with foreigners, where we speak nothing but English and think in English only, where the cares and duties of the day continually crowd in upon us, and where the little of a foreign language we learn today is almost forgotten by tomorrow? With all these drawbacks and disadvantages how can we learn to think in a foreign tongue?

No adult can learn as a child learns. In mastering its own tongue, the child reaches not only the power of expression but also the ability to think. From the perception of external facts he proceeds to mental conceptions. Each new word is a discovery to him. Each sound reveals to him a new world. Language is the basis of the child's whole mental development and underlies the acquisition of all his knowledge.

The adult, on the other hand, has passed beyond these preliminary stages. His intellect has been developed and trained. His memory is not nearly so fresh and retentive as that of an untutored child. He can already express his thoughts in one language, and in studying other tongues he aims solely at the acquirement of a new vehicle of sounds which will enable him to convey to natives of other countries the thoughts he expresses at home.

What is the meaning of the phrase, "to learn a foreign language"? It means to translate our thoughts into words and to express them in the foreign tongue. It must be accomplished by a sort of mental reconstruction. Life's scenes have to be represented anew in strange sounds which, constantly repeated, will become second nature to us. Again and again we have to *hear* and *repeat* these sounds. Again and again we must apply them until at last they are as familiar to us as the sounds of our native speech. The learner can, of course, *repeat* aloud over and over again and gain a great deal in this way. It is a valuable adjunct to this book to have also the set of Language Phone Method recordings, made by native-born speakers of the language that is being studied. This way the beginner can *hear* the language, properly pronounced, as often as he wishes.

Then there will no longer be talk of translation from one language into another. The words will have become so deeply impressed upon our memory that we shall utter them as unconsciously as we speak our mother tongue.

Language appeals, at first at least, chiefly to the *ear*, *tongue*, and *memory*, but though our intellect superintends the whole initiatory process, it cannot come into real action until the foreign sounds come just as unconsciously to us as the sounds of our mother tongue.

Remember also—the ear is the natural organ of language. If you desire to speak in a foreign language, listen to foreign speech and imitate what you have heard until the habit becomes second nature to you. This is The Method of Nature and this is

THE SECRET OF MASTERING A LANGUAGE

Thousands of persons have been successfully instructed by this method. Pupils as well as teachers of languages have testified to the splendid results that have been achieved by following this system. In the first place, all sentences are practical phrases based on the actual occurrences of every-day life.

After a few preliminary exercises, an advance is made with phrases that refer to speaking and understanding a language. Thereafter, as an introduction to life in a foreign land, the student continues his studies by entering a store to make some purchases. The next lesson takes him to the railway station. He buys railway tickets, checks his baggage, boards the train, arrives at his destination, takes a taxicab, drives to his hotel, engages a room, goes to the dining-room, gives his order to the waiter, eats his meal, and at the end of the day retires to his room.

Surely these are actual scenes in every-day life and occurrences with which every adult is familiar.

When such lessons have been thoroughly mastered, the next advance is to conversational exercises. English is now discarded and the foreign language alone is used. No new words are introduced and

EVERY SENTENCE IS BASED ON EXERCISES PREVIOUSLY LEARNED

By a conscientious use of this book the person who works with it will gain a mastery of foreign words, phrases, and sentences. Each phrase gradually presents conceptions and facts as clearly to the student as the English equivalents. Translation becomes unnecessary. The student's life is thus lived over again in the foreign language. His individuality is reconstructed and in this way the foreign language becomes in reality a "tongue" to the learner.

The study of it is no longer a laborious translation. The words cease to be meaningless printed signs and are immediately associated with living facts. The student no longer doubts and hesitates, but expresses his ideas as readily in the foreign language as in his own. He has acquired a new instrument of thought and action in his career. He is looking down a new vista of progress and achievement.

DIRECTIONS FOR PRIVATE STUDY

It has been made clear in the preceding pages that this book places its principal emphasis on the language of practical, every-day life. The words which the beginner is about to learn are therefore divided into the *necessary* and the *less necessary* ones. This is a simple, common-sense division. The necessary words, the expressions all men use and understand, must be mastered first.

How the necessary words were chosen can easily be illustrated. Consider, for instance, the three words, *money*, *fan*, and *chisel*. How do they compare with each other?

The word *money* is so important that no one can get on without the use of it—and, we might add, the substance of it. Everybody has to employ it and everyone must consequently know it. It is plainly a necessary word.

Fan belongs to a different class of expressions. Though no doubt necessary, the word, as well as the object itself, is by no means so imperatively necessary as *money;* it therefore belongs to another class, namely, the class of words which, though they ought to be learned, may be learned later.

Finally, there is the word *chisel.* One might live for twenty years in a foreign country without having any use for this word which to a carpenter is an absolute necessity. For the ordinary student the word belongs in the class of scarcely necessary expressions.

The user of this book must realize that what he is learning is basic. Every effort has been made to give only phrases and sentences used in the common transactions of life. The selection of the words used in this book is based on wide scientific research.

As the reader proceeds with the study of these pages and begins to acquire a vocabulary of essential terms, he should stop from time to time to test the various uses he can make of the words he has at his command. Lepsius, the famous Egyptologist, limited the number of words necessary for conversation on all general subjects to six hundred. Ogden and Richards' vocabulary for basic English is only eight hundred words. As his vocabulary grows from page to page, the student of this book will be surprised at the number of ideas it will enable him to express.

The learner may be puzzled at first by the long and sometimes complex sentences to which he is introduced, but he will soon realize that these are sentences we are in the habit of using in ordinary circumstances. This book rightly places an emphasis on idiomatic sentences constructed in a manner utterly foreign to our way of speaking.

The student must strive constantly to free himself from the habit of thinking in English. He must master each idiom to which he is introduced. These peculiar forms of expression common to every language are the lifeblood of language.

The complete mastery of a foreign tongue is best attained by training the eye, ear, tongue, and memory at one and the same time: the ear by giving the sound and intonation of every word and phrase; the eye by seeing the spelling; the tongue by pronouncing the words; and the memory by the continuous repetition of words and phrases so that the student no longer thinks *about* them but *in* them.

The person studying with this book should practice aloud as much as possible, for it is helpful to exercise the tongue and the ear at the same time. When he has read the English equivalent of a sentence and knows its meaning perfectly, he should read and pronounce the foreign sentence again and again until the words have become associated with their meaning. As stated earlier, it is also very helpful to have a set of the Language Phone Method recordings, in order to *hear* the language spoken with exact native pronunciation.

After the main sentence has been mastered, the student will proceed with the variations given in the exercises. Study should be pursued without undue haste. One should be sure that he has thorough mastery of each section he studies before he proceeds to the next. In a few days the phrases will become second nature to the learner. He will no longer think *about* them but *in* them. He will begin to think in the foreign language itself, and will be able to form hundreds of new phrases by inserting a new noun here, a verb there, an adverb in another place, and so on.

The study of grammar is carried on with each sentence. The footnotes, which explain the grammatical peculiarities, *must* therefore be carefully studied. A full grammatical outline is found at the end of the book.

The vocabularies included in the book have been especially designed to increase the student's knowledge of *necessary* words and phrases.

The proverbs that have been included contain some of the basic folk wisdom common to so many nations. To learn the foreign equivalents of proverbs familiar to all of us is an easy and effective method of fixing words and phrases in the memory.

NEW FRENCH SELF TAUGHT

PART ONE

CONTENTS

PHONETIC SYMBOLS

In this text, pronunciation is indicated by the phonetic symbols used by the International Phonetic Association.[1]

Each phonetic symbol represents only one sound.

A single letter of the alphabet may have several different pronunciations. For example, *s* in phra*s*e is pronounced [z], whereas *s* in *s*imple is pronounced [s].

Several letters of the alphabet combined frequently represent only one sound, but a single sound can never be represented by more than one symbol. For example, *beau* has four letters but only two sounds, and will therefore be represented by only two symbols: [bo].

Sometimes there are several ways of spelling the same sound, but this sound is always represented by the same symbol.

Thus in [bo], [o] is spelled eau: beau
in [po:z], [o] is spelled o: pose
in [fo], [o] is spelled au: faux

[1] *Cassell's New French Dictionary* uses these same symbols to indicate the pronunciation of each word.

PRONUNCIATION

VOWELS

General Instructions

Pronounce the English word *I* very slowly. You will notice that you are really saying a series of vowel sounds, starting with *a* as in f*a*ther, with the mouth wide open, and ending with *i* as in mach*i*ne, with the mouth almost closed. This composite sound is called a diphthong. The five basic English vowels, a, e, i, o, u, are diphthongs. No French vowel is ever pronounced as a diphthong. In pronouncing the English word *I* the open mouth produced an *a* as in f*a*ther, the closed mouth produced an *i* as in mach*i*ne. Each position of the mouth produces a different sound. Therefore, in pronouncing French vowels, be sure to keep tongue, lips and jaw tense and firm in exactly the same position throughout the entire sound. Otherwise you will produce a diphthong.

All French sounds are produced with the tongue convex (⌒), never concave (‿). The tip of the tongue must not be permitted to turn up and back.

Vowel Sounds

A. There are sixteen vowel sounds in French. Four of these are nasal vowels.

Symbol	*Tongue*
i	Very high in front of mouth, tip pressed firmly against lower teeth
e	Still very high in front, but not quite so high as for [i]. Tip still firmly against lower teeth
ɛ	A little lower in front than for [e]. Tip still against lower teeth
a	Only slightly raised, with tip still against lower teeth
ɑ	Lowered, with tip still against lower teeth
ɔ	Slightly raised toward back of mouth. Tip no longer touches teeth
o	A little higher in back of mouth than for [ɔ]. Tip a little further from teeth
u	Very high and pulled well back in the mouth
y	As for [i]
ø	As for [e]
œ	As for [ɛ]
ə[2]	Between [ø] and [œ]

[2] This sound is not to be pronounced by itself. It is heard only when surrounded by consonants.

Lips	*Jaw*	*Examples*
Corners drawn well back	Almost closed	i si vi zit si vil
Corners drawn back a little less than for [i]	Slightly more open than for [i]	si te e te i de
Corners drawn back a little less than for [e]	More open than for [e]	la bɛl ɛl mɛ:m[3] vi lɛ:n
Corners drawn back a little less than for [ɛ]	Moderately open	ma dam sa lad la bal
Relaxed	Well open	a ʃɑ la bɑ nɛs pɑ
Rounded and slightly protruding	A little less open than for [ɑ]	pɔm bɔ nɔm pɔ sɪbl
Quite far forward and tightly pursed	Very much more closed than for [ɔ]	ɔ po:z ʃa po o si
As far forward as possible	Almost closed	blu:z ʒa lu gu te
As for [u]	As for [i]	mi nyt py ni my zik
As for [o]	As for [e]	i dø:z e mø de ʒø ne
As for [ɔ]	As for [ɛ]	ɛl vœ:l il pœ:v i mœbl
Between [ø] and [œ]	Between [e] and [ɛ]	ʒən se pɑ kɛl kə za mi ta blə do:t

[3] Dots (:) after a vowel sound indicate that it is prolonged.

B. Nasal vowels.

There are no nasal vowels in English.

Open your mouth wide before a mirror. In the back of the mouth you will notice a small tongue-like extension of the soft palate, pointing downward. This is the uvula. It can be raised or lowered easily.

To produce a nasal vowel, lower the uvula just enough to allow a large part of the air rising from the throat to be expelled through the nose. Be sure that the back of the tongue does not touch the roof of the mouth, for this will add to the nasal vowel an English consonant sound (*ng*).

Symbol	*Tongue, Lips*	*Jaw*	*To Nasalize*	*Examples*
ɑ̃	As for [ɑ]	A little more open than for [ɑ]	Lower the uvula and force the air through the nose	ma mɑ̃ ɑ̃ fɑ̃ i mɑ̃:s
ɔ̃	As for [ɔ]	A little more closed than for [ɔ]		bɔ̃ bɔ̃ dɑ̃ sɔ̃ a lɔ̃
ɛ̃	As for [ɛ]	A little more open than for [ɛ]		mɛt sɛ̃ ɑ̃ fɛ̃ la mɛ̃
œ̃	As for [œ]	A little more open than for [œ]		œ̃ bɛ̃ œ̃ sɛ̃ kɛl kœ̃

SEMI-VOWELS

When the sounds [u, i, y] are pronounced immediately before any vowel, a new sound is produced which is halfway between a consonant and a vowel. This is called a semi-vowel. The semi-vowel and the accompanying vowel are always in the same syllable.[4]

---

[4] A semi-vowel cannot be pronounced by itself. It must be accompanied by a vowel.

Symbol	Derived from	Examples	
w	u	ui *becomes* wi	lwi:z (*not* lu i:z)
		uɛ *becomes* wɛ	swɛ te (*not* su ɛ te)
j	i	ia *becomes* ja	pja no (*not* pi a no)
		iɔ̃ *becomes* jɔ̃	de fi ni sjɔ̃ (*not* de fi ni si ɔ̃)
ɥ[5]	y	yi *becomes* ɥi	kɥi zin (*not* ky i zi:n; *not* kwi zi:n)
			lɛ̃ gɥist (*not* lɛ̃ gy ist; *not* lɛ̃ gwist)
		ye *becomes* ɥe	si tɥe (*not* si ty e; *not* si twe)
			a bi tɥe (*not* a bi ty e; *not* a bi twe)

CONSONANTS

General Instructions

French consonants, like French vowels, are pronounced with the tongue convex, the tip pointed downward.[6]

Try to pronounce each consonant with the tongue in the same position as the accompanying vowel. Do not permit the consonant to spoil the purity of the vowel.

The final consonant sound of a group of syllables must be very clearly and neatly articulated.

A. Breath consonants: In pronouncing consonants like [p, t, k], use as little breath as possible, saying the consonant and the accompanying vowel almost simultaneously, without any breath between them.
Examples: pa pa, ta pe, pa kɛ.

B. Dental consonants: [l, n, t, d, s, z] are produced with the tongue firmly against the upper teeth, the tip of the tongue pointing down towards the lower teeth. In English the tongue is concave, with the tip touching the upper gums.[6]
Examples: mad mwa zɛl, vi lɛ:n.

---

[5] Do not confuse with [w]. Be sure the tip of the tongue is firmly against the lower teeth as for [y].

[6] See page 3.

C. The Parisian [r]: This sound is pronounced by forcing the air between the back of the tongue and the back of the palate pressed firmly together. It resembles a dry gargling sound.[7] Be sure to keep the tip of the tongue lightly touching the lower teeth. If it curls up, you will probably pronounce an English *r*.[8] *Examples:* pa ri, mar sɛ:j, la frɑ̃:s.

D. Special consonants: The phonetic symbol for most consonants is the same as the corresponding small printed letter. Three consonant sounds have special symbols.

1. [ʃ] pronounced like *sh* in *she*.
   Examples: ʃɛ:z, aʃ te.
2. [ʒ] pronounced like *s* in plea*s*ure.
   Examples: a:ʒ, ʒa mɛ.
3. [ɲ]. Place the tip of the tongue against the lower teeth, pronounce [n] with the tongue touching the palate[9] as for [j]. The nearest English sound is [nj] as in onion. The French sound is like [nj] pronounced so close together that they form one sound.
   Examples: si ɲe, kɔ̃ pa ɲi, mɔ̃ taɲ.

SYLLABIFICATION

In English, most written letters are pronounced. French, on the other hand, is characterized by the fact that written letters are often silent.[10] It is particularly important to learn how to separate the letters of a French word into syllables, because the position of some letters in a syllable determines whether or not they are pronounced.

A single vowel sound, with or without accompanying consonants or semi-vowels, forms a syllable. Thus, in English, *I* is a syllable, *tie* is a syllable, so is *twin*. In French, [ɛ] is a syllable, so is [sɛ], so is [swɛt].

Each of the following groups of letters in French, with or without accompanying consonants or semi-vowels, forms just one syllable.

---

[7] There are regions in France where *r* is like a lightly trilled Italian or Spanish *r*.

[8] See page 3.

[9] Not the upper teeth.

[10] Silent letters are indicated in this introduction by a slanted line, as in *es̸t* and *comme̸*.

Spelling	*Pronunciation*[11]
ai	ɛ
au	o
eau	o
ei	ɛ
eu	œ
œu	œ
oi	wa
ou	u

Rules of Syllabification[12]

A. Whenever possible, a syllable starts with a consonant.

divisibilité—di vi si bi li té
inutile—i nu ti le[13]

B. Two consonants are generally separated.

partir—par tir
intacte—in tac te

1. However, r and l are combined with a preceding consonant to start the new syllable.

secrétaire—se cré tai re
probablement—pro ba ble ment

Exceptions: r, l are separated from a preceding r, l, n or m.

parlé—par lé
intelligent—in tel li gent
Henri—Hen ri

2. nn, mm, mn generally start the new syllable together.

immense—i mmen se
personne—per so nne
automne—au to mne

---

[11] This is the most frequent pronunciation. There are naturally some variants. These are indicated in the Reference List of Spellings, page 14.

[12] We are referring here to letters of the alphabet, not to their pronunciation.

[13] The method of syllabification used here will sometimes not correspond to the hyphenating method based on etymology. We are concerned only with pronunciation, not with meaning: inutile, from the point of view of meaning ("not useful") would be hyphenated in-u-ti-le.

3. ss preceded by the prefix re generally start the new syllable together.

   ressource—re ssour ce
   ressentiment—re ssen ti ment

4. ch, gn, ph, th represent only one consonant sound, so they must not be separated.

   achat—a chat
   signature—si gna tu re

C. When there are more than two consonants, separate the first consonant from the rest.

   surprendre—sur pren dre
   semblant—sem blant
   instructif—in struc tif

D. The letters i, u, and ou are in the same syllable as a vowel which follows.

   nation—na tion
   cuisinière—cui si niè re
   avoué—a voué

Spelling, Syllabification, and Pronunciation

A. A consonant or a group of consonants at the end of a *word* are generally silent.

   résultat—ré sul tat̸—pronounced re zyl tɑ
   palais—pa lais̸—pronounced pa lɛ
   portant—por tan̸t̸—pronounced pɔr tɑ̃

   Exceptions: c, f, l, r at the end of a word are frequently pronounced as in lac, actif, bal, amer—pronounced lak, ak tif, bal, a mɛ:r.

B. When the letter e (without any accent marks) is the last letter of a *syllable*, it is called a *mute e* and is generally silent.

   avenir—a ve̸ nir—pronounced av ni:r
   faire—fai re̸—pronounced fɛ:r

   Sometimes, however, there are so many consonants surrounding the mute e that it would be difficult to omit it altogether without omitting one of the consonants too. In that case, it is pronounced [ə].

   bretonne—br(e) to nne̸—pronounced brə tɔn
   je ne vois pas—j(e) ne̸ vois̸ pas̸—pronounced ʒən vwɑ pɑ

C. In all other positions the letter e (without any accent marks) is pronounced [ɛ].

respect—res pec̸t̸—pronounced rɛs pɛ

D. When n or m is the last letter of the *syllable*, it is silent.

menton—men̸ ton̸—pronounced mã tõ
importe—im̸ por te̸—pronounced ɛ̃ pɔrt

E. Whenever n or m is silent, no matter what the reason, the preceding vowel is nasalized.

menton—men̸ ton̸—pronounced mã tõ
important—im̸ por tan̸t̸—pronounced ɛ̃ pɔr tã

F. The letter h is silent.

Homme—h̸o mme̸—pronounced ɔm

G. Double consonants are generally pronounced like a single consonant.

confesseur—con̸ fes seur—pronounced kõ fɛ sœ:r
immense—i mmen̸ se̸—pronounced i mã:s

LA LIAISON

Just as in separating the letters of a word into syllables we start each syllable with a consonant *letter*, so in pronouncing a series of syllables we start each syllable with a consonant *sound*. This is so basic to the flow of the music of a French phrase, that when a word starts with a vowel sound, if a consonant sound is available at the end of the preceding word, it is borrowed for the beginning of the next one. Comme̸ il es̸t̸ gran̸d̸ is not pronounced kɔm il ɛ grã, but comme̸⁀il⁀es̸t̸ gran̸d̸[14]—kɔm⁀il⁀ɛ grã (really pronounced kɔ mi lɛ grã).

The need for starting syllables with a consonant sound is so marked that even a final consonant that is normally silent is very frequently pronounced at the beginning of the following word if it starts with a vowel.

Do not say Quan̸d̸ il es̸t̸ arrivé, j'étais̸ très̸ occupé.
Kã il ɛ a ri ve, ʒe tɛ trɛ ɔ ky pe.

Say Quan̸d̸‿il⁀es̸t‿arrivé, j'étais̸ très‿occupé.
Kã til⁀ɛ ta ri ve, ʒe tɛ trɛ zɔ ky pe.

[14] In this chapter as elsewhere, the linking of the final consonant sound of a word to the initial vowel of the next word is indicated by ⁀.

This pronunciation of a normally silent final consonant before the initial vowel of the next word is called la liaison (la ljɛ zɔ̃).[15]

In liaison d is pronounced [t]—prend‿il prɑ̃ til.
g is pronounced [k]—sang‿impur sɑ̃ kɛ̃ py:r.
s is pronounced [z]—pas‿ici pɑ zi si.
x is pronounced [z]—deux‿ans dø zɑ̃.

The liaison is permissible only when the two words to be linked are in the same thought group and are closely connected grammatically. However, some people make the liaison more often than others, and on the whole it is less frequent in familiar conversation than in formal speech. Take note of the phonetic transcription in your text and listen carefully to French recordings. You will get the "feel" of the liaison as your fluency increases.

CONNECTED SPEECH

A French thought group is pronounced as a single unit composed of a series of syllables, and not as a series of words.

The following sentence contains nine words, but only three thought groups.

Je voudrais partir | par le premier train | pour Paris.
ʒə vu drɛ par ti:r | par lə prə mje trɛ̃ | pur pa ri
(*not* ʒə vudrɛ partir par lə prɔmje trɛ̃ pur pari).

In pronouncing a series of French syllables, whether they form one word or a group of words, it is important to articulate clearly and accurately, saying exactly the vowel that the spelling requires, and no other. This is sometimes difficult for the English-speaking student, for in English, an unstressed vowel frequently deteriorates and becomes a mute [ə]: The English word attention is pronounced [ə tɛn ʃən]. A Frenchman with a heavy accent would pronounce it [a tɛn ʃɔn]. Ambassador is pronounced [am ba sə dər]. The same Frenchman would pronounce it [am ba sa dɔr].

Pronounce la salle d'attente—la sal da tɑ̃:t (*not* lə sal də tɑ̃:t).

Pronounce divisibilité—di vi zi bi li te (*not* də viz ə bil ə te).

[15] The liaison is indicated by ‿.

STRESS

In English, it is difficult for a foreigner to determine which syllables to stress. We say em'phatic,[16] but 'emphasis; re'fer, re'ferral, but 'reference. In French, all syllables are of equal importance and should be pronounced with equal intensity.

Pronounce the following sentences without stress:

Que voulez̸-vous̸ faire̸? Kə vu le vu fɛ:r?
Il⁀es̸t̸ ve̸nu me̸ voir. il⁀ɛ vnym vwa:r.

In emphatic speech, the last syllable of the last word of a thought group is stressed.

Mais̸ pourquoi | ne voulez̸-vous̸ pas̸ | me le̸ donner̸?
mɛ·pur 'kwa | nə vu le vu 'pɑ | məl dɔ 'ne?
C'es̸t̸ parce̸ que j'en̸‿ai besoin̸ | moi-même̸.
sɛ par skə ʒɑ̃ ne bə 'zwɛ̃ | mwa 'mɛ:m.

INTONATION

There is no resemblance between English and French intonation. A good French pronunciation can be badly marred by English intonations. Listen carefully to French records. You will notice that French intonation is generally a rising intonation. The voice rises smoothly throughout each thought group and in ordinary speech usually falls at the end of a sentence. Naturally, the greater the emphasis or the emotion, the higher the pitch of the stressed syllable. At such times the sentence may end on a high note instead of falling in the usual manner.

When practicing pronunciation or in working with your French records, try to imitate not only the pronunciation of individual syllables, but also the melody and rhythm of each thought group considered as a unit, and finally, the music of the entire sentence.

---

[16] In this chapter as elsewhere, ' is used before the stressed syllable.

REFERENCE LIST OF SPELLINGS, WITH THEIR REGULAR PRONUNCIATION[17]

Spelling	*Pronunciation*	*Examples*
a	a	place—pla ce̸—plas
a before a silent final consonant	ɑ	achat—a chat̸—a ʃɑ
à	a	là-bas—là bas̸—la bɑ
â	ɑ	âme—â me̸—ɑ:m
ai last letters of a *word*	e	serai—se̸ rai—sre
ai elsewhere	ɛ	grammaire—gra mmai re̸—gra mɛ:r
aim̸ } in the same ain̸ } syllable	ɛ̃	saint—sain̸t̸—sɛ̃
am̸ } in the same an̸ } syllable	ɑ̃	grande—gran̸ de̸—grɑ̃:d
au	o	autre—au tre̸—o:tr
b, bb	b	banane—ba na ne̸—ba nan
b before s	p	absent—ab sen̸t̸—ap sɑ̃
c, cc	k	fracas—fra cas̸—fra kɑ
c before e	s	lance—lan̸ ce̸—lɑ̃:s
cc before e	ks	accepte—ac cep te̸—ak sɛpt
c before i	s	civile—ci vi le̸—si vil
cc before i	ks	accident—ac ci den̸t̸—ak si dɑ̃
c before y	s	cynique—cy ni que̸—si nik
ç	s	français—fran̸ çais̸—frɑ̃ sɛ
ch	ʃ	achat—a chat̸—a ʃɑ
d, dd	d	madame—ma da me̸—ma dam
d in liaison	t	quand il parle—quan̸d‿il par le̸—kɑ̃‿til parl

[17] Irregularities will be treated as they occur. Watch for them carefully.

Spelling	*Pronunciation*	*Examples*
e last letter of a *syllable*	silent, or ə	serai—s~~e~~ rai—sre parlera—par le ra—par lə ra
e before mm	a	femme—fe mm~~e~~—fam
e before nn	ɛ	antenne—a~~n~~ tenn~~e~~—ã tɛn
e not last letter of a *syllable*	ɛ	secret—s~~e~~ cre~~t~~—skrɛ
é	e	dansé—da~~n~~ sé—dã se
è	ɛ	achète—a chè t~~e~~—a ʃɛ:t
ê	ɛ	rêverie—rê v~~e~~ ri ~~e~~—rɛ: vri
eau	o	beauté—beau té—bo te
ei	ɛ	veine—vei n~~e~~—vɛ:n
ei~~m~~, ei~~n~~ } in the same syllable	ɛ̃	déteint—dé tei~~nt~~—de tɛ̃
e~~m~~, e~~n~~ } in the same syllable	ɑ̃	entendre—e~~n~~ te~~n~~ dr~~e~~—ɑ̃ tɑ̃:dr
e~~n~~ last letters of a *word*	ɛ̃	lycéen—ly cé e~~n~~—li se ɛ̃
~~ent~~ verb ending	silent	ils désirent—il~~s~~ dé si r~~ent~~—il de zi:r
e~~r~~, last letters of a *word*	e	parler—par le~~r~~—par le
er, last letters of a few words	ɛ:r	cher—ʃɛ:r hiver—~~h~~i ver—i vɛ:r
~~es~~, verb ending	silent	tu parles—tu par l~~es~~—ty parl
~~es~~, plural ending	silent	trois livres—troi~~s~~ li vr~~es~~—trwɑ li:vr
e~~s~~, in monosyllables	e	me~~s~~—me
eu, last *sound* of a *word*	ø	dangereux—da~~n~~ g~~e~~ reu~~x~~—dã·ʒ rø
eu, before s	ø	dangereuse—da~~n~~ g~~e~~ reu s~~e~~—dã·ʒ rø:z
eu, before t	ø	feutre—feu tr~~e~~—fø:tr
eu, elsewhere	œ	empereur—e~~m~~ p~~e~~ reur—ã prœ:r

Spelling	*Pronunciation*	*Examples*
e~~z~~, last letters of a *word*	e	fermez—fer me~~z~~—fɛr me
f, ff	f	affaire—af fai r~~e~~—a fɛ:r
f in neuf, when linked	v	neuf ans—neuf‿a~~n~~~~s~~—nœ vɑ̃
g, gg	g	grandeur—gra~~n~~ deur—grɑ̃ dœ:r
g before e	ʒ	agent—a ge~~n~~~~t~~—a ʒɑ̃
gg before e	gʒ	suggéré—sug gé ré—syg ʒe re
g before i or y	ʒ	Égypte—é gyp t~~e~~—e ʒipt
g in liaison	k	sang impur—sa~~n~~g‿i~~m~~ pur—sɑ̃ k‿ɛ̃ py:r
gn	ɲ	signé—si gné—si ɲe
gu before e or i	g	guichet—gui che~~t~~—gi ʃɛ
~~h~~	silent[18]	haricot—~~h~~a ri co~~t~~—a ri ko
i	i	cheminée—ch~~e~~ mi n~~é~~~~e~~—ʃmi:ne
î	i	épître—é pî tr~~e~~—e pi:tr
i before a vowel	j	violet—vio le~~t~~—vjɔ lɛ
il at the end of a *word* after any vowel but o	j	travail—tra vail—tra va:j
ill after a vowel	j	travaillait—tra va illai~~t~~—tra va jɛ
ill after a consonant	ij	famille—fa mi ll~~e~~—fa mi:j
ill in a few words	il	ville—vi ll~~e~~—vil
i~~m~~, i~~n~~ } in the same syllable	ɛ̃	infinitif—i~~n~~ fi ni tif—ɛ̃ fi ni tif
j	ʒ	jamais—ja mai~~s~~—ʒa mɛ

[18] h is always silent. An initial h therefore leaves a vowel sound at the beginning of the word and we generally make the liaison with the final consonant of the preceding word: en‿~~h~~iver ɑ̃ ni vɛ:r. Sometimes, however, an initial h, though silent, prevents the liaison. This h is called "aspirated". Dictionaries and vocabularies indicate this type of h by placing a mark such as † before the word. For example †honte. Je n'ai pas honte j~~e~~ n'ai pa~~s~~ ho~~n~~ t~~e~~—ʒne pɑ ɔ̃:t (Do *not* say ʒne pɑ zɔ̃:t.)

Spelling	*Pronunciation*	*Examples*
k	k	képi—ké pi—ke pi
l, ll	l	embellir—em̸ bel lir—ã bɛ li:r
m, mm	m	comment—co mmen̸t̸—kɔ mã
mn	n	automne—au to m̸ne̸—o tɔ:n
n, nn	n	personne—per so nne̸—pɛr sɔ:n
o, before a final silent consonant	o	haricot—h̸a ri cot̸—a ri ko
o, before one s	o	arroser—ar ro ser̸—a ro ze
o, elsewhere	ɔ	forteresse—for te res se̸—fɔr tə rɛs
ô	o	hôte—h̸ô te̸—o:t
œu, last *sound* of a *word*	ø	nœud—nœud̸—nø
œu, elsewhere	œ	œuvre—œu vre̸—œ:vr
oi	wa	voilà—voi là—vwa la
oin̸ in the same syllable	wɛ̃	besoin—be soin̸—bə zwɛ̃
om̸, on̸ } in the same syllable	ɔ̃	chanson—chan̸ son̸—ʃã sɔ̃
ou	u	route—rou te̸—rut
ou, before a vowel	w	avouer—a vouer̸—a vwe
p, pp	p	apparent—ap pa rent̸—a pa rã
p, between two consonants	silent	compter—com̸ p̸ter̸—kɔ̃ te
ph	f	camphre—cam̸ phre̸—kã:fr
q	k	coq—kɔk
qu	k	question—ques tion̸—kɛs tjɔ̃
r, rr	r	guerre—guer re̸—gɛ:r
s, ss	s	sagesse—sa ges se̸—sa ʒɛs
s, between two vowels	z	caserne—sa ser ne̸—ka zɛ:rn
s, in liaison	z	pas ici—pas‿ici—pa‿zi si

Spelling	*Pronun-ciation*	*Examples*
t, tt	t	toilette—toi let te̸—twa lɛt
th	t	thèse—thè se̸—tɛ:z
t, before the *sound* j	s	initial—i ni tial—i ni sjal définition—dé fi ni tion̸—de fi ni sjɔ̃
t, before the *sound* j but after s	t	digestion—di ges tion̸—di ʒɛs tjɔ̃
u	y	punition—pu ni tion̸—py ni sjɔ̃
u, before a vowel	ɥ	intuition—in̸ tui tion̸—ɛ̃ tɥi sjɔ̃
v	v	arrivera—ar ri ve̸ ra—a ri vra
w	v	wagon—wa gon̸—va gɔ̃
x	ks	expert—ex per̸t̸—ɛk spɛ:r
x, before ce	k	exception—ex cep tion̸—ɛk sɛp sjɔ̃
x, before ci	k	exciter—ex ci ter̸—ɛk si te
x, before a vowel	gz or ks	examen—e xa men̸—ɛg za mɛ̃ fixer—fi xer̸—fik se
x, in liaison	z	deux amis—deux‿a mis̸—dø za mi
y	i	typique—ty pi que̸—ti pik
y, before a vowel	j	yeux—yeux̸—jø
y, after a vowel = ii		paysan—pai i san̸—pɛ i zɑ̃
y, between two vowels = ii		envoyez—en̸ voi iez̸—ɑ̃ vwa je
ym̸ } in the same yn̸ } syllable	ɛ̃	sympathie—sym̸ pa thi e̸—sɛ̃ pa ti
z	z	douzaine—dou zai ne̸—du zɛ:n

THE FRENCH ALPHABET

The French alphabet has 25 letters. W is used, but as a foreign letter only.

A	a	N	n
B	b	O	o
C	c	P	p
D	d	Q	q
E	e	R	r
F	f	S	s
G	g	T	t
H	h	U	u
I	i	V	v
J	j	X	x
K	k	Y	y
L	l	Z	z
M	m		

For alphabet sounds, examples and explanations, see pages 14 to 18.

PHRASE PRINCIPALE

Que voulez-vous faire ce matin? Je voudrais partir par le premier‿ avion pour Paris, mais, malheureusement, ceci est‿impossible, car j'attends un ami de la Nouvelle Orléans et dois rester à New York jusqu'à ce qu'il⁀arrive par l'autobus, par le train, ou par le bateau.

PRONONCIATION

Kə vu le vu fɛ:r sma tɛ̃? ʒə vu drɛ par ti:r par lə prə mje r‿a vjɔ̃ pur pa ri, mɛ, ma lø rø·z mɑ̃, sə si ɛ t‿ɛ̃ pɔ si:bl, kar ʒa tɑ̃ œ̃ n‿a mi d la nu vɛl⁀ɔr le ɑ̃ e dwa rɛs te a nœ jɔrk ʒys ka skil⁀a ri:v par lɔ tɔ bys, par lə trɛ̃, u par lə ba to.

Que voulez-vous faire ce matin?

Kə vu le vu fɛ:r s ma tɛ̃?

Que (kə)
voulez-vous (vu le vu)

faire (fɛ:r)
ce matin? (sma tɛ̃)

---

1. Que voulez-vous?
2. Que voulez-vous faire?
3. Que voulez-vous faire ce matin?
4. Que voulez-vous faire demain? (də mɛ̃)
5. Voulez-vous le[1] faire? (vu le vul fɛ:r)
6. Voulez-vous le faire demain?

---

[1] The *conjunctive personal pronouns*, me, thee, him, her, it, us, you, them, are placed *before* the verb in French. The pupil should commit these pronouns to memory:

me, *me* (to me)	lui, *to him, to her* (to it)
te, *thee* (to thee)	nous, *us* (to us)
le, *him* (it)	vous, *you* (to you)
la, *her* (it)	les, *them*

leur, *to them*

MAIN SENTENCE

What do you want to do this morning? I would like to leave by the first plane for Paris, but, unfortunately, this is impossible, for I expect a friend from New Orleans and must stay in New York until he arrives by the bus, by the train, or by the boat.

What do you want to do this morning?

What
do you want? do you wish? (Questions in English are asked with the auxiliary verb **to do.** We say: What do you want? The French say simply: What want you? We say: Do you go? The French: Go you?)
to do
this morning?

---

1. What do you want?
2. What do you want to do?
3. What do you want to do this morning?
4. What do you want to do to-morrow?
5. Will you do it?
6. Do you want to do it to-morrow?

Watch carefully the position of the object pronouns in French and in English in the following sentences. We say in English: Will you **tell me?** In French: *Voulez-vous **me dire?*** We say: He has written to him; the French: *Il lui a écrit.*

I want to do it, *Je veux **le faire**.* Do you understand it? ***Le comprenez-vous?*** Yes, I understand it. *Oui, **je le comprends**.* He has sent them a letter. ***Il leur a envoyé** une lettre.*

7. Voulez-vous le faire‿aujourd'hui? (o ʒur dyi)

je veux (ʒə vø)	nous voulons (nu vu lɔ̃)
tu veux (ty vø)	vous voulez (vu vu le)
il veut (il vø)	ils veulent (il vœ·l)

8. Je ne veux pas[1] le faire ce matin. (ʒən vø pɑl fɛ:r sma tɛ̃)

9. Pourquoi ne voulez-vous pas[2] le faire‿aujourd'hui? (pur kwa)

je ne veux pas	nous ne voulons pas
tu ne veux pas	vous ne voulez pas
il ne veut pas	ils ne veulent pas

10. Quand voulez-vous le faire? (kɑ̃)

11. Pouvez-vous le faire ce matin? (pu ve vu)

12. Non, je ne peux pas le faire ce matin. (nɔ̃, ʒə n pø pɑ)

je peux (ʒə pø)	nous pouvons (nu pu vɔ̃)
tu peux (ty pø)	vous pouvez (vu pu ve)
il peut (il pø)	ils peuvent (il pœ·v)

13. Pouvez-vous le faire demain? Oui, je peux le faire demain.

Parler

par le

14. Parlez-vous français? (par le vu frɑ̃·sɛ)

15. Oui, un peu. (wi, œ̃ pø)

16. Est-ce que[3] vous le parlez bien? (ɛs kə vul par le bjɛ̃)

---

[1] English negative statements are formed with the auxiliary verb *to do.* We say: I *do* not want to do it. In French such an auxiliary verb is not used. They simply say: Je ne veux pas le faire.

The negation, however, consists of two words, viz.: *ne-pas.*

Ne must be placed *before* the verb. This *ne* was formerly the real negation, but has now become a simple *warning,* so to say, that something *negative* is about to be stated.

The real negation *pas* is usually placed *after* the verb, that is to say, the verb (in simple tenses at least) is, so to speak, *sandwiched* between *ne* and *pas.*

As: I speak	*Je parle*
I do not speak	*Je ne parle pas*
We speak	*Nous parlons.*
We don't speak.	*Nous ne parlons pas.*
Speak!	*Parlez!*
Don't speak!	*Ne parlez pas!*

7. Do you want to do it to-day [aujourd'hui]?

I want	we want
thou wantest	you want
he wants	they want

8. I don't want [je ne veux pas[1]] to do it this morning.

9. Why don't you want [ne voulez-vous pas[2]] to do it to-day?

I do not want	we do not want
thou dost not want	you do not want
he does not want	they do not want

10. When do you want to do it?

11. Can you [pouvez-vous] do it this morning?

12. No, I cannot [je ne peux pas] do it this morning.

I can	we can
thou canst	you can
he can	they can

13. Can you do it to-morrow? Yes, I can do it to-morrow.

To Speak

14. Do you speak French [français]?

15. Yes, a little [un peu].

16. Do you speak it well [bien]?

---

[2] In negative questions the negation *ne-pas* is placed in the following manner:

Do you speak?	*Parlez-vous?*
Don't you speak?	*Ne parlez-vous pas?*
He wants to do it.	*Il veut le faire.*
Doesn't he want to do it?	*Ne veut-il pas le faire?*
Does he speak French?	*Parle-t-il français?*
Doesn't he speak French?	*Ne parle-t-il pas français?*

[3] We have seen that the interrogative form in French is obtained by inverting the subject: Vous voulez—You want. *Voulez-vous?*—Do you want? There exists however another way of asking a question. The normal order of words is kept: vous voulez, but it is preceded by ***est-ce que***: *Est-ce que vous voulez?*—Do you want? Other examples of both forms of interrogation: *Pouvez-vous?* or *Est-ce que vous pouvez?* Can you?; *Parlez-vous français* or *Est-ce que vous parlez français?* Do you speak French?; *Pourquoi ne pouvez-vous pas le faire?* or *Pourquoi est-ce que vous ne pouvez pas le faire?* Why can't you do it?

17. Oh, pas[1] très bien. (o, pa trɛ bjɛ̃)

je parle (ʒə parl)	nous parlons (nu par lɔ̃)
tu parles (ty parl)	vous parlez (vu par le)
il parle (il parl)	ils parlent (il parl)

18. Est-ce que vous pouvez vous‿exprimer facilement? (vu zɛk spri me fa sil mɑ̃)

19. Je le parle suffisamment pour me faire comprendre. (ʒə l parl sy fi za mɑ̃ pur mə fɛ:r kɔ̃ prɑ̃:dr)

20. Je ne sais pas très bien m'expliquer[2] en français, mais je le parle suffisamment pour me faire comprendre. (ʒən se pa mɛk spli ke)

21. Ce monsieur parle-t-il[3] français? (sə məsjø par lə t‿il frɑ̃·sɛ?)

22. Oui, il le parle couramment. (wi ku ra mɑ̃.)

23. Est-il français? (ɛ til frɑ̃ sɛ)

24. Oui, monsieur, il‿est français. (wi msjø il‿ɛ frɑ̃ sɛ)

je suis (ʒə sɥi)	nous sommes (nu sɔm)
tu es (t͡ɥɛ)	vous‿êtes (vu zɛt)
il‿est (il‿ɛ)	ils sont (il sɔ̃)
elle‿est (ɛl‿ɛ)	elles sont (ɛl sɔ̃)

25. Et, vous, monsieur, êtes-vous américain ou français?[4] (e vu, ɛt vu a me ri kɛ̃ u frɑ̃ sɛ)

26. Pourquoi me demandez-vous cela? (pur kwa mə dmɑ̃ de vu sla?)

---

[1] Note that when there is no verb in the sentence the negation affecting a noun, a pronoun, an adjective, an adverb, is *pas* (and not ne . . . pas). Examples: *pas bien*, not well; *pas beau*, not beautiful; *pas vous*, not you; *pas Robert*, not Robert.

[2] It seems as though it should be—*me expliquer;* but when monosyllables ending in *e* or *a* are followed by a word commencing with a vowel or silent h, these vowels are elided. As: *de aller, d'aller; me écrire, m'écrire; le ami, l'ami; la amie, l'amie; le homme, l'homme.*

[3] The French do not employ the English auxiliary verb *to do* when asking a question. Thus: Do you speak French? is simply rendered: *Parlez-vous français?*

17. Oh! not[2] very well.

I speak	we speak
thou speakest	you speak
he speaks	they speak

18. Can you express yourself readily?

19. I speak it sufficiently to make myself understood. (Literally: I speak sufficiently [suffisamment] in order to [pour] make (people) understand me [me faire comprendre].)

20. I can not explain myself very well in French, but I speak it sufficiently to make myself understood.

21. Does this gentleman speak French? (Literally: This gentleman [ce monsieur] does he speak [parle-t-il[3]] French?)

22. Yes, he speaks it fluently.

23. Is he [est-il] a Frenchman?

24. Yes, sir, he is [il est] a Frenchman.

I am	we are
thou art	you are
he is (it is)	they are
she is	they are (fem.)

25. And you, sir, are you [êtes-vous] an American or [ou] a Frenchman?

26. Why do you ask me that?

---

[3] When, however, the subject of a question is a *noun*, the inverted form of speech is used, that is to say, the noun begins the sentence and the verb and its corresponding pronoun (*il, elle, ils* or *elles*) are placed after it.

Does this gentleman speak French? Literally: This gentleman does he speak French?

Ce monsieur parle-t-il français?

Is Madam B. here? Literally: Madam B. is she here?

Madame B. est-elle ici?

However, it would also be correct to say: *Est-ce que vous parlez français?; Est-ce que ce monsieur parle français? Est-ce que Madame B. est ici?*

[4] We say in English: Are you *a* Frenchman? The French express this by saying: Are you French? *Êtes-vous français?* No, I am an American. *Non, je suis américain.*

27. Je vous pose cette[1] question, parce que vous parlez si bien l'anglais.[2] (ʒə vu po:z sɛt kɛs tjɔ̃, par skə vu par le si bjɛ̃ lɑ̃ glɛ)

28. Je suis français, mais ma[3] mère‿était‿anglaise[4], et je parle couramment le français et l'anglais. (ma mɛ:r‿e tɛ tɑ̃ glɛ:z)

29. Le français est-il difficile[5] à apprendre? (di fi sil)

30. Je suis né[6] à Paris et le[7] français est ma langue maternelle. (ma tɛr nɛl)

31. Est-ce que la prononciation française‿est très difficile? (la prɔ nɔ̃ sja sjɔ̃ frɑ̃·sɛ:z trɛ di fi sil)

32. La prononciation française n'est pas très difficile, au contraire. (o kɔ̃ trɛ:r)

33. J'ai beaucoup de difficulté à prononcer correctement[8] des phrases entières en français.

34. Au contraire, c'est la prononciation anglaise qui est bien plus difficile.

35. L'anglais est ma langue maternelle.

---

[1] There are two forms in French for this, viz.: *ce* this, for the masculine, and *cette* this, for the feminine.

Nouns ending in *ion* are feminine, consequently we say *cette* question.

[2] After *parler* the definite article is (generally) *not* used before names of languages, as: *Je parle français*, I speak French. *Parlez-vous‿anglais?* Do you speak English?

But when an adverb follows the verb *parler*, the definite article *must* be used, as: *Je ne parle pas bien le français*, I do not speak French well. *Vous parlez si bien l'anglais*, you speak English so well.

[3] There are two forms for my (*singular*), namely *mon* for the masculine and *ma* for the feminine, as: *mon père*, my father; *ma mère*, my mother.

[4] The feminine of adjectives is generally formed by adding *e* to the masculine, as *anglais, anglaise; petit, petite.*

27. I ask you [put to you, *vous pose*] this question, because [parce que] you speak English so [si] well.

28. I am French, but [mais] my mother was [était] English, and I speak French and English fluently.

29. Is it difficult to learn French? (Literally: Is French difficult to learn?)

30. I was born [né] in Paris and French is my mother [maternelle] tongue.

31. Is the French pronunciation very difficult?

32. On the contrary [au contraire]—French pronunciation is not very difficult.

33. It is very difficult for me to pronounce correctly whole French sentences. (Literally: I have much difficulty to pronounce correctly [correctement[8]] some entire phrases in French.)

34. On the contrary, it is the English pronunciation which is much more difficult.

35. English is my mother tongue.

---

[5] It would also be correct to say: *Est-ce que le français est difficile à apprendre?*

[6] This is an unusual construction: *Il est né à Paris.* He was born in Paris. *Où êtes-vous né?* Where were you born?—Similarly, the French say *Il est mort hier.* He died yesterday.

[7] The definite article is very generally employed. It must be used in French before all nouns employed in a general or indefinite sense, as:

L'homme, man; *la nature,* nature; *la fortune,* fortune; *le français est ma langue maternelle,* French is my mother tongue.

[8] The usual position of adverbs is immediately after the verb, if the verb stands in a simple tense, as: *Vous prononcez très bien,* you pronounce very well. Compare the above phrase. Other rules follow later.

36. Êtes-vous né à New York? Non monsieur, je suis né à Londres.

37. Le français est beaucoup plus facile‿à prononcer que[1] l'anglais. En‿effet, les régles de la prononciation française sont‿invariables.

38. L'accent est toujours sur la dernière syllabe d'un mot. Exemples: **Prononcer, général, correctement, difficile.**

AFFIRMATIVE

j'ai (ʒe)	nous‿avons (nu za vɔ̃)
tu as (tɥa)	vous‿avez (vu za ve)
il a (il‿a)	ils‿ont (il zɔ̃)
elle a (ɛl‿a)	elles‿ont (ɛl zɔ̃)

NEGATIVE

je n'ai pas	nous n'avons pas
tu n'as pas	vous n'avez pas
il n'a pas	ils n'ont pas
elle n'a pas	elles n'ont pas

QUESTION	NEGATIVE QUESTION
ai-je? (ɛ:ʒ)	n'ai-je pas? (nɛ:ʒ pa)
as-tu?	n'as-tu pas?
a-t-il?	n'a-t-il pas?
a-t-elle?	n'a-t-elle pas?
avons-nous?	n'avons-nous pas?
avez-vous?	n'avez-vous pas?
ont-ils?	n'ont-ils pas?
ont-elles?	n'ont-elles pas?

[1] *Than* after an adjective used in the comparative is generally rendered by *que*.

36. Were you born in New York? No sir, I was born in London. (Literally: **Are** you born in New York? No, sir, I **am** born in London.)

37. French is much easier [plus facile] to pronounce than[1] English. In fact [En effet] the rules [les règles] for [de] the French pronunciation are invariable.

38. The accent is always on the last syllable of each word. Examples: To pronounce, general, correctly, difficult.

AFFIRMATIVE

I have	we have
thou hast	you have
he has (it has)	they have (mas.)
she has	" " (fem.)

NEGATIVE

I have not	we have not
thou hast not	you have not
he has not	they have not (mas.)
she has not	" " " (fem.)

QUESTION	NEGATIVE QUESTION
have I?	have I not?
hast thou?	hast thou not?
has he?	has he not?
has she?	has she not?
have we?	have we not?
have you?	have you not?
have they (mas.)?	have they not (mas.)?
" " (fem.)?	" " " (fem.)?

CONJUGATION OF THE PRESENT TENSE

FIRST CONJUGATION[1]

Prononc-er

AFFIRMATIVE	NEGATIVE[2]
je prononc**e** (ʒə prɔ nɔ̃:s)	je ne prononc**e** pas
tu prononc**es** (ty prɔ nɔ̃:s)	tu ne prononc**es** pas
il prononc**e** (il prɔ nɔ̃:s)	il ne prononc**e** pas
nous prononç**ons**[3] (nu prɔ nɔ̃•sɔ̃)	nous ne prononç**ons** pas
vous prononc**ez** (vu prɔ nɔ̃•se)	vous ne prononc**ez** pas
ils prononc**ent** (il prɔ nɔ̃:s)	ils ne prononc**ent** pas

QUESTION	NEGATIVE QUESTION
est-ce que je prononc**e**[4]?	est-ce que je ne prononc**e** pas?
prononc**es**-tu?	ne prononc**es**-tu pas?
prononc**e**-t-il?[5]	ne prononc**e**-t-il pas?
prononç**ons**-nous?	ne prononç**ons**-nous pas?
prononc**ez**-vous?	ne prononc**ez**-vous pas?
prononc**ent**-ils? (prɔ nɔ̃•s til)	ne prononc**ent**-ils pas?

---

[1] Verbs of the first conjugation end in *er* in the infinitive, as parl*er*, to speak; donn*er*, to give; trouv*er*, to find; achet*er*, to buy; arriv*er*, to arrive.

The infinitive is the *ground form* of the verb, on which its conjugation depends. *Er* is called the ending.

By striking off the *er* we get the root or stem of the verb.

Thus *parl* is the stem of the verb *parler; arriv* the stem of *arriver; prononc* the stem of *prononcer*.

The stem remains unaltered in all regular verbs.

To the stem various terminations are added, by which persons, tenses and moods are distinguished, and which are common to all verbs of the same conjugation.

CONJUGATION OF THE PRESENT TENSE

FIRST CONJUGATION[1]

To Pronounce

AFFIRMATIVE	NEGATIVE
I pronounce	I do not pronounce
thou pronouncest	thou dost not pronounce
he pronounces	he does not pronounce
we pronounce	we do not pronounce
you pronounce	you do not pronounce
they pronounce	they do not pronounce

QUESTION	NEGATIVE QUESTION
Do I pronounce?	Do I not pronounce?
dost thou pronounce?	dost thou not pronounce?
does he pronounce?	does he not pronounce?
do we pronounce?	do we not pronounce?
do you pronounce?	do you not pronounce?
do they pronounce?	do they not pronounce?

In the present tense of the first conjugation the following terminations are added:

je ——— e
tu ——— es
il ——— e
nous ——— ons
vous ——— ez
ils ——— ent

The endings of the whole singular and of the third person plural are *never* pronounced. These verb forms sound like the stems of regular verbs.

[2] In the negative and interrogative forms the English auxiliary *to do* must not be expressed.

[3] In verbs ending in *cer*, as *prononcer*, *commencer*, *placer*, a cedilla must be placed under the *c*, whenever this letter is followed by *a* or *o*, as: *nous prononçons*, *nous commençons*, *nous plaçons*.

[4] This form with *est-ce-que* is always used instead of the obsolete *prononcè-je?* Literally it means: is it that I pronounce? It is sounded (ɛskə).

[5] The t- is inserted for euphony; as: *il a*, he has; *a-t-il?* has he? *parle-t-il?* does he speak? *arrive-t-il?* does he arrive? *trouve-t-il?* does he find?

THE PRESENT TENSE

Penser

AFFIRMATIVE	NEGATIVE
je pens**e**	je ne pens**e** pas
tu pens**es**	tu ne pens**es** pas
il pens**e**	il ne pens**e** pas
nous pens**ons**	nous ne pens**ons** pas
vous pens**ez**	vous ne pens**ez** pas
ils pens**ent**	ils ne pens**ent** pas

QUESTION	NEGATIVE QUESTION
est-ce que je pens**e**?	est-ce que je ne pens**e** pas?
pens**es**-tu?	ne pens**es**-tu pas?
pens**e**-t‿il?[5]	ne pens**e**-t‿il pas?
pens**ons**-nous?	ne pens**ons**-nous pas?
pens**ez**-vous?	ne pens**ez**-vous pas?
pens**ent**‿ils?	ne pens**ent**‿ils pas?

1. Voudriez-vous me prononcer ce mot.

2. Voudriez-vous le prononcer encore une fois. (ɑ̃ kɔr‿yn fwa)

3. Comment prononce-t-on ce mot? (kɔ mɑ̃)

4. Je ne puis pas prononcer ce mot; voudriez-vous me le répéter une fois de plus, s'il vous plaît? (re pe te)

5. Savez-vous maintenant comment ce mot se prononce? (sa ve vu mɛ̃·t nɑ̃)

6. Oui, maintenant je sais[1] le prononcer.

7. Est-ce que vous comprenez le[2] français? (kɔ̃ prə ne)

---

[1] I know, *je sais*, belongs to the irregular verbs. The present tense is conjugated thus:

je sais	I know
tu sais	thou knowest
il sait	he knows
nous savons	we know
vous savez	you know
ils savent	they know

THE PRESENT TENSE

To Think

AFFIRMATIVE	NEGATIVE
I think	I do not think
thou thinkest	thou dost not think
he thinks	he does not think
we think	we do not think
you think	you do not think
they think	they do not think

QUESTION	NEGATIVE QUESTION
Do I think?	Do I not think?
dost thou think?	Dost thou not think?
does he think?	does he not think?
do we think?	do we not think?
do you think?	do you not think?
do they think?	do they not think?

1. Would you please pronounce this word for me? (Literally: Would you me pronounce this word?)
2. Would you please pronounce it once more? (Literally: Would you it pronounce yet [encore] one time [une fois]?)
3. How is this word pronounced? (Literally: How does one pronounce this word?)
4. I cannot pronounce this word; would you please repeat it [le répéter] once more?
5. Do you know now [savez-vous] how this word is pronounced? (Literally: how this word pronounces itself?)
6. Yes, now I know how [je sais[1]] to pronounce it.
7. Do you understand French?

[2] The definite article before names of languages is used with all verbs, except *parler*, where it is employed only when used with an adverb, as: *Comprenez-vous le français?* Do you understand French? *Je ne parle pas bien le français*, I do not speak French well. But without an adverb: *Parlez-vous allemand?* Do you speak German?

8. Je le comprends[1]‿un peu. (ʒə l kɔ̃ prɑ̃ zœ̃ pø)

9. Me[2] comprenez-vous quand je vous[2] parle français?

10. Je vous[2] comprends quand vous parlez lentement. (lɑ̃·t mɑ̃)

11. Est-ce que vous me[2] comprenez quand je parle vite? (vit)

12. Non, monsieur, je ne vous[2] comprends pas bien quand vous parlez rapidement. (ra pid mɑ̃)

13. Ayez la bonté de me parler très lentement. Je suis‿américain et je comprends difficilement quand‿on me parle trop vite.

14. Voudriez-vous répéter cette phrase? Vous parlez‿un peu trop vite.

15. Me comprenez-vous maintenant?

16. Oui, maintenant je vous comprends parfaitement. (par fɛt mɑ̃)

17. Qu'est-ce que vous dites?[3] (kɛs kə vu dit)

18. Qu'est-ce qu'il dit?

19. Qu'est-ce que cet‿homme[4] dit? (sɛ t‿ɔm)

20. Comprenez-vous ce que[5] cet‿homme dit? Non, je ne le comprends pas.

---

[1] The present tense of *comprendre*, to understand, is conjugated:

je comprends (kɔ̃ prɑ̃)	I understand
tu comprends	thou understandest
il comprend	he understands
nous comprenons (kɔ̃ prə nɔ̃)	we understand
vous comprenez	you understand
ils comprennent (kɔ̃ prɛ:n)	they understand

[2] Note the position of the object pronouns *me*, me; *vous*, you, to you, before the verb.

[3] The present tense of the irregular verb *dire*, to say, to tell, is conjugated thus:

je dis	I tell
tu dis	thou tellest
il dit	he tells
nous disons	we tell
vous dites	you tell
ils disent	they tell

8. I understand it [je le comprends[1]] a little [un peu].

9. Do you understand me when I speak French to you?

10. I understand you when you speak slowly [lentement].

11. Do you understand me when I speak fast [vite]?

12. No sir, I do not understand you well when you speak fast.

13. Will you kindly (Have the kindness to) speak very slowly? I am an American and I understand with difficulty when one speaks too rapidly.

14. Would you please [Voudriez-vous] repeat [répéter] this phrase (cette phrase)? You speak a little too quickly.

15. Do you understand me now [maintenant]?

16. Yes, now I understand you perfectly [parfaitement].

17. What do you say? (Literally: What is it that you say [dites]?)

18. What does he say? (Literally: What is it that he says?)

19. What does this man say? (Literally: What is it that this man says?)

20. Do you understand what [ce que] this man says? No, I don't understand him.

---

[4] Before masculine nouns beginning with a vowel or silent *h* the French use *cet*, as: *cet‿ami*, this friend, *cet‿homme*, this man.

We have, therefore, three forms for our demonstrative pronoun, this, viz.: *ce*, *cet* and *cette*, used as follows:

ce (masculine), as: *ce monsieur*, this gentleman.
cet (masculine), as: *cet‿ami*, this friend; *cet‿homme*, this man.
cette (feminine), as: *cette dame*, this lady.

[5] What (if not used in a question) is usually expressed by *ce que*, that which. Observe that the relative pronoun must always be expressed in French. In English it is frequently omitted. This can never be done in French.

21. Comprenez-vous ce que je vous dis?

22. Oui, je peux comprendre tout ce que vous dites si vous parlez lentement. (tu skə vu dit)

23. Je ne comprends pas ce mot; voudriez-vous le répéter encore‿une fois?

24. Le comprenez-vous maintenant? Oui, maintenant je le comprends.

25. Que signifie ce mot? (si ɲi fi)

26. Que signifie ce mot en‿anglais? (ɑ̃ nɑ̃ glɛ)

27. Qu'est-ce que cela veut dire? (sla vø di:r)

28. Voudriez-vous me répéter cela?

29. Pourriez-vous m'expliquer ce mot? (mɛk spli ke)

30. Voudriez-vous m'expliquer ce mot une fois de plus?

31. Savez-vous maintenant ce que ce mot signifie en‿anglais?

32. Oui, maintenant je sais ce que ce mot signifie.

33. Auriez-vous la bonté de m'expliquer cette phrase française? Je ne sais pas ce que cela veut dire.

34. Comprenez-vous maintenant ce que cette phrase signifie? (skə sɛt fra·z si ɲi fi)

35. Oui, maintenant je sais ce que cette phrase signifie et je puis la[1] dire en français et en‿anglais (di:r)

36. Savez-vous ce que veut dire "dire encore"? Non, je ne sais pas.[2]

37. "Dire‿encore" signifie "répéter." Je peux dire: "Veuillez répéter cela." ou "Veuillez le dire‿encore." Ces[3] deux phrases signifient la même chose. (se dø frɑ:z si ɲi fi la mɛ:m ʃo:z)

---

[1] *La*, because it refers to the feminine word *cette phrase*.

[2] No, I don't, must be expressed by the repetition of the full phrase.

21. Do you understand what [ce que] I say to you?

22. Yes, I can understand everything (all that which) you say, if [si] you speak slowly.

23. I don't understand this word; would you please repeat it once more (again once)?

24. Do you understand it now? Yes, now I understand it.

25. What does this word mean? (Literally: What means this word?)

26. What does this word mean in [en] English?

27. What does that mean (wishes to say)?

28. Would you please repeat that to me?

29. Could you [Pourriez-vous] explain this word to me?

30. Would you please explain this word once more [une fois de plus] to me?

31. Do you know now what [ce que] this word means in English?

32. Yes, now I know what [ce que] this word means.

33. Would you kindly (Would you have the kindness to) explain this French phrase to me; I don't know what it means (wishes to say).

34. Do you understand now what this phrase means?

35. Yes, now I know what this phrase means and I can say it [je puis la dire] in French and in English.

36. Do you know the meaning of (what means, *ce que veut dire*) "dire encore"? No, I don't (I do not know it).[2]

37. "Dire encore" means "to repeat." I can [Je peux] say: "Will you please (be willing, *veuillez*) repeat that?" or "Will you please say it again?" These two phrases have the same meaning (mean the same thing, *signifient la même chose*).

---

[3] The plural of *ce, cet* and *cette* is *ces*, both for the masculine and feminine.

38. Il m'est très difficile de prononcer correctement toutes (tut) ces phrases. Je trouve la prononciation française bien difficile.

39. Au contraire, la prononciation française‿est très facile.

40. Il‿y a des règles fixes pour prononcer les mots français.

Dans‿un Magasin

(dɑ̃ zœ̃ ma ga zɛ̃)

1. Qu'est-ce que vous voulez faire dans ce magasin? J'ai quelque chose‿à acheter.

2. Qu'est-ce que vous voulez acheter?—Je désire‿acheter un[1] chapeau. (ʒə de zi:r‿aʃ te œ̃ ʃa po)

3. Veuillez m'accompagner. Je veux‿acheter un chapeau et je ne parle pas‿assez bien le français. (vœ je ma kɔ̃ pa ɲe)

4. Bonjour,[2] monsieur. Mon‿ami voudrait acheter un chapeau. (bɔ̃ ʒu:r, mə sjø—mɔ na mi)

je voudrais (ʒə vu drɛ)
tu voudrais (ty vu drɛ)
il voudrait (il vu drɛ)
nous voudrions (nu vu dri jɔ̃)
voux voudriez (vu vu dri je)
ils voudraient (il vu drɛ)

5. Quelle sorte de chapeau désirez-vous? (kɛl sɔrt)

6. Je désire‿un chapeau de feutre. (fø:tr)

---

[1] For the indefinite article there are two forms, viz.: *un*, a (for masculine nouns) and *une*, a (for feminine nouns). As: *un chapeau*, a hat; *une paire*, a pair. *Un frère*, a brother; *une sœur*, a sister.

38. It is very hard for me (to me, *m'*) to pronounce all these phrases [toutes ces phrases] correctly. I think (I find, *je trouve*) the French pronunciation is very [bien] difficult.

39. On the contrary, the French pronunciation is very easy.

40. French words are pronounced in accordance with fixed rules. (Literally: There are fixed rules in order to pronounce the French words.)

In a Store

1. What do you want to do in this store? I have to buy something. (Literally: What is it that you want to do in [dans] this store [ce magasin]? I have something to buy.)

2. What do you want to buy? I wish [Je désire] to purchase a hat [un chapeau].

3. Please (Be willing, *Veuillez*) accompany me. I want to buy a hat and I don't speak French well enough [assez bien].

4. Good morning [Bonjour],[2] sir. My friend would like [voudrait] to buy a hat.

I should like
thou wouldst like
he would like
we should like
you would like
they would like

5. What kind of a hat do you want?

6. I want a felt hat. (Literally: I desire a hat of felt [de feutre].)

---

[2] *Good morning* or *good afternoon* are not used in French, but bonjour, *good day;* bonsoir, *good evening.*

CARDINAL NUMBERS

NOMBRES CARDINAUX

Un	(œ̃)	1	Dix-neuf	(diz nœf)	19
Deux	(dø)	2	Vingt	(vɛ̃)	20
Trois	(trwɑ)	3	Vingt‿et un	(vɛ̃ te œ̃)	21
Quatre	(katr)	4	Vingt-deux	(vɛ̃·t dø)	22
Cinq[1]	(sɛ̃·k)	5	Vingt-trois	(vɛ̃ trwa)	23
Six[2]	(sis)	6	Vingt-quatre	(vɛ̃t katr)	24
Sept[3]	(sɛt)	7	Vingt-cinq	(vɛ̃t sɛ̃·k)	25
Huit[3]	(ɥit)	8	Vingt-six	(vɛ̃t sis)	26
Neuf[3]	(nœf)	9	Vingt-sept	(vɛ̃t sɛt)	27
Dix[2]	(dis)	10	Vingt‿huit	(vɛ̃ tɥit)	28
Onze	(ɔ̃:z)	11	Vingt-neuf	(vɛ̃t nœf)	29
Douze	(du:z)	12	Trente	(trɑ̃:t)	30
Treize	(trɛ:z)	13	Trente⁀et un	(trɑ̃·t⁀e œ̃)	31
Quatorze	(ka tɔrz)	14	Trente-deux	(trɑ̃:t dø)	32
Quinze	(kɛ̃:z)	15	Quarante	(ka rɑ̃:t)	40
Seize	(sɛ:z)	16	Quarante⁀et un[4]	(ka rɑ̃:t⁀e œ̃)	41
Dix-sept	(di sɛt)	17	Quarante-deux, etc.		42
Dix‿huit	(di zɥit)	18			

[1] *Cinq* is pronounced sɛ̃k, when alone, or before a word beginning with a vowel (*or* silent h). Otherwise, sɛ̃. *Cinq‿heures,* sɛ̃ k‿œ:r, five o'clock. *Cinq minutes,* sɛ̃ mi nyt, five minutes.

[2] *Six* and *dix* are pronounced sis and dis, when alone. When before a vowel (*or* silent h) x is linked to the next word as z. *Six‿heures,* si zœ:r, six o'clock. Before a consonant or aspirate h, this x is silent. *Six minutes,* si mi nyt, six minutes.

[3] *Huit* before a consonant is generally pronounced ɥi: huit̸ livres—ɥi li:vr. Otherwise pronounce ɥit: huit‿amis—ɥi t‿a mi; j'en ai huit (ɥit).

CARDINAL NUMBERS

NOMBRES CARDINAUX

Cinquante	(sɛ̃ kɑ̃:t)	50	Quatre-vingt-dix		90
Cinquante‿et un[4]		51	Quatre-vingt-onze		91
Soixante	(swa sɑ̃:t)	60	Quatre-vingt-douze		92
Soixante‿et un[4]		61	Quatre-vingt-treize		93
Soixante-dix		70	Quatre-vingt-quatorze		94
Soixante‿et onze		71	Quatre-vingt-quinze		95
Soixante-douze		72	Quatre-vingt-seize		96
Soixante-treize		73	Quatre-vingt-dix-sept		97
Soixante-quatorze		74	Quatre-vingt-dix‿huit		98
Soixante-quinze		75	Quatre-vingt-dix-neuf		99
Soixante-seize		76	Cent	(sɑ̃)	100
Soixante-dix-sept		77	Cent un	(sɑ̃ œ̃)	101
Soixante-dix‿huit		78	Mille (mil), A thousand		
Soixante-dix-neuf[5]		79	Un million (mi ljɔ̃), a million		
Quatre-vingts	(ka trə vɛ̃)	80	Un milliard (mi lja:r), a billion		
Quatre-vingt-un[6] (ka trə vɛ̃[7] œ̃)		81			

[4] Ka rɑ̃·t‿e œ̃, sɛ̃ kɑ̃·t‿e œ̃, swa sɑ̃·t‿e œ̃. The t of the conjunction *et* is never linked.

[5] As will have been observed, the French count from 60 to 100 in two series of twenty each, instead of four series of ten. Thus they say, *sixty-nine, sixty-ten, sixty-eleven, sixty-twelve . . . sixty-nineteen, eighty;* and *eighty-nine, eighty-ten, eighty-eleven . . . eighty-nineteen, hundred.*

[6] After eighty the word *et* is dropped from before *un.* Thus, *quatre-vingt-un,* not *et* un; *quatre-vingt onze,* not *et* onze; *cent un,* not *et* un.

[7] The t of *vingt* is silent in the numbers from 80 to 99, but is pronounced in the numbers from 21 to 29.

7. Quel numéro portez-vous? (kɛl ny me ro pɔr te vu?)

8. Je porte du sept.[1] (ʒə pɔrt dy sɛt)

9. Je voudrais‿acheter aussi une paire de gants. (ʒə vu drɛ za‿ʃ te o si yn pɛːr də gɑ̃)

10. Quelle sorte de gants portez-vous?—Des gants de chevreau. (kɛl sɔrt—ʃə vro)

11. Et quel numéro portez-vous?—Du six. (sis)

12. Est-ce que ces gants vous vont[2] [3] bien?—Oui, ces gants me vont très bien.

je vais (ʒə ve)	nous‿allons (nu za lɔ̃)
tu vas (ty va)	vous‿allez (vu za le)
il va (il va)	ils vont (il vɔ̃)

13. Et comment est-ce que ce chapeau vous va?—Il me va très bien. (kɔ mɑ̃)

14. Montrez-moi d'autres[4] gants; ceux-ci ne me vont pas. (mɔ̃ tre mwa do·trə gɑ̃—sø si)

---

[1] The numerals are most important and ought to be mastered at once. They are very difficult, but the pupil must learn them so thoroughly that he can give any number at once and without hesitation.

[2] *Je vais,* etc., is the present tense of the irregular verb *aller,* to go. Pupils generally experience great difficulties in mastering this verb. The conjugation of the present tense resembles that of *avoir,* to have. When the two verbs are learned *together* all difficulties vanish. The student ought therefore to learn the two verbs as per following table:

I HAVE	I GO
j'ai	je vais
tu as	tu vas
il‿a	il va
nous‿avons	nous‿allons
vous‿avez	vous‿allez
ils‿ont	ils vont

It will be found that the two verbs rhyme, as: *j'ai—je vais; tu as—tu vas; il a—il va,* etc.

7. What size do you wear? (Literally: What number [quel numéro] do you wear [portez-vous]?)

8. I wear size seven [du sept[1]].

9. I would like to buy also a pair of gloves [une paire de gants].

10. What kind [quelle sorte] of gloves do you wear?—Kid gloves.—(Literally: Some [des] gloves of kid [de chevreau].)

11. And what size do you wear?—Size six [du six].

12. Do these gloves fit you [vous vont bien]?—Yes, these gloves fit me [me vont] very well.

I go	we go
thou goest	you go
he goes	they go

13. And how [comment] does this hat fit you [vous va]?—It fits me very well.

14. Show me some other [d'autres[4]] gloves; these [ceux-ci] do not fit me.

---

[3] *Aller* is here used idiomatically for *to fit.*

[4] We shall see that *some* or *any* must always be rendered in French by *du, de la, de l'* in the singular and by *des* in the plural, except in three cases, when it is given by *de* (or *d'*):

These are

1. Before an adjective.
2. After an adverb of quantity.
3. After a negation.

15. Combien vaut ce chapeau? Ce chapeau vaut deux mille francs. (kɔ̃ bjɛ̃ vo—dø mil frɑ̃)

16. Et quel‿est le prix de ces gants? Mille francs. (kɛl‿ɛl pri)

17. C'est très cher.—Oh, non, monsieur, c'est très bon marché. (ʃɛr—bɔ̃ mar ʃe)

18. Voulez-vous payer[1] ces gants maintenant? (pɛ je—mɛ̃:t nɑ̃)

19. Oui, je vais les payer[1] maintenant. Voici.—Merci beaucoup, monsieur. (vwa si—mɛr si bo ku)

20. Voulez-vous payer ce chapeau maintenant?

21. Non, veuillez m'envoyer ce chapeau à l'hôtel‿avec la facture. Je remettrai l'argent au porteur. Je n'ai pas‿assez d'argent[2] sur moi. (nɔ̃, vœ je mɑ̃ vwa je sʃa po a lɔ tɛl‿a vɛk la fak ty:r. ʒər mɛ tre lar ʒɑ̃ o pɔr tœ:r. ʒə ne pa za se dar ʒɑ̃ syr mwa.)

22. Avez-vous de l'argent sur vous?

23. Combien d'argent[2] avez-vous sur vous?

24. Avez-vous beaucoup d'argent[2] sur vous?

25. J'ai très peu d'argent[2] sur moi.

26. Je n'ai pas beaucoup d'argent[2] sur moi. Envoyez-moi ce chapeau à mon‿hôtel; je paierai là-bas. (ɑ̃·vwa je—mɔ nɔ tɛl—ʒə pe re la bɑ)

---

[1] Note that *payer* takes a direct object: *payer un chapeau*, to pay for a hat; *le payer* to pay for it.

As: *Montrez-moi d'autres gants*, show me some other gloves. *Avez-vous de bonnes plumes?* Have you good pens? *J'ai assez d'argent*, I have money enough. *Je ne bois pas de vin*, I don't drink wine.

[2] *De* must be employed after the following *adverbs of quantity*:

Assez, enough
Beaucoup, much; a great deal; a great many
Combien, how much? how many?
Peu, little; few
Moins, less
Rien, nothing + adjective
Trop, too much; too many
Tant, so much; so many
Quelque chose, something + adjective

15. How much is (is worth, *vaut*) this hat?—This hat costs 2000 francs.

16. And what [quel] is the price of these gloves?—A thousand francs.

17. That is very dear [cher].—Oh no, sir, that is very inexpensive [bon marché].

18. Do you want to pay for[1] these gloves now?

19. Yes, I am going to pay for[1] them now. Here you are [Voici].—Many thanks [merci beaucoup], sir.

20. Do you want to pay for this hat now?

21. No, please (be willing to, *veuillez*) send this hat and your bill [facture] to the hotel. I will pay the delivery man. I have not money enough with me. (Literally: I will remit the money to the bearer. I do not have enough money on me.)

22. Have you any money with you (upon you, *sur vous*)?

23. How much [Combien d'[2]] money have you with you?

24. Have you much [beaucoup d'] money with you?

25. I have very little [peu d'] money with me.

26. I haven't much money with me. Send this hat to my hotel; I'll pay [paierai] for it there [là-bas].

EXAMPLES

J'ai vu beaucoup de personnes.	I have seen a great many persons.
J'ai très peu d'argent sur moi.	I have very little money with me.
Combien d'argent avez-vous sur vous?	How much money have you with you?
Montrez-moi quelque chose de beau.	Show me something nice.
Vous avez fait trop de fautes.	You have made too many mistakes.
Je ne sais rien de nouveau.	I don't know anything new.

The future tense of regular verbs of the first conjugation has already been given. The future terminations of verbs of the other conjugations and of irregular verbs are almost similar and present few difficulties.

The future tense of *prendre*, to take, and *comprendre*, to understand, is formed thus:

je prend*rai*, I shall take	je comprend*rai*, I shall understand
tu prend*ras*, thou wilt take	tu comprend*ras*, thou wilt understand
il prend*ra*, he will take	il comprend*ra*, he will understand
nous prend*rons*, we shall take	nous comprend*rons*, we shall understand
vous prend*rez*, you will take	vous comprend*rez*, you will understand
ils prend*ront*, they will take	ils comprend*ront*, they will understand

CONJUGATION OF THE FUTURE TENSE[1]

First Conjugation

Prononc-er

AFFIRMATIVE	NEGATIVE
je prononc**erai** (ʒə prɔ nɔ̃ sre)	je ne prononc**erai** pas
tu prononc**eras**	tu ne prononc**eras** pas
il prononc**era**	il ne prononc**era** pas
nous prononç**erons**	nous ne prononc**erons** pas
vous prononc**erez**	vous ne prononc**erez** pas
ils prononc**eront**	ils ne prononc**eront** pas

QUESTION	NEGATIVE QUESTION
prononc**erai**-je? (prɔ nɔ̃ srɛ:ʒ)	ne prononc**erai**-je pas?
prononc**eras**-tu?	ne prononc**eras**-tu pas?
prononc**era**-t-il?	ne prononc**era**-t-il pas?
prononc**erons**-nous?	ne prononc**erons**-nous pas?
prononc**erez**-vous?	ne prononc**erez**-vous pas?
prononc**eront**-ils? (prɔ nɔ̃ srɔ̃ til)	ne prononc**eront**-ils pas?

[1] The future tense of regular verbs of the first conjugation is formed by adding *erai, eras, era, erons, erez, eront* to the stem. (Compare note page 45). We have therefore the following table:

je	—— erai
tu	—— eras
il	—— era
nous	—— erons
vous	—— erez
ils	—— eront

CONJUGATION OF THE FUTURE TENSE[1]

First Conjugation

To Pronounce

AFFIRMATIVE	NEGATIVE
I shall pronounce	I shall not pronounce
thou wilt pronounce	thou wilt not pronounce
he will pronounce	he will not pronounce
we shall pronounce	we shall not pronounce
you will pronounce	you will not pronounce
they will pronounce	they will not pronounce

QUESTION	NEGATIVE QUESTION
shall I pronounce?	shall I not pronounce?
wilt thou pronounce?	wilt thou not pronounce?
will he pronounce?	will he not pronounce?
shall we pronounce?	shall we not pronounce?
will you pronounce?	will you not pronounce?
will they pronounce?	will they not pronounce?

Form and conjugate the future tense of the following verbs: *penser*, to think; *arriver*, to arrive; *demander*, to ask; *trouver*, to find; *manger*, to eat; *dîner*, to dine; *causer*, to chat; *chercher*, to seek; *prier*, to beg; *donner*, to give.

The future must be used in French for the English "I will" when futurity is expressed, that is to say whenever "I will" cannot be changed to "I want to, I wish to, I desire," as:

Quand parlerez-vous à Robert?, When will you speak to Robert? *Je lui parlerai demain*, I shall speak to him tomorrow.

L'Arrivée — A L'Hôtel — Les Chambres
(la ri ve) le ʃã:br

1. Que voulez-vous faire‿en‿arrivant? (ã na ri vã)

2. Je suis très fatigué. Je voudrais‿aller directement à un bon‿ hôtel. (fa ti ge—di rɛk tə mã a œ̃ bɔ nɔ tɛl)

3. A quel‿hôtel voulez-vous‿aller?—A l'Hôtel de l'Opéra. (lɔ tɛl dlɔ pe ra)

4. Voulez-vous y aller à pied? Non, je vais prendre‿un taxi. (vu le vu ja le a pje—prã:dr‿œ̃ tak si)

5. Je me sens fatigué. Je ne pourrais pas aller à l'hôtel‿à pied. Je vais prendre‿un taxi. (ʒəm sã—ʒən pu rɛ pa)

6. Voulez-vous aller à l'hôtel‿à pied, ou préférez-vous prendre‿un taxi?

7. Je ne suis pas fatigué. J'irai à pied. (ʒi re)

8. Avez-vous des bagages? (ba ga:ʒ)

9. Avez-vous beaucoup de bagages?

10. Combien de bagages avez-vous? (kɔ̃ bjɛ̃)

11. J'ai beaucoup de bagages. Je ne puis pas‿aller à l'hôtel à pied. Je vais prendre un taxi.

The Arrival — At the Hotel — The Rooms

1. What do you want to do upon arriving [en‿arrivant]?

2. I am very tired. I should like [voudrais] to go directly [directement] to a good hotel.

3. To which [A quel] hotel do you want to go?—To the Opéra Hotel.

4. Do you want to walk there (to go there on foot, *y aller a pied*)? No, I am going to take [prendre] a taxicab.

5. I feel [Je me sens] very tired. I could not walk to the hotel. I am going to take a taxicab.

6. Do you want to walk to your hotel, or do you prefer to take a taxicab?

7. I am not tired. I shall walk [J'irai à pied].

8. Have you any baggage (des bagages)?

9. Have you much baggage [beaucoup de bagages]?

10. How much baggage have you?

11. I have a great deal of [beaucoup de] baggage. I cannot walk to my hotel. I am going to take a taxicab.

VOCABULAIRE	VOCABULARY
La Langue; les langues	**The Language; the languages**
Vous‿avez‿une bonne prononciation. (bɔn)	You have a good pronunciation.
Sa prononciation est très mauvaise. (mɔ vɛ:z)	His pronunciation is very bad.
L'accent (lak sɑ̃)	The accent
Les‿accents (le z‿ak sɑ̃)	The accents
Vous ne mettez pas l'accent où il faut. (mɛ te—u il fo)	You do not put the accent where it belongs.
Accentuez bien cette syllabe. (ak sɑ̃ tɥe)	Put the right accent on this syllable.
Prononcer	To pronounce
Vous prononcez bien.	You pronounce well.
Vous prononcez mal. (mal)	You pronounce badly.
Vous ne prononcez pas ce mot correctement.	You do not pronounce this word correctly.
Vous ne prononcez pas ce mot comme il faut.	You do not pronounce this word correctly.
Corriger (kɔ ri ʒe)	To correct
La faute (la fo:t)	The mistake
Les fautes	The mistakes
Ayez la bonté de me corriger quand je fais des fautes de prononciation. (ɛ je la bɔ̃·te)	Will you kindly correct me when I make mistakes in pronunciation.
Vous‿avez fait une faute.	You have made a mistake.

PART TWO

CONTENTS

L'Arrivée — L'Hôtel — Les Chambres

(*Suite*)

12. J'ai beaucoup de bagages. Je ne peux pas‿aller à l'hôtel⁀à pied. Je vais prendre⁀un taxi.

13. Chauffeur, à l'Hôtel d'Angleterre. (ʃo fœ:r—dɑ̃ glə tɛ:r)

14. Bonjour, monsieur;pouvez-vous me donner une bonne[1] chambre? (bɔn ʃɑ̃:br)

15. Pouvez-vous me donner une bonne[1] chambre⁀au premier‿étage (*or* au premier[2])? (o prə mje re ta:ʒ)

16. Je suis très fatigué et désire me coucher[3] tout de suite. (de zi:r mə ku ʃe tut sɥit)

17. Veuillez me donner une bonne chambre⁀au premier‿étage.

18. Veuillez me montrer une bonne chambre⁀au deuxième⁀étage (*or* au second). (o dø·zje:m⁀e ta:ʒ—o zgɔ̃)

19. A quel prix pouvez-vous me donner cette chambre?

20. Quel⁀est le prix de cette chambre par jour? (par ʒu:r) De quel prix cette chambre est‿elle par jour?

21. Combien louez-vous cette chambre par jour? (lwe vu)

22. Cette chambre se loue seize cents francs par jour. (s lu) Cette chambre est de seize cents francs par jour.

---

[1] Adjectives ending in *on* or *ien* form their feminine forms by doubling the *n* and adding *e*, as: *bon*, *bonne*, good; *ancien*, *ancienne*, old. It has been stated before that all adjectives agree in gender and number with the nouns they qualify.

[2] In French hotels the *first* floor frequently corresponds to our *second* floor. The first or ground floor is *le rez-de-chaussée;* the American second floor is *le premier;* the American third, *le second;* the fourth, *le troisième*, etc.

The word *étage* may be omitted. *Au premier*, *au second*, *au troisième*, etc., are in fact much more frequently used than *au premier‿étage*, *au deuxième⁀étage*, *au troisième⁀étage*, etc.

The Arrival — At the Hotel — The Rooms

(*Continuation*)

12. I have a great deal of [beaucoup de] baggage. I cannot walk (go on foot) to my hotel. I am going to take a taxi.

13. Driver [Chauffeur], to the Hotel of England [l'Hôtel d'Angleterre].

14. Good morning, sir; can you [pouvez-vous] give me a good room [chambre]?

15. Can you give me a good room on the [au] second floor [premier‿étage[2]]?

16. I am very tired and wish to go to bed [me coucher] at once.

17. Please give me a good room on the second floor.

18. Please show me a good room on the third floor.

19. At what price can you give me this room [cette chambre]?

20. What is the price [le prix] of this room per day [par jour]?

21. How much [Combien] do you rent [louez-vous] this room for per day?

22. This room rents [se loue] for sixteen hundred francs per day. *Or:* This room is sixteen hundred francs per day.

---

[3] *Se coucher* is a so-called reflexive verb. Reflexive verbs are those in which the action is reflected upon the subject, as: I wash myself; she flatters herself, etc. Many verbs, however, are reflexive in French which are not so in English, as: *se coucher*, to retire, to go to bed.

For full rules and conjugation see Part X.

23. C'est très cher; pourriez-vous m'en[1] donner une‿à douze cents francs? (sɛ trɛ ʃɛ:r; pu rje vu mɑ̃ dɔ ne yn)

24. La chambre ne me convient pas; montrez m'en une autre. (*Or:* Veuillez m'en montrer une‿autre). (la ʃɑ̃:brə nəm kɔ̃ vjɛ̃ pɑ; mɔ̃ tre mɑ̃ yn‿o:tr)

25. Je n'ai pas d'autre chambre‿à cet‿étage-ci, mais je puis vous donner une très grande chambre, à très bon marché, au troisième. (o trwa zjɛ:m)

26. Je ne voudrais pas me loger trop haut et avoir trop d'escaliers à monter. Pourrais-je‿avoir‿une chambre‿au rez-de-chaussée? (ʒən vu drɛ pam lɔ ʒe trɔ o e a vwar trɔ dɛs ka lje a mɔ̃ te.—o rɛt ʃo se)

27. Cette chambre‿est très grande‿et très belle. Pour combien pouvez-vous me la donner? (grɑ̃:d)

Conditional of "Pouvoir"

Je pourrais	(ʒə pu rɛ)
tu pourrais	(ty pu rɛ)
il pourrait	(il pu rɛ)
nous pourrions	(nu pu rjɔ̃)
vous pourriez	(vu pu rje)
ils pourraient	(il pu rɛ)

---

[1] The proper use of *en* presents great difficulties, as it is scarcely ever expressed in English.

In English we give as a general rule short replies to preceding questions. Not so in French where anything expressed in a previous question must be referred to again. Thus we say in English:

Question: Have you a pen?
Answer: ENGLISH: Yes, I have one.
FRENCH: Yes, I have one *of them*, *Oui, j'en‿ai une.*

Question: Did Mr. B. give you any money?
Answer: ENGLISH: No, he didn't.
FRENCH: No, he didn't give me *any*, *Non, il ne m'en‿a pas donné.*

As seen from these examples *en* means of it, of them, from it, from them, for it, for them, about it, about them, some, any, from there, and must be supplied in sentences though it may not be expressed in English.

23. That's very dear. Could you [Pourriez-vous] give me one for [à] 1200 francs?

24. The room does not suit me [ne me convient pas]; show me another one. *Or:* Will you please show me [m'en montrer] another.)

25. I haven't another (any other) room on [à] this floor, but I can [je puis] give you a very large and very moderately priced [à très bon marché] room on the [au] fourth floor.

26. I would not like to be [me loger] too high up and to have to climb [monter] too many stairs [trop d'escaliers]. Could I get [Pourrais-je avoir] a room on the first floor [au rez-de-chaussée]?

27. This room is very large and very beautiful. At what price [Pour combien] can you give it to me?

Conditional of "Pouvoir, To can,[2] to be able"

I could
thou couldst
he could
we could
you could
they could

The position of *en* is always immediately before the verb (with the exception of the affirmative imperative when *en* is placed after the verb).

This mode of employing *en* is by no means restricted to answers, but *en* must be used whenever anything previously mentioned is referred to again.

EXAMPLES

S'il vous faut du sucre, nous pouvons vous‿en fournir à bien bon marché.	If you need sugar, we can furnish you some at very cheap rates.
Regardez ces roses! Je vais‿en acheter une douzaine.	Look at those roses! I am going to buy a dozen.
Garçon, je n'ai pas de serviette. En voici une, monsieur.	Waiter, I have no napkin. Here is one, sir.
Je ne trouve pas d'allumettes. Ah, en voici.	I don't find any matches. Ah, here are some.

[2] This ungrammatical form is used here for convenience only.

28. Cette chambre‿est très bon marché. Elle n'est que[1] de douze cents francs par jour.

29. Très bien, je la prends. Veuillez faire[2] monter mes bagages, et payez le chauffeur. (mɔ̃·te—pɛ je)

30. Concierge, à quel‿étage pouvez-vous nous loger? (kɔ̃ sjɛ:rʒ)

31. Je ne peux pas vous le dire; il faut que j'appelle le patron. (il fo k ʒa pɛl lə pa trɔ̃)

32. Bonjour, monsieur. Vous voudriez des chambres?

33. Combien de chambres voudriez-vous?

34. Pourriez-vous nous donner un salon et deux chambres‿à coucher qui communiquent? (œ̃ sa lɔ̃ e dø ʃɑ̃:br‿a ku ʃe ki kɔ my nik)

35. Où pourriez-vous nous donner ces chambres?

36. Au second.—C'est trop haut. Ma femme ne peut pas monter si haut. Ne pourriez-vous pas nous donner des chambres plus bas? (ma fam—si o—ply bɑ)

37. Si, certainement. (si, sɛr tɛn mɑ̃)

38. A quel‿étage,‿alors?—Au rez-de-chaussée. (a lɔr)

39. Quel‿est le prix de ces chambres par jour?

40. C'est trois mille francs par jour.

41. C'est très cher. (sɛ trɛ ʃɛ:r)

---

[1] *Ne—que,* only. *Cette chambre ne coûte que quinze francs,* this room costs only fifteen francs.

[2] There is some difficulty in regard to *faire* when employed together with another verb. The difficulty, however, does not lie so much in the French, as in the English language.

We say in English: I have done it, *je l'ai fait,* expressing thereby a past action. So far the two languages correspond in the use of the verb "to have," *avoir.*

But we also say: I will have it done, meaning thereby: I will *cause* some other person to do something for me. This is expressed in French by *faire,* as: *Je veux le faire faire.* I want to have it done.

28. This room is very cheap. It costs only[1] 1200 francs a day.

29. Very well, I take it. Please have my baggage sent up and pay the chauffeur. (Literally: Please **make** [someone] bring up [faire[2] monter] my baggages.)

30. Porter, on [à] what floor can you put us [nous loger]?

31. I can not tell you. I must call the proprietor. (Literally: It is necessary that I call the manager.)

32. Good day, sir. You would like [voudriez] some [des] rooms?

33. How many rooms would you like?

34. Could you give us a parlor [salon] and two adjoining bedrooms? (Literally: two bedrooms [chambres à coucher] which communicate?)

35. Where could you give us these rooms?

36. On the third floor. That is too high up. My wife can not climb up [monter] so high. Couldn't you give us some rooms on a lower floor [plus bas]?

37. Yes, certainly.

38. On what floor then [alors]?—On the first floor [au rez-de-chaussée].

39. What is the price of these rooms per day?

40. It is 3000 francs per day. (Literally: That is 3000 francs a day.)

41. That's very dear.

A few examples will make this clear:—

Je veux le faire.	I want to do it.
Je veux le faire faire.	I want to *have* it done.
Voulez-vous porter votre sac de voyage?	Do you want to carry your valise?
Voulez-vous faire porter votre sac de voyage?	Do you wish to *have* your valise carried?
Voulez-vous‿enregistrer vos bagages?	Do you want to check your baggage?
Voulez-vous faire‿enregistrer vos bagages?	Do you want to *have* your baggage checked?

42. Je puis[1] vous donner des chambres moins chères. (mwɛ̃ ʃɛ:r)

43. Au deuxième‿étage, probablement? Non, monsieur, à l'entresol. (o dø·zjɛ·m‿e ta:z, prɔ ba blə mɑ̃? nɔ̃, a lɑ̃ trə sɔl.)

44. Et de quel prix seraient-elles[2]?

Je serais	(ʒə srɛ)
tu serais	(ty srɛ)
il serait	(il srɛ)
nous serions	(nu sə rjɔ̃)
vous seriez	(vu sə rje)
ils seraient	(il srɛ)

45. Ce serait deux mille sept cents francs par jour.

46. Bien! Je prendrai les chambres à l'entresol.

47. Désirez-vous diner maintenant, monsieur? (di ne)

48. Non, merci; je suis très fatigué et je veux‿aller me coucher[3] tout de suite.

---

[1] *Je puis* is a somewhat weaker form than *je peux*, I can, I am able.

Special Note: *N'est-ce pas* is used in place of the English *has he? has he not? is he? is he not? do you? don't you? will you? won't you?* etc. A few examples will make its use clear:

Elle chante bien, n'est-ce pas?	She sings well, doesn't she?
Elle ne chante pas bien, n'est-ce pas?	She doesn't sing well, does she?
Il est malade, n'est-ce pas?	He is ill, is he not?
Elle n'a pas de frère, n'est-ce pas?	She has no brother, has she?
Vous connaissez mon beau-frère, n'est-ce pas?	You know my brother-in-law, don't you?
Vous comprenez l'anglais, n'est-ce pas?	You understand English, do you not?
Vous devriez‿apprendre le français, n'est-ce pas?	You ought to learn French, ought you not?
Il ne partirait pas, n'est-ce pas?	He would not start, would he?

[2] *Elles* (fem. plur.), they, must be used here, because it refers to *les chambres* (fem. plur.), the rooms.

[3] A reflexive verb. The conjugation of these verbs presents but slight difficulties. In their simple tenses they are conjugated like the regular verbs of the conjugation to which they belong. Two pronouns are used in the conjugation, viz.:

Je me, I myself	*Nous nous*, we ourselves
tu te, thou thyself	*vous vous*, you yourself, yourselves
il se, he himself	*ils se* / *elles se* } they themselves
elle se, she herself	

42. I can[1] give you less expensive [des chambres moins chères]. rooms.

43. On the third floor, probably?—No, sir, on the mezzanine floor [à l'entresol].

44. And what price would they be [seraient-elles[2]?

I should be
thou wouldst be
he would be
we should be
you would be
they would be

45. It would be 2700 francs a day.

46. All right [Bien!]! I'll take the rooms on the mezzanine.

47. Do you wish to dine [diner] now, sir?

48. No, thanks, I am very much fatigued and want to go to bed [me coucher[3]] at once [tout de suite].

Therefore *s'habiller*, to dress one's self, is conjugated:

Je m'habille	I dress myself
tu t'habilles	etc.
il / *elle* } *s'habille*	etc.
nous nous‿habillons	we dress ourselves
vous vous‿habillez	etc.
ils / *elles* } *s'habillent*	etc.

All reflexive verbs are conjugated with *être*, to be, in their compound tenses, as:

Je me suis‿habillé (ée)	I have dressed myself
tu t'es‿habillé (ée)	thou hast dressed thyself
il s'est‿habillé	he has dressed himself
elle s'est‿habillée	she has dressed herself
nous nous sommes‿habillés (ées)	we have dressed ourselves
vous vous‿êtes‿habillé (és) (ée) (ées)	you have dressed yourself, yourselves
ils se sont‿habillés / *elles se sont‿habillées* }	they have dressed themselves

The participle agrees in gender and number with the pronoun object, which is also the subject it relates to.

49. Monsieur désire-t-il autre chose?

il me faut[2]
il te faut
il lui faut (il lɥi fo)

il nous faut
il vous faut
il leur faut (il lœːr fo)

50. Oui, des‿allumettes. (wi, de za ly mɛt)

51. Voici[3] des‿allumettes, monsieur. Monsieur a-t-il besoin d'autre chose? (bə zwɛ̃)

52. Non, merci, j'ai tout ce qu'il me faut maintenant. Je vais me coucher tout de suite. (tu skil mə fo)

Je dors[2]	(ʒə dɔr)
tu dors	
il dort	
nous dormons	(nu dɔr mɔ̃)
vous dormez	(vu dɔr me)
ils dorment	(il dɔrm)

53. Bonne nuit, monsieur. (bɔn nɥi)

---

[1] In France, servants and clerks address their masters and customers in the third person: *Madame, est-elle contente?* Are you pleased, Madam? Is the lady satisfied? *Monsieur a-t-il besoin d'un chapeau?* Do you need a hat, Sir? Does the gentleman need a hat?

To need is either expressed by *il faut* (impersonal verb used with *me, te, lui, nous, vous, leur*), or by *avoir besoin de* (to have need of). A few examples will suffice to make this construction clear:

Il me faut des gants *J'ai besoin de gants*	I need (I want) gloves.
Est-ce tout ce qu'il vous faut? *Est-ce tout ce dont vous‿avez besoin?*	Is that all you need?

49. Do you wish anything else, sir[1]? (Literally: Does Monsieur want anything else?)

I need[2]
thou needest
he } needs
she }
we need
you need
they need

50. Yes, some matches.

51. Here are [Voici[3]] some matches, sir. Do you need anything else, sir?

52. No, thanks, I have everything I need now. I am going (to go) to bed at once. (Literally: I have all that is necessary to me.)

I sleep	*or*	I am sleeping[2]
thou sleepest	"	thou art sleeping
he sleeps	"	he is sleeping
we sleep	"	we are sleeping
you sleep	"	you are sleeping
they sleep	"	they are sleeping

53. Good night, sir.

C'est tout ce qu'il me faut / *C'est tout ce dont j'ai besoin*	That's all I need (want).
Il vous faut‿un plus grand bureau	You need a larger office.
N'avez-vous pas besoin d'un bon domestique?	Don't you need a good servant?

Falloir, to be wanting, to be needed, to be necessary, is an impersonal verb (subject *il*, it). What is necessary, needed, wanting or wanted follows the impersonal *il faut*, etc.

[2] The pupil must not forget that we have no progressive conjugation in French. Whether we say in English: I am going or I go, in French we can only render it *je vais*. Where are you going? *Où allez-vous?* He is sleeping, *il dort*.

[3] *Voici*, here is, here are. *Me voici*, here I am. *Voilà*, there is, there are. *Vous voilà*, there you are.

Phrase Principale

Je voudrais partir par le premier train pour Paris,
ʒə vu drɛ par ti:r par lə prə mje trɛ̃ pur pa ri,
mais, malheureusement cela est‿impossible.
mɛ, ma lø rø:z mɑ̃ sla ɛ t‿ɛ̃ pɔ sibl.

Je voudrais (ʒə vu drɛ)
partir[1] (par ti:r)
par (par)
le premier train (lə prə mje trɛ̃)
pour (pur)
Paris (pa ri)
mais (mɛ)
malheureusement (ma lø rø:z mɑ̃)
cela (sla)
est‿impossible (ɛ tɛ̃ pɔ sibl)

Un Voyage

(œ̃ vwa ja:ʒ)

1. Que désirez-vous faire demain matin. Je voudrais partir pour Boulogne par le premier train. (pu:r bu lɔ·ɲ)
2. Pardon, monsieur; je voudrais‿aller à Boulogne. Pouvez-vous me dire⁀où est la gare du Nord? (par dɔ̃—la ga·r dy nɔ:r)
3. Pardon, monsieur; la gare du Nord, s'il vous plaît[2]? (sil vu plɛ)
4. Pardon, monsieur; quel⁀est le chemin pour⁀aller à la gare du Nord. (lə ʃmɛ̃)
5. Pardon, madame; où est la salle d'attente? (la sal da tɑ̃:t)
6. Je vous demande pardon, où est le guichet? (ʒə vu dmɑ̃:d par dɔ̃—lə gi ʃɛ)

---

[1] *Partir*, to leave, to start, is followed by *pour; aller* by *à*.

Special Note: *Moi* must be used in connection with prepositions, as: *Venez‿avec moi*, come with me. This is also the case with *toi*, thee; *lui*, him; *elle*, her; *nous*, us; *vous*, you; *eux* (masc.), them; *elles* (fem.), them. These are the so-called disjunctive personal pronouns.

When the verb is in the affirmative imperative *moi* and *toi* must always be used instead of *me* and *te*.

Excusez-moi	Excuse me
apportez-moi	bring me
donnez-moi	give me

Main Sentence

I should like to leave by the first train for Paris, but, unfortunately, that is impossible.

I should like (I would like)
to leave (to start, to set out)
by
the first train
for[1]
Paris,
but
unfortunately
that
is impossible

A Journey

1. What do you want [désirez-vous] to do tomorrow morning? I should like to leave [partir] by the first train for Boulogne.
2. Excuse me [Pardon], sir, I should like to go to Boulogne. Can you tell me where the North Station is [où est la gare du Nord]?
3. Pardon, sir; where is the North Station, please?
4. Pardon, sir; which is the way [le chemin] (to go) to the North Station?
5. Pardon, madam; where is the waiting-room [la salle d'attente]?
6. I beg (ask) your pardon, where is the ticket-office [le guichet]?

---

[2] This form of inquiry is very generally used. Thus we say:

Pardon, monsieur, l'opéra, s'il vous plaît? — Excuse me, sir, where is the opera-house?

Pardon, monsieur, la gare du Nord, s'il vous plaît? — Pardon, sir, which is the way to the North Station?

7. Pourriez-vous m'indiquer le guichet pour Versailles? (mɛ̃ di ke—vɛr sɑ:j)

8. Pardon, monsieur, voudriez-vous m'indiquer la gare de l'Est? (la ga:r də lɛst)

9. Oui, Monsieur; c'est[1] là, tout droit devant vous. Merci, monsieur. (sɛ la, tu drwɑ dvɑ̃ vu)

10. Pardon, monsieur; je voudrais prendre l'express d'Orléans. Pourriez-vous me dire‿où est le guichet? (lɛk sprɛs dɔr le ɑ̃)

11. Allez tout droit!
Droit devant vous!
En face! (ɑ̃ fas)

12. Le guichet est‿à droite (à gauche). (lə gi ʃɛ ɛ ta drwat—a go:ʃ)

13. Pardon de vous déranger; de quel côté se trouve[2] le guichet? A votre droite (gauche). De ce côté. De l'autre côté.[3]

14. De quel côté est le guichet? A droite! A gauche. De ce côté-ci. De ce côté-là.

15. Où prend‿on[4] les billets pour Versailles? (u prɑ̃ tɔ̃ le bi jɛ)

---

[1] Pupils frequently experience great difficulty in the proper use of *c'est*, it is. He, she, it or they before the verb *être* are rendered by *ce* instead of *il* or *ils*.

a. Before a noun: He is my brother, *c'est mon frère.*
They are my brothers, *ce sont mes frères.*

b. Before a pronoun: It is I, *c'est moi.*
It is he, *c'est* lui.

c. Before an adjective (when *c'est* means it or that and is not followed by a verb in the same clause):

It is just, *c'est juste.*
It is easy, *c'est* facile.

But: It is just to do that, *il est juste de faire cela.* This rule does not hold if the adjective is followed by *à, pour* or *sans.* For instance:

That's easy to do, *c'est facile‿à faire.*

d. Before a possessive pronoun: It is mine, *c'est le mien* (mjɛ̃)
They are mine, *ce sont les miens.*

7. Could you show me [m'indiquer] the ticket-office for Versailles?

8. I beg your pardon, sir; would you please [voudriez-vous] show me where the East Station is [où est la gare de l'Est]?

9. Yes, sir, it is there [c'est là[1]] straight [tout droit] ahead of [devant] you.—Thank you, sir.

10. Pardon me, sir, I should like to take the express train for Orléans [l'express d'Orléans]. Could you please [Pourriez-vous] tell me where the ticket-office is?

11. Go straight ahead [tout droit].
Straight ahead!
Right opposite [en face].

12. The ticket-office is on the right side [à droite] (on the left side [à gauche]).

13. Pardon me for disturbing you [de vous déranger], could you please tell me on which side [de quel côté] the ticket-office is? To your right [droite] (left [gauche]), on this side, on the other side.

14. On which side [De quel côté] is the ticket-office?—On the right. On the left. On this side [De ce côté-ci]. On that side [De ce côté-là].

15. Where does one get [Où prend‿on[1]] tickets for Versailles?

---

e. Before a demonstrative pronoun: It is that one, *c'est celui-là* (sə lyi la)

f. Before a superlative: It is the finest, *c'est le plus beau.*

But whenever with a single adjective we cannot say *that* instead of *it* or *he* in English, as for instance: He is tall, *il‿est grand,* the personal pronoun must be used.

[2] *se trouver,* to be, expresses location: *Où se trouve l'université?* Where is the university?

[3] *De ce côté,* on this side; *de l'autre côté,* on the other side.

[4] *On,* one, has no exact equivalent in English. *On* is very frequently used and applies to persons only. It is always followed by the third person singular and is used for our *one, they, people, we,* etc., and for our passive voice.

On cherche toujours le bonheur,	People always seek for happiness. We always seek for happiness. One always seeks for happiness.
On‿a déchiré mon‿habit,	My coat has been torn.
On nous‿a dit qu'elle viendra.	We have been told she will come.
Que dit‿on de moi?	What do they say of me?
On me dit que vous nous quittez.	I am told you are about to leave us.

16. Pourriez-vous me dire‿où l'on[1] prend les billets pour Versailles?

17. Oui, monsieur; de l'autre côté, au[2] troisième guichet.

18. Je vous remercie beaucoup. (ʒə vu rmɛ:r si)

19. Le guichet est-il⁀ouvert? (ɛ til⁀u vɛ:r) Est-ce que[3] le guichet est‿ouvert? (ɛs kə)

20. Est-ce[4] le guichet pour Asnières? (ɛs)

21. Je voudrais un billet pour⁀Asnières. (pur⁀a njɛ:r)

22. Quelle classe[5]?—Seconde, s'il vous plait. (kɛl klɑ·s—sə gɔ̃:d)

23. Donnez-moi une seconde[6] pour Versailles.

24. Aller seulement? Aller et retour? (a le sœ·l mɑ̃—rə tu:r)

25. Combien est-ce? Deux cent cinquante francs.

26. Combien coûte⁀une seconde⁀aller et retour pour⁀Enghien? (kut—ɑ̃ gjɛ̃)

27. Quel⁀est le supplément pour le wagon-lit? (sy ple mɑ̃—va gɔ̃ li)

28. Environ les trois quarts du prix d'un billet de première.[6] (ɑ̃ vi rɔ̃ le trwɑ kar dy pri dœ̃ bi jɛd prə mjɛ:r)

29. Vous trouverez un‿indicateur⁀au kiosque à journaux pour trente francs. (vu tru vre œ̃ nɛ̃ di ka tœ:r⁀o kjɔsk⁀a ʒu·r no)

30. Les‿indicateurs français donnent les‿heures d'arrivée et de départ des trains, les distances et les prix des billets pour chaque classe. (le zœ:r da ri ve e də de par—le dis tɑ̃:s)

31. Avez-vous des bagages?—Oui, j'ai une malle. (mal)

32. Je voudrais faire⁀enregistrer ma malle. La salle des bagages, s'il vous plait? (ɑ̃·r ʒis tre)

---

[1] After *où*, where, *si*, if, *que*, that, *l'on* is often used instead of *on*. Also in some other cases for euphony.

[2] The definite articles *le* (masc.), and *la* (fem.), the, are declined:

le	la	the
du	de la	of the
au	à la	to the

There is only one form for the plural:

les	the
des	of the
aux	to the

16. Could you tell me where one gets (takes, *prend*) tickets for Versailles?

17. Yes, sir, on the other side, at the [au] third window.

18. I thank you.

19. Is the ticket window open [ouvert]?

20. Is this[4] the ticket window for Asnières?

21. I would like a ticket [un billet] for Asnières.

22. Which [quelle] class?—Second, please.

23. Give me a second class ticket [une seconde] for Versailles.

24. One way [Aller] only? Round trip [Aller et retour]?

25. How much is it [est-ce]? 250 francs.

26. How much is [coûte] a second class round-trip ticket to [pour] Enghien?

27. What is the extra fare [supplément] for the sleeping car [le wagon-lit]?

28. About [Environ] ¾ [les trois quarts] of a first class ticket.

29. You will find a time-table at the news-stand for thirty francs.

30. French time-tables give the hours of arrival and departure of the trains, the distances and the prices of tickets of each class.

31. Have you any baggage?—Yes, I have a trunk [une malle].

32. I would like to have my trunk checked. The baggage room, if you please? (Literally: I would like **to make** (someone) check [faire enregistrer] my trunk [ma[7] malle].)

---

[3] Similarly we say: *Est-ce ici chez Monsieur Dumont?* Is this Mr. Dumont's place?

[4] This form of question with *est-ce que* is very frequently used, especially with the first person singular of the indicative present, often with other persons and tenses.

[5] The trains on French railways have first and second class compartments.

[6] Used very frequently. Similarly we say: *Une seconde*, a second class ticket.

Footnotes continued on page 68.

33. Facteur[1], voulez-vous m'indiquer la salle des bagages? La voilà, madame, à droite. (fak tœ:r)

34. Auriez-vous l'obligeance de me dire⁀où est la salle des bagages? J'ai une malle⁀à enregistrer. (ɔ·rje vu lɔ bli ʒɑ:s)

J'aurais	(ʒɔ rɛ)
tu aurais	(tɥ⁀ɔ rɛ)
il⁀aurait	(il ɔ rɛ)
nous‿aurions	(nu z͜ɔ rjɔ̃)
vous‿auriez	(vu z͜ɔ rje)
ils‿auraient	(il z͜ɔ rɛ)

35. Je vais‿appeler le facteur; il va enregistrer votre malle. (ʒə ve z͜a ple)

36. Facteur, ce monsieur voudrait faire⁀enregistrer sa malle.

37. Où allez-vous, monsieur? Quelle⁀est votre destination? (vɔ trə dɛs ti na sjɔ̃)

38. Je vais‿à Orléans.

39. Vous‿avez votre billet?—Non, pas‿encore.—Il faut votre billet[2] pour⁀enregistrer vos bagages. (pa z͜ɑ̃ kɔ·r)

40. Avez-vous votre billet? Le voilà.

41. Donnez-le moi. Entrez dans la salle d'attente. Je vais‿enregistrer vos colis et je vous‿apporterai le bulletin. (ɑ̃·tre—vo kɔ li—vu z͜a pɔr tə rel byl tɛ̃)

42. Porteur, voici mon billet. Faites‿enregistrer mes bagages et apportez-moi le bulletin et le billet au buffet. (o by fɛ)

Footnotes continued from page 67.

[7] The possessive pronouns are:

MASCULINE	FEMININE	PLURAL	
Mon	ma	mes	my
ton	ta	tes	thy
son	sa	ses	his, her, its
notre	notre	nos	our

33. Porter [Facteur], will you please show me [m'indiquer] the baggage room?—There it is [La voilà], madam, to your right.

34. Would you be kind enough to tell me where the baggage room is? I would like to check this trunk. (Literally: Would you have the kindness [l'obligeance] to tell me where is the baggage room? I have a trunk to check.)

I should have
thou wouldst have
he would have
we should have
you would have
they would have

35. I am going to call [appeler] the porter; he will (is going to) check your trunk.

36. Porter, this gentleman would like to have his trunk checked. (Literally: Porter, this gentleman [ce monsieur] would like **to make** (someone) check [faire enregistrer] his trunk [sa malle].

37. Where are you going, sir? What is your destination?

38. I am going to Orléans.

39. Have you your ticket?—No, not yet [pas encore].—You must have your ticket (your ticket is needed) in order to [pour] check your baggage.

40. Have you your ticket?—There it is [Le voilà].

41. Give it to me. Go into [Entrez dans] the waiting-room [salle d'attente]. I am going to check your baggage (*vos colis*, your packages) and I will bring you the check [le bulletin].

42. Porter, here is [voici] my ticket. Have [Faites] my baggage checked and bring me the check and the ticket to the buffet.

---

[1] *Facteur* signifies either porter (in a railroad station), or postman, letter-carrier.

votre	votre	vos	your
leur	leur	leurs	their

The possessive pronouns agree in gender and number with the object possessed (*not* with the possessor, as in English).

[2] Note again the use of *il faut* followed by a noun: *Il faut de l'argent*, Money is needed; *Il faut votre billet*, Your ticket is necessary, is needed.

VOCABULAIRE	VOCABULARY
Suite	*Continuation*
Qu'est-ce que cela signifie? (si ɲi fi)	What does that mean?
Le sens. (lə sã·s)	The sense.
Employer. (ã·plwɑ je)	To use, to employ.
Ce mot n'est pas‿employé dans ce sens.	This word is not used in this sense.
Comment ce mot est‿il employé?	How is this word used?
La phrase; les phrases. (la frɑ:z)	The sentence; the sentences.

Pour Faire Des‿Achats (Des‿Emplettes)	To make purchases; to do some shopping
Je voudrais faire quelques‿achats. (kɛl kə za ʃɑ)	I would like to make some purchases.
Je voudrais faire des‿emplettes. (de zã plɛt)	I should like to do some shopping.
Combien cela coûte-t-il? (ku tə til)	How much does that cost?
Quel‿est le prix de ceci?	What is the price of this?
Est-ce le meilleur marché? (lə mɛ jœ·r mar ʃe)	Is that the cheapest price?
Je ne peux pas vous le donner à meilleur marché.	I cannot give it to you any cheaper.
La facture. (fak ty:r)	The bill.
L'addition. (la di sjɔ̃)	The bill (at a restaurant only).
Le reçu. (lə rsy)	The receipt.

PART THREE

CONTENTS

Un Voyage

Suite

43. Voici votre bulletin, monsieur. Il y a[1] de l'excédent à payer. (il ja dlɛk se dɑ̃ a pɛ je)

44. Combien ai-je d'excédent?—Vous‿avez trente francs d'excédent. (kɔ̃ bjɛ̃ ɛ:ʒ)

45. Voici l'argent pour l'excédent. Et combien vous dois-je? (dwa:ʒ)

46. Il n'y a pas de tarif. Ce sera ce que vous voudrez.[2]

Je voudrai	(ʒə vu dre)
tu voudras	(ty vu dra)
il voudra	(il vu dra)
nous voudrons	(nu vu drɔ̃)
vous voudrez	(vu vu dre)
ils voudront	(il vu drɔ̃)

47. Ah oui! Voici tout ce que j'ai de monnaie. (mɔ nɛ)

48. Merci bien, monsieur. Les‿Américains[3] donnent toujours de généreux[4] pourboires. (le za me ri kɛ̃ dɔn tu ʒu:r də ʒe ne rø pur bwa:r)

---

[1] *Il y a* (there is, there are) is an idiomatic French expression.

Qu'y a-t-il de nouveau?	What is the news?
Il n'y a rien de nouveau.	There is no news.
Y a-t-il des lettres pour moi?	Are there any letters for me?
Y a-t-il de la place?—Non, monsieur, ce compartiment est‿au complet.	Is there any room here?—No, sir, this compartment is full.
Il y a beaucoup de monde.	There are a great many people here.
Y a-t-il quelque chose pour moi, garçon?	Anything for me, waiter?
Il y a déjà du monde.	There are already some people here.
Il y avait beaucoup de monde au concert.	There were a great many people at the concert.

For full rules and further idiomatic expressions see Part X.

[2] *Vouloir,* to be willing, to wish, to want has a full conjugation in French.

A Journey

Continuation

43. Here is [Voici] your check, sir. There is [Il y a[1]] some overweight [de l'excédent] to pay.

44. How much overweight have I?—Thirty francs, sir.

45. Here is the money for the overweight. And how much do I owe you [vous dois-je]?

46. We have no tariff. You may give what you like. (Literally: There is no tariff [tarif]. It will be what you will wish.)

Future

I shall want
you will want
he will want
we shall want
you will want
they will want

47. Oh yes! Here is all the small change I have. (Literally: all that which I have in change.)

48. Thank you very much, sir. Americans [Les Américains[3]] always give generous tips [de généreux[4] pourboires].

---

[3] The article is not only used before nouns used in a *definite*, but also before nouns employed in a *general* sense, as:

Les‿enfants aiment le jeu,	Children like games.
La vertu est‿aimable,	Virtue is lovable.
Les petites filles aiment les poupées,	Little girls like dolls.
Les‿hommes sont‿égoïstes,	Men are selfish.

[4] The plural of nouns and adjectives is formed by adding a (silent) *s* to the singular, as:

L'homme	les‿hommes	The man	the men
L'ami	les‿amis	The friend	the friends
Une jolie demoiselle		A pretty young lady	
De jolies demoiselles		Pretty young ladies	
Un‿habit noir		A black coat	
Des‿habits noirs		Black coats	

Footnotes continued on page 74.

49. A quelle‿heure partons-nous? (a kɛl‿œ:r)

Je pars	(ʒə pa:r)
tu pars	(ty pa:r)
il part	(il pa:r)
nous partons	(nu par tɔ̃)
vous partez	(vu par te)
ils partent	(il part)

50. A quelle‿heure arrivons-nous à Lyon? (ljɔ̃)

51. Est-ce qu'il y a un‿arrêt?—Vingt minutes, buffet. (œ̃ na rɛ)

52. Les voyageurs pour Marseille‿en voiture, s'il vous plaît. (le vwa ja ʒœ:r pur mar sɛ:j‿ɑ̃ vwa ty:r)

53. Quel‿est le signal du départ? Le coup de sifflet du chef de gare. lə si ɲal—lə kud si flɛ dy ʃɛf də ga:r)

Footnotes continued from page 73.

Words ending in *s*, *x* or *z* remain unchanged in the plural:

Le fils	les fils	The son	the sons
La voix	les voix	The voice	the voices
Heureux (sing. and plural)		Happy	

Words in *au* or *ou* take a (silent) *x*:

L'anneau	les‿anneaux	The ring	the rings
Le tableau	les tableaux	The picture	the pictures
Le beau jeu	les beaux jeux	The nice game	the nice games

Nouns in *al* (and a few in *ail*) change that termination into *aux*:

Le cheval	les chevaux	The horse	the horses
L'animal	les‿animaux	The animal	the animals
Le canal	les canaux	The canal	the canals

49. At what time [A quelle heure] do we leave?

I leave,	*or*	I am leaving
thou leavest,	*or*	thou art leaving
he leaves,	*or*	he is leaving
we leave,	*or*	we are leaving
you leave,	*or*	you are leaving
they leave,	*or*	they are leaving

50. At what time do we get to (do we arrive in) Lyons?

51. Is there[1] a stop [un‿arrêt]? Twenty minutes, buffet.[2]

52. Passengers for Marseilles all aboard [en voiture], please!

53. What is the signal for departure? The whistle (*coup de sifflet,* blow of the whistle) of the station-master [chef de gare].

---

[1] The interrogative form of *il y a* (There is, there are) is *y a-t‿il* or *est-ce qu'il y a.*

[2] *Vingt minutes, buffet.* Twenty minutes for a buffet lunch!—This abbreviated expression is found in a R.R. timetable or is announced by the train conductor.

CONVERSATIONAL EXERCISES

What they are and how they should be studied

Having thoroughly mastered the foregoing sentences, the student must now familiarize himself with the Conversational Exercises.

They consist of purely practical phrases, such as we are in the habit of using in common, every-day life. But as every person employs of necessity his own peculiar mode of diction,

Diversity of Expression

must be acquired from the very start by the student of foreign tongues.

The most commonplace thought can be expressed in numerous ways, and throughout these books, and especially in the Conversational Parts, are therefore given a vast number of sentences which, though worded differently, are identical in meaning.

The Advantages of this Plan

are self-evident. The pupil is no longer confined to a single phrase, but becomes familiar with a variety of expressions. He does not learn only **one** sentence by which he may state his wants, but controls **the whole colloquial vocabulary on any one subject,** and is thus enabled to sustain a conversation with almost anyone.

At the same time

The Conversations Are Graded

in such a manner that the only constructions, idioms, moods and tenses which are given are those which have been previously mastered by the student.

Mere questions and answers **of the guide-book style** have—as far as possible—been avoided. Later on all conversations are carried on in French.

All phrases used are, so to say,

Sentence-Molds

They are intended to teach the pupil to **think** in French, and with this end in view they must always be studied **aloud** and rendered frequently in French until the pupil can utter them just as smoothly and rapidly in the foreign language as in his own.

Let it always be remembered that:

"*Repetitio est mater studiorum.*"

("Repetition is the mother of studies.")

Nothing is so essential in the mastery of a foreign tongue as constant repetition because—

"*Gutta cavat lapidem, non vi, sed saepe cadendo.*"

("The drop hollows the stone, not by its force, but by its often falling.")

CONVERSATION

kɔ̃ vɛr sa sjɔ̃

Pour Demander Son Chemin

pur də mɑ̃ de sɔ̃ ʃmɛ̃

1. Pardon, monsieur. La rue Vivienne,[1] s'il vous plaît? (vi vjɛn)

2. Prenez[2] la troisième rue à droite, et ensuite suivez tout droit. (ry—ɑ̃ sɥit sɥi ve tu drwɑ)

3. Pardon, monsieur, voudriez-vous me dire‿où est la rue Royale?[3] (ry rwa jal)

4. Pardon, monsieur, voudriez-vous m'indiquer la rue de Rivoli? (mɛ̃ di ke la ry dri vɔ li)

5. Auriez-vous la bonté de me montrer le chemin pour‿aller au Boulevard des‿Italiens? (o bul vaːr de zi ta ljɛ̃)

6. Je vous demande pardon, quel‿est le chemin pour‿aller à la place de l'Opéra? (a la plas də lɔ pe ra)

7. Pardon, monsieur, j'ai perdu[4] mon chemin. Voudriez-vous m'indiquer l'Avenue de l'Opéra? (ʒe pɛr dy mɔ̃ ʃmɛ̃—la vny dlɔ pe ra)

8. Voudriez-vous‿être‿assez bon pour m'indiquer le chemin pour‿aller à la gare du Nord? (a se)

9. Prenez la deuxième rue à gauche, puis la troisième‿à droite,‿et ensuite suivez tout droit. Vous ne pouvez pas vous tromper de chemin. (trɔ̃·pe dʃmɛ̃)

10. Pourriez-vous me dire si cette rue conduit au Théâtre de la Renaissance? (kɔ̃·dɥi o te aːtrə dlar nɛ sɑ̃ːs)

---

[1] This abbreviated form of inquiry is very generally used.

[2] The imperative of the irregular verb *prendre*.

CONVERSATION

To Inquire One's Way

1. I beg your pardon, sir. (Where is) the rue Vivienne, please?

2. Take [Prenez] the third street to the right and then [ensuite] follow [suivez] straight ahead [tout droit].

3. Excuse me, sir; would you please [voudriez-vous] tell me where the rue Royale is?

4. Excuse me, sir, would you please show me the way to [m'indiquer] the rue de Rivoli?

5. Would you kindly (*Auriez-vous la bonté*, Would you have the kindness) show me the way [le chemin pour aller] to the Boulevard des‿Italiens?

6. Pardon me (I ask your pardon, *Je vous demande pardon*), which is the way [le chemin] to go to the Place de l'Opéra?

7. Excuse me, sir, I have lost [perdu[4]] my way. Would you show me the way to [m'indiquer] the Avenue de l'Opéra?

8. Would you be kind enough to [assez bon pour] tell me the way to (to go to, *pour‿aller*) the North Station [la gare du Nord]?

9. Take the second street on the left, then [puis] the third street on the right, and then go straight ahead [suivez tout droit]. You cannot miss your way [vous tromper de chemin].

10. Could you tell me whether [si] this street leads [conduit] to the Renaissance Theater?

---

[3] Literally: Royal Street.

[4] Past participle of *perdre*, to lose; *perdu*, lost.

11. Oui, allez tout droit, jusqu'à ce que vous‿arriviez à la Porte St. Martin. (ʒys ka skə vu za ri vje a la pɔrt sɛ̃ mar tɛ̃)

12. Pardon, l'hôtel des Deux-Mondes, s'il vous plaît? (dø mɔ̃:d)

13. Prenez la deuxième rue à droite͡ et ensuite continuez tout droit jusqu'à la place de l'Opéra. Une fois arrivé[2] là, suivez l'Avenue de l'Opéra, qui vous‿y conduira. (yn fwa a ri ve la—ki vu zi kɔ̃ dɥi ra)

14. Prenez la troisième rue à gauche͡ et allez tout droit, jusqu'à ce que vous‿arriviez à un square. (skwa:r)

15. Passez ce pont, puis traversez le square. Vous ne pouvez pas vous tromper de chemin. (pa se spɔ̃—tra vɛr se)

16. J'ai bien peur[4] de me perdre‿en route. (pœ:r—pɛ:rdr‿ɑ̃ rut)

---

[1] It is almost impossible to translate the so-called subjunctive into English. As a matter of fact we scarcely use the subjunctive mood in our language. Not so in French where this mood is very frequently employed.

Let the student remember that the subjunctive expresses uncertainty, indecision, doubt or fear existing in the mind of the speaker, as to the action referred to and that, therefore, it can be employed in subordinate sentences only.

The subjunctive is therefore always joined to the main sentence, generally by the conjunction *que* or by conjunctions compounded with *que* as *jusqu'à ce que,* till, *afin que,* in order that, etc.

Thus we say:

I know he will come, *Je sais qu'il viendra,*
using the indicative mood—as in English—because no doubt or uncertainty exists in the speaker's mind.

But:

Do you think he will come? *Croyez-vous qu'il vienne?*
using the subjunctive mood, because the question itself expresses doubt and uncertainty.

Or: I don't think he will come, *Je ne crois pas qu'il vienne,*
using again the subjunctive because the negative implies uncertainty.

This rule properly applied would illustrate the correct employment of this difficult mood. We shall be obliged, however, to give special rules later on.

As regards the formation of the present subjunctive of verbs of the first conjugation, we add the following endings to the stem.

11. Yes; go straight ahead till you reach [jusqu'à ce que vous arriviez[2] à] the Porte St. Martin.

12. Excuse me, the Hotel des Deux-Mondes, please? (Literally: Pardon, the Hotel of the Two Worlds, if you please?)

13. Take the second street to your right and then go straight ahead [continuez tout droit] as far as [jusqu'à] the Place de l'Opéra. Once there [une fois arrivé là], follow the Avenue de l'Opéra which [qui] will lead you there [vous‿y[3] conduira].

14. Take the third street to your left and go straight ahead till [jusqu'à ce que] you come [vous arriviez] to a square.

15. Go across (Pass over, *Passez*) this bridge [pont], then across [traversez] the square. You cannot miss (mistake, *vous tromper de*) your way.

16. I am afraid[4] I shall lose my way. (Literally: I have great [bien] fear [peur] of getting lost [de me perdre] on the way [en route].)

---

je	——	e
tu	——	es
il	——	e
nous	——	ions
vous	——	iez
ils	——	ent

It will therefore be seen that the subjunctive of the present differs only in the first and second person plural from the present indicative. Let the student remember this.

[2] Past participle of *arriver*, to arrive; *arrivé*, arrived. The past participles of all regular verbs of the first conjugation end in *é*, which is added to the stem, as: *trouver*, to find, *trouvé*, found; *montrer*, to show; *montré*, shown; *payer*, to pay; *payé*, paid; *donner*, to give; *donné*, given.

The pupil ought to observe that verbs expressing an *unfavorable* meaning are generally followed by *de*, as:

J'ai peur de me perdre en route,	I am afraid I shall lose my way.
Je crains de m'enrhumer,	I am afraid of catching cold.
Il refuse de le faire,	He refuses to do it.

All verbs of *command* or *request* take *de*, as:

Dites-lui de m'apporter mon déjeûner. Tell him to bring me my breakfast.

[3] *y* is an adverbial pronoun meaning there, to it, on it, etc.; *Nous allons à Paris. Nous‿y allons. La chaise est dans la chambre. Elle y est.*

[4] *J'ai peur* (literally: I have fear), I fear, I am afraid, is an idiomatic expression.

17. Désirez-vous que je vous‿accompagne?—Oui, s'il vous plaît. (kəʒ vu za kɔ̃ paɲ)

18. Si vous craignez de vous perdre, vous pourriez prendre⁀un taxi. (si vu krɛ ɲe dvu pɛ:r dr)

19. Est-ce loin d'ici? (lwɛ̃ di si)
Est-ce[1] près d'ici? (prɛ)

20. Non, ce n'est pas loin. (snɛ pɑ)

Faire des‿Achats — Faire des‿Emplettes

fɛ:r de za ʃɑ—de zɑ̃ plɛt

1. Que voulez-vous faire cet‿après-midi? (sɛ ta prɛ mi di)

2. Je voudrais‿aller faire[2] quelques‿achats. (kɛl kə za ʃɑ)

3. Et où désirez-vous aller faire vos‿emplettes? (vo zɑ̃ plɛt)

4. Je ne sais vraiment pas. Mais vous‿avez‿été plusieurs fois à Paris. Pouvez-vous me dire⁀où je pourrais‿acheter de bons gants? (vrɛ mɑ̃)

5. Est-ce tout ce dont vous‿avez besoin. (tu sdɔ̃)

6. Non, j'ai aussi quelques petites choses⁀à acheter pour[3] ma femme. (kɛl kə ptit ʃo:z⁀a aʃ te pu:r ma fam)

---

[1] Note: *C'est,* It is; *Est-ce?* Is it?; *Ce n'est pas,* It is not; *N'est-ce pas?* Is it not?

[2] There are about fifty verbs which do not require any preposition when governing another verb. A list of these is given in Part X. The following are most frequently used:

Aimer mieux	to prefer	*Falloir*	to be necessary
Aller	to go	*Oser*	to dare
Compter	to intend	*Pouvoir*	to be able to
Désirer	to wish	*Savoir*	to know
Envoyer	to send	*Venir*	to come (generally)
Espérer	to hope	*Voir*	to see
Faire	to make	*Vouloir*	to be willing

17. Do you want me to accompany you?—Yes, please. (Literally: Do you desire that I accompany you [que je vous‿accompagne]? —Yes, if you please.)

18. If you are afraid [Si vous craignez] of getting lost [de vous perdre] you might take a taxi.

19. Is it[1] far [loin] from here [d'ici]?

20. No, it is not far.[1]

To Make Purchases — To Go Shopping

1. What do you want to do this afternoon (cet‿après-midi?)

2. I would like to do some shopping. (Literally: I should like to go [aller] to make[2] some purchases [quelques‿achats].)

3. And where do you want to (go and) make your purchases?

4. I really [vraiment] don't know. But you have been [été] several [plusieurs] times [fois] in Paris. Can you tell me where I could [pourrais] buy some good gloves [de bons gants]?

5. Is that all you need? (Literally: Is this all of which [dont] you have need?)

6. No; I have also to buy a few [quelques] small things for[3] my wife [pour[3] ma femme].

EXAMPLES

Je compte‿acheter un chapeau neuf.	I intend buying a new hat.
J'ai fait raccommoder mon pantalon.	I have had my trousers mended.
Il me faut lui donner cet‿argent.	I must give him this money.
Je n'ose pas dire cela.	I don't dare to say that.
Venez dîner avec nous.	Come and dine with us.

[3] For (preposition), *pour;* for (conjunction, equivalent to as or because) *car.*

7. Elle‿a besoin d'épingles à cheveux, d'une brosse à dents, d'un peigne, d'une brosse à cheveux et d'autres bagatelles. (e pɛ̃:gl‿a ʃvø—brɔs‿a dɑ̃—pɛ:ɲ—ba ga tɛl)

8. Veuillez venir‿avec moi, car[1] je ne sais pas où trouver toutes ces choses. (vœ:je vni:r‿a vɛk mwa—tru ve)

9. Vous pouvez les trouver tout près d'ici. Voulez-vous sortir tout de suite? (sɔr ti:r)

10. Certainement, tout de suite. Ma femme désire sortir‿et elle‿a besoin de tous[2] ces‿articles. (tu se zar ti:kl)

11. Très bien; il y a juste‿en face un très bon magasin, où vous pouvez trouver tout ce dont vous‿avez besoin. (ʒyst‿ɑ̃ fas—ma ga zɛ̃)

12. Est-ce‿un magasin bon marché?

13. Oh oui, très bon marché. Vous savez que ces‿articles de toilette sont bien meilleur[3] marché ici qu'en[4]‿Amérique. (twa lɛt—mɛ jœ:r mar ʃe—kɑ̃ na me rik)

14. Voici notre magasin; il‿est très grand, n'est-ce pas?—Oui, c'est très grand et très beau.

15. Que désirez-vous‿acheter d'abord?—Des gants. (da bɔ:r)

16. J'ai besoin de deux paires de gants, une paire de noirs[5] et une paire de bruns. Veuillez me montrer de bons gants de chevreau, Mademoiselle. (nwa:r—brœ̃—mad mwa zɛl)

---

[1] See footnote, page 83.

[2] *Tout* (masc. sing.), *toute* (fem. sing.), *tous* (masc. plur.), *toutes* (fem. plur.), every, all.

[3] *Bon marché*, cheap; *meilleur marché*, cheaper.

[4] While *à* is generally used with towns, *en* is employed before most names of countries, as:

à Berlin,	at, in *or* to Berlin.
à Paris,	" " " " Paris.
à Londres,	" " " " London.
en France,	in *or* to France.
en‿Angleterre,	" " " England.
en‿Amérique,	" " " America.

7. She needs [a besoin d'] hairpins [épingles à cheveux], a toothbrush [d'une brosse à dents], a comb [d'un peigne], a hairbrush [d'une brosse à cheveux], and some other trifles [d'autres bagatelles].

8. Please [Veuillez] come with me as [car] I don't know where to find all these things [toutes[2] ces choses].

9. You can find them quite near [tout près] (from here, *d'ici*). Do you want to go out [sortir] at once?

10. Certainly [Certainement], at once. My wife wishes to go out and she needs [elle a besoin de] all[2] these articles.

11. All right; directly opposite is a very good store, where you can get everything you need. (Literally: Very well; there is [il y a] just [juste] opposite [en face] a very good store where you can find all this of which you have need.)

12. Is that a moderately priced [bon marché[3]] store?

13. Oh yes, quite low priced. You know that these toilet articles [ces articles de toilette] are much cheaper [bien meilleur marché[3]] here than [qu'] in America.

14. Here is [Voici] our store; (it is) very large [grand], isn't it [n'est-ce pas]?—Yes, it is very large and very beautiful [beau].

15. What do you want to buy first [d'abord]?—(Some) gloves.

16. I need [J'ai besoin de] two pairs of gloves, a pair of black[5] ones [de noirs] and a pair of brown ones [de bruns]. Please show me some good kid gloves [de bons gants de chevreau].

But with a few countries, the names of which are masculine in French, *au* or *aux* is used, as:

au Mexique, in *or* to Mexico.
aux‿États-Unis, in *or* to the United States.

[5] See footnote, page 86.

17. Désirez-vous un brun[1] clair? (klɛ:r)

18. Pas[2] trop clair; donnez-moi une bonne teinte moyenne, s'il vous plaît. (yn bɔn tɛ̃:t mwa jɛn)

19. Quel prix voulez-vous payer?—Pas trop cher.

20. Pour douze cents francs, je puis vous donner de très bons gants.

21. Combien cela fait‿il en monnaie américaine? (ɑ̃ mɔ nɛ a me ri kɛ·n)

Je fais	(ʒə fɛ)
tu fais	(ty fɛ)
il fait	(il fɛ)
nous faisons	(nu fzɔ̃)
vous faites	(vu fɛt)
ils font	(il fɔ̃)

22. Un dollar vaut environ quatre cents francs. (œ̃ dɔ la:r vo ɑ̃ vi rɔ̃)

23. Douze cents francs font[3] environ trois dollars.

24. Douze cents francs font environ une livre en monnaie anglaise. Ces gants ne sont pas chers, n'est-ce pas?

---

[1] The principal colors are:

Les Couleurs	**The Colors**
Blanc, blanche	White
noir, noire	black
bleu, bleue	blue
brun, brune	brown
châtain, châtaine	chestnut
rouge, rouge	red
roux, rousse	reddish
cramoisi, cramoisie	crimson
écarlate, écarlate	scarlet
vert, verte	green
jaune, jaune	yellow
olive, olive	olive
une couleur bon teint	a fast color
une couleur salissante	a color easily soiled

[2] When no verb is used the negation is expressed by *pas*, as: *pas‿aujourd'hui*, not to-day; *pas pour moi*, not for me.

17. Do you want a light brown [un brun clair]?

18. Not too [Pas trop] light; give me a good medium shade [teinte moyenne], if you please.

19. What price do you wish to pay?—Not too expensive [cher].

20. For twelve hundred francs I can give you (some, *de*) very good gloves.

21. How much is that [cela fait-il] in American money [monnaie américaine]?

I make	*or*	I am making
thou makest	"	thou art making
he makes	"	he is making
we make	"	we are making
you make	"	you are making
they make	"	they are making

22. A dollar is worth [vaut] about 400 francs.

23. 1200 francs are equal to [font] about 3 dollars.

24. 1200 francs are equal to [font] about one pound in English money. These gloves are not expensive, are they [n'est-ce pas]?

---

[3] Similarly we say:

Combien font vingt-quatre et cinquante?	How much is twenty-four and fifty?
Combien font dix-sept multiplié par six?	How much is six times seventeen?

Special Note: In speaking of the parts of the body or qualities of the mind, the French use *le, la, les,* instead of the possessive pronoun, or the indefinite article in English:

J'ai froid aux pieds.	My feet are cold.
Il s'est coupé les ongles.	He has cut his nails.
J'ai mal à la tête.	I have a headache.
Elle a mal aux dents.	She has a toothache.
Lavez-vous les mains et la figure.	Wash your hands and face.
Ne vous essuyez pas les mains à cette serviette.	Do not wipe your hands on this towel.

25. C'est très bon marché. Pour cinq **dollars** nous n'avons pas de gants comme ceux-ci aux‿États-Unis. (kɔm sø si o ze ta zy ni)

26. Quel numéro portez-vous, monsieur?—Je ne sais plus. J'oublie toujours mon numéro. (ʒu bli tu ʒu:r)

27. Très bien. Je vais vous prendre mesure. (prɑ̃: drm zy:r)

28. Voulez-vous essayer ces gants? (ɛ sɛ je)

29. Ces gants ne me vont pas; ils sont trop grands.—Je les trouve[1]⁀un peu longs. (œ̃ pø lɔ̃)

30. En[2] voici une paire qui vous‿ira. (ki vu zi ra)

Future of Aller

J'irai	(ʒi re)
tu iras	(ty i ra)
il⁀ira	(il⁀i ra)
nous‿irons	(nu zi rɔ̃)
vous‿irez	(vu zi re)
ils‿iront	(il zi rɔ̃)

31. Ils sont trop‿étroits. J'ai peur de les faire craquer. (e trwa—kra ke)

[1] To think is expressed by *croire*, when belief is implied, as:

Croyez-vous qu'il pleuve? — Do you think it is going to rain (*i.e.*, do you believe it)?

To think is given by *trouver*, when an opinion is implied, as:

Trouvez-vous cela bon? — Do you think this is good?

Of course, *penser* may be used in both instances, but a Frenchman would never

25. That is very cheap. For five dollars we cannot get gloves like these in the United States. (Literally: That is very cheap. For five dollars we have not gloves like [comme] these [ceux-ci] in the States United [aux‿États-Unis].)

26. What size [numéro] do you wear [portez-vous], sir?—I don't know any more [Je ne sais plus]. I always forget [oublie] my size.

27. Very well, I am going to take your measure [vous prendre mesure].

28. Will you try these gloves on [essayer ces gants]?

29. These gloves do not fit me [ne me vont pas]; they are too large [grands]. I find them a little long.

30. Here is [En[2] voici] a pair which will fit you [qui vous ira].

Future of Aller

I shall go
thou wilt go
he will go
we shall go
you will go
they will go

31. They are too narrow [étroits]. I am afraid I shall split them. (Literally: I have fear [peur] of making them split [craquer].)

---

think of doing so. With him *penser* expresses to think as an act of mental consideration, as:

A quoi pensez-vous? What are you thinking about?

With *que*, *penser* is generally followed by *de*, as:

Que pensez-vous de cet‿homme? What do you think of this man?

[2] In French the complete thought must be expressed: a pair of them. Hence: *en voici une paire.*

32. Attendez. Je vais‿y[1] mettre‿un peu de poudre. Maintenant, essayez-les. (a tɑ̃ de. ʒə vɛ zi mɛ·trœ pød pu·dr)

33. Combien cela fait-il en tout?

34. Cela fait trois mille francs en tout.

35. Combien coûtent ces‿épingles?—Elles coûtent quarante francs le paquet. (kut se ze pɛ̃:gl—pa kɛ)

36. Et ce démêloir[2], combien coûte-t-il?—Celui-là coûte cent cinquante francs. (de mɛ lwa:r—ku tə til—sə lɥi la)

37. Il me faut‿aussi un peigne fin. (œ̃ pɛ:ɲ fɛ̃)

38. Combien celui-là coûte-t-il?—Celui-là est de cent francs.

39. Très bien. Je prendrai cinq paquets d'épingles, le démêloir et ce peigne fin. Combien cela fait-il‿en tout?

40. Cela fait en tout quatre cent cinquante francs.

41. Envoyez tout cela chez[3] moi, s'il vous plait.

42. Très bien. Tout‿y sera dans[4]‿une‿heure. (tu ti sra dɑ̃ zyn‿œ:r)

---

[1] *Y, at, to it, to them, at it, at them, in it, on it, there* is placed in the same position as *en, i.e.*, it is placed immediately before the verb, except with the affirmative imperative when *en* and *y* come after the verb, like all other pronoun-objects.

Allez-y.	Go there.
N'y allez pas.	Don't go there.
Y pensez-vous?	Are you thinking of it?
Oui, j'y pense.	Yes, I am thinking of it.
Le livre est-il sur la table?—Oui, il‿y est.	Is the book on the table?—Yes, it is on it.

Exceptions: In some very rare cases *en* and *y* will appear together. In such cases *y* is placed before *en*, as:

Une seconde, Orléans, s'il vous plaît.	One second-class ticket for Orléans, if you please.
Il n'y en‿a pas; c'est‿un express. Il n'y a que des premières.	There are none for sale; this is an express train. Only first-class tickets sold.

[2] *Le démêloir*, the comb, the large comb; *un peigne fin*, a fine-tooth comb.

32. (Just) wait. I am going to put [Je vais‿y[1] mettre] a little powder [poudre] into them. Now, try them.

33. How much does that amount to? (Literally: How much does it make in all [en tout]?)

34. That amounts to [Cela fait] 3000 francs in all.

35. How much are (cost, *coûtent*) these pins [ces‿épingles]?—They cost 40 francs a [le] package.

36. And how much is this comb [ce démêloir]?—That one [celui-là] coûte cent cinquante francs.

37. I also need [Il me faut‿aussi] a fine-tooth comb [un peigne fin].

38. What's the price of that one?—That one costs ten francs. (Literally: How much does that one [celui-là] cost? That one costs [est de] 100 francs.)

39. All right [Très bien], I'll take five packages [paquets] of pins, the large comb and this fine-tooth comb. How much does that come to [cela fait-il]?

40. The total amount is [Cela fait en tout] 450 francs

41. Please send [envoyez] all these things (all that, *tout cela*) to my place [chez[3] moi].

42. All right. You'll get them within an hour. (Literally: Very well. All will be there [y sera] within [dans] an hour.)

---

[3] The French have no word for *home*. They render it by *chez*, as:

Est-il chez lui? — Is he at home?
Est-elle chez‿elle? — Is she at home?
Je suis chez moi. — I am at home.
Allez-vous chez vous? — Are you going home?

Chez, like any preposition, is followed by a disjunctive pronoun: *pour moi; avec lui; chez elle;* etc.

[4] *Dans* with reference to *time* denotes *when* a certain thing will occur, as:
Je reviendrai dans trois jours. — I shall return in (after) three days.

En with reference to *time* denotes how long a certain thing will last, as:
Il fera ce voyage en trois jours. — He will make (*i.e.*, complete) this journey within three days.

En with reference to place is rarely followed by the article or an adjective and expresses something *indefinite; dans,* something *definite. Dans* is always followed by the article, as:

Il est‿en ville. — He is in town.
Il est dans la ville. — He is in (inside) the city.

Compare with Part X.

VOCABULAIRE *Suite*	VOCABULARY *Continuation*
Veuillez envoyer ces‿articles⁀ avec la facture⁀acquittée. (a ki te)	Please send these goods with a receipted bill.
Le bureau (by ro)	The office
Le caissier (kɛ sje)	The cashier
Le bureau du caissier	The cashier's desk
Payer (pɛ je)	To pay
Quel‿est le total? (tɔ tal)	What is the total?
L'argent (lar ʒɑ̃)	The money
La monnaie (mɔ nɛ)	The change
Je n'ai pas de monnaie sur moi.	I have no change with me. (Literally: upon me)
Avez-vous de la monnaie sur vous?	Have you any change with you?
Vous ne me donnez pas mon compte. (mɔ̃ kɔ̃·t)	You did not give me the correct change (my reckoning).
Changer (ʃɑ̃ ʒe)	To change
Pouvez-vous me changer un billet de mille francs?	Can you change a thousand franc bill for me?
Le billet de banque (bɑ̃·k)	The bank-note
Voulez-vous de gros billets? (gro)	Do you want large denominations?
Vendre (vɑ̃·dr)	To sell
A quel prix vendez-vous ceci? (pri)	At what price do you sell this?

PART FOUR

CONTENTS

Chez Une Modiste

1. Bonjour,[1] madame. Que puis-je vous montrer ce matin?[2] (ma dam —pɥi:ʒ)
2. Je voudrais un chapeau.[3]
3. Comment madame le voudrait-elle?[4]
4. Je le voudrais haut et garni[5] de dentelles. (gar ni də dɑ̃·tɛl)
5. En voici un bien joli, madame. C'est tout ce qu'il y a de plu nouveau. (ʒɔ li—sɛ tu skil ja də ply nu vo)
6. Essayez-le, s'il vous plaît.
7. Comment me va-t-il?
8. Il ne pourrait pas mieux aller. (mjø)
9. Ce chapeau vous va à merveille. (mɛr vɛ:j)
10. Quel est le prix de ce chapeau?—C'est deux mille francs.
11. Vous me le laisserez à moins? (lɛ sre a mwɛ̃)
12. Je voudrais bien, mais c'est impossible. Nous ne vendons qu'à[6] prix fixe. (sɛ tɛ̃ pɔ sibl—nu n vɑ̃·dɔ̃ ka pri fiks)
13. Est-ce là votre dernier prix?—Oui, madame, c'est notre prix le plus bas. (dɛr nje—lə ply bɑ)
14. Je ne veux pas marchander, mais cela me semble hors de prix. (mar ʃɑ̃ de—slam sɑ̃·blə ɔr də pri)

---

[1] The French do not say "Good morning," but *bonjour*.

[2] A French phrase much used by shopkeepers. Another phrase also very frequently used is:

Qu'y a-t-il pour votre service?	What can I do for you? (Literally: What is there at your service)?

[3] *Un chapeau* means not only a hat, but also a bonnet.

[4] A form of question very generally used by shopkeepers. In the same manner a waiter will announce: *Monsieur est servi, Madame est servie.*

At a Milliner's

1. Good morning,[1] madam. What can I [puis-je] show[2] you this morning?
2. I should like a hat.[3]
3. What kind would madam like? (Literally: How would madam like it?[4])
4. I want a high one, trimmed with lace. (Literally: I would like it high and trimmed [garni[5]] with [de] lace [dentelles].)
5. Here is a very pretty one [bien joli], madam. It is the very latest style. (Literally: It is all that there is [c'est tout ce qu'il y a] of most new [de plus nouveau]; **or** it's the newest thing there is.)
6. Please try it on.
7. Is it becoming to me? (Literally: How does it become me?)
8. It could not fit (become you) better [mieux].
9. This hat is exceedingly becoming to you. (Literally: This hat becomes you (fits you) wonderfully [à merveille].)
10. What's the price of this hat? It is 2000 francs.
11. Will you let me have it cheaper? (Literally: You will leave it to me for less [à moins].)
12. I should like to, but it is impossible. We only[6] sell [Nous ne vendons qu'] at fixed prices [à prix fixe].
13. Is that your best (last, *dernier*) price?—Yes, madam, it's our very lowest price [notre prix le plus bas].
14. I don't want to bargain [marchander], but that seems exorbitant [hors de prix] to me.

---

[5] *Garnir*, to trim; *faire garnir*, to have trimmed.

Comment voulez-vous faire garnir ce chapeau?	How do you want to have this hat trimmed?
Je veux le faire garnir de rubans.	I want to have it trimmed with ribbons.

[6] Note again the translation of only by *ne . . . que* when only accompanies a verb; *que* bears upon the noun object or an adverb or adjective:

Il ne parle qu'avec les enfants.	He speaks only to the children.
Elle n'achètera que ce chapeau.	She will only buy this hat.
Il ne parle qu'avec difficulté.	He speaks only with difficulty.

15. Ne pourriez-vous pas me rabattre quelque chose sur le prix? (ra ba tr)

16. Enfin, comme vous‿êtes‿une nouvelle cliente, je vous ferai une diminution, pour cette fois-ci. Je vous le laisserai à dix-huit cents francs. (yn nu vɛl kli jɑ̃:t—ʒə vu fre yn di mi ny sjɔ̃)

Je ferai	(ʒə fre)
tu feras	(ty fra)
il fera	(il fra)
nous ferons	(nu frɔ̃)
vous ferez	(vu fre)
ils feront	(il frɔ̃)

17. Dans ce cas-là, envoyez-le moi. Voici mon‿adresse. (dɑ̃ skɑ la, ɑ̃ vwa je lə mwa—mɔ n‿a drɛs)

Pour Saluer

pu·r sa lɥe

1. Bonjour, comment vous portez-vous?[1] (kɔ mɑ̃ vu pɔr te vu)
Comment‿allez-vous? (kɔ mɑ̃ t‿a le vu)
Comment cela va-t‿il?
Comment ça va-t‿il?

2. Je vais‿assez bien, merci.
Je me porte‿assez bien, merci.
Merci, cela va assez bien.
Ça va assez bien, merci.

[1] All the above expressions are used for our: How do you do? How are you? It must, however, be observed that the two latter expressions: *Comment cela va-t‿il? Comment ça va-t-il?* or the frequently heard inquiry: *Comment ça va?* are very familiar.

Similarly we say:

Comment va la santé?	How is your health?
Cela va assez bien, merci.	Pretty good, thank you.
Ça va mieux.	Better.
Ça va beaucoup mieux.	Much better.

15. Couldn't you give me a reduction? (Literally: Could you not, for me [me], come down [rabattre] something [quelque chose] in [sur] price?)

16. Well [Enfin], as you are a new customer [cliente], I will—for once [pour cette fois-ci]—make you a reduction [une diminution]. I shall let you have it for 1800 francs.

I shall make
thou wilt make
he will make
we shall make
you will make
they will make

17. In that case, send it to me. Here is [Voici] my address.

Salutations

1. Good morning, how do you feel? How are you? How goes it?[1] (Literally: Good day, how do you bear yourself? **Or**: How do you go? **Or**: How goes it?)

2. I feel pretty [assez] well, thank you.

---

[1] It must be remembered that questions about one's health, when asked in the *past* tense, must always be rendered with the reflexive verb *se porter* (and *never* with *aller*), as:

Comment vous‿êtes-vous porté depuis que je ne vous‿ai vu? How have you been since I saw you?

3. Et comment se porte madame Morin?[1] (kɔ mɑ̃ spɔrt ma dam mɔ rɛ̃)
Et comment va votre femme?

4. Elle va (Elle se porte) très bien, je vous remercie. (ʒə vur mɛr si)

5. Et comment‿allez-vous, vous-même?—Très bien, merci. (vu mɛ:m)

6. Et comment se porte (va) votre frère? J'espère[2] qu'il va tout‿à fait bien maintenant. (vɔ trə frɛ:r—ʒɛs pɛ:r—tu t‿a fɛ)

7. Je vais très bien, merci, mais mon pauvre frère, ne peut pas‿ encore sortir. Il est‿encore très faible. (mɔ̃ po•vrə frɛ:r—pɑ z‿ɑ̃ kɔ•r)

8. Mais j'espère qu'il sera bientôt rétabli. Il est très jeune͡ il a une[3] solide constitution,[4] et à son‿âge͡ on se remet très vite. (bjɛ̃ to re ta bli—ʒœ•n—yn sɔ lid kɔ̃ sti ty sjɔ̃—a sɔ n‿a:ʒ͡ ɔ̃ sər mɛ trɛ vit)

9. Espérons[5]-le. (ɛs pe rɔ̃ lə)

---

[1] When speaking about other people's relatives—unless a certain degree of familiarity exists—*madame*, *monsieur* and *mademoiselle* are used, as:

Comment va monsieur?	How is your husband?
Comment se porte madame?	How is your wife?
Comment se porte madame votre mère?	How is your mother?

But *never* use them in speaking of your *own* relatives (i.e., *never* say: Monsieur mon père, madame ma mère). It would sound exceedingly ridiculous.

[2] Verbs of the first conjugation having an *é* preceding the infinitive termination, as *espérer*, *régler*, *considérer*, etc., change it into *è* before an *e mute*. Thus: *Espérer*, To hope.
Pres: J'espère, tu espères, il͡ espère, nous‿espérons, vous‿espérez, ils‿espèrent.
Imp: J'espérais, tu espérais, il͡ espérait, etc.
Fut: J'espèrerai, tu espèreras, il͡ espèrera, etc.

[3] The indefinite article is declined:

un,	*une,*	a
d'un,	*d'une,*	of a
à un,	*à une,*	to a
un,	*une,*	a

[4] Nouns ending in *ion* are generally spelled in the same manner in French and English, and are (generally) feminine, as: *opinion*, opinion; *nation*, nation; *constitution*, constitution.

3. And how is [se porte] Mrs. Morin? And how is [va] your wife?

4. She is [se porte] very well, thank you.

5. And how are you [allez-vous] yourself?—Quite [Très] well, thanks.

6. And how is your brother? I hope [J'espère[2]] he is quite [tout à fait] well now.

7. I am very well, thanks, but my poor [pauvre] brother can not go out [sortir] yet. He is still very weak [faible].

8. But I hope (that) he will soon be recovered [rétabli]. He is quite [très] young, his constitution[4] is sturdy, and at his age people recover [on se remet] very rapidly [vite].

9. Let us hope so (espérons[5]-le).

A large number of words in the English language were derived from the French. In the course of time these words have undergone slight changes in each language. Thus, many English words become French by changing their terminations, as:

ary becomes *aire:*	honorary, *honoraire;*	ordinary, *ordinaire*
ory " *oire:*	victory, *victoire;*	glory, *gloire*
cy " *ce:*	constancy, *constance;*	urgency, *urgence*

Several nouns ending in *ce* have the same spelling and usually the same meaning, as: Silence, *silence;* prudence, *prudence;* science, *science;* conscience, *conscience*, etc.

ty, changes into *té:*	Trinity, *Trinité;*	charity, *charité*
ous, " " *eux:*	virtuous, *vertueux;*	generous, *généreux*
or, " " *eur:*	doctor, *docteur;*	honor, *honneur*
y, " " *ie:*	folly, *folie;*	modesty, *modestie*

Several verbs ending in *ate* correspond to the French verbs in *er*, as: To animate, *animer;* to illustrate, *illustrer.*

fy corresponds to *fier:* to modify, *modifier;* to simplify, *simplifier.*
ish " to *ir:* to finish, *finir;* to polish, *polir;* to tarnish, *ternir.*
de, dis " to *dé, dés:* defeat, *défaite;* despair, *désespoir;* disguise, *déguisement;* to disown, *désavouer.*
mis " to *mal:* to misjudge, *juger mal;* misfortune, *malheur;* misinterpret, *interpréter mal*, etc.

[5] Imperative of *espérer*, to hope.

10. Demain j'irai vous voir. J'irai prendre des nouvelles de votre frère. En‿attendant faites-lui mes‿amitiés. Au revoir. (ɑ̃ na tɑ̃ dɑ̃ —me za mi tje. o·r vwa:r)

Phrases Employées en Faisant une Visite

fra:z‿ɑ̃ plwa je ɑ̃ fzɑ̃ yn vi zit

1. Monsieur Carnot est-il chez lui[1]?—Non, monsieur, il n'y est pas. (kar no—ʃe lɥi—il njɛ pɑ)

2. Oh, je regrette infiniment. (ʒə rgrɛt‿ɛ̃ fi ni mɑ̃)

3. Mais monsieur ne tardera pas‿à[3] rentrer. Donnez-vous la peine[3] d'entrer et de vous‿asseoir. (tar də ra—rɑ̃ tre—la pɛ·n—vu za swa:r)

4. Non merci, je ne puis pas‿attendre. Vous lui remettrez ma carte. Je regrette beaucoup de ne pas l'avoir trouvé.

5. Est-il venu[4] quelqu'un pour me voir? (ɛ til və ny kɛl kœ̃)

6. Non, madame, personne[5] n'est venu. (pɛr sɔn)

---

[1] Note again: *Chez lui,* At (his) home; *chez Robert,* at Robert's house; *chez le dentiste,* at the dentist's (office).

[2] *Tarder à* means to delay, as:

Ne tardez pas‿à lui envoyer cette lettre.	Do not delay sending him this letter, *i.e.,* Hasten to send him this letter.
Le train ne tardera pas‿à venir.	The train will soon be here.

Tarder de used impersonally signifies to long, as:

Qu'il me tarde de vous revoir.	How I long to see you again.

[3] This form: *donnez-vous la peine de* (literally: give yourself the trouble of) is considered very polite and is very frequently used. Of course, we can also say:

Asseyez-vous, s'il vous plaît *Veuillez vous‿asseoir*	Please be seated.

10. To-morrow I will call on you. I shall see how your brother is getting along. Meanwhile give him my kindest regards. Good-bye. (Literally: To-morrow I shall go to see [voir] you. I shall go to get [prendre] news of your brother. In the meanwhile [en‿attendant] give him [faites-lui] my regards [mes‿amitiés]. Good-bye [au revoir].)

Phrases Used During a Call

1. Is Mr. Carnot at home[1]?—No, sir, he is not (there, *y*).

2. Oh, I am very sorry. (Literally: Oh, I regret infinitely.)

3. But Mr. Carnot will return very soon. Please walk in and take a seat. (Literally: But mister will not delay to return [ne tardera pas‿à rentrer]. Give yourself the trouble [la peine] to enter [d'entrer] and to seat yourself [de vous‿asseoir].)

4. No, thanks; I cannot wait [attendre]. Please give him my card. I am very sorry to have missed him. (Literally: You will hand [remettrez] him my card [ma carte]. I regret much not to have found him.)

5. Has anyone been to see me? (Literally: Has someone come [Est‿il venu quelqu'un] in order to [pour] see me?)

6. No, madam, nobody [personne n'] came.

---

[4] The following verbs of motion must be conjugated with *être*, to be, while we in English use *to have:*

Aller,	to go	*Partir pour,*	to leave, to start for
Venir,	to come	*Entrer,*	to enter
Parvenir,	to reach, to attain	*Sortir,*	to go out
Retourner / *Revenir*	to come back, to return	*Naître,*	to be born
Arriver,	to arrive	*Mourir* / *Décéder*	to die

As: *Je suis‿allé,* I have gone; *il est parti,* he has left; *il est‿arrivé,* he has arrived; *je suis venu,* I have come, etc.

[5] The negation *ne* must be used with *personne* whether it appears as subject or object of a verb, as:

Personne n'est venu.	Nobody came.
Je n'ai vu personne.	I did not see anyone.

7. On‿a sonné; allez donc[1]⁀ouvrir la porte. (ɔ̃ na sɔ ne; a le dɔ̃·k⁀u vri:r)

8. C'est[2] monsieur Dubois qui[3] voudrait vous voir. (dy bwa)

9. Faites-le entrer au salon, et dites-lui que j'y serai dans quelques‿instants. (kɛl kə zɛ̃ stɑ̃)

10. Madame Arnaud est‿elle visible?[4] (ar no—vi zi·bl)

11. Oui, madame; donnez-vous la peine d'entrer au salon.

12. Ah! bonjour, ma chère. Je suis si contente de vous voir. (kɔ̃·tɑ̃:t)

13. Est-ce que je vous dérange?

14. Mais, pas du tout; au contraire, je suis‿enchantée[5] de vous voir. Donnez-vous la peine de vous‿asseoir. (Asseyez-vous, s'il vous plaît.) (o kɔ̃ trɛ:r, ʒə sɥi zɑ̃ ʃɑ̃ te—a sɛ je vu)

15. N'aimeriez-vous pas mieux[6] le sofa? (nɛ mə rje vu pa mjøl sɔ fa)

16. Merci, je suis[7] très bien ici.

17. Merci, j'ai très peu de temps, je ne veux pas m'asseoir.

---

[1] *donc* is often used to emphasize the act expressed by the verb: *allez donc*, do go, please go; *écoutez donc*, listen carefully; *répondez donc*, why don't you answer?

[2] If special emphasis is placed on a noun *c'est . . . qui* must be used with the *subject* of a sentence, as:

C'est votre sœur qui me l'a dit.	*Your sister* told me.
C'est votre patron qui l'a envoyé.	*Your employer* sent it.

Before all other members of a sentence *c'est . . . que* must be employed, as:

C'est votre mère que j'ai vue.	It is your mother (whom) I saw.

[3] Who, which, that, is rendered by *qui*, when the relative pronoun is the subject of the next verb and refers to persons or things in the singular as well as in the plural.

L'employé qui a écrit cette lettre n'est pas‿ici.	The clerk who wrote this letter is not here.
Passez-moi le plat qui est sur la table.	Hand me the dish which is on the table.

7. The bell is ringing; go and open the door. (Literally: Someone rang the bell [a sonné]; go to open [ouvrir] the door [la porte].)

8. (It's, *C'est*[2]) Mr. Dubois (who, *qui*[3]) would like to see you.

9. Show him into (make him enter, *faites-le entrer au*) the parlor [salon] and tell him I shall be there in a few moments [dans quelques‿instants].

10. Is Madam Arnaud at home [visible]?

11. Yes, madam; please [donnez-vous la peine d'] walk into the parlor.

12. Ah, good morning, my dear [ma chère]. I am so glad [contente] to see you.

13. Am I disturbing you?

14. Oh [Mais], not at all; on the contrary, I am delighted [enchantée] to see you. Please be seated. (Give yourself the trouble to sit down, *Donnez-vous la peine de vous‿asseoir.*)

15. Wouldn't you rather sit on the sofa? (Literally: Would you not like the sofa better [mieux]?)

16. Thanks, this will do nicely. (Literally: Thanks, I am very comfortable [bien] here.)

17. Thank you, I have but very little time; I don't want to sit down. (Literally: Thanks, I have very little [peu] of time; I don't want to sit myself.)

---

[4] A phrase frequently used.

[5] The feminine form *enchantée* must be used, because a lady is speaking.

[6] The infinitive without any preposition is used after *aimer*, to like (when used in the conditional), *préférer*, to prefer, *aimer mieux*, to like better, to prefer, *il vaut mieux*, it is better, as:

J'aimerais le voir.	I should like to see him.
Je préfère rester à la maison.	I prefer to stay at home.
Il vaut mieux céder.	It is better to yield.

[7] *Etre* sometimes means *to stand.*

Il était‿à la fenêtre.	He was standing at the window.

18. Il‿y a un siècle qu'on ne[1] vous‿a vue.[2] (œ̃ sjɛ·klə kɔ̃n vu za·vy)

19. Comme vous devenez rare.

20. J'ai été à la campagne. (a la kɑ̃ paɲ)

21. Et donnez-moi donc des nouvelles de votre famille? (vɔ trə fa mi:j)

22. Merci, nous sommes tous bien portants. (tus bjɛ̃ pɔr tɑ̃)

23. Ça me fait plaisir d'apprendre cela. (plɛ·zi:r)

24. Et chez vous?—Tout le monde se porte bien, merci.

25. Que je suis contente de vous revoir!

26. Quand‿avez-vous reçu des nouvelles de monsieur votre frère? (kɑ̃ ta ve vur sy)

27. Avez-vous‿eu de[3] ses nouvelles? (a ve vu zy)

28. Il‿y a longtemps que nous n'avons‿eu de ses nouvelles. (lɔ̃ tɑ̃)

---

[1] The use of *ne* in this connection is difficult to explain. *Ne* must be used after *il‿y a* when the action did *not* take place during the time mentioned, as:

Il‿y a quinze jours que je ne l'ai vu.	It is a fortnight since I saw him.

This in other words would mean: I have not seen him for a fortnight, consequently *ne* must be used.

If, however, the action *did* take place during the time mentioned, *ne* is *not* used, as:

Y a-t-il longtemps que vous avez ces livres?	Is it long since you had these books?

This in other words would signify: Have you had these books for a long time, consequently *ne* cannot be used.

[2] When a verb is conjugated with the auxiliary verb *être* the participle must agree with the subject in gender and number, as:

Mon frère‿est venu (masc. sing.).	My brother came.
Mes frères sont venus (masc. plur.).	My brothers came.
Ma sœur‿est venue (fem. sing.).	My sister came.
Mes sœurs sont venues (fem. plur.).	My sisters came.

18. It has been an age since I have seen you. (Literally: It has [il y a] a century [un siècle] that one has **not** seen you.)

19. You are becoming quite a stranger! (Literally: How you become rare.)

20. I have been in the country. (à la campagne)

21. Please [donc] tell me about your family. (Literally: Give me some news of your family.)

22. Thank you, we are all [tous] well [bien portants].

23. I am very glad to hear that. (Literally: That gives me [me fait] pleasure to learn that.)

24. And at your home [chez vous]?—Everybody [Tout le monde] is well [se porte bien], thank you.

25. I am so happy to see you again! (Literally: How happy I am [Que je suis contente] to see you again [revoir].)

26. When did you hear from your brother? (Literally: When have you received [reçu] news [des nouvelles] from your brother?)

27. Have you heard from him? (Literally: Have you had [eu] any news from him [de ses nouvelles]?)

28. We have not had any news from him for a long time. (Literally: It is a long time since [Il‿y a longtemps que] . . .)

But when the verb is conjugated with the auxiliary verb *avoir*, the participle remains unchanged:

Ma mère a acheté cette maison. My mother bought this house.

When, however, the object precedes the verb which can be the case *only* when the object is a *pronoun* (personal, relative or other), the participle must agree with its object, as:

Je les‿ai oubliés. I have forgotten them.
Je l'ai vue. I saw her.

[3] These phrases with *nouvelles* cannot be translated literally; the use of *de* and the possessive adjective is idiomatic. Similarly we say:

J'attendrai de vos nouvelles pour écrire
Je n'écrirai pas‿avant d'avoir de vos nouvelles } I shall wait till I hear from you before writing.

29. Nous‿attendons[1] de ses nouvelles de jour⁀en jour. (də ʒu·r⁀ɑ̃ ʒu:r)

30. Comment? Vous voulez me quitter déjà? (ki te de ʒa)

31. Êtes-vous donc si pressée? (prɛ se)

32. Il faut que je m'en‿aille[2]; mon mari m'attend. (il fo kəʒ mɑ̃ nɑ:j; mɔ̃ ma ri)

33. Je vous quitte⁀à regret, mais‿il le faut. (rə grɛ)

---

[1] The infinitive of this verb is *attendre*, to wait, to expect.

Verbs of the fourth conjugation end in *re*, as *vendre*, to sell; *entendre*, to hear; *rendre*, to render, to give back.

By striking off this ending we get the stem of the verb, as: *vendre*, vend; *entendre*, entend; *rendre*, rend; *attendre*, attend.

To the stem of the verb the following endings are added in the

PRESENT

INDICATIVE		SUBJUNCTIVE	
je ———	s	je ———	e
tu ———	s	tu ———	es
il ———	—	il ———	e
nous ———	ons	nous ———	ions
vous ———	ez	vous ———	iez
ils ———	ent	ils ———	ent

Vendre, To Sell

PRESENT

INDICATIVE	SUBJUNCTIVE
je vend*s*	que je vend*e*
tu vend*s*	que tu vend*es*
il vend	qu'il vend*e*
nous vend*ons*	que nous vend*ions*
vous vend*ez*	que vous vend*iez*
ils vend*ent*	qu'ils vend*ent*

Remember that the ending *ent* is never pronounced in conjugations.

29. We are in daily expectation of news from him. (Literally: We expect [nous‿attendons[1]] news from him from day to day [de jour⁀en jour].)

30. What [Comment]? You wish to leave me [me quitter] already [déjà]?)

31. Are you really [donc] in such a hurry [si pressée]?

32. I must go; my husband is expecting me. (Literally: It is necessary [il faut] that I go [que je m'en‿aille[2]]; my husband expects me [m'attend].)

33. I am sorry to leave you, but I have to. (Literally: I leave you with regret, but it is necessary.)

---

[2] After *il faut* we employ the subjunctive (although we may also use the infinitive with or without a pronoun). Compare Part X for full rules.

Il faut que je sonne la domestique.	I must ring for the servant.
Que faut-il que je fasse?	What have I to do? What must I do?
Il faut que vous‿y alliez de suite.	You must go there at once.

The French have no verb which corresponds to our "must." Let it be remembered that with *a noun* as subject of must *il faut* is always followed by the subjunctive with *que*, as:

Il faut que mon frère parte ce soir.	My brother must leave to-night.
Il faut que le cordonnier fasse mes bottes tout de suite, car je vais partir.	The shoemaker must make my boots at once, as I am going to leave.

For the conjugation of *s'en‿aller* see Part X. We conjugate:

Aller, To Go

PRESENT

INDICATIVE	SUBJUNCTIVE
je vais	que j'aille (kə ʒa:j)
tu vas	que tu ailles
il va	qu'il aille
nous‿allons	que nous‿allions
vous‿allez	que vous‿alliez
ils vont	qu'ils‿aillent (kil za:j)

34. Il faut que je sois[1] de retour‿à la maison à six heures.

35. Faites-moi le plaisir de renouveler bientôt votre visite. (lə plɛ·zi:r dər nu vle)

36. Alors, quand nous ferez-vous le plaisir de revenir nous voir?

37. Je reviendrai[2] sous peu, je vous le promets.[3] (ʒər vjɛ̃ dre su pø, ʒə vul prɔ mɛ)

38. N'y manquez pas. (ni mɑ̃ ke pa)

39. Ne vous dérangez pas, je vous prie.—Je vous‿accompagnerai jusqu'à[4] la porte. (ʒə vu pri—ʒə vu za kɔ̃ pa ɲə re)

40. Faites mes compliments à Monsieur Morin. Faites mes compliments à votre mari. (kɔ̃ pli mɑ̃)

41. Je n'y manquerai pas. Bien[5] des‿amitiés à votre sœur. (de za mi tje)

42. A qui ai-je l'honneur de parler?—Monsieur Barbou. (lɔ nœ:r—mə sjø bar bu)

43. Est-ce‿à Monsieur Goblet que j'ai l'honneur de parler? (gɔ blɛ)

44. C'est‿exact, monsieur. (sɛ tɛg zɑ‿kt)

---

[1] The subjunctive present of *être* is conjugated:

que je sois (kə ʒə swa)	that I (may) be
que tu sois	that thou (mayst) be
qu'il soit	that he (may) be
que nous soyons (swa jɔ̃)	that we (may) be
que vous soyez	that you (may) be
qu'ils soient (swa)	that they (may) be

[2] The future of *venir*, to come, and of verbs derived from it, is conjugated:

je viendrai (ʒə vjɛ̃ dre)	I shall come
tu viendras	thou wilt come
il viendra	he will come
nous viendrons	we shall come
vous viendrez	you will come
ils viendront	they will come

34. I am obliged to be back home at six o'clock. (Literally: It is necessary [il faut] that I be back [que je sois de retour] at the house [à la maison] at six hours.)

35. Please call soon again. (Literally: Do me the pleasure [le plaisir] to renew [renouveler] soon your visit.)

36. Well [Alors], when shall we have the pleasure of seeing you again? (Literally: Well, when will you do us [nous ferez-vous] the pleasure to return to see us?)

37. I shall soon call again, I promise you. (Literally: I shall return [je reviendrai] soon [sous peu **or** bientôt], I promise it to you [je vous le promets].)

38. Do not fail to do so [y].

39. Please (I beg you) don't disturb yourself.—I shall see (accompany) you to [jusqu'à[4]] the door.

40. Give my regards [Faites mes compliments] to your husband.

41. I shall surely (not fail to) do so. My kindest regards [Bien des‿amitiés] to your sister.

42. Whom have I the honor of addressing?—My name is Barbou. (Literally: To whom have I the honor of speaking?—Mr. Barbou.)

43. Am I speaking to Mr. Goblet? (Literally: Is it to Mr. Goblet that I have the honor of speaking?)

44. That's so [exact], sir.

---

[3] *Mettre*, to put, to place, and verbs derived from it are irregular. The present is conjugated:

je mets (mɛ)	I put
tu mets	thou puttest
il met	he puts
nous mettons	we put
vous mettez	you put
ils mettent (mɛt)	they put

[4] The French have three ways of saying *till, until:*

a. Jusque, which is used before an adverb, as: *Jusque là*, as far as there, to there.

b. Jusqu'à, as far as: *Jusqu'à Paris*, as far as Paris.

c. Jusqu'à ce que before a verb (in the subjunctive): *Jusqu'à ce que le vapeur arrive*, till the steamer arrives.

[5] After *bien*, used in the sense of *many, a great deal, du, de la* and *des* must be used, *i.e.*, the partitive follows *bien*.

45. Au revoir, monsieur.

46. Faites-moi le plaisir de renouveler bientôt votre visite.

47. Le plaisir est pour moi.

48. Vous‿êtes trop‿aimable.

49. Au revoir! Au plaisir![1]

50. Eh! bien, à tantôt. (tɑ̃ to)

CONVERSATION

kɔ̃ vɛr sa sjɔ̃

1. Comprenez-vous le français?

2. Je le comprends‿un peu, mais pas très bien.

3. Me comprenez-vous quand je parle vite? (vit)

4. Je vous comprends quand vous parlez lentement, mais quand vous parlez vite, ou plutôt, quand vous parlez naturellement, c'est‿à peine si je comprends‿un mot. (na ty rɛl mɑ̃, sɛ ta pɛ·n)

5. C'est probablement parce que vous manquez de pratique. (prɔ ba blə mɑ̃ par skə vu mɑ̃ ke)

6. Chaque fois qu'on parle français en votre présence, écoutez‿attentivement. (ɑ̃ vɔ trə pre zɑ̃:s—a tɑ̃ tiv mɑ̃)

7. Il me semble que les Francais parlent beaucoup plus vite[2] que nous‿autres.[3] (sɑ̃·bl—bo ku)

8. Une langue⁀étrangère donne toujours cette impression. (yn lɑ̃·g⁀e trɑ̃ ʒɛ:r—sɛt⁀ɛ̃ prɛ sjɔ̃)

---

[1] Note the following expressions which begin with *à* (until): *à demain,* see you to-morrow; *à bientôt,* see you soon; *au plaisir,* I hope I'll have the pleasure to see you soon again.

[2] The comparative of superiority is formed by placing *plus,* more, before the adjective, while *le plus, la plus* (fem.) is put before the superlative.

Positive		Comparative	
beau *belle* (fem.)	beautiful	*plus beau* *plus belle*	more beautiful

Superlative

le plus beau *la plus belle*	the most beautiful

45. Good day, sir.

46. Please call soon again. (Literally: Do me the pleasure of renewing your call soon.)

47. The pleasure is mine [pour moi].

48. You are very kind (too amiable).

49. Good-bye. Hope to see you again soon.

50. Hope to see you soon again.

CONVERSATION

1. Do you understand French?

2. I understand it a little, but not [pas] very well.

3. Do you understand me when I speak rapidly [vite]?

4. I understand you when you talk slowly [lentement], but when you speak rapidly, or rather [plutôt], when you talk naturally [naturellement], I can scarcely [à peine] understand a word.

5. This is probably because you lack [manquez de] practice.

6. Every time (that) anyone [on] speaks French in your presence, listen carefully [attentivement].

7. It seems to me that French people (the French, *les Français*) talk a great deal faster [plus vite] than we do.

8. A foreign language always gives that impression.

The comparative is generally followed by *que*, than, as:

La paresse͡ est plus dangereuse que la vanité.	Idleness is more dangerous than vanity.

The comparative of inferiority is formed with *moins*, less, *le moins*, the least, as: *beau*, fine; *moins beau*, less fine; *le moins beau*, the least fine.

Il est moins pauvre que moi.	He is not as poor as (less poor than) I am.

[3] *Autres* sometimes accompanies *nous* or *vous* for emphasis sake: *Vous autres‿ Américains vous‿êtes plus‿optimistes que nous autres Français.*

9. Avec le temps et de la pratique votre‿oreille se formera. Vous suivrez sans peine n'importe[1] quelle conversation, vous verrez. (vɔtr‿ɔ rɛ:j sə fɔr mə ra. vu sɥi vre—nɛ̃ pɔrt—vu vɛ re)

10. Je l'espère. Mais, pardon; vous‿avez‿employé[2] une expression qui est toute nouvelle[3] pour moi. Quelle‿est la signification littérale de "n'importe quelle"? (vu za ve zɑ̃·plwa je yn‿ɛk sprɛ sjɔ̃—tut nu vɛl—la si ɲi fi ka sjɔ̃ li te ral)

---

[1] "N'importe" means "no matter! never mind!" but in this instance it means: Any conversation whatever; it does not matter what conversation.

Finir, to finish.

	Present	
	Indicative	Subjunctive
	Je fin*is*	Que je fin*isse*
	tu fin*is*	que tu fin*isses*
	il fin*it*	qu'il fin*isse*
	nous fin*issons*	que nous fin*issions*
	vous fin*issez*	que vous fin*issiez*
	ils fin*issent*	qu'ils fin*issent*

Imperfect: Je fin*issais*, tu fin*issais*, il fin*issait*, nous fin*issions*, vous fin*issiez*, ils fin*issaient*.

Future: Je fin*irai*, tu fin*iras*, il fin*ira*, nous fin*irons*, vous fin*irez*, ils fin*iront*.

Conditional: Je fin*irais*, tu fin*irais*, il fin*irait*, nous fin*irions*, vous fin*iriez*, ils fin*iraient*.

[2] It has already been explained that the French have no progressive conjugation, *i. e.*, they cannot say: *I am writing*, but only: *I write*.

Neither do they use the auxiliary verb *to do* in questions or negations. They can only say: *Je ne vais pas*, I do not go, I am not going. *Allez-vous?* Do you go? Are you going? *N'allez-vous pas?* Don't you go? Are you not going? etc.

9. In time and by practice your ear will get accustomed to it. You will follow without difficulty any conversation whatsoever. You will see. (Literally: With the time [le temps] and some practice [de la pratique] your ear [oreille] will adjust itself [se formera]. You will follow without difficulty [sans peine], no matter what conversation. You will see.)

10. I hope so. But pardon me, you used an expression which is quite new [toute nouvelle[3]] to [pour] me. What is the literal meaning [signification] of: "N'importe quelle"?

They consequently say:

Avez-vous‿écrit? Did you write?	Have you written?
Je n'ai pas‿écrit, I did not write.	I have not written.

On the other hand, it must be understood that the French very rarely use our perfect tense, which is so generally employed in English when talking about past events.

We say:	I saw him.	The French:	I have seen him.	*Je l'ai vu.*
"	I received it.	"	I have received it.	*Je l'ai reçu.*
"	I did it.	"	I have done it.	*Je l'ai fait.*
"	Did you write him?	"	Have you written to him?	*Lui avez-vous‿écrit?*

[3] Adjectives in *eau* and *ou* form their feminine as follows:

Beau,	beautiful;	*belle*
nouveau,	new;	*nouvelle*
mou,	soft;	*molle*
fou,	foolish;	*folle*

This is due to their old masculine forms: *bel, nouvel, mol, fol,* which are still used before *masculine nouns beginning with a vowel or silent h,* as:

Un nouvel‿opéra	A new opera
un bel‿homme	A fine looking man

VOCABULAIRE	**VOCABULARY**
Suite	*Continuation*
Combien prenez-vous pour cela? (prə ne vu)	How much do you take for that?
Combien demandez-vous pour cela?	How much do you ask for that?
Combien vendez-vous cela?	How much do you sell that for?
Combien vaut cet‿objet? (sɛt‿ ɔb ʒɛ)	How much is this object?
C'est trop cher; je n'en veux pas‿à ce prix.	That is too dear; I don't want to take it at this price.
La qualité (ka li te)	The quality
Je n'aime pas cette qualité.	I don't like this quality.
Comment trouvez-vous celle-ci? (sɛl si)	How do you like this one? (How do you find this one?)
Je la préfère. (pre fɛ:r)	I like it better (I prefer it).
Le drap (drɑ)	The cloth
La soie (swa)	The silk
La laine (lɛ:n)	The wool
Le coton (kɔ tɔ̃)	The cotton
La robe (rɔb)	The dress
Une robe de soie	A silk dress (a dress of silk)
Une robe de laine	A woolen dress (a dress of wool)
Une robe de coton	A cotton dress (a dress of cotton)
Porter	To wear
Durer (dy·re)	To wear, *i.e.*, to last
Ces‿articles sont d'un bon‿usage. (bɔ ny za:ʒ)	These goods wear very well.

PART FIVE

CONTENTS

Conversation

(*Suite*)

11. "Alors vous verrez" signifie: "Then you will see."

PRESENT	FUTURE
je vois (ʒə vwa)	je verrai (ʒə vɛ re)
tu vois	tu verras (ty vɛ ra)
il voit (il vwa)	il verra (il vɛ ra)
nous voyons (vwa jɔ̃)	nous verrons (nu vɛ rɔ̃)
vous voyez (vwa je)	vous verrez (vu vɛ re)
ils voient (vwa)	ils verront (il vɛ rɔ̃)

12. Ah, je vous comprends maintenant. Je désire que vous me donniez[1] toujours des traductions littérales.[2] (dɔ nje—tra dyk sjɔ̃)

13. Les traductions littérales, mon cher monsieur, sont dans la plupart des cas, une impossibilité. (dɑ̃ la ply pa:r de ka, yn‿ɛ̃ pɔ si bi li te)

14. Pourquoi donc?[3]

15. Parce que chaque langue a ses propres particularités, ses propres‿idiotismes et des formes d'expressions particulières qui ne peuvent jamais[4]‿être traduites littéralement.[5] (ʃak lɑ̃:g‿a se prɔ prə par ti ky la ri te, se prɔ prə zi djɔ tis mə—fɔr mə dɛk sprɛ sjɔ̃ par ti ky ljɛ:r—tra dɥit li te ral mɑ̃)

---

[1] The subjunctive is used after verbs denoting a wish or desire.

[2] Adjectives are generally placed after the noun.

[3] *Donc* is used frequently to stress the preceding word.

[4] *Ne* must be used in connection with *jamais, personne, rien*, etc.

N'ont‿ils jamais‿écrit?	Did they never write?
Personne n'est venu.	No one came.
Je n'ai rien fait.	I didn't do anything.
Je n'ai vu personne.	I have not seen anyone.

[5] Most adverbs are formed by adding the syllable *ment* (corresponding to our *ly*) to the adjective, as:

sage,	wise	*sagement,*	wisely
ferme,	firm	*fermement,*	firmly
agréable,	agreeable	*agréablement,*	agreeably

ment is added to the masculine adjective if the adjective ends with a vowel; if not, to the feminine, as:

utile,		useful	*utilement,*	usefully
doux,	*douce,*	sweet	*doucement,*	sweetly
certain,	*certaine,*	certain	*certainement,*	certainly

Conversation

(Continuation)

11. "Alors vous verrez" means: "Then you will see."

PRESENT	FUTURE
I see	I shall (will) see
thou seest	thou wilt see
he sees	he will see
we see	we shall see
you see	you will see
they see	they will see

12. Ah, now [maintenant] I understand you. I wish[1] you would (I wish that you) always give me literal translations.

13. Literal translations, my dear sir, are in the majority [la plupart] of cases an impossibility.

14. And why?

15. Because every [chaque] language possesses [a] its own peculiarities, its own idioms and particular modes [formes] of expression which [qui] can never be translated [traduites] literally [littéralement].

The adjectives *beau, nouveau, fou* and *mou,* whose feminine is *belle, nouvelle, folle* and *molle,* form their adverbs by adding *ment* to the feminine, as:

bellement,	beautifully	*follement,*	foolishly
nouvellement,	newly	*mollement,*	softly

The usual place of adverbs is immediately after the verb, if the verb stands in a simple tense, as:

Vous prononcez bien. — You pronounce well.

If the adverb stands in a compound tense, the adverb is placed between the auxiliary and past participle, as:

Vous‿avez bien prononcé. — You have pronounced well.

Hier, aujourd'hui, demain, ici, là and adverbial expressions are placed after both parts of the verb, as:

Il est venu hier. — He came yesterday.

Hier, aujourd'hui and *demain* are sometimes placed at the beginning of sentences for the sake of emphasis.

16. Y a-t-il beaucoup d'expressions idiomatiques françaises? (i djɔ ma tik)

17. La langue française, mon cher monsieur, est‿une des plus riches du monde. Parmi les langues modernes, le français et l'allemand sont‿au premier rang pour le nombre des‿expressions et des formes idiomatiques. (de ply riʃ dy mɔ̃·d. par mi—mɔ dɛrn—lal mɑ̃—prə mje rɑ̃—lə nɔ̃:br)

18. Voulez-vous avoir la bonté de me citer quelques‿uns des‿idiotismes les plus‿employés; je veux dire ceux usités dans‿une conversation ordinaire. (si te kɛl kə zœ̃ de ply zɑ̃ plwa je—y zi te—ɔr di nɛ:r)

19. Avec plaisir. Vous rappelez-vous le verbe⁀**avoir** que nous‿avons‿ étudié dans le premier livre? (ra ple—lə vɛrb—nu za vɔ̃ ze ty dje)

20. Oui, je me le rappelle fort bien; mais nous n'avons‿étudié que[1] le présent de l'indicatif. (pre zɑ̃ dlɛ̃ di ka tif)

21. Très bien; mais vous devez‿étudier le verbe⁀entier, car⁀il⁀est d'un‿usage très fréquent et présente beaucoup de difficultés pour les‿Anglais et les‿Américains. (vu dve ze ty dje lə vɛrb⁀ɑ̃ tje—dœ̃ ny za:ʒ trɛ fre kɑ̃—pre zɑ̃·t—le zɑ̃ glɛ— le za me ri kɛ̃)

Present

Je dois	(ʒə dwa)
tu dois	(ty dwa)
il doit	(il dwa)
nous devons	(nu dvɔ̃)
vous devez	(vu dve)
ils doivent	(il dwa·v)

22. Eh bien, étudiez-le. Vous le trouverez dans le dixième livre qui contient la grammaire de la langue française. (di zjɛ:m—ki kɔ̃·tjɛ̃ la gra mɛ:r)

23. Étudiez-le bien et dans la prochaine leçon je vous‿enseignerai les‿idiotismes du verbe⁀**avoir.** Au revoir! (dɑ̃ la prɔ ʃɛ·n lə sɔ̃ ʒə vu zɑ̃·sɛ ɲə re)

24. Au revoir, monsieur.

---

[1] Note again the use of *ne . . . que*, not . . . except, only, accompanying a verb: *Il ne parle que l'anglais*, He speaks only English (nothing but English).

16. Are there [Y a-t-il] many idiomatic expressions in French?

17. The French language, my dear sir, is one of the richest (languages) in the world. Among [Parmi] modern languages French and German rank highest [sont au premier rang] as regards [pour] the number [le nombre] of the idiomatic expressions and forms.

18. Would you have the kindness to mention [de me citer] some [quelques uns] of the most widely used [les plus employés] idioms? I mean [Je veux dire] which come up (used, *usités*) in ordinary conversation.

19. With pleasure. You remember [Vous rappelez-vous] the verb **avoir** which we studied in the first book?

20. Yes, I remember it very well [fort bien], but we studied only[1] the present indicative.

21. Well, you ought to study the whole verb [le verbe entier], as [car] the use of it is very common [il est d'un‿usage très fréquent] and presents many difficulties to English speaking persons.

Devoir, To have to, be to, must, ought, should

PRESENT TENSE

I ought to, am to, must
thou oughtest to
he ought to
we ought to
you ought to
they ought to

22. Well, study it. You will find it in the tenth [dixième] book which contains [contient] the grammar of the French language.

23. Study it well and in our next [prochaine] lesson I will teach you [vous‿enseignerai] the idioms of the verb **avoir.** Good-bye!

24. Good-bye, sir.

Faire

1. Ah, bonjour, cher monsieur. Je suis‿enchanté de vous voir. Comment‿allez-vous?

2. Très bien, merci. Et vous, comment vous portez-vous aujourd' hui?

3. Fort bien, je vous remercie. Ce temps de printemps me plaît beaucoup. (sə tɑ̃ də prɛ̃ tɑ̃)

4. "Temps de printemps?" Excusez-moi, si je répète ces mots après vous, mais l'expression[1] est tout‿à fait nouvelle pour moi et je ne sais pas du tout ce qu'elle signifie. (ɛk sky ze mwa siʒ re pɛ:t se mo a prɛ vu—tu ta fɛ)

5. Vous savez sans doute, que nous‿avons quatre saisons, qui sont: Le printemps, l'été, l'automne‿et l'hiver, mais je pense que ces mots français sont nouveaux pour vous. (sɑ̃ dut—ka trə sɛ·zɔ̃—lə prɛ̃ tɑ̃, le te, lo tɔ·nɛ li vɛ:r)

6. Ils le[2] sont‿en‿effet. Laissez-moi les répéter après vous: Le printemps, l'été, l'automne et l'hiver. (ɑ̃ ne fɛ)

7. C'est très bien[2]! Votre prononciation est‿excellente. (ɛk sɛ lɑ̃:t)

8. Vous me flattez, monsieur. Vous‿autres[2] Français vous‿aimez[3] faire des compliments. (vum fla te—vu zɛ me fɛ:r de kɔ̃ pli mɑ̃)

9. Nous ne faisons pas de compliments, nous sommes polis. Les Français sont polis par nature. La politesse française‿est‿innée, générale et se rencontre‿aussi bien[4] dans la classe pauvre que dans la classe riche. (pɔ li—par na ty:r—la pɔ li tɛs—i ne, ʒe ne ral—srɑ̃ kɔ̃:tr‿o si)

---

[1] Before nouns beginning with a vowel or an unaspirated (*i. e.*, mute) *h*, *le* and *la* are changed into *l'*, thus forming but one word with the noun, as:

L'oncle	the uncle	*L'amie,*	the woman friend
l'ami,	the friend	*l'assiette,*	the plate
l'homme,	the man	*l'habitude,*	the habit

The declension of these nouns presents no difficulties.

Singular		Plural	
l'ami,	the friend	*les‿amis,*	the friends
de l'ami,	of the friend	*des‿amis,*	of the friends
à l'ami,	to the friend	*aux‿amis,*	to the friends
l'ami,	the friend	*les‿amis,*	the friends

To Make; To Do

1. Ah! good morning, my dear sir. I am delighted [enchanté] to see you. How are you?

2. Very well, thanks. And how do you feel [comment vous portez-vous] to-day? (Literally: Very well, thanks. And you, how do you carry yourself to-day?)

3. (I am) very [fort] well, thank you. This (beautiful) spring weather just suits me (pleases me [me plaît] much).

4. Spring weather? Pardon me for repeating (if I repeat, *si je répète*) these [ces] words after you, but the expression is quite [tout‿à fait] new to me and I don't really [du tout] know what it means [ce qu'elle signifie].

5. You know of course (without doubt, *sans doute*) that we have four seasons viz. [qui sont]: spring, summer, autumn and winter [le printemps, l'été, l'automne, et l'hiver], but I suppose (that) these French words are new to [pour] you.

6. Quite so (They are so, indeed, *Ils le sont‿en effet*); let me [laissez-moi] repeat them after you: spring, summer, autumn, winter.

7. That is very good [bien]! Your pronunciation is excellent!

8. You flatter me, sir. You Frenchmen are always so complimentary. (Literally: You flatter me, sir. You French people [Vous‿autres Français], you like [vous‿aimez] to pay [faire] compliments.)

9. We do not make compliments, we are polite. French people [Les Français] are polite by nature. French politeness is inborn [innée] and general; and is found [se rencontre] among the poor as well as among the rich (as well [aussi bien] in the poor class of people as [que] in the rich class of people).

---

[2] Idiomatic usage.

[3] *Aimer*, to like, to love, refers to settled tastes or affections.

But when *to like* expresses merely an opinion or an impression, the French prefer—as far as practicable—to use some indirect form of speech, as: That does not please me, That does not suit me, *cela ne me plaît pas, cela ne me convient pas.*

[4] *Aussi . . . que*—as . . . as, is used in comparisons of equality, as:

Il est‿aussi heureux que son frère. He is just as happy as his brother.

In negative comparisons *aussi . . . que . . .*, or *si . . . que . . .* may be used:

Il n'est pas si riche (aussi riche) que vous. He is not so rich as you.

10. Je souhaiterais de pouvoir‿en[1] dire‿autant de mes compatriotes. Je crains[2] que nos manières ne vous paraissent plutôt rudes. (ʒə swɛ trɛd pu vwa:r‿ɑ̃ di:r‿o tɑ̃ də me kɔ̃ pa tri ɔt. ʒə krɛ̃ kə no ma njɛ:r nə vu pa rɛs ply to ry:d)

11. A parler franchement, je crois que sous ce rapport,[3] les‿Anglais ont‿encore beaucoup à apprendre de nous; d'un‿autre côté, il y a beaucoup de choses plus‿importantes que la politesse que[4] nous devrions‿apprendre d'eux. Mais revenons‿à notre conversation. (frɑ̃·ʃ mɑ̃, ʒə krwa kə su sra pɔ:r—ply zɛ̃ pɔr tɑ̃:t—nu də vri jɔ̃ za prɑ̃:drə dø—rə vnɔ̃)

CONDITIONNEL de Devoir (də vwar)

Je devrais	(ʒə də vrɛ)
tu devrais	(ty də vrɛ)
il devrait	(il də vrɛ)
nous devrions	(nu də vri jɔ̃)
vous devriez	(vu də vri je)
ils devraient	(il də vrɛ)

---

[1] Note again that *en*, which is not expressed in English, completes the French sentence: *en . . . autant*, as much concerning this (*en*).

[2] The verbs *craindre, avoir peur*, to fear, *trembler*, to tremble, *appréhender*, to apprehend, *empêcher*, to hinder, require the particle *ne* before the verb in the subjunctive mood, when these verbs themselves are affirmative or negative-interrogative, as:

Je crains qu'il ne vienne.	I am afraid he will come.
Ne craignez-vous pas qu'il ne vienne?	Aren't you afraid he will come?

But if the sentence be simply negative or simply interrogative, *ne* is *not* used, as:

Je ne crains pas qu'il vienne.	I don't fear his coming.
Craignez-vous qu'il vienne?	Are you afraid he is coming?

Still after *craindre, avoir peur* and *trembler* we use *pas* after *ne* when we wish for the accomplishment of the action expressed by the second verb, which must stand in the subjunctive:

J'ai peur qu'elle ne vienne pas.	I fear she will not come.
J'ai peur qu'elle ne vienne.	I fear she will come.
Je crains qu'il n'écrive pas.	I fear he will not write.
Je crains qu'il n'écrive.	I fear he will write.

The subjunctive mood will be treated fully in a later lesson.

10. I wish I could say the same thing about my countrymen. I am afraid our manners must appear rather rude to you. (Literally: I should wish [je souhaiterais] to be able [de pouvoir] to say as much [autant] of my countrymen [mes compatriotes]. I fear [je crains] that our manners [nos manières] may seem to you [ne vous paraissent] rather rude [plutôt rudes].

11. Frankly speaking (To speak frankly, *à parler franchement*), I think that Englishmen in that respect [sous ce rapport] still have much to learn from us; on the other hand [d'un autre côté], there are many more important things than [que] politeness which [que] we ought [devrions] to learn from them [d'eux]. But let us return to [revenons‿à] our conversation.

CONDITIONAL of Devoir

I ought to
thou oughtest to
he ought to
we ought to
you ought to
they ought to

---

[3] In every respect, *à tous les égards.*—In this respect, *à cet‿égard.*—In no respect, *sous‿aucun rapport.*—To pay one's respects, *présenter ses‿hommages.*—

Pourrais-je présenter mes‿hommages à madame?	May I pay my respects to your wife?

[4] We have already learned that *who, which* and *that* are rendered by *qui,* when they are in the nominative case, whether they refer to persons or things, both for the singular and plural, as:

Les dames qui l'ont dit, sont parties hier soir.	*The ladies who said so, left last night.*

The same relative pronouns, when direct objects, *i. e., whom, which* and *that* are rendered by *que,* as:

Est-ce là le chapeau que vous avez acheté?	Is this the hat you bought?
La leçon que vous m'avez donnée est très difficile.	The lesson (task) you gave me is very difficult.

Observe that in French the relative pronoun must always be expressed, though it is frequently omitted in English.

12. J'ai totalement oublié de quoi nous parlions. (ʒe tɔ tal mɑ̃ u bli je də kwa nu par ljɔ̃)

IMPARFAIT[1]

Je parlais	(ʒə par lɛ)
tu parlais	(ty par lɛ)
il parlait	(il par lɛ)
nous parlions	(nu par ljɔ̃)
vous parliez	(vu par lje)
ils parlaient	(il par lɛ)

13. Nous parlions des saisons et je venais[2] de vous dire leurs noms. Vous les rappelez-vous encore? (ʒə vnɛ—lœ·r nɔ̃)

14. Parfaitement: Le printemps, l'été, l'automne et l'hiver.

15. C'est très bien!—Quel temps fait‿il aujourd'hui? (o ʒu·r dɥi)

16. Pardonnez-moi de vous‿interrompre; mais pourquoi dites-vous "fait‿il"? (par dɔ ne mwad vu zɛ̃ tɛ rɔ̃:pr)

Je dis	(ʒə di)
tu dis	(ty di)
il dit	(il di)
nous disons	(nu di zɔ̃)
vous dites	(vu dit)
ils disent	(il di:z)

---

[1] As a general thing the Perfect Tense is used in French in speaking of past actions or events, as:

Je l'ai vu hier. — I saw him yesterday.

The Imperfect in French is used:

a. when referring to habitual or repeated actions, as:

L'hiver passé je faisais‿une promenade tous les matins. — Last winter I took a walk every morning.

Je lisais beaucoup. — I used to read a great deal.

b. when denoting a continued action, as:

Tandis que j'écrivais, il parlait. — While I was writing, he was talking.

c. when referring to an action which was going on while another one took place, as:

Quand je suis‿entré, il lisait. — When I entered he was reading.

12. I have quite [totalement] forgotten [oublié] what we were talking [nous parlions] about.

IMPERFECT[1]

I was speaking
thou wast "
he was "
we were "
you were "
they were "

13. We were talking about the [des] seasons and I had just mentioned [dire] their names to you. Do you still [encore] remember them?

14. Perfectly: spring, summer, autumn and winter.

15. Very good [bien]! What is [fait-il] the weather to-day?

16. Pardon me for interrupting you [de vous‿interrompre]; but why do you say "fait-il"?

I say	*or*	I am saying
thou sayest	"	thou art "
he says	"	he is "
we say	"	we are "
you say	"	you are "
they say	"	they are "

[2] The English *just, just now,* used with a verb, is rendered in French by *venir de,* as:

Je viens de recevoir‿une lettre.	I have just received a letter. (Lit.: I come from receiving a letter.)
Le facteur vient d'apporter une lettre pour vous.	The postman just brought a letter for you.
Je suis‿allé chez‿elle, mais je ne l'ai pas trouvée. Elle venait de sortir.	I went to her house, but did not find her. She had just gone out.

17. Parce que **faire** s'emploie[1] en parlant du temps. (sã·plwa ã par lã)

18. C'est très bizarre! Et cela ne devrait pas me paraître si bizarre, car les‿Espagnols se servent[2] du même verbe. (bi za:r—pa rɛ:tr—le zɛs pa ɲɔl sə sɛrv dy mɛ:m vɛrb)

19. C'est vrai. Maintenant afin de vous familiariser avec cet‿idiotisme, nous ferons‿un certain nombre de phrases⁀avec ce verbe. (fa mi lja ri ze—œ̃ sɛr tɛ̃ nɔ̃:br)

20. Puis-je vous‿adresser une question, monsieur? (yn kɛs tjɔ̃)

21. Autant qu'il vous plaira. (o·tã kil vu plɛ ra)

22. De quelle langue⁀est dérivé le verbe **faire**? Vient‿il du latin?[3] (de ri ve—vjɛ̃ til dy la tɛ̃)

Je viens	(ʒə vjɛ̃)
tu viens	(ty vjɛ̃)
il vient	(il vjɛ̃)
nous venons	(nu vnɔ̃)
vous venez	(vu vne)
ils viennent	(il vjɛ·n)

23. Certainement, il vient du mot latin **"facere."**

24. Ah, je vois maintenant son‿origine latine. A l'avenir je ne vous‿interromprai plus. Je désire faire quelques phrases sur le temps, afin d'apprendre⁀à m'en servir correctement. (sɔ nɔ ri ʒi:n la ti:n. a la vni:r ʒən vu zɛ̃ tɛ rɔ̃ pre ply—a mã sɛr vi:r kɔ rɛk tə mã)

---

[1] Verbs ending in *yer* like *employer*, to employ, *essuyer*, to wipe, to dry, change the *y* into *i* before *e* mute, *i. e.*, wherever *y* comes before *e*, *es*, *ent* and the *erai* of the future and conditional, as:

Pres: J'emploie, tu emploies, il emploie, nous‿employons, vous‿employez, ils‿emploient.
Impf: J'employais, tu employais, il employait, etc.
Fut: J'emploierai, tu emploieras, il emploiera, etc.
Cond: J'emploierais, tu emploierais, il emploierait, etc.

Verbs ending in *ayer* or *eyer* like *payer*, to pay, *grasseyer*, to roll one's *r*'s, may retain the *y* or change it into *i*, as:

Pres: Je paye, tu payes, il paye, etc.
Or: Je paie, tu paies, il paie, etc.

17. Because **faire** is used with reference to the weather. (Literally: Because [parce que] **faire** is used [s'emploie] in speaking [en parlant] of the weather.)

18. That's very strange [bizarre]. And yet it [cela] ought not to appear [paraître] so strange to me, as [car] the Spaniards use [se servent] the same verb [du même verbe].

19. That is true [vrai]. Now in order to [afin de] make you familiar [vous familiariser] with this idiom, we will form [nous ferons] a certain number of sentences with this verb.

20. May I [Puis-je] ask you [vous‿adresser] a question, sir?

21. As many as you like. (Literally: As many as it will please you [autant qu'il vous plaira].)

22. From which language is the verb **faire** derived [dérivé]? Does it come [vient‿il] from the Latin?

I come	*or*	I am coming
thou comest	"	thou art "
he comes	"	he is "
we come	"	we are "
you come	"	you are "
they come	"	they are "

23. Certainly, it comes from the Latin word **"facere."**

24. Ah, now I see its Latin origin. From now on [A l'avenir] I shall not interrupt you any more [je ne vous‿interromprai plus]. I am anxious to form [Je désire faire] some phrases about [sur] the weather in order to [afin d'] learn to use them correctly [à m'en servir correctement].

---

[2] *Servir,* to serve, *se servir,* to make use of, to help oneself, and *desservir,* to clear the table are conjugated in the

PRESENT

Je sers	I serve
tu sers	thou servest
il sert	he serves
nous servons	we serve
vous servez	you serve
ils servent	they serve

[3] Adjectives denoting nationality are written with small letters, as allemand, German; français, French, italien, Italian, etc.

Faire

(Suite)

1. Bonjour, mon‿ami. Je suis ravi de vous voir! Comment vous‿êtes-vous porté depuis que je n'ai eu le plaisir de vous voir? La dernière fois que vous‿étiez‿ici, vous‿aviez mal⁀à la tête. J'espère que vous‿allez mieux aujourd'hui (or que vous‿êtes mieux aujourd'hui). (ra vi—mal⁀a la tɛ:t)

2. Merci, je me porte beaucoup mieux; en‿effet, je me sens très bien et tout disposé à continuer notre leçon. (ʒəm sɑ̃—tu dis po ze a kɔ̃ ti nɥe nɔ trɔlə sɔ̃)

3. J'en suis‿enchanté, mais veuillez retirer votre pardessus et vous‿asseoir. (ʒɑ̃ sɥi zɑ̃ ʃɑ̃ te—rə ti re vɔ trə par də sy)

4. Où m'assiérai-je, monsieur? (u ma sje rɛ:ʒ)

PRESENT[1]

je m'assieds	(ʒə ma sje)
tu t'assieds	(ty ta sje)
il s'assied	(il sa sje)
nous nous‿asseyons	(nu nu za sɛ jɔ̃)
vous vous‿asseyez	(vu vu za sɛ je)
ils s'asseient	(il sa sɛj)

FUTURE[1]

je m'assiérai	(ʒə ma sje re)
tu t'assiéras	
il s'assiéra	
nous nous‿assiérons	
vous vous‿assiérez	
ils s'assiéront	

---

[1] Also:

Present	Future
Je m'assois	*Je m'assoirai*
tu t'assois	*tu t'assoiras*
il s'assoit	*il s'assoira*
nous nous‿assoyons	*nous nous‿assoirons*
vous vous‿assoyez	*vous vous‿assoirez*
ils s'assoient	*ils s'assoiront*

To Make; To Do

(Continuation)

1. Good morning, my friend. Delighted [ravi] to see you! How have you been [vous‿êtes-vous porté] since I had [depuis que je n'ai eu] the pleasure of seeing you? The last time [La dernière fois que] you were here, you were suffering with a headache [aviez mal‿a la tête]. I hope (that) you feel better [allez mieux] to-day.

2. Thanks, I am [je me porte] a great deal better [beaucoup mieux]; in fact, I am quite well [je me sens très bien] and ready [tout disposé] to go on with [à continuer] our lesson.

3. I am very glad [enchanté] of that, but please [veuillez] take off [retirer] your overcoat [pardessus] and sit down [vous‿asseoir].

4. Where shall I sit, sir?

PRESENT

I sit down
thou sittest down
he sits down
we sit down
you sit down
they sit down

FUTURE

I shall sit down
thou wilt sit down
he will sit down
we shall sit down
you will sit down
they will sit down

5. Là sur cette chaise. Maintenant commençons![1] De quoi parlions-nous la dernière[2] fois? (kɔ mɑ̃ sɔ̃—la dɛr njɛ:r fwa)

6. Vous‿avez‿expliqué l'emploi de **faire** en parlant du temps. (vu za ve zɛk spli ke)

7. Ah oui, je me le rappelle. Avez-vous‿appris[3] par cœur la conjugaison du verbe **faire**? (a ve vu za pri par kœ:r la kɔ̃ ʒy gɛ·zɔ̃)

8. Oui, monsieur. **Faire**‿est très‿irrégulier, mais je crois que j'en sais toute la conjugaison. (trɛ zi re gy lje)

9. Très bien, voyons! Conjuguez le présent de l'indicatif. (vwa jɔ̃. kɔ̃ ʒy ge lə pre zɑ̃ dlɛ̃ di ka tif)

Je fais	(ʒə fɛ)
tu fais	(ty fɛ)
il fait	(il fɛ)
nous faisons	(nu fzɔ̃)
vous faites	(vu fɛ·t)
ils font	(il fɔ̃)

10. Très bien! Maintenant le présent du subjonctif. (syb ʒɔ̃k tif)

Que je fasse	(kəʒ fas)
que tu fasses	(kə ty fas)
qu'il fasse	(kil fas)
que nous fassions	(kə nu fa sjɔ̃)
que vous fassiez	(kə vu fa sje)
qu'ils fassent	(kil fas)

---

[1] Verbs ending in *cer* as *commencer*, to begin; *placer*, to put, place a *cedilla* under the *c* when this letter is followed by *a* or *o*.

Pres: Je commence, tu commences, il commence, nous commençons, etc.
Imp: Je commençais, tu commençais, il commençait, nous commencions, etc.

[2] Some adjectives have a different meaning when placed *before* or *after* a noun, as:

5. Right here [Là] on this chair. And now let us commence. Of what were we talking the last time [la dernière[2] fois]?

6. You explained the use of **faire** in reference to the [en parlant du] weather.

7. Ah, yes, I remember (it). Have you learned [appris] the conjugation of **faire** by heart [par cœur]?

8. Yes, sir. **Faire** is very irregular, but I believe (that) I know the whole conjugation [toute la conjugaison] (of it: *en*).

9. Very well, let us see [voyons]! Conjugate the present indicative.

I do	*or*	I am	doing
thou dost	"	thou are	"
he does	"	he is	"
we do	"	we are	"
you do	"	you are	"
they do	"	they are	"

10. Very good! And now the present subjunctive (le présent du subjonctif)

that I may	make or do
thou mayest	"
he may	"
we may	"
you may	"
they may	"

L'année dernière	Last year (the year just expired)
La dernière‿année	The last year (of a series)
Un grand‿homme	A great man
Un‿homme grand	A tall man
Mon cher père	My dear father
Un tableau cher	A dear (expensive) picture
Un brave‿homme	An honest (good sort of a) man
Un‿homme brave	A brave (courageous) man

[3] *Appris*, learned, is the irregular past participle of *apprendre*, to learn. In the same way *prendre*, to take, gives *pris*, taken; *comprendre*, to understand; *compris*, understood.

11. Excellent! L'imparfait! (lɛ̃ par fɛ)

Je faisais	(ʒə fzɛ)
tu faisais	
il faisait	
nous faisions	(nu fə zjɔ̃)
vous faisiez	(vu fə zje)
ils faisaient	(il fə zɛ)

12. Maintenant le prétérit[1] ou passe défini: (pre te rit—pa se de fi ni)

Je fis	(ʒə fi)
tu fis	(ty fi)
il fit	(il fi)
nous fîmes	(nu fi:m)
vous fîtes	(vu fi:t)
ils firent	(il fi:r)

13. Bien! Le futur: (fy ty:r)

Je ferai	(ʒə fre)
tu feras	
il fera	
nous ferons	
vous ferez	
ils feront	

14. C'est très bien! Le conditionnel: (kɔ̃ di sjɔ nɛl)

Je ferais	(ʒə frɛ)
tu ferais	
il ferait	
nous ferions	(nu fə rjɔ̃)
vous feriez	(vu fə rje)
ils feraient	(il frɛ)

---

[1] The *prétérit* or *passé défini* is scarcely ever used in conversation, but is always employed in narration, as: *Le président le vit et dit.* The president saw him and said.

11. Excellent! And now the imperfect [l'imparfait].

I was	making **or** doing		
thou wast	"	"	"
he was	"	"	"
we were	"	"	"
you were	"	"	"
they were	"	"	"

12. Now the historical tense [le prétérit ou passé défini].

I did	**or**	I made
thou didst	"	thou madest
he did	"	he made
we "	"	we "
you "	"	you "
they "	"	they "

13. Good! And the future [le futur]:

I shall	do	**or**	make
thou wilt	"	"	"
he will	"	"	"
we shall	"	"	"
you will	"	"	"
they will	"	"	"

14. That's very good! And now the conditional:

I should	do	**or**	make
thou wouldst	"	"	"
he would	"	"	"
we should	"	"	"
you would	"	"	"
they would	"	"	"

15. Vraiment, vous‿êtes un‿excellent‿élève! Conjuguez maintenant l'imparfait du subjonctif.

que je fisse	(kəʒ fis)
que tu fisses	(kə ty fis)
qu'il fît	(kil fi)
que nous fissions	(kə nu fi sjɔ̃)
que vous fissiez	(kə vu fi sje)
qu'ils fissent	(kil fis)

16. Bravo! Je ne doute pas que bientôt vous‿aurez vaincu toutes les difficultés de la langue française. (bra vo—ʒən dut pa—vɛ̃ ky)

17. Vous ne savez pas combien j'ai à cœur de l'apprendre. Aucune[1] autre langue n'est‿aussi importante pour un‿homme d'affaires que la belle langue de Corneille. (o•ky:n—pur œ nɔm da fɛ:r—kɔr nɛ:j)

[1] *Aucun* (masc.), *aucune* (fem.), none, not one, is always used with *ne* (like *personne, rien, jamais*), as:

Avez-vous toutes les boîtes?	Have you all the boxes?
Je n'en‿ai aucune.	I haven't any.
Aucun paquet n'est arrivé.	No parcel came.

15. Really [Vraiment], you are an excellent pupil [élève]. Conjugate now the imperfect tense of the subjunctive mood.

that I might make or do
thou mightest make
he might make
we might make
you might make
they might make

16. Bravo! I have no doubt [Je ne doute pas] that you will soon have [aurez] mastered [vaincu] all the difficulties of the French language.

17. You do not know how anxious I am [combien j'ai à cœur de] to learn it. No other [Aucune autre] tongue is [n'est] so important for a businessman as [que] the beautiful language of Corneille.

VOCABULAIRE (*Suite*)	**VOCABULARY** (*Continuation*)
Le magasin	The store; the shop
Le magasin de nouveautés (nu vo te)	The dry goods store
Le chapeau; les chapeaux (ʃa po)	The hat; the hats; the bonnet; the bonnets
Le chapelier (ʃa pə lje)	The hatter
La modiste (mɔ dist)	The milliner
Le magasin de la modiste	The millinery store
La librairie (li brɛ·ri)	The bookstore
Le papier (pa pje)	The paper
La papeterie (pap tri)	The stationery store
Le cordonnier (kɔr dɔ nje)	The shoemaker
Des souliers (su lje)	Shoes
Des bottines (fem.) (bɔ tin)	High shoes; ladies' boots
La montre (mɔ̃:tr)	The watch
La pendule (pɑ̃ dy·l)	The clock
L'horloge (lɔr lɔ·ʒ)	The (large) clock
L'horloger (lɔr lɔ ʒe)	The watchmaker
Le marchand (mar ʃɑ̃)	The merchant
Le pain (pɛ̃)	The bread
Le petit pain	The roll
Le gâteau (gɑ·to)	The cake
Le boulanger (bu lɑ̃ ʒe)	The baker
La boulangerie (bu lɑ̃·ʒ ri)	The bakery
Le boucher (bu ʃe)	The butcher
La boucherie (buʃ ri)	The butcher-shop

PART SIX

CONTENTS

FAIRE[1] ET SON‿USAGE IDIOMATIQUE

(*Suite*)

18. Vous‿avez raison. Le français n'est pas seulement la langue de la diplomatie, elle est‿aussi celle des classes instruites de la société dans toute l'Europe et l'Asie. Un‿homme qui sait la langue française peut voyager partout. Les Turcs, les‿Égyptiens, les‿Espagnols, les‿Italiens, les Brésiliens, les‿Allemands, parlent notre belle langue de préférence à toute autre, parce que les‿idées ne peuvent‿être exprimées dans‿aucune autre langue aussi clairement qu'en français. (vu za ve rɛ·zɔ̃—la di plɔ ma si—de klɑ·s‿ɛ̃ strɥit də la sɔ sje te—vwa ja ʒe—tyrk—e ʒip sjɛ̃—bre zi ljɛ̃—pre fe rɑ̃:s—le zi de—ɛk spri me—klɛ·r mɑ̃)

19. "N'importe quelle conversation" signifie "toute conversation," "une conversation quelconque."

20. Maintenant nous‿allons voir quelques gallicismes où entre le verbe **faire**: (ga li sism)

21. Parlez-moi un peu du temps qu'il fait aujourd'hui.

---

[1] Besides the idioms taught in this lesson, the student should study the following phrases in which *faire* is used idiomatically:

Vous‿avez fait‿attendre mon employé.	You kept my clerk waiting.
Il a fait des‿embarras.	He made a great fuss.
Il fait semblant d'être malade.	He pretends to be ill.
Je vais faire ma malle à présent.	I am now going to pack my trunk.
Pourquoi n'avez-vous pas fait ma chambre?	Why didn't you put my room in order?
Il fait des contes.	He tells stories.
Il fait le grand seigneur‿à Paris.	He plays the great lord in Paris.
Il fait le bon‿apôtre.	He acts the part of a saint.
Il s'est fait des‿affaires.	He got himself into a scrape.

FAIRE[1] AND ITS IDIOMATIC USE

(*Continuation*)

18. You are (quite) right [Vous‿avez raison]. French is not only [seulement] the language of diplomacy; it is also that [celle] of the cultivated [instruites] classes of society in all Europe and Asia. A man who knows French can travel anywhere [voyager partout]. The Turks, the Egyptians, the Spaniards, the Italians, the Brazilians, the Germans, speak our beautiful language in [de] preference to any other [à toute autre], because [parce que] ideas [les idées] cannot be expressed in any other [dans‿aucune autre] language as [aussi] clearly [clairement] as [qu'] in French.

19. "N'importe (Literally: It does not matter) quelle conversation" means [signifie], "any conversation," "any conversation whatsoever."

20. Now we shall see some [quelques] gallicisms in which [où] the verb **faire** is used (enters, *entre*).

21. Talk to me about to-day's weather.[1] (Literally: Speak to me a little of the weather we have [qu'il fait] to-day.)

---

[1] The following expressions in regard to the weather are formed with *faire:*

Il fait beau (temps).	The weather is fine.
" *mauvais (temps).*	" " " bad.
" *magnifique.*	" " " splendid.
" *un temps magnifique.*	" " " "
" " " *abominable.*	" " " horrid.
" " " *sombre.*	" " " gloomy.
Il fait chaud.	It is warm.
" *froid.*	" cold.
" *humide.*	" damp.
" *sec.*	" dry.
" *lourd.*	" sultry.
" *jour.*	" daylight.
" *nuit.*	" dark.
" *du vent.*	" windy.
" *du brouillard.*	" foggy.
" *de la poussière.*	" dusty.
" *de l'orage.*	" stormy.
" *du soleil.*	The sun is shining.
" *clair de lune.*	The moon is shining.
" *une chaleur‿étouffante.*	It is stiflingly hot.

22. Hier il faisait très mauvais temps, mais‿aujourd'hui il fait très beau. Le temps est‿agréable; il fait chaud, mais pas trop. (a gre abl—ʃo)

23. Est-ce qu'il fait du vent? (dy vɑ̃)

24. Il faisait beaucoup de vent la nuit dernière, mais‿aujourd'hui il⁀en fait‿à peine. (il⁀ɑ̃ fɛ̃ ta pɛ·n)

25. Avez-vous lu les journaux? Savez-vous quel⁀est le temps probable pour demain?

26. Voici le journal. Laissez-moi voir; c'est‿ici. Le bulletin météorologique annonce de forts vents d'ouest (d'est, du nord, du sud), et des‿averses. (dwɛst, dɛst, dy nɔr, dy syd—de za vɛrs)

27. Vous traduisez[1] très bien. La prochaine fois je vous donnerai d'autres phrases sur le temps où entre encore le verbe **faire.** (tra dɥi ze)

28. Quel temps fait-il aujourd'hui?—Magnifique; le temps est délicieux. (ma ɲi fik—de li sjø)

29. Ouvrez la fenêtre et regardez comment est le temps.[2] (u·vre la fnɛ:tr)

30. Il fait‿un soleil magnifique, mais‿il fait froid. (sɔ lɛ:j)

---

[1] *Traduire*, to translate, *conduire*, to conduct, to lead, to take, *construire*, to construct, *instruire*, to instruct, *cuire*, to cook and all verbs ending in *duire*, are slightly irregular and are conjugated:

Pres: Je traduis, tu traduis, il traduit, nous traduisons, vous traduisez, ils traduisent.
Imp: Je traduisais, tu traduisais, etc.
Fut: Je traduirai, tu traduiras, il traduira, etc.
Cond: Je traduirais, tu traduirais, il traduirait, etc.
Pres. Subj: Que je traduise, que tu traduises, etc.
Part. Passé: Traduit.

22. Yesterday the weather was very bad, but to-day we have most beautiful weather. It is pleasant, it is warm, and yet not too warm. (Literally: Yesterday it was [il faisait] very bad weather, but to-day it is [il fait] very beautiful. The weather is agreeable; it is [il fait] warm [chaud], but not too much so [pas trop].

23. Is it windy? (Literally: Is there [Est-ce qu'il fait] any wind [du vent]?)

24. It was quite windy last night, but to-day there is scarcely any breeze. (Literally: There was [Il faisait] much wind last night [la nuit dernière], but to-day there is [il‿en fait] scarcely [à peine] any.)

25. Have you read [lu] the papers [les journaux]? Do you know what is the weather forecast [le temps probable] for to-morrow?

26. Here is the paper. Let me see; here it is! The weather bulletin [bulletin météorologique] announces strong westerly winds [de forts vents d'ouest] (easterly [d'est], northerly [du nord], southerly [du sud]) and showers [des‿averses].

27. You translate [Vous traduisez] very well. Next time I will give you other phrases about [sur] the weather in which [où] the verb **faire** is again used [entre‿encore].

28. What kind of weather is it [fait‿il] to-day? Splendid; the weather is delightful [délicieux].

29. Open [Ouvrez] the window [la fenêtre] and see [regardez] how the weather is.

30. The sun is shining beautifully, but it is cold. (Literally: There is [il fait] a magnificent sun [un soleil magnifique], but it is [il fait] cold.)

---

[2] Note that the subject is often inverted, especially in short sentences, as: *Je ne sais pas où est Robert.*

31. Il me semble que nous‿allons avoir du mauvais temps; le baromètre annonce de la pluie (le baromètre est‿à la pluie). (lə ba rɔ mɛ:tr⁀ɛ ta la plɥi)

32. Vous‿avez raison; le baromètre est descendu[1]; je crains qu'il ne pleuve. (de sɑ̃ dy—plœ:v)

33. C'est parfait! Je vois que vous comprenez très bien ces gallicismes. (par fɛ—ga li sism)

34. Sont-ce là tous les idiotismes dans lesquels[2] **faire** est‿employé? (dɑ̃ le kɛl)

35. Oh! non, nous‿employons surtout **faire** avec d'autres verbes; comme par⁀exemple avec le verbe écrire, faire écrire. (par⁀ɛg zɑ̃:pl)

36. Ah, je m'en souviens; vous m'avez déjà expliqué ces‿idiotismes.

37. C'est vrai, mais à présent montrez-moi si vous savez les‿employer convenablement. Formez‿une phrase. (kɔ̃ vna blə mɑ̃)

38. Sur quel sujet, monsieur?—Oh, sur celui qui vous plaira.[3] (sy ʒɛ—sə lɥi ki vu plɛ·ra)

39. Fort bien. Je vais‿essayer de faire de mon mieux.[4]—Où allez-vous?—Je vais chez[5] le tailleur. (mjø—tɑ·jœ:r)

40. Qu'allez-vous‿y faire?—Je vais me faire faire un complet neuf. (kɔ̃ plɛ nœf)

41. Parfait! A propos, comment diriez-vous:— (a prɔ po)

---

[1] Similarly:

Le baromètre est monté,	The barometer has risen.
Le baromètre est‿au beau,	The barometer points to fair.
" " " *à la pluie,*	" " " " rain.
" " " *à variable,*	" " " " change.

[2] *Lequel* (masc.), *laquelle* (fem.), *lesquels* (m. plur.), *lesquelles* (f. plur.), must be used after prepositions when reference is made to things:

Voilà le banc sur lequel je me suis‿assis.	There stands the bench on which I sat.
C'est‿une condition sans laquelle⁀il ne veut rien faire.	That is a condition without which he will do nothing.

Compare Part X for full rules.

31. It seems to me we are going to have bad weather; the barometer points to [annonce] rain [de la pluie].

32. You are (quite) right; the barometer has fallen [est descendu]; I am afraid [je crains] it is going to (that it may) rain [qu'il ne pleuve].

33. Excellent [C'est parfait]! I see that you understand these French idioms [gallicismes] very well.

34. Are these [Sont-ce là] all the idiomatic expressions in which [dans lesquels] **faire** is used [est‿employé]?

35. Oh no, we use [employons] especially [surtout] **faire** with other [avec d'autres] verbs, as for instance [par‿exemple] with **écrire,** to write, faire écrire, to cause to be written.

36. Ah, I remember [je m'en souviens]; you have already explained [déjà expliqué] these idioms to me.

37. That's true, but show me now [à présent] if you can [savez] use them properly [convenablement]. Form a phrase.

38. Upon [Sur] what subject, sir?—Oh, on any you like (on the one [celui] which will please you [qui vous plaira[3]].)

39. Very [Fort] well; I am going to try [essayer] to do my best [de mon mieux].—Where are you going?—I am on my way [Je vais] to [chez] the tailor [le tailleur].

40. What [Qu'] are you going to do there [y]?—I am going to have a new suit made [faire faire‿un complet neuf].

41. Excellent [Parfait]! By the way [A propos], how would you say:—

---

[3] *Plaire,* to please, is slightly irregular.

Pres: Je plais, tu plais, il plaît, nous plaisons, vous plaisez, ils plaisent.
Imp: Je plaisais, tu plaisais, il plaisait, etc.
Fut: Je plairai, tu plairas, il plaira, etc.
Cond: Je plairais, tu plairais, il plairait, etc.
Pres. Subj: Que je plaise, que tu plaises, qu'il plaise, que nous plaisions, que vous plaisiez, qu'ils plaisent.

Part. Passé: Plu.

[4] Idiomatic expression.

[5] *Chez* must always be used with persons.

42. Ma sœur se fait faire une robe chez[1] Madame Élise. (sœ:r—ʃe ma dam͡e li:z)

43. Très bien! Maintenant traduisez-moi:

44. Comment voulez-vous que votre chapeau soit garni? Comment voulez-vous faire garnir votre chapeau?

45. Vous le garnirez de fleurs et d'un ruban bleu. Prenez‿un joli bleu marine; cela ira bien avec ma toilette. (flœ:r—ry bã blø—ma rin)

Avoir et Son‿Usage Idiomatique

1. Voyons[2] maintenant le verbe avoir. Je suppose que vous‿avez‿ appris par cœur la conjugaison de ce verbe? (vwa jɔ̃—sy po:z—vu za ve za pri par kœ:r la kɔ̃ ʒy gɛ·zɔ̃)

---

[1] *At home*, is rendered either by *à la maison*, or by *chez moi, chez toi, chez lui, chez‿elle, chez nous, chez vous, chez‿eux, chez‿elles.*

Je vais chez moi. *Je vais‿à la maison.*	I am going home.
Est‿il chez lui?	Is he at home?
Est‿elle chez‿elle?	Is she at home?
Allez-vous chez vous?	Are you going home?
Ils restent chez‿eux aujourd'hui.	They remain at home to-day.
Venez chez moi.	Come to my house.
Elles ne sont pas chez‿elles.	They are not at home.
Allons chez‿eux.	Let us go to their house.
Ne sont-ils pas chez vous?	Are they not at your house?
Chez qui demeurez-vous?	At whose house do you live?
Je demeure chez madame Renard.	I live at Mrs. Renard's.
Quand viendrez-vous chez moi?	When will you come to my house?
Aussitôt que je le pourrai.	As soon as I can.
Les Messieurs Marcel sont‿ils chez eux?	Are the Messrs. Marcel at home?
Ils ne sont pas chez‿eux; ils sont‿allés chez Monsieur Le Gros.	They are not at home; they have gone to Mr. Le Gros's.
Madame Didier est‿elle chez‿elle?	Is Mrs. Didier in?
Non, mais mademoiselle Didier y est.	No, but Miss Didier is.
Mes‿enfants sont‿à la maison, (not, *chez‿eux.*)	My children are at home.

42. My sister is having a dress made [se fait faire une robe] at [chez] Mme. Elise's.

43. Very good [bien]! Now translate for me:

44. How do you wish to have your hat trimmed (that your hat should be [soit] trimmed [garni])? How do you want to have your bonnet trimmed [faire garnir votre chapeau]?

45. You will trim it with flowers [de fleurs] and a blue ribbon [d'un ruban bleu]. Take [Prenez] a pretty navy blue [bleu marine]. That will match [ira bien avec] my dress [ma toilette].

Avoir and Its Idiomatic Use

1. Let us consider [voyons] now the verb **avoir.** I suppose (that) you have learned [appris] the conjugation by heart [par cœur]?

---

[2] For conversational purposes only five forms of the verb need be mastered, viz., the Indicative of the Present, Imperfect, Future and Conditional and the Subjunctive mood of the Present.

The compound tenses are conjugated with *avoir* or *être*, as the case may be; these can be formed by the pupil himself as soon as he knows the conjugation of these two auxiliary verbs.

When it comes to reading, the *prétérit* or *passé défini* must be thoroughly mastered, as it is constantly employed when past actions or events are referred to.

At present, however, the necessary forms for conversation only are given in the conjugation of the irregular verbs of which complete tables are given in Part X.

Voir, to see; *voyant*, seeing; *vu*, seen.

Pres: Je vois, tu vois, il voit, nous voyons, vous voyez, ils voient.
Imp: Je voyais, tu voyais, il voyait, etc.
Fut: Je verrai, tu verras, il verra, nous verrons, vous verrez, ils verront.
Cond: Je verrais, tu verrais, il verrait, etc.
Pres. Subj: Que je voie, que tu voies, qu'il voie, que nous voyions, que vous voyiez, qu'ils voient.

2. Je l'ai étudié et je crois[1] que j'en[2] sais[3] tous les modes et tous les temps. (e ty dje—krwa—ʒɑ̃ se—mɔd)

3. Très bien! Voyons! Dites-moi le présent de l'indicatif.

J'ai
tu as
il⁀a
nous‿avons
vous‿avez
ils‿ont

4. Très bien! Maintenant le présent du subjonctif.

Que j'aie	(kə ʒε)
que tu aies	(kə ty ε)
qu'il⁀ait	(kil⁀ε)
que nous‿ayons	(kə nu z͜ε jɔ̃)
que vous‿ayez	(kə vu z͜ε je)
qu'ils‿aient	(kil z͜ε)

5. Parfait! L'imparfait, s'il vous plaît.

J'avais	(ʒa vε)
tu avais	(ty a vε)
il⁀avait	(il⁀a vε)
nous‿avions	(nu z͜a vjɔ̃)
vous‿aviez	(vu z͜a vje)
ils‿avaient	(il z͜a vε)

---

[1] *Croire*, to believe; *croyant*, believing; *cru*, believed.

Pres: Je crois, tu crois, il croit, nous croyons, vous croyez, ils croient.
Imp: Je croyais, tu croyais, il croyait, etc.
Fut: Je croirai, tu croiras, il croira, etc.
Cond: Je croirais, tu croirais, il croirait, etc.
Pres. Subj: Que je croie, que tu croies, qu'il croie, que nous croyions, que vous croyiez, qu'ils croient.

2. I have studied it and think (that) I know all its moods and tenses. (Literally: I have studied [étudié] it and I believe [je crois] that I know all the moods [tous les modes] and all the tenses [tous les temps] of it [en].)

3. Well, let us see! Give me (Tell me, *Dites-moi*) the Present Indicative.

I have
thou hast
he has
we have
you have
they have

4. Very well! Now the Present Subjunctive.

That I may have
that thou mayest have
that he may have
that we may have
that you may have
that they may have

5. Excellent! Now the Imperfect, if you please.

I had, **or**, I used to have
thou hadst, **or**, thou used [st] to have
he had, **or**, he used to have
we had, **or**, we used to have
you had, **or**, you used to have
they had, **or**, they used to have

---

[2] Note the use of *en* when in English a possessive would be used: *j'en sais tous les temps*, I know all the tenses of it (*en*), I know all its tenses.

[3] *Savoir*, to know; *sachant*, knowing; *su*, known.

Pres: Je sais, tu sais, il sait, nous savons, vous savez, ils savent.
Imp: Je savais, tu savais, il savait, nous savions, vous saviez, ils savaient.
Fut: Je saurai, tu sauras, il saura, nous saurons, vous saurez, ils sauront.
Cond: Je saurais, tu saurais, il saurait, nous saurions, vous sauriez, ils sauraient.
Pres. Subj: Que je sache, que tu saches, qu'il sache, que nous sachions, que vous sachiez, qu'ils sachent.

6. Excellent! Le prétérit.

J'eus	(ʒy)
tu eus	(ty y)
il‿eut	(il‿y)
nous‿eûmes	(nu zy:m)
vous‿eûtes	(vu zyt)
ils‿eurent	(il zy:r)

7. C'est[1] très bien! Conjuguez maintenant l'imparfait du subjonctif.

Que j'eusse	(kə ʒys)
que tu eusses	(kə ty ys)
qu'il eût	(kil‿y)
que nous‿eussions	(kə nu zy sjɔ̃)
que vous‿eussiez	(kə vu zy sje)
qu'ils‿eussent	(kil zys)

8. Vraiment, vous‿êtes‿un‿excellent‿élève. Conjuguez maintenant le futur. (fy ty:r)

J'aurai	(ʒɔ re)
tu auras	(ty ɔ ra)
il‿aura	(il‿ɔ ra)
nous‿aurons	(nu zɔ rɔ̃)
vous‿aurez	(vu zɔ re)
ils‿auront	(il zɔ rɔ̃)

9. Excellent! Et le conditionnel, s'il vous plaît. (kɔ̃ di sjɔ nɛl)

J'aurais	(ʒɔ rɛ)
tu aurais	(ty ɔ rɛ)
il‿aurait	(il‿ɔ rɛ)
nous‿aurions	(nu zɔ rjɔ̃)
vous‿auriez	(vu zɔ rje)
ils‿auraient	(il zɔ rɛ)

---

[1] The pupil should familiarize himself with the conjugation of the verb *être,* to be.

Pres: Je suis, tu es, il‿est, nous sommes, vous‿êtes, ils sont.
Imp: J'étais, tu étais, il‿était, nous‿étions, vous‿étiez, ils‿étaient.
Fut: Je serai, tu seras, il sera, nous serons, vous serez, ils seront.
Cond: Je serais, tu serais, il serait, nous serions, vous seriez, ils seraient.
Pres. Subj: Que je sois, que tu sois, qu'il soit, que nous soyons, que vous soyez, qu'ils soient.

6. Excellent! Now the historical tense (le prétérit).

I had
thou hadst
he had
we had
you had
they had

7. That's fine [très bien]! Now conjugate the Imperfect Subjunctive.

That I might have
that thou mightest have
that he might have
that we " "
that you " "
that they " "

8. You are really [vraiment] an excellent student. Now conjugate the Future tense [le futur].

I shall have
thou wilt "
he will "
we shall "
you will "
they will "

9. Very good! And the Conditional, if you please.

I should have
thou wouldst "
he would "
we should "
you would "
they would "

Le temps passé et son emploi

10. Très bien! Maintenant, pouvez-vous[1] me dire[2] comment on‿emploie **avoir** dans la conjugaison d'autres verbes?

11. Nous l'employons comme verbe auxiliaire, exactement comme en‿anglais, dans la formation des temps composés, par⁀exemple: J'ai écrit; je l'aurais fait. Qu'auriez-vous fait si vous‿aviez‿été à ma place? (ɔk si ljɛːr—ɛg zak tə mɑ̃—fɔr ma sjɔ̃—kɔ̃ po·ze—par⁀ɛg zɑ̃·pl—kɔ rje vu fɛ)

12. Très bien! Mais je dois‿appeler votre attention sur un point important où les deux langues diffèrent entièrement. (a tɑ̃·sjɔ̃—pwɛ̃ ɛ̃ pɔr tɑ̃—di fɛ·r⁀ɑ̃ tjɛ·r mɑ̃)

13. En‿anglais, le prétérit est généralement employé quand‿on parle de faits ou d'actions passés.[3] Par⁀exemple: **"I saw him yesterday morning."** En français, on‿emploie rarement le prétérit, mais plutôt le passé indéfini, ainsi l'on dit. "Je l'ai vu hier matin." (fɛ u ak sjɔ̃ pa·se—ra·r mɑ̃—ɛ̃·si)

14. Est-ce toujours ainsi?

15. Généralement, oui. (ʒe ne ral mɑ̃)

16. Sans doute, il y a des règles pour l'emploi de l'imparfait et du prétérit. Ce dernier est‿employé seulement dans les récits, mais ces règles nous les verrons plus tard. (dɛr nje)

---

[1] *Pouvoir,* to be able; *pouvant; pu.*—

Pres. Je peux (je puis), tu peux, il peut, nous pouvons, vous pouvez, ils peuvent.

Imp: Je pouvais, tu pouvais, il pouvait, etc.

Fut: Je pourrai, tu pourras, il pourra, nous pourrons, vous pourrez, ils pourront.

Cond: Je pourrais, tu pourrais, il pourrait, nous pourrions, vous pourriez, ils pourraient.

Pres. Subj: Que je puisse, que tu puisses, qu'il puisse, que nous puissions, que vous puissiez, qu'ils puissent.

10. Very well! Now can you [pouvez-vous] tell me how we use [on emploie] **avoir** in the conjugation of other verbs?

11. We use it as an auxiliary verb, exactly as in English, for [dans] the formation of compound [composés] tenses, as for instance [par exemple]: I have written; I would have done it. What would you have done if you had been [été] in [à] my place?

12. Very good! But I should call [je dois appeler] your attention to [sur] an important point of difference between the two languages (where the two languages differ [diffèrent] entirely [entièrement].)

13. In English, the perfect tense is generally used when talking about (when one speaks of, *quand on parle de*) past events [faits] or actions. For instance [Par exemple]: **"I saw him yesterday morning."** In French, we rarely use [on emploie rarement] the perfect [le prétérit ou passé défini], but the past perfect tense [passé indéfini] and therefore [ainsi] we say [l'on dit]: **"I have seen him yesterday morning."**

14. Is this always the case (thus, *ainsi*)?

15. Generally (speaking), yes.

16. Of course [Sans doute], there are rules [des règles] for the use of the Imperfect and the Historical Tense [et du prétérit]. The latter [le dernier] is used in narratives [dans les récits] only; but these rules we shall take (we shall see them, *nous les verrons*) later [plus tard]. (Literally: Without doubt, there are some rules [des règles] for the use [l'emploi] of the imperfect and of the preterit [du prétérit]. This last [ce dernier] is employed only in the narratives [dans les récits], but these rules we shall see them later [plus tard].)

---

[2] *Dire*, to say, to tell; *disant*, saying; *dit*, said.

Pres: Je dis, tu dis, il dit, nous disons, vous dites, ils disent.

Imp: Je disais, tu disais, il disait, nous disions, vous disiez, ils disaient.

Fut: Je dirai, tu diras, il dira, nous dirons, vous direz, ils diront.

Cond: Je dirais, tu dirais, il dirait, nous dirions, vous diriez, ils diraient.

Pres. Subj: Que je dise, que tu dises, qu'il dise, que nous disions, que vous disiez, qu'ils disent.

[3] When two or more nouns of different genders are qualified by the *same* adjective, the adjective takes the masculine termination.

17. Pour le moment je tiens[1]‿à vous rappeler que généralement nous‿employons le passé indéfini en français quand nous voulons[2] parler de faits passés. C'est‿une règle très‿importante et vous devez vous la rappeler, surtout quand vous traduirez[3] des questions. (ʒə tjɛ̃—syr tu—kɛs tjɔ̃)

18. Pourquoi des questions?

19. Parce qu'en français il n'y a pas de verbe auxiliaire correspondant à notre verbe anglais "**did.**" (kɔ rɛs pɔ̃ dɑ̃)

20. Par‿exemple, quand nous disons en‿anglais: "**Did you do this?—Did he tell you so?—Why didn't you pay him the money which I handed you this morning?—Did you send him a dispatch or did you write to him?**"—En français nous disons: Avez-vous fait ceci?—Vous l'[4]a-t-il dit?—Pourquoi ne lui[4] avez-vous pas remis l'argent que je vous‿ai donné ce matin?—Lui[4] avez-vous‿envoyé une dépêche ou lui avez-vous‿écrit? (rə mi—de pɛ·ʃ)

21. Je comprends cela parfaitement et m'efforcerai de toujours me rappeler cette règle. (me fɔr sə re)

22. C'est très bien, mais vous devez la pratiquer et en faire l'application. Les règles sont bonnes en théorie, mais la pratique est la chose principale pour bien posséder une langue étrangère. (la pli ka sjɔ̃—te ɔ ri—prɛ̃ si pal—pɔ se de—e trɑ̃·ʒɛːr)

---

[1] *Tenir*, to hold; *tenant*, holding; *tenu*, held.—*Tenir à*, to want badly, to care to, to insist upon.

Pres: Je tiens, tu tiens, il tient, nous tenons, vous tenez, ils tiennent.
Imp: Je tenais, tu tenais, il tenait, nous tenions, vous teniez, ils tenaient.
Fut: Je tiendrai, tu tiendras, il tiendra, nous tiendrons, vous tiendrez, ils tiendront.
Cond: Je tiendrais, tu tiendrais, il tiendrait, nous tiendrions, vous tiendriez, ils tiendraient.
Pres. Subj: Que je tienne, que tu tiennes, qu'il tienne, que nous tenions, que vous teniez, qu'ils tiennent.

[2] *Vouloir*, to be willing, to wish, to want; *voulant; voulu*.

Pres: Je veux, tu veux, il veut, nous voulons, vous voulez, ils veulent.
Imp: Je voulais, tu voulais, il voulait, etc.
Fut: Je voudrai, tu voudras, il voudra, etc.
Cond: Je voudrais, tu voudrais, il voudrait, etc.
Pres. Subj: Que je veuille, que tu veuilles, qu'il veuille, que nous voulions, que vous vouliez, qu'ils veuillent.

17. Just now [Pour le moment] I want [je tiens[1] à] to remind you [vous rappeler] that we generally use the past perfect tense in French when we wish to speak of past actions. This is a very important rule and you ought [vous devez] to remember it, especially [surtout] when you translate [traduirez[3]] questions.

18. And why questions?

19. Because in French there is no auxiliary verb corresponding to [correspondant à] our English **"did."**

20. For instance, when we say in English: **"Did you do this?—Did he tell you so?—Why didn't you pay him the money which I handed you this morning?—Did you send him a dispatch or did you write to him?"**—In French we say: Have you done this [ceci]?—Has he told you so [Vous l'a-t-il dit]?—Why haven't you paid him (haven't you handed him, *ne lui avez-vous pas remis*) the money that I gave you this morning?—Have you sent him a dispatch or have you written to him?

21. I understand this [cela] perfectly and shall try [je m'efforcerai] always to remember [me rappeler] this rule.

22. Very well, but you must [vous devez] practise [la pratiquer] and apply it [en faire l'application]. Rules are good in theory, but practice is the main thing [la chose principale] in mastering [pour bien posséder] a foreign tongue.

---

[3] The French employ the future after *quand, lorsque,* when; *aussitôt que,* as soon as, to express a future action or state; though in English the present tense is often used, as:

Quand vous‿aurez fini, venez.	Come, when you are done.
Aussitôt qu'il saura lire, il‿aura ces livres.	As soon as he knows how to read, he shall have these books.
Quand vous viendrez, elle sera ici.	When you come she will be here.
Lorsqu'il sera ici, je lui donnerai cet‿argent.	When he is here I'll give him this money.

[4] Compare Part X on the position of pronoun-objects and study the tables given there carefully. Exercises on the use of the pronoun-objects are given in a later lesson.

VOCABULAIRE / VOCABULARY

(Suite) / *(Continuation)*

VOCABULAIRE	VOCABULARY
La viande (vjɑ̃:d)	The meat
Le mètre (mɛ·tr)	The metre; (a few inches more than a yard)
Le kilo (ki lo)	The kilo; (a little more than two English pounds avoirdupois)
Une livre (li:vr)	A pound; (a little more than an English pound avoirdupois)

Manger et Boire / Eating and Drinking

Manger et Boire	Eating and Drinking
Manger (mɑ̃·ʒe)	To eat
Boire (bwa:r)	To drink
Déjeuner (de ʒø ne)	To breakfast; to luncheon
Dîner (di ne)	To dine
Souper (su pe)	To take supper
L'appétit (la pe ti)	The appetite
Je n'ai pas d'appétit.	I have no appetite.
Avoir faim (fɛ̃)	To be hungry (to have hunger)
Avez-vous faim?	Are you hungry?
Oui, j'ai faim.	Yes, I am hungry.
Avoir soif (swaf)	To be thirsty (to have thirst)
Avez-vous soif?	Are you thirsty?
Non, je n'ai pas soif.	No, I am not thirsty.

Le Déjeuner / The Breakfast

Le Déjeuner	The Breakfast
Le petit déjeuner	The (first) breakfast (consisting of coffee and rolls)
Le goûter (gu te) Le thé (te)	Light afternoon meal; tea
Le café (ka fe)	The coffee
Une tasse de café (tɑ·s)	A cup of coffee

VOCABULAIRE	VOCABULARY
Une tasse de thé	A cup of tea
Le chocolat (ʃɔ kɔ lɑ)	The chocolate
Que voulez-vous pour votre déjeuner? Du café, du thé ou du chocolat?	What do you wish for breakfast? Coffee, tea, or chocolate?
Je bois du café, mais ma femme prend du thé.	I drink coffee, but my wife takes tea.
N'aimez-vous pas le thé?	Don't you like tea?
Je préfère le café.	I prefer coffee.
Commander (kɔ mɑ̃ de)	To order
Avez-vous commandé?	Did you order?
Que voulez-vous commander?	What do you want to order?
Le bifteck (bif tɛk)	The beefsteak
Bien cuit (kɥi)	Well done
Garçon, apportez moi un bifteck et une tasse de café.	Waiter, bring me a beefsteak and a cup of coffee.
Le voulez-vous bien cuit?	Do you want it well done?
Non, saignant, s'il vous plaît. (sɛ·ɲɑ̃)	No, rare, please (*i.e.*, saignant, bleeding).
La côtelette (ko·t lɛt)	The chop
La côtelette de mouton (mu tɔ̃)	The mutton-chop
La côtelette de veau (vo)	The veal chop
La côtelette de porc (pɔr)	The pork chop
Des pommes de terre (pɔm də tɛ:r)	Potatoes
Des pommes de terre frites (frit)	French fried potatoes
Apportez-moi une côtelette de mouton et des pommes de terre frites.	Bring me a mutton-chop and French fried potatoes.
Un‿œuf (œ̃ nœf)	An egg
Des‿œufs (de zø)	Eggs

VOCABULAIRE	VOCABULARY
Des‿œufs à la coque (a la kɔk)	Soft-boiled eggs (eggs in the shell)
Des‿œufs durs (dy:r)	Hard-boiled eggs (eggs hard)
Des‿œufs brouillés (bru je)	Scrambled eggs
Des‿œufs sur le plat (plɑ)	Fried eggs (eggs on the dish)
Des‿œufs pochés (pɔ ʃe)	Poached eggs
Des‿œufs frais (frɛ)	Fresh eggs
Une‿omelette (ɔm lɛt)	An omelette
Comment désirez-vous les‿œufs, à la coque ou durs?	How do you want the eggs, soft boiled or hard?
Faites-les bouillir trois minutes. (bu•ji:r trwɑ mi nyt)	Let them boil three minutes.
Le sel (sɛl)	The salt
Le poivre (pwa:vr)	The pepper
Le sucre (sy:kr)	The sugar
Le lait (lɛ)	The milk
La crême (krɛ:m)	The cream
Le vinaigre (vi nɛ:gr)	The vinegar
L'huile (lɥi•l)	The oil
La moutarde (mu tard)	The mustard
La salière (sa ljɛ:r)	The salt-cellar
Le sucrier (sy kri je)	The sugar-bowl
La cafetière (kaf tjɛ:r)	The coffee-pot
La théière (te jɛ:r)	The tea-pot
Le coquetier (kɔk tje)	The egg-cup
Verser (vɛr se)	To pour out
Versez-moi une tasse de thé, s'il vous plaît.	Please pour me out a cup of tea.
De l'eau fraîche (də lo frɛ:ʃ)	Fresh water
Un verre d'eau (vɛ:r)	A glass of water

VOCABULAIRE	VOCABULARY
Versez-moi un verre d'eau, s'il vous plaît.	Please pour me out a glass of water.
De l'eau froide (frwad)	Cold water
De l'eau chaude (ʃo·d)	Warm water
De l'eau bouillante (bu jɑ̃:t)	Boiling water
De l'eau tiède (tjɛ·d)	Lukewarm water
De l'eau minérale (mi ne ral)	Mineral water
De l'eau glacée (gla se)	Ice-water
Une carafe (ka raf)	A decanter

Les Plats (plɑ) **La Vaisselle**[1] (vɛ sɛl)	**The Dishes**
Mettre la table	To set the table
Mettez la table	Set the table
Une assiette (a sjɛt)	A plate
Propre (prɔpr)	Clean
Veuillez donner des‿assiettes propres.	Please serve (give) clean plates.
L'assiette à soupe (sup)	The soup-plate
Le plat	The dish
La cuiller (kɥi jɛ:r)	The spoon
La grande cuiller (la cuiller à soupe)	The large spoon
La cuiller‿à thé	The teaspoon
Une cuillerée (kɥi jə re)	A spoonful
La fourchette (fu·r ʃɛt)	The fork
Le couteau (ku to)	The knife
Les couteaux (ku to)	The knives
Donnez-moi un couteau propre.	Give me a clean knife.

[1] *La Vaisselle* means dishes in general; table service.

VOCABULAIRE	VOCABULARY
La nappe (nap)	The table-cloth
La serviette (sɛr vjɛt)	The napkin
Vous ne m'avez pas‿apporté de serviette.	You did not bring me a napkin.
Le couvert (ku vɛ·r)	The cover
Le verre	The glass
Un verre d'eau	A glass of water
Un verre de vin (vɛ̃)	A glass of wine
Un verre‿à vin	A wine glass
Un bock (bɔk)	A glass of beer
Boire dans‿un verre[1]	To drink out of a glass
La tasse	The cup
La soucoupe (su kup)	The saucer
Le tirebouchon (ti:r bu ʃɔ̃)	The corkscrew
Servez le café (sɛr ve)	Serve the coffee
Desservez la table (de sɛr ve)	Clear the table

[1] Idiomatic use of *dans*.

PART SEVEN

CONTENTS

Avoir

(Suite)

23. Ecrivez[1] chez vous un certain nombre de phrases à différentes personnes et à différents temps, apportez-les-moi et je vous les corrigerai. (e kri ve—œ̃ sɛr tɛ̃ nɔ̃•br—di fe rɑ̃:t pɛr sɔn—kɔ riʒ re)

24. Je le ferai. Mais parlez-moi du participe passé qui est‿accompagné de l'auxiliaire‿**avoir** dans les temps composés. (par ti sip pa•se—a kɔ̃ pa ɲe—tɑ̃ kɔ̃ po se)

25. Ah, je suis content que vous m'adressiez[2] cette question. Nous‿avons‿en français quatre conjugaisons.[3] (kɔ̃ tɑ̃—ma drɛ sje—kɔ̃ ʒy gɛ zɔ̃)

26. Je sais cela. Est-ce que les verbes de la première conjugaison ne finissent pas‿en **er**?[4] (fi nis)

27. Oui; les verbes de la première conjugaison se terminent‿en **er**; ceux de la seconde‿en **ir**; ceux de la troisième‿en **oir** et ceux de la quatrième en **re.** (tɛr min)

28. En supprimant ces terminaisons, nous‿avons le radical du verbe qui dans les verbes réguliers demeure toujours le même. A ces radicaux nous‿ajoutons les terminaisons des diverses conjugaisons. Vous trouverez dans le livre X un tableau complet de ces terminaisons que vous ferez bien d'étudier. (ɑ̃ sy pri mɑ̃—ra di kal—də mœ:r—nu za ʒu tɔ̃—di vɛrs—ta blo kɔ̃ plɛ—de ty dje)

29. Je le ferai. Mais je voudrais savoir comment est formé le participe passé[5] de ces quatre conjugaisons.

---

[1] *Ecrire,* to write; *écrivant,* writing; *écrit,* written.

Pres: J'écris, tu écris, il écrit, nous écrivons, vous écrivez, ils écrivent.
Imp: J'écrivais, tu écrivais, il écrivait, nous écrivions, etc.
Fut: J'écrirai, tu écriras, il écrira, nous écrirons, vous écrirez, ils écriront.
Cond: J'écrirais, tu écrirais, il écrirait, nous écririons, etc.
Pres. Subj: Que j'écrive, que tu écrives, qu'il écrive, que nous écrivions, que vous écriviez, qu'ils écrivent.

[2] The Subjunctive Mood must be used after verbs (or sentences) expressing pleasure, wonder, surprise, wish, desire, will, command, doubt, fear or sorrow, as:

Je suis content que vous l'ayez vu. — I am glad you saw him.
Je regrette que vous soyez malade. — I am sorry you are ill.

Avoir

(*Continuation*)

23. Write at home [Écrivez chez vous] a certain number of sentences in various [à differentes] persons and in various tenses; bring them to me and I shall correct them for you [et je vous les corrigerai].

24. I'll do so. But speak to me of the past participle [du participe passé] which is accompanied by the [de l'] auxiliary **avoir** in the compound [composés] tenses.

25. Ah, I am glad [content] that you asked me [que vous m'adressiez] this question. We have four conjugations in French.

26. I know that. The verbs of the first conjugation end in **er**, do they not? (Literally: I know that. Don't the verbs of the first conjugation end in **er?**)

27. Yes, the verbs of the first conjugation end [se terminent] in **er;** those [ceux] of the second in **ir;** those of the third in **oir**, and those of the fourth in **re**.

28. By dropping (In suppressing, *en supprimant*) these endings we get [nous avons] the root [le radical] of the verb which [qui] in the regular verbs remains [demeure] unchanged [toujours le même]. To these roots [radicaux] we add [ajoutons] the endings of the respective [diverses] conjugations. You will find a complete list [tableau] of these endings in Book X which [que] you will do well to study.

29. I will do so. But I would like to know how the past participle of the four conjugations is formed.

---

[3] Compare Part X The Conjugations.

[4] Note the use of *Est-ce que* followed by a negative statement to express a negative question. Other examples:

Est-ce que Robert n'est pas venu?	Hasn't Robert come?
Est-ce que vous ne savez pas cela?	Don't you know that?

[5] Note the inversion of the subject.

30. D'une manière très simple. Le participe passé de la première conjugaison se termine en é, comme: aimer, aimé; payer, payé; donner, donné; parler, parlé, etc. (ma njɛ:r sɛ̃:pl)

31. Quelle est la terminaison du participe passé des verbes de la deuxième conjugaison?

32. Ils se terminent en **i**, comme finir, fini; remplir, rempli; rétablir, rétabli. (rɑ̃·pli:r, rɑ̃·pli; re ta bli:r, re ta bli)

33. Ah, c'est très simple. Quelle est la terminaison des participes passés des verbes de la troisième conjugaison?

34. Ils se terminent en **u**: apercevoir, aperçu; concevoir, conçu; recevoir, reçu, etc. (y: a pɛr sə vwa:r, a pɛr sy; kɔ̃ sə vwa:r, kɔ̃ sy; rə sə vwa:r, rə sy)

35. Quelle est la terminaison des participes passés des verbes de la quatrième conjugaison?

36. Ils se terminent en **u**: vendre, vendu; rendre, rendu; descendre, descendu, etc. (rɑ̃·dr, rɑ̃·dy; de sɑ̃·dr, de sɑ̃·dy)

37. Mais ces règles s'appliquent seulement aux verbes réguliers, n'est-ce-pas? (sa plik—re gy lje)

38. Certainement. Nous‿avons‿un grand nombre de verbes‿irréguliers. Vous‿en trouverez une table complète dans le volume X. (kɔ̃·plɛt—vɔ lym dis)

39. Et tous les verbes se conjuguent[1]-ils avec **avoir?** (sə kɔ̃ ʒyg til)

VERBES NEUTRES, PASSIFS ET RÉFLÉCHIS

40. Tous les verbes‿actifs et presque tous les verbes neutres[2] se conjuguent avec **avoir.** Cependant les douze verbes neutres suivants se conjuguent avec **être**: (nø:tr)

aller	entrer
rester	sortir
venir	arriver
revenir	monter
retourner	descendre
partir	tomber

[1] Note that the French reflexive verb often translates an English verb in the passive.

30. In a very simple way [D'une manière très simple]. The past participle of the first conjugation ends [se termine] in é, as [comme]: aimer, aimé; payer, payé; donner, donné; parler, parlé, etc.

31. What is the ending of the past participle of verbs of the second conjugation?

32. They end in **i** as finir, fini; remplir, rempli; rétablir, rétabli, etc.

33. Ah, that is very simple. And what is the ending of the past participle of the verbs of the third conjugation?

34. They end in **u**, as apercevoir, aperçu; concevoir, conçu; recevoir, reçu, etc.

35. What is the ending of the past participle of the verbs of the fourth conjugation?

36. They end in **u**, as vendre, vendu; rendre, rendu; descendre, descendu, etc.

37. But these rules refer solely [s'appliquent seulement] to the regular verbs, do they not [n'est-ce pas]?

38. Certainly. We have a large number of irregular verbs. You will find a complete list of them [en] in Part X.

39. And are all verbs conjugated [se conjuguent-ils[1]] with **avoir?**

NEUTER, PASSIVE AND REFLEXIVE VERBS

40. All active verbs and almost [presque] all neuter verbs are conjugated with **avoir.** The following [suivants] twelve neuter verbs, however, are conjugated [se conjuguent] with **être.**

to go	to enter
to stay	to go out
to come	to arrive
to come back	to get in
to return	to get out
to leave	to fall

---

[2] Neuter or intransitive verbs admit no direct object, as *aller*, to go; *arriver*, to arrive, etc.

41. Nous conjuguons‿aussi avec⁀**être** les verbes **devenir, parvenir,** etc., qui sont dérivés du verbe **venir.** Ainsi que **naître**[1] et **mourir.**[2] Nous disons: "Où êtes-vous né?—Je suis né à Paris. Il⁀est mort. Elle est morte." (də vni:r, par və ni:r—de ri ve—nɛ:tr, mu ri:r—mɔ·r—mɔrt)

42. Je crois que je comprends cette règle; nous‿avons‿eu dans nos leçons précédentes un certain nombre d'exemples. Mais·dites-moi, quels sont les verbes conjugués avec⁀**être?** (nu za vɔ̃ zy—lə sɔ̃ pre se dɑ̃·t—œ̃ sɛr tɛ̃ nɔ̃·br dɛg zɑ̃·pl)

43. Le verbe auxiliaire **être** est‿employé avec tous les verbes passifs[3] et aussi avec tous les verbes réfléchis.[4] (re fle ʃi)

44. Étudiez les verbes réguliers avec⁀attention; pratiquez-les tant que vous pourrez, afin d'en réciter n'importe quel temps ou n'importe quel mode. (nɛ̃·pɔrt)

45. N'apprenez[5] pas la table par cœur, mais pratiquez‿un certain nombre de verbes réguliers, jusqu'à ce que vous puissiez les dire ainsi: "Il parle. Il aurait parlé. Qu'auriez-vous payé? Il faut que nous vendions[6] cette maison, etc." (ʒys ka skə vu pɥi sje)

---

[1] *Naître,* to be born; *naissant, né,* born.

Pres: Je nais, tu nais, il naît, nous naissons, vous naissez, ils naissent.
Imp: Je naissais, tu naissais, il naissait, etc.
Fut: Je naîtrai, tu naîtras, il naîtra, etc.
Cond: Je naîtrais, tu naîtrais, il naîtrait, etc.
Pres. Subj: Que je naisse, que tu naisses, qu'il naisse, que nous naissions, que vous naissiez, qu'ils naissent.

[2] *Mourir,* to die; *mourant,* dying; *mort,* dead.

Pres: Je meurs, tu meurs, il meurt, nous mourons, vous mourez, ils meurent.
Imp: Je mourais, tu mourais, il mourait, etc.
Fut: Je mourrai, tu mourras, il mourra, nous mourrons, vous mourrez, ils mourront.
Cond: Je mourrais, tu mourrais, il mourrait, etc.
Pres. Subj: Que je meure, que tu meures, qu'il meure, que nous mourions, que vous mouriez, qu'ils meurent.

41. We also conjugate with **être** the verbs **devenir,** to become, **parvenir,** to come to, etc., which are derived from [dérivés de] **venir,** to come. Also [Ainsi que] **naître,** to be born, and **mourir,** to die. We say: *Où êtes-vous né?* Where were you born?—*Je suis né à Paris.* I was born in Paris.—*Il est mort.* He died *or* He is dead.—*Elle est morte.* She died *or* She is dead.

42. I think (that) I understand this rule; we have had in our previous lessons quite a number [un certain nombre] of examples. But tell me which verbs are conjugated with **être.**

43. The auxiliary verb **être** is used [employé] with all passive verbs and also with all reflexive verbs.

44. Study the regular verbs thoroughly [avec attention]; practise them as much as you can [tant que vous pourrez], in order to recite [afin d'en réciter] any (no matter what, *n'importe quel*) tense or any (no matter what, *n'importe quel*) mood.

45. Do not learn the table by heart, but practise a certain number of regular verbs until [jusqu'à ce que] you can [vous puissiez] say them like this [ainsi]: "He is speaking. He would have spoken. What would you have paid? We must sell this house, etc."

---

[3] Passive verbs are formed in French—as in English—by joining the past participle of an active verb to the auxiliary verb *to be,* être; as: donner, to give; être donné, to be given; finir, to finish; être fini, to be finished.

The past participle in French must agree in gender and number with the noun or pronoun it relates to and which stands as the subject of the sentence.

[4] All reflexive verbs are conjugated with être.

[5] *Apprendre,* to learn; *comprendre,* to understand, etc., are conjugated like the irregular verb *prendre.*

Prendre, to take; *prenant,* taking; *pris,* taken.

Pres: Je prends, tu prends, il prend, nous prenons, vous prenez, ils prennent.
Imp: Je prenais, tu prenais, il prenait, nous prenions, etc.
Fut: Je prendrai, tu prendras, il prendra, nous prendrons, etc.
Cond: Je prendrais, tu prendrais, il prendrait, nous prendrions, etc.
Pres. Subj: Que je prenne, que tu prennes, qu'il prenne, que nous prenions, que vous preniez, qu'ils prennent.

[6] As explained before, the subjunctive must be used after *il faut.*

46. Mais‿il faut que je parte,[1] monsieur. Je vois que la leçon est finie; onze heures viennent de sonner.[2]

47. Oui, il est onze heures cinq.—Eh bien, pour la prochaine leçon, écrivez quelques‿exercices, des phrases courtes, mais usuelles, en‿observant les règles que je vous‿ai données; étudiez‿aussi les verbes réguliers. (kurt—y zɥɛl)

48. Je ferai mon possible, monsieur. Je désire tant posséder votre belle langue!

49. Au revoir, monsieur.

50. Au revoir.

Avoir

(*Suite*)

1. Voudriez-vous me donner une règle de l'emploi du verbe **avoir** au lieu du verbe **"to be"** en‿anglais. (lã•plwa—o ljø)

2. Avec plaisir. **Avoir**⁀est‿employé dans le sens de **"to be"** en‿ anglais, quand‿il⁀exprime un désir⁀ou un sentiment. (lə sã•s—kã til⁀ɛk sprim⁀œ̃ de•zi:r—œ̃ sã ti mã)

3. Je regrette de vous dire que je ne comprends pas très bien ce que vous voulez dire. Voudriez-vous donc me citer des‿exemples. (rə grɛt—si te de zɛg zã:pl)

4. Vous‿avez raison. Nous‿apprenons par la pratique et les‿ exemples. (rɛ•zɔ̃—pra tik)

---

[1] *Partir*, to leave, to start; *partant*, leaving; *parti*, left.

Pres: Je pars, tu pars, il part, nous partons, vous partez, ils partent.
Imp: Je partais, tu partais, il partait, etc.
Fut: Je partirai, tu partiras, il partira, etc.
Cond: Je partirais, tu partirais, il partirait, etc.
Pres. Subj: Que je parte, que tu partes, qu'il parte, que nous partions, que vous partiez, qu'ils partent.

46. But I must go, sir. I see our lesson is over; it has just struck eleven. (Literally: But it is necessary that I leave [que je parte], sir. I see that the lesson is finished; eleven o'clock [onze heures] has just struck [viennent de sonner].)

47. Yes, it is five minutes past eleven.—Well, write some [quelques] exercises for the next [prochaine] lesson, short, practical [usuelles] phrases, applying [en observant] the rules I have given you; also study the regular verbs.

48. I shall do my best, sir. I am anxious to master your beautiful language. (Literally: I shall do my possible, sir. I desire so much [tant] to master [posséder] your beautiful language.)

49. Good-bye, sir.

50. Good-bye.

Avoir

(Continuation)

1. Will you please give me a rule about [de] the use of the verb **avoir** in place [au lieu] of the verb **"to be"** in English.

2. With pleasure. **Avoir** is used in the sense of **"to be"** in English, when it expresses [il exprime] desire or sensation [un sentiment].

3. I am sorry to say that I can't quite understand what you mean by this. Kindly give me some illustrations. (Literally: I am sorry [Je regrette] to tell **you** that I do not understand very well what you wish to say [ce que vous voulez dire]. Will you please give me [me citer] some examples.)

4. You are quite right [Vous avez raison]. We learn by practice and (through) examples.

[2] The time of the day and how to say it in French will be taught in a later lesson.

5. C'est mon‿avis. Le tort de presque tous les‿auteurs c'est d'être plus théoriques que pratiques. (mɔ na vi—tɔ:r—le zo tœ:r)

6. En deux mots: le verbe **avoir** est‿employé à la place de notre verbe anglais **"to be,"** quand‿il est joint avec les mots suivants: faim,[1] soif, froid, chaud, sommeil, honte, raison, tort, envie et peur. (ʒwɛ̃—sɥi vɑ̃—fɛ̃, swaf, frwɑ, ʃo, sɔ mɛ:j, ɔ̃:t, rɛ·zɔ̃, tɔr, ɑ̃·vi, pœ:r)

7. Ah, je comprends fort bien, quoique je craigne[2] qu'il ne[3] me soit difficile de me rappeler un si grand nombre de mots‿isolés. (kwak ʒə krɛ·ɲ—mo zi zɔ le)

8. Les mots‿isolés, mon‿ami, sont toujours très difficiles à retenir. Les mots qui ne sont pas joints à d'autres ne font pas‿une langue. Une personne peut‿apprendre par cœur tout le dictionnaire et être parfaitement incapable de tenir‿une conversation. La nature nous‿enseigne par des phrases et ce sont les phrases que nous devons‿apprendre. (rə tni:r—par kœ:r—dik sjɔ nɛ:r—ɛ̃ ka pabl—kɔ̃ vɛr sa sjɔ̃. la na ty:r nu zɑ̃ sɛ·ɲ)

---

[1] There are a number of idiomatic expressions in connection with *avoir* with which the student ought to familiarize himself:

J'ai froid.	I am cold. (I have cold.)
J'ai froid aux mains.	My hands are cold. (I have cold in the hands.)
J'ai chaud.	I am warm. (I have warmth.)
Avez-vous faim?	Are you hungry? (Have you hunger?)
J'ai bien soif.	I am very thirsty. (I have great thirst.)
A-t-il sommeil?	Is he sleepy? (Has he sleep)?
Avez-vous peur?	Are you afraid? (Have you fear?)
N'avez-vous pas honte?	Aren't you ashamed? (Have you no shame?)
J'avais raison.	I was right. (I had right.)
J'avais tort.	I was wrong. (I had wrong.)
Quel‿âge avez-vous?	How old are you? (What age have you?)
J'ai vingt‿ans.	I am 20 years old. (I have 20 years.)
J'ai besoin de.	I need. (I have need of.)
J'ai envie de.	I desire to, I feel inclined to. (I have inclination of.)
Qu'avez-vous?	What is the matter with you? (What have you?)

5. That is my opinion [mon‿avis]. The error [le tort] of almost [presque] all the authors [les‿auteurs] is [c'est] to be more theoretical [théoriques] than practical [pratiques].

6. In plain words [En deux mots]: **"avoir"** is used in place of our English verb "to be", when it is connected [joint] with the following words [les mots suivants]: hunger [faim], thirst [soif], cold [froid], warm [chaud], sleep [sommeil], shame [honte], right [raison], wrong [tort], inclination [envie] and fear [peur].

7. Ah, this I understand, though I am afraid [quoique je craigne[2]] it will be quite difficult for me [qu'il ne[3] me soit difficile] to remember such a [un si grand] number of isolated words.

8. Isolated words, my friend, are always hard to remember. Disconnected words are not language. A person might learn the whole dictionary by heart and yet would not be able to carry on a conversation. Nature teaches by sentences, and sentences you will have to learn. (Literally: Isolated words, my friend, are always very difficult to [à] retain [retenir]. Words which are not joined [joints] to others [à d'autres], do not make a language. A person may [peut] learn by heart [par cœur] all the dictionary [le dictionnaire] and be perfectly incapable [incapable] to sustain [tenir] a conversation. Nature [la nature] teaches us [enseigne] by phrases [des phrases] and it's [ce sont] phrases which we ought to learn.)

Qu'a-t-elle?	What is the matter with her? (What has she?)
Elle n'a rien.	Nothing is the matter with her. (She has nothing.)
Vous n'avez pas bonne mine.	You do not look well. (You have not good appearance.)
Il a mauvaise mine.	He looks badly. (He has a bad appearance.)

Observe also the following expressions:

J'ai mal‿à la tête.	I have a headache	(pain in the head).
J'ai mal‿aux dents.	I have a toothache	(" " " teeth).
J'ai mal‿à la gorge.	My throat pains me	(" " " throat).
J'ai mal‿au ventre.	I have a belly-ache	(" " " abdomen).
J'ai mal‿aux‿yeux.	My eyes pain me	(" " " eyes).
J'ai mal‿aux‿oreilles.	My ears pain me	(" " " ears).
J'ai mal‿au cœur.	I feel sick	(" " " heart).

This latter expression is used of nausea only.

[2] The subjunctive follows *quoique*, although, though.

[3] The subjunctive with *ne* follows after craindre, to fear. See Part X.

9. J'en suis persuadé, aussi vous serais-je[1] très‿obligé si vous pouviez me faire quelques phrases avec ces mots. (pɛr sɥa de)

10. Avec plaisir, mais dans le but d'obtenir le plus grand profit de ces‿exemples, que je vais vous donner, vous devrez‿essayer de faire chez vous un certain nombre de phrases semblables et me les‿apporter pour que[2] je les corrige. (by dɔp tə ni:r—prɔ fi—vu də vre zɛ sɛ je—kɔ ri:ʒ)

11. Je le ferai. Je mettrai[3] les verbes de vos phrases à différents temps et différentes personnes. (di fe rɑ̃—di fe rɑ̃:t)

12. Très bien. Maintenant commençons. Qu'avez-vous donc? Vous n'avez pas l'air très bien. (ka ve vu)

13. Formez maintenant une phrase semblable, mais mettez-la au passé. (sɑ̃ blabl)

---

[1] A pronoun used as subject of a sentence generally precedes the verb, except in questions, as: Va-t-il? Does he go?—Donnons-nous? Do we give?

But in affirmative or negative sentences beginning with au moins, du moins, *at least;* à peine, *scarcely;* encore, *still, yet;* en vain, *in vain;* aussi, *also, so, therefore;* combien, *how much;* que de fois, *how many times, etc.*, the inverted form is frequently used, as:

A peine étais-je parti qu'elle vint.	I had scarcely left when she came.
Au moins, me l'a-t-il dit.	At least, he told me so.
Peut-être quitterons-nous Paris.	Perhaps we shall leave Paris.
A plus forte raison, n'irai-je pas.	For a still greater reason, I shall not go.

This rule, however, is not imperative. We could and do say:

Peut-être quitterons-nous Paris *Peut-être que nous quitterons Paris* *Nous quitterons peut-être Paris*	Perhaps we shall leave Paris.

9. I am convinced of that and should feel obliged to you if you would form some sentences with these words for me. (Literally: I am convinced [persuadé] of it [en], therefore [aussi] I would be very obliged to you if you could make for me [me faire] some phrases with these words.)

10. With pleasure, but in order to derive the full benefit of the examples which I am going to give you, you ought to form a number of similar phrases at home and bring them to me for correction. (Literally: With pleasure, but in the aim [le but] to obtain [obtenir] the greatest profit [profit] of these examples which I am going to give you, you will have [vous devrez] to try to make at home [chez vous] a certain number of similar [semblables] phrases and bring them to me so that [pour que] I may correct them [je les corrige].)

11. I'll do so. I shall put [Je mettrai] the verbs of your sentences into [à] different tenses and persons.

12. Very well! Now let us begin. What is the matter with you [Qu'avez-vous donc]? You do not look [Vous n'avez pas l'air] very well.

13. Now form a similar [semblable] sentence, but put it into the [au] past tense.

---

[2] The subjunctive must be employed after *pour que*, in order that.

[3] *Mettre*, to put, to place; *mettant*, putting; *mis*, put.

Pres: Je mets, tu mets, il met, nous mettons, vous mettez, ils mettent.
Imp: Je mettais, tu mettais, il mettait, etc.
Fut: Je mettrai, tu mettras, il mettra, etc.
Cond: Je mettrais, tu mettrais, il mettrait, etc.
Pres. Subj: Que je mette, que tu mettes, qu'il mette, que nous mettions, que vous mettiez, qu'ils mettent.

In the same way we conjugate: *admettre*, to admit; *commettre*, to commit; *omettre*, to omit; *permettre*, to permit, to allow; *promettre*, to promise; *compromettre*, to compromise, to expose; *remettre*, to replace, to hand; *soumettre*, to submit, etc.

Se mettre à means to begin, as:

Il se mit‿à rire.	He commenced to laugh.

14. J'ai rencontré votre cousin et il avait l'air très souffrant. Qu'est-ce[1] qu'il a? (rɑ̃ kɔ̃ tre—ku zɛ̃—su frɑ̃)

15. C'est très bien! Faites maintenant une phrase avec "faim" et "soif," mais ne la faites pas trop courte. (kurt)

16. Lundi[2] dernier j'ai attrapé un gros rhume, et je n'ai pas d'appétit. Ce matin je n'ai pris qu'une tasse[3] de café. Je n'ai rien pu prendre[4] à déjeuner. (lœ·di dɛr nje ʒe a tra pe œ̃ gro ry:m)

17. Eh bien, n'avez-vous pas faim à présent? N'accepteriez-vous pas‿un déjeuner avec moi? (a pre sɑ̃)

18. Non, je vous remercie beaucoup; je n'ai pas faim du tout; il me serait‿impossible de manger une bouchée. Mais vous seriez bien aimable de me donner un verre d'eau. J'ai très soif (bien soif). (il mə srɛ tɛ̃ pɔ si bl də mɑ̃ ʒe yn bu ʃe)

---

[1] Instead of the simple form *que*, what? the form *qu'est-ce que?* or even *qu'est-ce que c'est que?* is frequently used (but only for the objective case).

Qu'est-ce que vous voulez?	What do you want?
Qu'est-ce que vous faites là?	What are you doing there?

What, when subject, may be rendered by *qu'est-ce qui?* (It must always be the *subject* of the sentence, and must not be confounded with *qui est-ce qui?* who?)

Qu'est-ce qui vous‿afflige?	What afflicts you?
Qu'est-ce qui vous manque?	What are you missing? (What is lacking to you?)

[2] The days of the week are:

lundi	Monday
mardi	Tuesday
mercredi	Wednesday
jeudi	Thursday
vendredi	Friday
samedi	Saturday
dimanche	Sunday

Lundi prochain, next Monday.—*Mardi dernier*, last Tuesday.—*Lundi*, on Monday.—*Le lundi, les lundis*, every Monday.

14. I met [J'ai rencontré] your cousin and he seemed very ill [souffrant]. What is the matter with him [Qu'est-ce qu'il a]?

15. That's very good! Now form [faites] a phrase with "hunger" and "thirst," but don't make it too short [courte].

16. Last Monday [Lundi dernier] I caught [j'ai attrapé] a bad cold [un gros rhume] and I have no appetite. This morning I took only a cup of coffee. I could not eat anything [Je n'ai rien pu prendre] at breakfast.

17. Well, don't you feel hungry now [à présent]? Wouldn't you accept a light lunch [déjeuner] with me? (Literally: Well, don't you have hunger at present [à présent]? Would you not accept a light lunch [un léger déjeuner] with me?)

18. No, thank you very much; I am not at all hungry; it would be impossible for me to eat a mouthful [une bouchée]. But you would be very kind [aimable] to give me a glass of water [un verre d'eau]. I am very thirsty [J'ai très soif].

Quel quantième sommes-nous? / *Quel jour du mois sommes-nous?*	What date is to-day?
C'est‿aujourd'hui le sept.	To-day is the seventh.
Quel jour de la semaine sommes-nous?	What day of the week is it?
C'est‿aujourd'hui mardi.	To-day is Tuesday.
C'était hier lundi.	Yesterday was Monday.
Ce sera demain mercredi.	To-morrow will be Wednesday.
C'était hier le six.	Yesterday was the sixth.
Ce sera demain le huit.	To-morrow will be the eighth.

[3] Note again the use of *ne . . . que*, only: *je n'ai pris qu'une tasse*, I took only a cup.

[4] *Prendre*, to take, is used to form many idiomatic expressions. Here are only a few of them:

Ne le prenez pas‿en mauvaise part.	Do not take it amiss. (Don't be offended at it.)
Il prend tout cela au pied de la lettre.	He takes all this for gospel truth (literally).
Elle est‿assez simple pour prendre tous ses compliments au pied de la lettre.	She is foolish enough to take all his compliments literally.
Comment vous‿y prenez-vous?	How do you manage?
Comment vous‿y prenez-vous pour préparer vos leçons sans dictionnaire?	How do you manage to prepare your lessons without a dictionary?
Comment vous‿y êtes-vous pris?	How did you manage it?

19. Faites quelques phrases avec **envie, honte,** et **peur.** Je voudrais voir comment vous vous‿y prendrez. (kɔ mɑ̃ vu vu zy prɑ̃·dre)

20. J'ai envie de faire un voyage en‿Italie dans[1] la Calabre, mais à vous parler franchement j'ai peur des brigands. (ɑ̃ ni ta li—dɑ̃ la ka la·br)

21. N'ayez‿aucune inquiétude à ce sujet. Les brigands jadis⁀ont terrorisé cette province, mais, actuellement, le brigandage en[2] Calabre n'est plus qu'une légende. (nɛ je zo ky·n⁀ɛ̃ kje tyd—le bri gɑ̃ ʒa dis⁀ɔ̃ tɛ rɔ ri ze—prɔ vɛ̃:s—ak tɥɛl mɑ̃—bri gɑ̃ da:ʒ—le ʒɑ̃:d)

22. A présent, vous‿avez des‿exemples de l'emploi idiomatique du verbe **avoir.** J'espère que vous les comprenez très bien.

23. Oh parfaitement. Mais dites-moi s'il y a d'autres‿expressions dans lesquelles on‿emploie[3] **avoir?** (do:trə zɛk sprɛ sjɔ̃)

---

[1] *Dans*, before la Calabre.

[2] *En*, before Calabre, when the definite article is omitted. *En*, with reference to place, is rarely followed by the article, and expresses something indefinite.

19. Form [Faites] some sentences with **inclination, shame** and **fear.** I should like to see how you will go about it [vous vous y prendrez].

20. I have a mind [envie] to take a journey [faire un voyage] through Calabria in Italy, but, to speak frankly [franchement], I am afraid [j'ai peur] of brigands.

21. Don't have any worry [aucune inquiétude] on that account [à ce sujet]. Formerly [Jadis], brigands terrorized this province, but nowadays [actuellement] brigandage in Calabria is nothing more than [n'est plus qu'] a legend.

22. Now, you have some examples of the idiomatic use of the verb **avoir.** I trust (I hope that) you understand them very well.

23. Oh, perfectly. But tell me whether there are [s'il y a] other expressions in which [lesquelles] **avoir** is used [on emploie **avoir**]?

Dans expresses something definite and is always followed by the article, as: *Ils est‿en ville.* He is in town. *Il⁀est dans la ville.* He is in the city.

[3] *Pres:* J'emploie, tu emploies, il⁀emploie, nous‿employons, vous‿employez, ils‿emploient.

LE VOYAGE (lə vwa ja:ʒ)	THE JOURNEY
Faire un voyage	To make (to take) a journey, a trip
Allez-vous faire un voyage?	Are you going to make a journey?
Je suis sur le point de partir pour l'Europe. (pwɛ̃—lœ·rɔp)	I am on the point of leaving for Europe.
Faire un voyage; aller à; partir pour	To take a journey; to go to; to leave for
Où allez-vous?	Where are you going?
Je pars pour la France. (la frɑ̃:s)	I am leaving for France.
Quitter la ville (ki te la vil)	To go out of town
Je pars en voyage demain.	I am going on a trip tomorrow.
Votre mari est-il en ville? (ma ri)	Is your husband in town?
Avez-vous fait un bon voyage?	Did you have a good journey?
Au revoir, j'espère que vous ferez un bon voyage.	Good-bye, I hope you will have a pleasant journey.

Le Chemin de fer (lə ʃmɛ̃ tfɛ:r)	The Railroad
La gare (ga:r)	The terminal; the station
La station (sta sjɔ̃)	The (way) station; the stop
De quelle gare partez-vous?	From which station are you leaving?
Je pars de la gare du Nord.	I leave from the North Station.

Le Billet (lə bi jɛ)	The Ticket
Le guichet	The ticket-window
Pouvez-vous me dire où est le guichet?	Can you tell me where the ticket office is?
Où puis-je prendre mes billets, s'il vous plaît? / Où prend-on ses billets?	Where does one get one's tickets, please?
La seconde porte à droite	Second door to the right
De ce côté	On this side

En face (ɑ̃ fas) Devant vous (dvɑ̃)	Right opposite; straight before you
Donnez-moi un billet pour Londres. (lɔ̃:dr)	Give me a ticket to London.
Un billet de première	A first-class ticket
Un billet de seconde	A second-class ticket
Voulez-vous‿un billet de première ou de seconde classe?	Do you want a first or a second class ticket?
Le billet de retour (rə tu:r)	The return-ticket
Pendant combien de temps les billets de retour sont-ils valables? (pɑ̃·dɑ̃—va labl)	How long are return tickets good?
Les billets d'aller et retour sont valables pendant un mois. (mwɑ)	Round-trip tickets are good for a month.
Pouvez-vous me donner un billet direct pour Paris? (di rɛkt)	Can you give me a through ticket for Paris?
Combien coûte un billet d'ici à Bordeaux? (bɔr do)	How much is a ticket from here to Bordeaux?
Le porteur	The porter
Porteur, veuillez‿enregistrer mes bagages.	Porter, please check my baggage.
Combien de colis avez-vous? (kɔ li)	How many pieces have you?
La malle; la valise (la mal; la va li:z)	The trunk; the valise
Le carton à chapeaux (kar tɔ̃)	The hat-box
Ayez soin de mon carton à chapeaux. (ɛ je swɛ̃)	Be careful with my hat-box.
Le bulletin de bagages (byl tɛ̃)	The baggage check
Veuillez me donner votre billet; je vous‿apporterai le bulletin tout de suite. (tut sɥit)	Please give me your ticket; I'll bring your check at once.
Les bagages en franchise (frɑ̃·ʃi:z)	Free baggage.
A combien de kilos a-t-on droit?	How much baggage is allowed free? (To how many kilos has one right?)

Les chemins de fer français accordent seulement cent cinquante livres. (a kɔrd)	French railroads grant only one hundred and fifty pounds of baggage free.
Le poids (pwɑ)	The weight
L'excédent (lɛk se dɑ̃)	The overweight
Est-ce que j'ai de l'excédent?	Have I any overweight?
Vous‿avez cinq cents francs d'excédent.	You have 500 francs overweight.
On ne peut pas voyager en France avec beaucoup de bagages; c'est trop coûteux. (ku tø)	People cannot travel with much baggage in France. It is too expensive.
Pardon, où est la salle d'attente?	Where is the waiting-room, please?

Faire un Voyage en Chemin de Fer	**To Take a Railroad Trip**
Le voyageur	The traveler; the passenger
En voiture, s'il vous plaît!	All aboard, please!
En voiture! Montez!	All aboard!
Le train express (ɛk sprɛs)	The fast train
Le rapide (ra pid)	The express
Le train spécial (spe sjal)	The special train
Le train omnibus (ɔm ni bys)	The local train
Est-ce le train express pour Paris?	Is this the Paris express?
Le contrôleur (kɔ̃ trɔ lœ:r)	The conductor
Partir	To leave; to start
Le train part dans‿une minute. (mi ṅyt)	The train leaves in a minute.
En voiture; le train va partir.	All aboard! The train is going to start.
Le wagon (va gɔ̃)	The coach
Le compartiment (kɔ̃ par ti mɑ̃)	The compartment
La place; les places	The seat; the seats

PART EIGHT

CONTENTS

Avoir

(*Suite*)

24. Certainement. Nous l'employons par‿exemple en parlant de l'âge des personnes. Ainsi nous disons:
Quel‿âge avez-vous?
Quel‿âge peut‿avoir sa sœur?
Je ne sais pas‿exactement quel‿âge elle a, mais je pense qu'elle a vingt-et-un ou vingt-deux‿ans.
Je ne crois pas qu'elle soit[1] aussi âgée.

25. Cette manière de s'exprimer est la même‿en espagnol. (sɛt ma njɛ:r də sɛk spri me)

26. C'est‿exact. Nous‿employons‿aussi le verbe‿**avoir**‿en parlant en général des dimensions des monuments, des rivières, des routes, etc. Comme par‿exemple:
Cette rivière a quatre-vingts mètres de largeur‿et cinquante mètres de profondeur. (ɛg zɑkt—di mɑ̃ sjɔ̃—mɔ ny mɑ̃, ri vjɛ:r—ru·t—lar ʒœ:r—prɔ fɔ̃·dœ:r)

27. Quelles dimensions a cette chambre?—Je crois qu'elle a vingt-cinq pieds de long sur quinze de large. (pje—lɔ̃—la:rʒ)

28. Cette maison n'a-t-elle pas soixante pieds de hauteur?—Elle a au moins quatre-vingts pieds! (o·tœ:r—o mwɛ̃)

29. Trouverai-je tous ces‿idiotismes dans la grammaire?—Certainement; étudiez-les avec soin et répétez-les avec‿attention jusqu'à ce qu'ils vous soient tout‿a fait familiers. (swɛ̃—a vɛk‿a tɑ̃·sjɔ̃—fa mi lje)

---

[1] The subjunctive must be used here as uncertainty is implied.

Avoir

(*Continuation*)

24. Certainly. We employ it for instance in speaking of the age of persons. Thus [Ainsi] we say: How old are you [Quel‿âge avez-vous]? How old may his sister be [Quel‿âge peut‿avoir sa sœur]? I don't know exactly how old she is, but I think she is [qu'elle a] twenty-one or twenty-two. I don't think she is as old as that [aussi âgée].

25. This mode [manière] of expressing oneself is the same in Spanish.

26. Precisely [C'est‿exact]. We also use the verb **avoir** in speaking generally [en général] of the dimensions of monuments, rivers [des rivières], roads [des routes], etc. As for instance: This river is [a] 80 meters broad [de largeur] and 50 meters deep [de profondeur].

27. What are the dimensions of this room?—I think it is [qu'elle‿a] 25 feet [pieds] long [de long] by [sur] 15 wide [de large].

28. Isn't this house 60 feet high [de hauteur]?—It is [Elle‿a] at least [au moins] 80 (feet).

29. Shall I find all these idioms in the grammar?—Certainly; study them carefully [avec soin] and repeat them attentively [avec attention], until they will be [jusqu'à ce qu'ils vous soient] quite [tout à fait] familiar to you.

PHRASE PRINCIPALE

Car j'attends‿un‿ami de Chicago et dois rester à Boulogne jusqu'à ce que le vapeur‿arrive

kar ʒa tɑ̃ zœ̃ na mid ʃi ka go e dwa rɛs te a bu lɔ·ɲ ʒys ska skəl va pœːr‿a riːv.

Car (kar)
j'attends (ʒa tɑ̃)
un ami (œ̃ na mi)
de Chicago (də ʃi ka go)
et (e)
dois[1] (dwa)
rester (res te)
à Boulogne (a bu lɔ·ɲ)
jusqu'à ce que[2] (ʒys ka skə)
le vapeur (lə va pœːr)
arrive (a riːv)

---

[1] *Devoir* means to owe, ought to, should, to have to, must.

Monsieur Goulet me doit cent francs; il devrait me payer.	Mr. Goulet owes me a hundred francs; he ought to pay me.
Vous devriez‿écrire‿à votre père.	You should (ought to) write to your father.
Je pense que vous devriez lui faire‿une visite.	I think you ought to pay her a visit.
Vous devriez sortir‿avec moi.	You ought to go out with me.
Je ne peux pas; je dois faire‿une visite.	I can't; I have to pay a call.
Vous‿auriez dû venir plus tôt.	You ought to have come sooner.
J'aurais dû le payer hier.	I should have paid him yesterday.

[2] The subjunctive mood must be employed after the following compound conjunctions:

Afin que	in order that	*Pour que*	in order that
à moins que (ne)	unless	*pourvu que*	provided
au cas que	in case that	*non pas que*	not that

MAIN SENTENCE

For I expect a friend from Chicago and must stay in Boulogne until

the steamer arrives

For
I expect
a friend
from Chicago
and
must
stay
in Boulogne
until
the steamer
may arrive.

---

avant que	before	*pour peu que*	however little
bien que	though	*quoique*	though
de crainte que (ne)	for fear that	*sans que*	without
de peur que (ne)	for fear that	*si tant est que*	if it is true that
en cas que	in case that	*soit que*	whether
encore que	although	*supposé que*	suppose that
loin que	far from	*supposons que*	let us suppose that
malgré que	notwithstanding	*jusqu'à ce que*	till, until

Afin que vous sachiez — In order that you may know
En cas que vous restiez‿ici — In case you remain here
A moins que vous ne lui écriviez — Unless you write to him

The negative *ne* is used after the following conjunctions (*without implying negation*): *à moins que; de peur que; de crainte que.*

A moins que vous ne soyez laborieux — Unless you are industrious
De peur (de crainte) qu'il ne se plaigne — For fear he might complain

Le Cinéma — Le Théatre — Le Concert

1. Pourquoi restez-vous à Boulogne? La ville n'est pas très‿intéressante; il y a peu de choses à voir. (trɛ zɛ̃ te rɛ sɑ̃:t)

2. Je ne reste pas‿à Boulogne pour ce qu'il⁀y a à voir, mais parce que j'attends‿une personne qui vient d'Amérique. (pur skil ja a vwa:r)

3. Qui attendez-vous?

4. Une jeune dame qui arrivera très probablement par le prochain bateau. (prɔ ʃɛ̃)

5. Une jeune dame! Je croyais que vous‿étiez marié. (ma rje)

6. En‿effet, je suis marié. La dame en question est‿une de mes parentes. C'est ma cousine. (ɑ̃ kɛs tjɔ̃—pa rɑ̃·t—ku zi:n)

7. Oh, c'est différent. Veuillez me pardonner ma plaisanterie. (plɛ zɑ̃ tri)

8. Boulogne est‿un peu monotone et je ne sais[1] comment tuer le temps. Comme je regrette de ne pas‿avoir⁀emporté mon poste de radio! (mɔ nɔ tɔn—tɥe)

9. Vous vous‿ennuyez? Pourquoi n'allez-vous pas‿au cinéma, au théâtre ou au concert? (vu vu zɑ̃ nɥi je—si ne ma—te ɑ:tr—kɔ̃ sɛ·r)

10. J'aime beaucoup le théâtre et le concert, et je serais très‿heureux d'y aller, mais je crains de ne rien[2] comprendre. (trɛ zø rø—rjɛ̃)

Special Note: The subjunctive is used after impersonal verbs expressing *doubt, wish, fear, necessity, indecision, supposition* or *surprise.*

Il⁀est‿important qu'il⁀écrive.	It is important that he should write.
Il⁀est temps que nous partions.	It is time we should leave.
Il ne me semble pas qu'il⁀ait tort.	It doesn't seem to me that he is wrong.

When, however, a positive fact is expressed, the indicative mood must be employed.

Il me semble qu'il⁀a tort.	It seems to me that he is wrong.

The Movies — The Theater — The Concert

1. Why do you stay in Boulogne? The town is not very interesting [intéressante]; there are but few [peu de] things to [à] see.

2. I don't remain in Boulogne on account of the sights [pour ce qu'il y a à voir], but because I expect a person who comes from America.)

3. Whom do you expect?

4. A young lady [dame] who will very probably arrive by the next boat [le prochain bateau].

5. A young lady! I thought [Je croyais que] you were married [marié].

6. Certainly [En effet], I am married. The lady in question is a relative of mine [une de mes parentes]. She is my cousin [ma cousine].

7. Oh, that's different. Please excuse my joking [ma plaisanterie].

8. Boulogne is rather [un peu] monotonous and I don't know how to kill [tuer] time. How [Comme] I regret not to have [de ne pas‿avoir] brought my radio along!

9. You are bored [Vous vous‿ennuyez]! Why don't you go to the movies, to the theater or to the concert?

10. I am very fond of the theater and concert and I should be very happy [très‿heureux] to go there, but I fear not to understand anything [de ne rien comprendre].

---

[1] With *savoir*, to know, *pouvoir*, to be able, *oser*, to dare, *cesser*, to cease, *pas* may be omitted. The use of *pas* is, however, always correct.

[2] *Ne pas, ne rien* are usually placed before the infinitive:

Je lui ai dit de ne pas courir.	I told him not to run.
Tâchez de ne pas‿être en retard.	Try not to be late.
Il‿est difficile‿à un garçon de ne pas courir.	It is difficult for a boy not to run.

11. Alors, pourquoi n'allez-vous pas‿aux concerts? Il⁀y a[1] ici une salle de concerts. Vous n'aimez peut-être pas la musique? (la my zik)

12. Au contraire, je l'adore⁀et à Chicago j'assistais[2] tous les samedis aux concerts symphoniques. (ʒə la dɔ:r—sɛ̃ fɔ nik)

13. C'est bien, alors venez‿avec moi cet‿après-midi au concert. L'orchestre Poulet est‿ici en ce moment. (lɔr kɛs trə pu lɛ—ɑ̃ smɔ mɑ̃)

14. Quelle chance! Est-ce[3] le célèbre Roi de la Valse? (kɛl ʃɑ̃:s—lə se lɛ:brə rwɑ dla vals)

15. Non, Jean Poulet est mort⁀il y a quelque temps. (ʒɑ̃)

16. Alors, c'est son fils, le compositeur? Je l'ai vu à Boston il⁀y a quelques‿années. (kɔ̃ po zi tœ:r—bɔs tɔ̃—kɛl kə za ne)

17. Non, ce[3] n'est pas lui non plus.[4] Il ne donne jamais de concerts. Il demeure⁀à Lyon et n'est que compositeur.

18. Alors, qui est-ce? C'est peut-être⁀un parent éloigné? (pa rɑ̃ e lwa ɲe)

---

[1] *Il⁀y a* is also used to express *time.* It must be observed that in speaking of actions or conditions begun in the past, but still continuing, the French use the present indicative, while we employ the past perfect tense in English:

Combien de temps y a-t‿il que vous‿êtes à Paris?	How long have you been in Paris?
Il⁀y a quinze jours que j'y suis.	I have been here a fortnight.
Il⁀y a deux mois que j'apprends le français.	I have been studying French for two months.
Il⁀y a dix‿ans que ma mère⁀est morte.	My mother has been dead ten years.

When, however, the action or state no longer continues, the past is used in French:

Il⁀y avait‿un mois que j'étais‿à Paris.	I had been in Paris a month.
Il⁀y avait quatre jours qu'il pleuvait.	It had been raining four days.
Il⁀y avait cinq⁀ans que je ne l'avais vue.	It was five years since I had seen her.

Ago is always translated by *il y a* and the French verb is put in the past tense:

Je suis venu à Paris il⁀y a trente⁀ans.	I came to Paris thirty years ago.

Il⁀y a is also used to denote distance:

Combien y a-t‿il de Paris à Boulogne?	How far is it from Paris to Boulogne?
Il⁀y a trois cents milles.	It is 300 miles.

11. Then why don't you go to concerts? There is a concert hall [une salle de concert] here. Perhaps you are not fond of [vous n'aimez pas] music?

12. On the [Au] contrary, I adore it and in Chicago I used to attend the [j'assistais aux] symphony concerts every [tous les] Saturday.

13. Very well; then come with me this afternoon to the concert. Poulet's Orchestra is here just now [en ce moment].

14. What luck [chance]! Is that [Est-ce] the celebrated Waltz-King?

15. No, John Poulet died [est mort] some time ago.

16. Then, it is his son, the composer [compositeur]? I saw him a few years ago [il‿y a quelques années] in Boston.

17. No, it is not he either [ce[3] n'est pas lui non plus[4]]. He never gives any concerts. He is living [demeure] at Lyons and is only a composer [n'est que compositeur].

18. Well, who is it? Perhaps it is a distant relative [un parent éloigné]?

---

[2] A peculiar French expression; *assister* in this connection, *attend.*

[3] After *c'est*—expressed or understood—we use the personal disjunctive pronouns, as:

C'est moi qui ai.	It is I who have	*or I* have.
C'est toi qui as.	It is thou who hast	" *thou* hast.
C'est lui qui a.	It is he who has	" *he* has.
C'est‿elle qui a.	It is she " "	" *she* "
C'est nous qui avons.	It is we who have	" *we* have.
C'est vous qui avez.	It is you " "	" *you* "
Ce sont‿eux qui ont.	It is they " "	" *they* "
Ce sont‿elles qui ont.	It is they " "	" *they* "

Examples

C'est vous qui avez raison.	It is you who are right.
Ce sont‿eux qui doivent payer.	It is they who ought to pay.

[4] Note the use of *non plus*, either, neither:

Allez-vous‿au concert?	Are you going to the concert?
Non, je n'y vais pas.	No, I am not.
Ni moi non plus.	Neither am I.

19. Au contraire, c'est‿un très proche parent, c'est‿Édouard Poulet, le frère de Jean. (prɔʃ—e dwa:r)

20. Oh, maintenant je me le rappelle. Il y a quelques‿années il⁀est venu en‿Amérique avec son‿orchestre et a fait plusieurs tournées aux‿États-Unis. (ply zjœ:r tur ne)

21. L'avez-vous‿entendu? Comment le trouvez-vous? Il conduit magnifiquement. N'est-ce pas que lui et son‿orchestre interprètent la musique de danse mieux que tous les‿autres musiciens? (il kɔ̃ dɥi ma ɲi fik mɑ̃—ɛ̃ tɛr prɛ·t—my zi sjɛ̃)

22. Je ne sais pas. Quant‿à lui, je le déteste. (kɑ̃ t‿a lɥi, ʒəl de tɛst)

23. Pourquoi? C'est‿un bel⁀homme, très‿attrayant! (œ̃ bɛl⁀ɔm, trɛ z‿a trɛ jɑ̃)

24. C'est vrai, mais c'est justement pour cette raison que je ne l'aime pas. (ʒys tə mɑ̃)

25. C'est‿une contradiction! Comment expliquez-vous cela? (kɔ̃ tra dik sjɔ̃)

26. C'est facile⁀à comprendre, je pense. Il⁀est beau garçon et comme beaucoup de beaux garçons il⁀est vaniteux. (va ni tø)

27. Vous‿avez raison. Les beaux‿hommes sont généralement plus vains et plus poseurs que les jolies femmes. Un poseur me semble toujours⁀insupportable. (vɛ̃—po·zœ:r—ɛ̃ sy pɔr tabl.)

28. Je suis de votre⁀avis; un vaniteux me dégoûte. (de gu·t)

29. Et Poulet vous‿a dégoûté? (de gu te)

30. Oui, il me dégoûte. Il danse⁀en conduisant son‿orchestre⁀et il⁀est maniéré comme⁀une jeune fille dans sa première robe de bal. (ma nje re—ʒœ·n fi:j—rɔb də bal).

19. On the contrary, it is a very near (proche) relative. It is Edward Poulet, the brother of John.

20. Ah, now I remember him [je me le rappelle]. Some years ago he came to America with his orchestra and made several tours [plusieurs tournées] in the [aux] United States.

21. Did you hear him? How do you like him [le trouvez-vous]? He conducts [conduit] splendidly [magnifiquement]. Don't you think that [N'est-ce pas que] he [lui] and his orchestra interpret [interprètent] dance music better than [mieux que] all the other musicians [musiciens]?

22. I don't know (about that). As for him [Quant‿à lui], I detest him.

23. And why? He is a handsome and very attractive man. (Literally: Why? He is a handsome man [bel⁀homme], very attractive [attrayant].

24. That's true, but it is exactly [justement] for that reason that I dislike him.

25. That is a contradiction! How do you explain that?

26. That's easy to understand, I think. He is handsome [beau garçon], and like many handsome fellows he is conceited [vaniteux].

27. You are right. Handsome men are generally more vain and conceited [poseurs] than beautiful women, and a conceited man [un poseur] always seems unbearable [insupportable] to me.

28. I agree with you [Je suis de votre⁀avis]; a vain man disgusts me [me dégoûte].

29. And Poulet has disgusted you?

30. Yes, he is distasteful to me. He dances while leading [en conduisant] his orchestra and is as affected as [maniéré comme] a young girl in her first party dress [robe de bal]

31. Oui, il‿est maniéré et très vain. Mais savez-vous quelle est la différence entre **"vain"** et **"vin"?** (di fe rɑ̃:s—vɛ̃—vɛ̃)

32. Non, je n'en sais rien. Ces deux mots ont le même son. (sɔ̃)

33. Ils ont le même son, oui, mais c'est la seule ressemblance qu'ils‿aient. Leur signification est très différente. (la sœ·l rə sɑ̃ blɑ̃:s)

34. Veuillez me l'expliquer. J'aime toujours à apprendre quelque chose de nouveau.

35. Est-ce simple curiosité ou désir de vous‿instruire? (sɛ̃·plə ky rjo zi te u de zi:r də vu zɛ̃ strɥi:r)

36. Non, je ne suis pas curieux. (ky rjø)

37. Est-ce également l'opinion de votre femme? J'ai toujours remarqué que les hommes étaient au moins aussi curieux que les femmes.

38. Oui, en général, mais‿en ce qui me concerne, vraiment ce n'est pas le cas. (ɑ̃ ʒe ne ral—kɔ̃ sɛ·rn—snɛ pal ka)

39. Il n'y a pas de règle sans‿exception. (sɑ̃ zɛk sɛp sjɔ̃)

40. Est-ce un proverbe français? Je l'aime mieux que le nôtre. (prɔ vɛ·rb—no:tr)

41. Oui, le proverbe anglais semble absurde. Comment une exception peut-elle confirmer la règle? (kɔ̃ fir me)

42. Ne discutons pas si c'est‿absurde ou non. Je n'aime pas les discussions. Je préfère que vous m'expliquiez la différence entre "vain" et "vin." (dis ky sjɔ̃—ʒə pre fɛ:r kə vu mɛk spli kje)

43. Je n'aime pas beaucoup les discussions moi-même. A quoi aboutissent-elles? (a bu tis tɛl)

31. Yes, affected and conceited he is. But do you know what the difference between [entre] **"vain"** [conceited] and **"vin"** [wine] is?

32. No, I don't know at all (I don't know (anything) about it [en]). These two words have the same sound.

33. Yes, they have the same sound, but that is the only resemblance [la seule ressemblance] they have [qu'ils aient]. Their meaning [signification] is very different.

34. Please explain it to me. I always like to learn something new [quelque chose de nouveau].

35. Is this simple curiosity [curiosité] or desire [désir] to learn [de vous‿instruire]?

36. No, I am not curious [curieux].

37. Is this also [également] the opinion of your wife? I have always found [remarqué] that men are at least as curious as women.

38. Yes, in general; but as far as I am concerned (in what concerns me, *en ce qui me concerne*), it is really not the case.

39. There is no rule without exception.

40. Is that a French proverb? I like it better than ours [le nôtre].

41. Yes, the English proverb seems absurd. How can an exception prove [confirmer] the rule?

42. Let us not discuss whether [si] it is absurd or not. I don't like discussions. I prefer that you explain to me the difference between **"vain"** and **"vin."**

43. I am not particularly fond of [Je n'aime pas beaucoup] discussions myself [moi-même]. What do they amount to in the end? (To what do they lead [aboutissent‿elles]?)

44. A rien du tout dans la plupart des cas, surtout quand la discussion porte sur la politique ou la religion. (syr tu—pɔ li tik—rə li ʒjɔ̃)

45. La politique est‿une question d'opinions et la religion parfois une affaire de sentiment. Par conséquent il‿est préférable de ne pas‿aborder ces sujets. (par fwa—yn‿a fɛːr də sɑ̃ ti mɑ̃—par kɔ̃ se kɑ̃—a bɔr de se sy ʒɛ)

46. Le catholicisme est la religion de la majorité des Français. (lə ka tɔ li sism—la ma ʒɔ ri te)

47. En français le mot église s'applique exclusivement aux‿édifices du culte catholique. On dit un temple protestant et une synagogue juive, un prêtre catholique, un pasteur protestant, un rabbin juif. (e gliːz—sa plik—o ze di fis—dy kylt—œ̃ tɑ̃ːplə prɔ tɛs tɑ̃—yn si na gɔg ʒɥiːv—œ̃ prɛːtr—œ̃ pas tœːr—œ̃ ra bɛ̃ ʒɥif)

48. En France, l'église est, comme en‿Amérique, entièrement séparée de l'État. (ɑ̃·tjɛ·r mɑ̃)

44. To nothing at all in most [la plupart] of cases, especially [surtout] when the discussion bears [porte] upon politics [sur la politique] or religion [la religion].

45. Politics is a question of opinion and religion sometimes [parfois] a matter of feeling [une affaire de sentiment]. Consequently [Par conséquent] it is preferable not to touch upon [de ne pas aborder] those subjects.

46. Catholicism is the religion of the majority of Frenchmen. (Literally: of the French.)

47. In French the word church designates (Literally: applies to) exclusively the buildings [édifices] of the Catholic faith [culte]. One says: a Protestant temple, a Jewish [juive] synagogue, a Catholic priest, a Protestant minister, a Jewish rabbi.

48. In France, the Church is, as in America, completely [entièrement] separated from the State.

Personal Conjunctive Pronouns

The personal conjunctive pronouns present great difficulty to the English-speaking student.

	Singular		Plural	
	First Person		First Person	
Sujet	*je*	I	*nous*	we
Complément indirect	*me*	to me	*nous*	to us
Complément direct	*me*	me	*nous*	us
	Second Person		Second Person	
Sujet	*tu*	thou	*vous*	you
Complément indirect	*te*	to thee	*vous*	to you
Complément direct	*te*	thee	*vous*	you
	Third Person (Masc.)		Third Person (Masc.)	
Sujet	*il*	he, it	*ils*	they
Complément indirect	*lui*	to him, to it	*leur*	to them
Complément direct	*le*	him, it	*les*	them
	Third Person (Fem.)		Third Person (Fem.)	
Sujet	*elle*	she, it	*elles*	they
Complément indirect	*lui*	to her, to it	*leur*	to them
Complément direct	*la*	her, it	*les*	them

Rules in regard to the Position of the Personal Conjunctive Pronouns

1. In affirmative and negative sentences the nominative cases **je, tu, il, elle, nous, vous, ils, elles** precede the verb, as in English: **Je parle,** I speak; **nous‿envoyons,** we send; **elle n'apportera pas,** she will not bring, etc.
2. In interrogative sentences they are placed immediately after the verb (**do you, does he, did she, did we?** etc., is not expressed), as:

Parle-t-il?	Does he speak?
Comprenez-vous?	Do you understand?
Qu'a-t-il dit?	What did he say?
Avez-vous reçu?	Did you receive? etc.

3. The pronoun-objects, *i.e.*, the indirect and direct objects **me, te, lui, le, la, nous, vous, leur, les** are placed **immediately before** the verb in a simple tense, and before the auxiliary in a **compound** one, as:

Je vous vois.	I see you.
Il me parle.	He speaks to me.
Nous vous‿envoyons.	We send you.
Vous lui apportez.	You bring him (to him).
Je vous‿ai compris.	I have understood you.

Il m'a vu.	He has seen me.
Je lui ai écrit.	I wrote her (to her).
Je leur͡ai dit.	I told them (to them).

4. In negative sentences **ne** is placed directly after the subject (and before the pronoun-object), as:

Il ne me voit pas.	He does not see me.
Je ne lui parle pas.	I do not speak to him.
Vous ne me comprenez pas.	You don't understand me.
Je ne vous‿ai pas compris.	I did not understand you.
Il ne lui a pas‿écrit.	He did not write to her.
Il ne leur͡a rien‿envoyé.	He has not sent anything to them.

5. When a verb governs **two** pronouns they are both placed immediately before the verb (so that the indirect comes first and the direct follows).

   However, this rule applies only to **me le** (or **la, les**), **te le** (or **la, les**), **nous le** (or **la, les**), **vous le** (or **la, les**).

   When the indirect pronoun is either **lui** or **leur,** the direct pronoun object precedes the indirect, as in: **Je le lui ai dit.** I said it to him (or to her). **Il les leur͡a donnés.** He gave them to them. Simple as these rules are, their practical application gives great trouble to the student, especially in compound tenses.

A Useful Table Showing the Position of the Pronoun-Objects in Simple Tenses

Affirmative	Negative	Question	Negative Question
je ‿—	je ne ‿—pas	‿—je?	ne‿—je pas?
tu ‿—	tu ne ‿—pas	‿—tu?	ne‿—tu pas?
il ‿—	il ne ‿—pas	‿—il?	ne‿—t-il pas?
nous‿—	nous ne‿—pas	‿—nous?	ne‿—nous pas?
vous‿—	vous ne‿—pas	‿—vous?	ne‿—vous pas?
ils ‿—	ils ne ‿—pas	‿—ils?	ne‿—ils pas?

Key to the Table

This sign ‿ indicates the place where the pronouns should be put.

Whether there are one or two pronouns, their place is always where this sign ‿ is.

The verb goes where this sign — stands, whether it is the Present, Imperfect, Historical Tense, Future or Conditional.

Examples

Affirmative

Je vous vois.	I see you.
Je le voyais.	I used to see him.
Je la verrai.	I shall see her.
Je les verrais.	I would see them.
Il me comprend.	He understands me.
Il vous le donnerait.	He would give it to you.
Nous le ferions.	We would do it.
Nous le leur‿enverrons.	We shall send it to them.
Vous me le donnerez.	You will give it to me.
Vous le lui direz.	You will tell it to him (*or* her).
Ils le font.	They do it.
Ils vous l'enverront.	They will send it to you.
Il le lui enverront.	They will send it to him (*or* her).

Negative

Je ne vous vois pas.	I do not see you.
Je ne le voyais pas.	I did not use to see him.
Je ne la verrai pas.	I shall not see her.
Je ne les verrais pas.	I would not see them.
Il ne me comprend pas.	He does not understand me.
Il ne vous le donnerait pas.	He would not give it to you.
Nous ne le ferions pas.	We would not do it.
Nous ne le leur‿enverrons pas.	We shall not send it to them.
Vous ne me le donnerez pas.	You will not give it to me.
Vous ne le lui direz pas.	You will not tell it to him (*or* her).
Ils ne le font pas.	They don't do it.
Ils ne vous l'enverront pas.	They will not send it to you.
Ils ne le lui enverront pas.	They will not send it to him (*or* her).

Questions

Vous vois-je? *Est-ce que je vous vois?*	Do I see you?
Le voyais-je? *Est-ce que je le voyais?*	Did I use to see him?
La verrai-je? *Est-ce que je la verrai?*	Shall I see her?
Les verrais-je? *Est-ce que je les verrais?*	Would I see them?
Me comprend-il?	Does he understand me?
Vous le donnerait-il?	Would he give it you?
Le ferions-nous?	Would we do it?
Le leur enverrons-nous?	Shall we send it to them?
Me le donnerez-vous?	Will you give it to me?
Le lui direz-vous?	Will you tell it to him (*or* her).
Le font-ils?	Do they do it?
Vous l'enverront-ils?	Will they send it to you?
Le lui enverront-ils?	Will they send it to him (*or* her)?

Negative Questions

Ne vous vois-je pas? *Est-ce que je ne vous vois pas?*	Don't I see you?
Ne le voyais-je pas? *Est-ce que je ne le voyais pas?*	Didn't I use to see him?
Ne la verrai-je pas? *Est-ce que je ne la verrai pas?*	Shall I not see her?
Ne les verrais-je pas? *Est-ce que je ne les verrais pas?*	Would I not see them?
Ne me comprend-il pas?	Does he not understand me?
Ne vous le donnerait-il pas?	Wouldn't he give it to you?
Ne le ferions-nous pas?	Would we not do it?
Ne le leur enverrons-nous pas?	Shall we not send it to them?
Ne me le donnerez-vous pas?	Will you not give it to me?
Ne le lui direz-vous pas?	Shall you not tell it to him?
Ne le font-ils pas?	Don't they do it?
Ne vous l'enverront-ils pas?	Will they not send it to you?
Ne le lui enverront-ils pas?	Will they not send it to him (*or* her)?

Position of the Pronoun-Objects in Compound Tenses

Affirmative	Negative
je ‿ai ——	je ne ‿ai pas ——
tu ‿as ——	tu ne ‿as pas ——
il ‿a ——	il ne ‿a pas ——
nous‿avons ——	nous ne‿avons pas——
vous‿avez ——	vous ne‿avez pas ——
ils ‿ont ——	ils ne ‿ont pas ——
Question	**Negative Question**
‿ai-je ——?	ne‿ai-je pas ——?
‿as-tu ——?	ne‿as-tu pas ——?
‿a-t-il ——?	ne‿a-t-il pas ——?
‿avons-nous——?	ne‿avons-nous pas——?
‿avez-vous ——?	ne‿avez-vous pas ——?
‿ont-ils ——?	ne‿ont-ils pas ——?

Key to the Table

This sign ‿ indicates the place where the pronouns should be put.

Whether there are two pronouns or one, their place is always where this sign ‿ is.

The past participle goes where this sign — stands, whether the verb stands in the Past Perfect, Pluperfect, the Future (past) or Conditional (past).

Examples

Affirmative

Je vous‿ai compris.	I have understood you.
Je l'ai vu.	I saw him.
Je l'aurais fait.	I would have done it.
Il vous l'a envoyé.	He sent it to you.
Il m'aurait vu.	He would have seen me.
Il me l'aurait dit.	He would have told me.
Nous le lui avons‿écrit.	We wrote it to him (*or* her).

Nous vous l'aurions donné.	We would have given it to you.
Vous l'avez‿acheté.	You bought it.
Vous le leur‿auriez‿apporté.	You would have brought it to them.
Ils l'ont refusé.	They refused it.
Ils nous l'auraient‿envoyé.	They would have sent it to us.

Negative

Je ne vous‿ai pas compris.	I did not understand you.
Je ne l'ai pas vu.	I did not see him.
Je ne l'aurais pas fait.	I would not have done it.
Il ne vous l'a pas‿envoyé.	He did not send it to you.
Il ne m'aurait pas vu.	He would not have seen me.
Nous ne le lui avons pas‿écrit.	We did not write it to him (*or* her).
Nous ne vous l'aurions pas donné.	We wouldn't have given it to you.
Vous ne l'avez pas‿acheté.	You did not buy it.
Vous ne le leur‿auriez pas‿apporté.	You would not have brought it to them.
Ils ne l'ont pas refusé.	They did not refuse it.
Ils ne nous l'auraient pas‿envoyé.	They would not have sent it to us.

Questions

Vous‿ai-je compris? *Est-ce que je vous‿ai compris?*	Did I understand you?
L'ai-je vu? *Est-ce que je l'ai vu?*	Did I see him?
L'aurais-je fait? *Est-ce que je l'aurais fait?*	Would I have done it?
Vous l'a-t-‿il envoyé?	Did he send it to you?
M'aurait-‿il vu?	Would he have seen me?
Me l'aurait-‿il dit?	Would he have told it to me?
Le lui avons-nous‿écrit?	Did we write it to him (*or* her)?
Vous l'aurions-nous donné?	Would we have given it to you?
L'avez-vous‿acheté?	Did you buy it?
Le leur‿auriez-vous‿apporté?	Would you have brought it to them?
L'ont-‿ils refusé?	Did they refuse it?
Nous l'auraient-‿ils envoyé?	Would they have sent it to us?

Negative Questions

Ne vous‿ai-je pas compris? *Est-ce que je ne vous‿ai pas compris?*	Did I not understand you?
Ne l'ai-je pas vu? *Est-ce que je ne l'ai pas vu?*	Did I not see him?
Ne l'aurais-je pas fait? *Est-ce que je ne l'aurais pas fait?*	Would I not have done it?
Ne vous l'a-t-il pas‿envoyé?	Didn't he send it to you?
Ne m'aurait-il pas vu?	Wouldn't he have seen me?
Ne me l'aurait-il pas dit?	Wouldn't he have told it to me?
Ne le lui avons-nous pas‿écrit?	Didn't we write him (*or* her) so?
Ne vous l'aurions-nous pas donné?	Wouldn't we have given it to you?
Ne l'avez-vous pas‿acheté?	Did you not buy it?
Ne le leur auriez-vous pas‿apporté?	Wouldn't you have brought it to them?
Ne l'ont-ils pas refusé?	Haven't they refused it?
Ne nous l'auraient-ils pas‿envoyé?	Wouldn't they have sent it to us?

Recapitulation of the Above Rules

1. The place of the pronoun-objects is before the verb.

2. When there are two pronoun-objects, **le, la,** or **les** take the second place, except when the other pronoun is **lui** or **leur.**

There is only

One Exception

to these rules:

When the verb stands in the affirmative Imperative, the pronoun-objects are placed just as in English:

Donnez-le moi.	Give it to me.[1]
Envoyez-le leur.	Send it to them.
Parlez-moi.	Speak to me.
Dites-le lui.	Tell it to him (*or* her).

[1] *Me* and *to me—me,* before the verb in all tenses and moods, except in the *affirmative Imperative,* when it is rendered by *moi.* The same is true of *te* and *toi, thee, to thee.*

The following simple table illustrates all possible positions of

Two Pronoun-Objects before the verb

Me *Te* *Nous* *Vous*	*Le* *La* *Les*	*Lui* *Leur*

Key to the Table

Cover the right-hand box (containing **lui** and **leur**) and you will see that **le, la** and **les** always follow after **me, te, nous** and **vous.**

Then cover the left-hand box (containing **me, te, nous** and **vous**), and it will be clear that **le, la,** and **les** always precede **lui** and **leur.**

Translation Exercise on the Pronouns

What did you write him?—I wrote him to send us these goods at once.—Has he sent them?—We received a letter yesterday that he had sent them, but we have not as yet received them.—What would you have done in my place? Would you have spoken to him about this matter or not?—If I had been in your place I would not have spoken to him about it. I would have handed him the money and that is all.—Did you buy these gloves in this store?—No, I bought them in London.—Have you worn them long?—I have worn them for two months.—If you see him, give him this package and tell him to come to see me.—Did you study the rules which I gave you?—I studied them and think I know them.—Did you write any exercises about the pronouns?—Yes, sir, but I left them at home. I forgot to bring them.—Bring them to me this afternoon and I will correct them.—I will do so without fail.—I should be very much obliged to you if you were to ask him to send me the patterns (les‿échantillons) which I selected a fortnight ago.—I beg your pardon, sir; I did not understand you.—I told you to ask him to send me the patterns which I selected.—When did you choose them?—I selected them a fortnight ago.—If Mr. Bronsard should come, tell him that I could not wait for him any longer.—Did you see him to-day?—No, I saw him yesterday when he was going to the post-office.—Did you speak to him?—No, sir, I did not. Hasn't the laundress (la blanchisseuse, blɑ̃ ʃi sø:z) brought my linen (mon linge, lɛ̃·ʒ) yet?—Yes, she brought it this morning and I put it on your bed.—Where did you put it?—

I put it on your bed, sir.—Did you brush (brossé) my clothes?—Yes, sir, I did. I put them on the chair in your room.—Did you tell him to go to the bank?—Yes, I told him so.—Did you check the baggage and did you give her the check?—I gave it to her last evening, but she has mislaid (égaré) it and cannot find it.—Did anyone call during my absence?—Two of your countrymen came to pay you a call.—Didn't they leave (laissé) their cards with you?—They told me their names, but upon my word (ma foi!), I have forgotten them. —Do not speak to him about this affair.—Don't tell them anything about my business.—Tell it to him.—Do not tell it to them.

En and Y

1. **En** and **y** are treated like pronoun-objects and stand always before the verb, except, of course, in the affirmative Imperative.

2. When **en or y** meets with another personal pronoun it is always placed **last,** as: **Je m'en souviens,** I remember.—**Je l'y ai mené,** I led him there.—**Je vous‿en‿ai parlé,** I spoke to you about it.

3. After the affirmative Imperative **en** and **y** come **after** the verb: **Donnez-m'en,** Give me some.—**Allez-y,** Go there. But with the negative Imperative they precede the verb: **Ne m'en donnez pas,** Don't give me any.—**N'y allez pas,** Don't go there.

Exercise On En and Y

Show me some good steel pens (de bonnes plumes métalliques).—Here are some excellent ones.—Waiter, I have no napkin.—Here is one, sir.—If you need good sugar, we can furnish (fournir) you some at a very low price (à bien bon marché).—No, thanks, I don't need any at present.—I do not like this room. Haven't you another one which you can give me?—We have none on this floor, sir.—Waiter, bring me a decanter of ice-water (une caraffe frappée), if you please.—We haven't any, sir, but I'll bring you some ice (de la glace) in a cup, if you like.—This roast-beef is excellent. May I not help you to some more (encore)?—This meat is very tender (tendre). May I offer you (puis-je vous‿en‿offrir) another piece (encore‿un morceau)?—Give me a very small piece only; I haven't any appetite.—You are giving me too much (trop); give me only half of it (la moitié).—Do you want a fork?—Thanks, I have one.—One second-class ticket for Boulogne, if you please!—There are none (sold); this is an express train. Only first-class tickets sold.—Please go into the waiting-room. I shall be there in two minutes.—Conductor, two seats for Lyons, please.—There are no more in these carriages; further down, perhaps (il‿y en‿a probablement à l'arrière).—Is it far from here to the Champs‿Élysées (ʃã ze lize)?—This street doesn't lead there at all.—Don't you need any gloves?—Yes, I need two pairs.—This pair is too narrow for me.—Pass the gloves to me, if you please; I'll put a little powder in them.

VOCABULAIRE (*Suite*)	**VOCABULARY** (*Continuation*)
Pour prendre une place	To take a seat
Puis-je monter ici?	Can I get in here?
Toutes les places sont prises. (pri:z)	All seats are taken.
Cette place est retenue. (rə tny)	This seat is engaged (reserved).
Cette place est-elle libre? (li·br)	Is this seat unoccupied (vacant)?
Cette place est-elle prise?—Non, elle est libre.	Is this seat taken?—No, it is vacant.
Retenez-moi une place.	Retain a seat for me.
J'ai retenu cette place.	I reserved this seat.
Excusez-moi, c'est ma place.	Pardon me, this is my seat.
Voulez-vous que nous changions de place?	Shall we change seats?
Ne pourriez-vous pas reculer un peu? Nous sommes trop serrés. (rə ky le—sɛ re)	Can you move a little further? We are sitting very close.
Je suis tout disposé à changer de place. (dis po·ze)	I am quite willing to change seats.
Êtes-vous bien assis?	Are you comfortably seated?
Y a-t-il un coin de libre?	Is there a corner seat vacant?
Pouvez-vous me donner une banquette à moi seul, conducteur? (bɑ̃ kɛt—kɔ̃ dyk tœ:r)	Can you give me a whole side (**une banquette**) to myself, conductor?
Je voudrais pouvoir dormir à mon aise.	I should like to sleep comfortably (at my ease).
Complet! (kɔ̃ plɛ)	Quite full!
Le compartiment est au complet.	All the seats in this compartment are taken.
Pardon, il y a place pour une huitième personne.	Pardon me, but there is room (place) for an eighth person.
Cela ne m'amuserait pas de rester en route.	It would inconvenience me to stay behind (It would not amuse me to be left behind.)

VOCABULAIRE	VOCABULARY
Conducteur, ces messieurs ne veulent pas me laisser monter. Il y a cependant deux places, qui ne sont pas‿occupées. (me sjø—ɔ ky pe)	Conductor, these gentlemen will not allow me to get in and there are still two vacant seats.
Y a-t-il des compartiments de fumeurs? (fy mœ:r)	Is there a smoking-car?
Fumer (fy me)	To smoke
La fumée (fy me)	The smoke
Fumez-vous?	Do you smoke?
Me permettriez-vous d'allumer un cigare?	Would you allow me to light a cigar?
Mais certainement! Faites, monsieur, faites!	Why certainly!
Le tabac vous gêne-t‿il?	Does tobacco smoke bother you?
Je ne peux pas supporter la fumée.	I cannot endure tobacco smoke.
Est‿il permis de fumer?	Is smoking permitted?
Défense de fumer.	Smoking is prohibited here.
Vous m'obligeriez infiniment, monsieur, si vous vouliez bien ne pas fumer. Je ne puis pas supporter la fumée.	You would greatly oblige me, sir, if you would not smoke. I cannot endure the smell of tobacco smoke.
Vous‿offrirai-je un cigare?	May I offer you a cigar?

La Fenêtre (la fnɛ:tr)	**The Window**
Ouvrez la fenêtre.	Open the window.
Fermez la fenêtre.	Shut the window.
Le courant d'air. (ku rɑ̃)	The draught.
Il‿y a un courant d'air.	There is a draught here.
Sentez-vous le courant d'air quand j'ouvre la fenêtre?	Do you feel the draught when I open the window?

VOCABULAIRE	VOCABULARY
Il fait‿un courant d'air très vif; laissez-la entr'ouverte. (ɑ̃·tru vɛrt)	There is a great draught here; leave it open just a little (half way).
Le vent vient de tous les côtés. (vɑ̃)	The wind blows from all sides.
Il fait du soleil; je vais baisser les stores.	The sun is shining; I will lower the blinds.
La poussière. (pu sjɛːr)	The dust.
Il fait de la poussière.	It is dusty.
Il fait tant de poussière; veuillez fermer la fenêtre.	There is so much dust here; please shut the window.

La Gare	**The Station**
Quel⁀est le nom de cette gare? / Quelle⁀est cette gare?	What is the name of this station? / What is this station?
Avez-vous saisi le nom que le conducteur⁀a crié?	Did you catch the name the conductor called out?
Conducteur,⁀où sommes-nous?	Conductor, where are we?
Sommes-nous loin de la prochaine gare?	Are we far from the next station?
A quelle gare peut‿on bien déjeuner?	At what station is there a chance of getting a good lunch?
Un wagon-lit	A sleeping-car

Arrêter	**To Stop**
Combien de temps le train s'arrête-t‿il⁀ici? (sa rɛ·tə til)	How long does the train stop here?
Conducteur, quand s'arrête-t‿on pour dîner?	Conductor, when do we stop for dinner?
Combien de temps s'arrête-t‿on ici?	How long do we stop here?
Combien de temps s'arrête-t‿on à la prochaine gare?	How long do we stop at the next station?
Où est-ce qu'on s'arrête⁀un peu plus longtemps?	Where do we stop a little longer?
Pourquoi y a-t‿il⁀un‿arrêt?	Why do they stop here?

VOCABULAIRE	VOCABULARY
Combien de temps s'arrête-t-on à Orléans?	How long do we stop at Orléans?
Rouen! Cinq minutes d'arrêt! (rwũ)	Rouen! We stop five minutes!

Changer De Voiture / **To Change Cars**

Changer De Voiture	To Change Cars
Faut-il changer? Dois-je changer de voiture? (vwa ty:r)	Have I to change cars?
Montrez-moi votre billet, s'il vous plaît.	Please show me your ticket.
Non, vous n'avez pas à changer de train; ce train va directement à Bordeaux.	No, you don't change; this train goes through to Bordeaux.
Vous changez à Blois. (blwa)	You change cars at Blois.
A-t-on la correspondance à Blois? (kɔ rɛs pɔ̃ dɑ̃:s)	Do we make connection at Blois?
Où allez-vous?—A Paris.	Where are you going?—To Paris.
Vous aurez quatre heures à attendre à Blois.	You will have to wait four hours at Blois.
Il n'y a pas de correspondance.	You don't make connection there.
Vous auriez dû changer à Orléans; c'est là que se font les correspondances.	You ought to have changed at Orléans; you make connection there.
Le train a manqué sa correspondance. (mɑ̃ ke)	The train has missed making connection.

La Frontière	The Frontier
Avons-nous déjà passé la frontière? (frɔ̃·tjɛ:r)	Have we already passed the frontier?
La douane; les droits. (dwan)	Customs, duties.
Où est la douane?	Where is the custom-house?
La visite de la douane, où a-t-elle lieu? (ljø)	Where does the customs' examination take place?
La visite est-elle minutieuse? (mi ny sjø:z)	Is the examination strict?

PROVERBES	PROVERBS
Assez a qui se contente.	Enough is as good as a feast.
Assez sait qui sait vivre et se taire.	He is wise enough who can live and keep his own counsel.
Au pays des‿aveugles les borgnes sont rois.	In the land of the blind the one-eyed are kings.
Bouche serrée, mouche n'y entre.	Keep your mouth shut and you will swallow no flies.
Ce qu'on apprend au berceau dure jusqu'au tombeau.	What is learned in the cradle remains with us until the grave.
De la main à la bouche se perd souvent la soupe.	There's many a slip twixt the cup and the lip.
Du dire au fait il y a grand trait.	Between word and deed is a long way to go.
Homme chiche jamais riche.	A stingy man is never rich.
Il faut casser la noix pour manger le noyau.	To eat the kernel you must break the shell.
Jamais bon chien n'aboie à faux.	A good dog never barks without cause.
La philosophie, qui nous promet de nous rendre heureux, nous trompe.	The philosophy, which promises to make us happy, deceives us.
L'avare et le cochon ne sont bons qu'après leur mort.	The miser and the pig are useless until after they are dead.
Les maux viennent‿à livres, et s'en vont‿à onces.	Troubles come in pounds and depart in ounces.

PART NINE

CONTENTS

PHRASE PRINCIPALE

Vous n'auriez pas dû sortir sans caoutchoucs par ce vilain temps. Par suite de votre étourderie vous‿avez pris froid, et vous serez obligé de garder la chambre quelque temps, avant de pouvoir continuer votre voyage.

(vɔtr‿e tur də ri—vu za ve pri frwɑ—gar de—kɔ̃ ti nɥe)

Vous n'auriez pas dû sortir sans caoutchoucs par ce vilain temps.

Vous n'auriez pas dû (vu nɔ rje pa dy)
sortir (sɔr tir)
sans (sɑ̃)
caoutchoucs (ka ut ʃu)
par (par)
ce vilain temps (sə vi lɛ̃ tɑ̃)

LE TEMPS

1. Pourquoi êtes-vous sorti[1] sans caoutchoucs par ce vilain temps? Vous n'auriez pas dû faire cela.

2. Je ne l'aurais pas fait, si[2] je n'avais cru que le temps s'éclaircirait. (se klɛr si rɛ)

3. Comment pouviez-vous supposer cela? Le temps a été affreux ces jours-ci. (sy po·ze—a frø)

---

[1] *Sortir*, to go out; *sortant*, going out; *sorti*, gone out.

Pres: *Je sors, tu sors, il sort, nous sortons, vous sortez, ils sortent.*
Imp: *Je sortais, tu sortais, il sortait, nous sortions*, etc.
Fut: *Je sortirai, tu sortiras, il sortira*, etc.
Cond: *Je sortirais, tu sortirais, il sortirait*, etc.
Pres. Subj: *Que je sorte, que tu sortes, qu'il sorte, que nous sortions, que vous sortiez, qu'ils sortent.*

The following verbs in *ir* are conjugated like *sortir:*

Consentir	to consent	*Repartir*	to set out again
Départir	to distribute	*Ressentir*	to resent
Desservir	to clear the table	*Ressortir*	to go out again
Dormir	to sleep	*Sentir*	to feel, to smell
Mentir	to lie	*S'endormir*	to fall asleep
Partir	to depart	*Sortir*	to go out

MAIN SENTENCE

You ought not to have gone out without your rubbers in this bad weather. In consequence of your carelessness you have caught a cold and will be obliged to stay at home some time before you will be able to continue your journey.

You ought not to have gone out without your rubbers in this bad weather.

You ought not to have
gone out
without
rubbers
by (in)
this bad weather.

THE WEATHER

1. Why did you go out [êtes-vous sorti] without (your) rubbers in [par] this bad [vilain] weather? You ought not to have [Vous n'auriez pas dû] done that [faire cela].
2. I would not have done it if I had not thought [je n'avais pas cru que] the weather would clear [s'éclaircirait].
3. How could you [pouviez-vous] suppose such a thing [cela]? The weather has been awful [affreux] these past days [ces jours-ci].

---

[2] After *si*, if, the French use either the present or imperfect tense, according to the sense of the phrase (and *not* the future or conditional, as we do in English):

Si je puis faire cela, je le ferai.	If I can do that, I will.
S'il pouvait‿écrire, ce serait mieux.	If he could write, it would be better.
Je vous serais bien‿obligé si vous lui disiez de m'envoyer ces livres.	I should be greatly obliged to you if you would tell him to send me these books.

Still, when *si* stands for *whether*, the future and conditional may be used in French:

Je ne sais pas si elle viendra.	I don't know whether she will come.
Je ne savais pas si vous‿iriez‿au théâtre.	I did not know whether you would go to the theater.

4. Oui, cette année le printemps a été assez mauvais; malgré tout, j'ai cru que le temps s'éclaircirait. (mal gre)

5. C'est‿une erreur, mon cher monsieur. Vous ne savez pas‿encore combien notre climat est variable. (nɔ trə kli ma ɛ va rjabl)

6. J'ai toujours entendu dire que le climat en France était‿excellent et, d'après le bulletin météorologique, j'ai cru que sûrement le temps s'éclaircirait. (lə byl tɛ̃ me te ɔ·rɔ lɔ ʒik)

7. Le bulletin météorologique? Êtes-vous donc[1] de ceux qui croient aux prédictions des météorologistes? (pre dik sjɔ̃)

8. En général je ne suis pas crédule, et je regrette cette fois de m'être laissé tromper par ces prédictions. (kre dyl—trɔ pe)

9. Oui, vous n'auriez pas dû y croire. Vous‿avez‿été trompé.

10. Il est très probable que nous resterons à la maison tout l'après-midi. Voici justement la pluie. (prɔ ba bl—la prɛ mi di—ʒys tə mɑ̃)

11. Oui, il pleut[2] à verse. Il‿est‿inutile de sortir par ce temps affreux. C'est bien‿ennuyeux, n'est-ce pas? (il pløta vɛ·rs. il‿ɛ ti ny til—sɛ bjɛ̃ nɑ̃ nɥi jø)

12. Certainement! Que diriez-vous d'une petite promenade en‿auto?[3] (dyn pətit prɔm nad‿ɑ̃ nɔ to.)

---

[1] *donc*, then, really, etc., is often merely an emphatic adverb.

[2] *Pleuvoir*, to rain, is an impersonal verb, used only in the third person singular:

Pleuvoir, to rain; *pleuvant*, raining; *plu*, rained.

Pres:	*il pleut*	it rains
Imp:	*il pleuvait*	it rained
Past Ind:	*il a plu*	it rained
Fut:	*il pleuvra*	it will rain
Cond:	*il pleuvrait*	it would rain
Pres. Subj:	*qu'il pleuve*	it may rain
Imp. Subj:	*qu'il plût*	it might rain

4. Yes, this year spring has been pretty bad [assez mauvais]; nevertheless (in spite of everything, *malgré tout*) I thought it would clear.

5. It was a mistake [une erreur], my dear sir. You don't know yet how [combien] changeable [variable] our climate is.

6. I've always heard (it said, *dire*) that the climate in France was very fine [excellent] and, according to [d'après] the weather report [bulletin météorologique], I believed that it was surely going to clear [s'éclaircirait].

7. The weather report [Le bulletin météorologique]? Are you (one) of those who believe in the [croient aux] predictions of meteorologists?

8. Generally [En général] I am not credulous [crédule], and I regret this time to have allowed myself to be deceived [de m'être laissé tromper] by these forecasts [prédictions].

9. Yes, you ought not to have [vous n'auriez pas dû] believed them [y croire]. You have been misled [trompé].

10. It is very probable that we shall stay in [à] the house all the afternoon. It is just beginning to rain. (Here is rain now, *Voici justement la pluie*).

11. Yes, it is pouring [Il pleut à verse]. It is useless to [inutile de] go out in [par] this fearful [affreux] weather. Very tiresome [bien ennuyeux], isn't it?

12. It certainly is [Certainement]! What would you say to a [d'une] short drive [petite promenade en auto]?

---

[3] We have no (single) expression for *driving* or a *drive* in French, but say:

Faire un voyage en chemin de fer	To take a railway trip
faire un tour en auto	To take a drive; to go out driving
" " " *en traîneau*	To take a sleigh-ride; to go out sleighing
" " " *à pied*	To take a walk
" " " *à cheval*	To take a ride (on horseback)

13. Croyez-moi. Restez à la maison. Voyez comme il fait des‿éclairs. (krwa je mwa—de ze klɛ:r)

14. Oui, il commence[1] à tonner. Mon Dieu,[2] quel coup de tonnerre! La foudre doit‿être tombée près d'ici! (il kɔ mɑ̃:s͡a tɔ ne. mɔ̃ djø, kɛl kud tɔ nɛ:r.)

15. Qu'est-ce qu'il͡y a? Un taxi devant[3] notre porte par͡un temps pareil? Qui cela peut-il bien[4]‿être? (kɛs kil͡ja?—par͡œ̃ tɑ̃ pa rɛ·j)

16. Si je ne me trompe, c'est votre compatriote, Monsieur X.

17. Qu'est-ce qui peut donc l'amener par ce temps affreux?—Ah! le voici!

18. Mon cher Louis, qu'est-ce qui vous‿amène par ce vilain temps? Vous‿êtes trempé jusqu'aux‿os. (vu zɛt trɑ̃ pe ʒys ko zo)

19. Je n'ai fait que traverser[5] la rue pour prendre un taxi et dans ces quelques‿instants, j'ai été trempé jusqu'aux‿os. (dɑ̃ se kɛl kə zɛ̃ stɑ̃)

20. Vous devriez changer de[6] vêtements tout de suite, autrement vous‿attraperez un rhume. (ʃɑ̃·ʒe·d vɛ·t mɑ̃—o·trə mɑ̃)

21. Venez vite dans ma chambre retirer vos vêtements mouillés. (mu je)

22. Je venais vous‿apporter une invitation. Notre ami, Monsieur Marchand, vous envoie ses‿amitiés et . . . (yn͡ɛ̃ vi ta sjɔ̃)

---

[1] *Commencer*, to begin, is generally followed by *à*, as:

On‿a commencé à jouer. — They have begun to play.

[2] Literally, "My God"; an exclamation commonly used by French people, but meaning no more to them than our "Good gracious!" "Goodness!"

[3] We have two French prepositions meaning before, viz.: *devant*, used in regard to place, and *avant*, used as to time.

13. Take my advice [Croyez-moi]. Stay at home. Just see [Voyez] how it lightens [il fait des‿éclairs]!

14. Yes, it begins to thunder [à tonner]. Goodness [Mon Dieu], what a clap [coup] of thunder [tonnerre]! The lightning [La foudre] must have struck (must have fallen, *doit‿être tombée*) near by [près d'ici]!

15. But what is that? (What's the matter? *Qu'est-ce qu'il⁀y a*?) A taxicab at [devant] our door [porte] in such weather [par⁀un temps pareil]? Who can that be?

16. If I am not mistaken [si je ne me trompe], it is your compatriot, Mr. X.

17. What can bring him here [l'amener] in this fearful weather?—Ah, here he is [le voici]!

18. My dear Louis, what brings you here in this foul [vilain] weather? You are wet to the skin! (You are soaked [trempé] to the bones [jusqu'aux‿os].)

19. I only went across [Je n'ai fait que traverser[5]] the street to take a taxi and in those few moments I got wet through and through (I have been soaked to the bones).

20. You ought to [devriez] change your clothes at once or (otherwise, *autrement*) you'll catch a cold [un rhume].

21. Come at once [vite] into my room and take off [retirer] your wet [mouillés] clothes.

22. I came to bring you an invitation. Our friend, Mr. Marchand, sends you his regards [ses‿amitiés] and . . .

---

[4] *bien* merely adds emphasis.

[5] When "only" bears upon the verb itself, *ne . . . que* may be used but *faire* must be introduced in the sentence, as in: *Il ne fait que rire,* He only laughs; He does nothing but laugh.

[6] *De* is used idiomatically with *changer*.

23. Pardonnez-moi de vous‿interrompre,[1] mais votre santé est plus‿importante qu'une invitation. Venez d'abord changer de vêtements et vous me direz‿ensuite ce qui vous‿amène. (ply zɛ̃ pɔr tɑ̃:t)

24. Comme vous voudrez. Je ne me refroidis pas aussi facilement que vous croyez. (ʒɔn mə rə frwɑ di pɑ)

25. Voici tout ce qu'il vous faut. Heureusement que nous sommes de la même taille; ces vêtements vous‿iront à merveille.

26. Ôtez donc vos vêtements mouillés tout de suite et mettez les miens. Aussitôt que vous serez‿habillé, je sonnerai le garçon. Il mettra vos habits à sécher. (le mjɛ̃)

PHRASE PRINCIPALE

(*Suite*)

Par suite de votre étourderie vous‿avez pris froid.

Par suite de (par sɥit də)
votre étourderie (vɔtr e tur də ri)
vous‿avez pris (vu za ve pri)
froid (frwɑ)

LA SANTÉ ET LES MALADIES

1. Quel est le sujet de la leçon d'aujourd'hui?

2. Dans la leçon d'aujourd'hui nous parlerons des maladies et de la santé—question fort importante.

---

[1] *Interrompre,* to interrupt, is conjugated like:

Rompre, to break; *rompant,* breaking; *rompu,* broken.

Pres: Je romps, tu romps, il rompt, nous rompons, vous rompez, ils rompent.
Imp: Je rompais, tu rompais, il rompait, nous rompions, etc.

23. Pardon me for [de] interrupting you, but your health [santé] is more important than an invitation. First [D'abord] come and change your [venez changer de] clothes and then [ensuite] you will tell me what [ce qui] brings you (here).

24. (Just) as you like [Comme vous voudrez]. I do not take cold [je ne me refroidis pas] as easily as you think.

25. Here is everything you need (all that which is necessary to you, *tout ce qu'il vous faut*). Fortunately [Heureusement] (that) we are of the same height [taille]. These clothes will fit you [vous iront] splendidly [à merveille].

26. Take off [Ôtez] your wet clothes at once and put on mine [mettez les miens]. As soon as you are dressed [vous serez‿habillé], I'll ring for the boy. He will put your clothes (away) to dry [à sécher].

MAIN SENTENCE

(*Continuation*)

In consequence of your thoughtlessness you have taken cold

In consequence of
your thoughtlessness
you have taken
cold

HEALTH AND ILLNESS

1. What is the subject of to-day's lesson?

2. In to-day's lesson we will talk about [des] diseases and about [de la] health,—quite an important question.

Fut: *Je romprai, tu rompras, il rompra, nous romprons,* etc.
Cond: *Je romprais, tu romprais, il romprait, nous romprions,* etc.
Pres. Subj: *Que je rompe, que tu rompes, qu'il rompe, que nous rompions, que vous rompiez, qu'ils rompent.*

3. Très probablement la conversation nous‿amènera à employer de nouvelles‿expressions. (prɔ ba blə mɑ̃ la kɔ̃ vɛr sa sjɔ̃—nu vɛl zɛk sprɛ sjɔ̃)

4. Sans doute. Voyons, commençons tout de suite. Comment vous portez-vous aujourd'hui? Il me semble que vous‿avez l'air fatigué et souffrant. (fa ti ge e su frɑ̃)

5. Je ne me sens pas très bien. Je crois qu'hier soir j'ai pris froid en sortant du théâtre. (ʒən mə sɑ̃ pɑ)

6. J'en[1] suis bien fâché. N'aviez-vous pas vos caoutchoucs?

7. Malheureusement non. Le temps était si beau, quand je suis parti pour le théâtre, que je n'[2]ai pensé à prendre ni[2] mon parapluie ni[2] mes caoutchoucs.

8. Vous‿avez‿un mauvais rhume. Vous semblez‿avoir⁀un très mauvais rhume.

9. J'espère que ce n'est qu'un rhume. Soyez prudent, portez des vêtements chauds, car dans notre climat variable, un rhume peut‿avoir des conséquences très sérieuses. (swa je pry dɑ̃—dɑ̃ nɔ trə kli ma va rjabl—de kɔ̃ se kɑ̃·s trɛ se rjø:z)

10. C'est vrai, à l'avenir je serai plus prudent. Ma gorge me fait mal.

11. Si j'étais‿à votre place, je consulterais sans retard⁀un bon médecin. Vous‿êtes très‿enroué. (trɛ zɑ̃ rwe)

12. Un‿enrouement n'est rien, je m'en débarrasse très‿aisément, mais le mal de gorge m'inquiète. (œ̃ nɑ̃ ru mɑ̃—mɛ̃·kjɛ·t)

---

[1] *en*, about this, completes the thought.

[2] Note the use of *ne* . . . *ni* . . . *ni*, neither . . . nor, not . . . or.

3. Very probably the conversation will lead us to the use of [à employer] new expressions [de nouvelles‿expressions].

4. Without doubt. Now [Voyons], let us begin at once. How are you [Comment vous portez-vous] to-day? It seems to me you are looking [vous‿avez l'air] tired and ill [souffrant].

5. I don't feel [Je ne me sens pas] very well. I think (that) I took cold last night on leaving the [en sortant du] theater.

6. I am very sorry [bien fâché]. Did you not have [N'aviez-vous pas] your rubbers?

7. Unfortunately no. The weather was so fine when I started [je suis parti] for the theater that I did not think to [je n'ai pas pensé à] take (either) [ni] my umbrella or [ni] my rubbers.

8. You have a bad cold. You seem to have a very bad cold.

9. I hope (that) it is nothing but [ce n'est qu'] a cold. Be careful [Soyez prudent], wear warm clothes, for [car] a cold in our changeable [variable] climate may have very serious consequences [des conséquences très sérieuses].

10. That's true. In [A] the future I shall be more prudent. My throat [Ma gorge] hurts me [me fait mal].

11. If I were in [à] your place I would consult [consulterais] a good physician without delay [retard]. You are quite hoarse [enroué].

12. Being hoarse does not trouble me much (Hoarseness is nothing, *Un‿enrouement n'est rien*), (for) I get rid of it very easily [je m'en débarrasse très‿aisément]; but the pain in my throat [le mal de gorge] makes me uneasy (worries me, *m'inquiète*).

1. Êtes-vous venu à pied?

2. Non, en taxi.—Pas dans‿une voiture découverte, je suppose?—Oh non, elle était bien fermée. (ʒə sy po:z)

3. C'était prudent. Évitez les courants d'air‿et le froid. Je vous ferai une ordonnance. Vous prendrez régulièrement ce médicament toutes les deux‿heures.

4. Ne vous‿arrêtez pas‿en route, mais rentrez chez vous.

5. Dois-je me mettre au lit?

6. Je vous‿ai déjà dit de vous mettre au lit sans plus tarder. Il faudra garder la chambre pendant plusieurs jours, car les bronchites avec notre climat ne sont pas‿une petite affaire. (pɑ̃ dɑ̃ ply zjœ:r ʒu:r—le brɔ̃·ʃit)

7. Suis-je sérieusement pris?

8. Non, pas tant que cela. Mais je dois vous‿avertir qu'il faudra garder le lit une semaine au moins. (yn smɛ:n‿o mwɛ̃)

9. Alors quand pourrai-je continuer mon voyage?

10. Cela dépend des circonstances. Tout d'abord il faut vous débarrasser de la fièvre. De toute façon attendez-vous à rester au moins quinze jours‿ici. (sla de pɑ̃ de sir kɔ̃ stɑ̃:s—da bɔ·r—la fjɛ:vr)

11. Quand viendrez-vous me voir? (kɑ̃ vjɛ̃·dre vu)

12. Il est maintenant midi moins le quart. Je reçois jusqu'à deux‿heures; j'ai à voir trois malades qui ne vont pas bien.

13. Vous‿êtes très‿occupé?—Oui, malheureusement; en ce moment il y a beaucoup de personnes malades en ville (mɔ mɑ̃—ɑ̃ vil)

14. Quand puis-je espérer vous voir?

15. Je viendrai entre quatre et cinq heures sans faute. En‿attendant prenez la potion que je vous‿ai ordonnée, une cuiller‿à bouche toutes les deux‿heures. (la po·sjɔ̃—yn kɥi jɛ:r‿a buʃ)

1. Did you come on foot [à pied]?

2. No, in a cab.—Not in an open cab [voiture découverte], I suppose?—Oh, no, it was closed tightly [bien fermée].

3. That was prudent. Avoid [Évitez] any draught [les courants d'air] or cold. I shall write [ferai] a prescription [une ordonnance] for you. You will take this medicine [médicament] regularly every two hours [toutes les deux‿heures].

4. Don't stop on your way [en route], but go back home [rentrez chez vous].

5. Have I got to [Dois-je] go to bed [me mettre au lit]?

6. I told you already [déjà] to go to bed without delay. You will have to (It will be necessary to, *Il faudra*) keep your room for some days [pendant plusieurs jours], for bronchitis [les bronchites] in our climate is not a petty affair.

7. Am I seriously ill (affected, taken, *pris*)?

8. Not as bad as that [pas tant que cela]. But I must warn you [vous avertir] that you will have to (it will be necessary to, *il faudra*) stay in bed for a week at least [au moins].

9. And when shall I be able [pourrai-je] to continue my journey?

10. That depends on [des] circumstances. In the first place [Tout d'abord], we must get rid of (it is necessary to get rid of, *il faut vous débarrasser de*) your fever. At any rate [De toute façon], be prepared (expect, *attendez-vous à*) to remain at least a fortnight [quinze jours] here.

11. When will you come to see me?

12. It is now a quarter to twelve [midi moins le quart]. My office hours last (I receive, *Je reçois*) till two. I have three patients [malades] to see who are not doing well [qui ne vont pas bien].

13. You are very busy [occupé]?—Unfortunately so. At present [En ce moment] there are many sick people in town [en ville].

14. When may I hope to see you?

15. I will call on you [Je viendrai] between four and five without fail [faute]. In the meanwhile [En‿attendant], take the medicine [la potion] (which) I have prescribed [ordonnée] for you; a tablespoonful [une cuiller‿à bouche] every two hours.

16. Ayez bien soin d'avoir toujours la même température dans votre chambre. Faites allumer du feu. (tɑ̃ pe ra ty:r—dy fø)

17. Tenez-vous au chaud et évitez le froid. Je serai chez vous entre quatre et cinq. Au revoir, j'espère que vous‿irez bientôt mieux.

Un Voyage en Afrique du Nord

1. Je vous remercie beaucoup de votre aimable invitation. Cette comédie m'a beaucoup‿amusé.
2. Tant mieux! J'en suis très‿heureux.
3. A mon tour j'aimerais vous‿inviter à assister avec moi aux finales de tennis du championnat de France. Elles vont‿avoir lieu la semaine prochaine. (o fi nal də tɛ nis dy ʃɑ̃ pjɔ na də frɑ̃:s)
4. C'est très gentil de votre part. Malheureusement je ne serai pas‿ici la semaine prochaine .(ʒɑ̃ · ti)
5. C'est vraiment dommage! Vous retournez déjà aux‿États-Unis? (o ze ta zy ni)
6. Non, pas‿encore. Je vais faire un petit voyage en‿Afrique du Nord.
7. Une excursion en‿Afrique du Nord! Vous partez seul?
8. Non, j'accompagnerai un de mes‿amis. Il va visiter plusieurs succursales de sa compagnie au Maroc, en‿Algérie et en Tunisie. (ply zjœ:r sy kyr sal də sa kɔ̃ pa ɲi o ma rɔk, ɑ̃ nal ʒe ri e ɑ̃ ty ni zi)
9. Prendrez-vous le bateau pour la traversée de la Méditerranée? (me di tɛ ra ne)
10. Non, notre voyage se fera par‿avion. Nous volerons directement de Paris au Maroc. Mon‿ami doit passer quelques jours à Casablanca et à Marrakech. (ka za blɑ̃ ka—ma ra kɛʃ)
11. J'ai eu l'occasion de visiter ces villes il‿y a quelques‿années. Elles sont très pittoresques. Les quartiers modernes font‿un contraste saisissant avec les‿anciens quartiers indigènes. (sɛ zi sɑ̃ —le zɑ̃ sjɛ̃ kar tje ɛ̃ di ʒɛ:n)

16. Be very careful to [Ayez bien soin d'] have always the same temperature in your room. Have a fire lighted (Make—someone—light a fire, *Faites‿allumer du feu*).

17. Keep yourself warm [au chaud] and avoid cold. I'll be with you [chez vous] between four and five. Good-bye; I hope (that) you'll soon be [vous‿irez bientôt] better.

A Trip to North Africa

1. Thank you very much for [de] your kind [aimable] invitation. That comedy amused me a great deal.

2. So much the better [Tant mieux]! I am very glad [heureux] of it.

3. In [A] my turn, I would like to invite you to attend [à assister] with me the [aux] tennis finals of the French championship. They will take place [Elles vont‿avoir lieu] next week.

4. That's very kind of you [gentil de votre part]. Unfortunately, I shall not be here next week.

5. That really is a pity [C'est vraiment dommage]! Are you returning so soon [déjà] to the United States?

6. No, not yet. I am going to take a short trip [faire‿un petit voyage] to [en] North Africa.

7. An excursion in North Africa! Are you going [Vous partez] alone?

8. No, I shall accompany one of my friends. He is going to visit several branches [plusieurs succursales] of his company in [au] Morocco, [en] Algeria and [en] Tunisia.

9. Will you take the boat for the Mediterranean crossing [traversée]?

10. No, our trip will be made [se fera] by plane [avion]. We shall fly directly from Paris to Morocco. My friend has to [doit] spend [passer] a few days in Casablanca and in Marrakech.

11. I had [J'ai eu] occasion to visit those cities a few years ago [il‿y a quelques‿années]. They [Elles] are very picturesque. The modern districts [quartiers] form a striking contrast to [font‿un contraste saisissant avec] the ancient native [indigènes] districts.

12. C'est ce que me disait mon‿ami. Il admire beaucoup le port de Casablanca. Je crois que la France a développé le Maroc d'une manière splendide. Maintenant le commerce et l'agriculture y sont très prospères. (lə kɔ mɛ·rs‿e la gri kyl ty:r—prɔs pɛ:r)

13. Vous‿avez tout‿à fait raison. Marrakech vous‿intéressera particulièrement, surtout la Place du Marché où se trouvent les fameux "souks"; sans guide on peut s'y perdre facilement (sɑ̃ gid)

14. Il parait que les "souks" sont très curieux à voir et qu'ils sont restés tels qu'ils‿étaient il‿y a plusieurs siècles. (sjɛ·kl)

15. C'est juste. Ils n'ont pas changé. On‿y vend des fruits, des légumes, de la viande, et toutes sortes d'articles de cuir‿artistiquement décorés à la main.

16. Je compte acheter plusieurs beaux portefeuilles et porte-monnaie en cuir marocain. Je les‿offrirai à mes‿amis à Noël. (pɔr tə fœ:j‿e pɔr tə mɔ nɛ ɑ̃ kɥi:r ma rɔ kɛ̃)

17. N'ayez pas peur de marchander. C'est la coutume là-bas. (la ku ty:m)

18. Merci pour le conseil. Je le suivrai. (lə kɔ̃·sɛ:j)

19. Resterez-vous longtemps à Alger?

20. Environ une semaine, d'après ce que m'a dit mon‿ami.

21. Alger vous‿enchantera. Là encore vous trouverez ce curieux et pittoresque mélange de l'ancien et du moderne qu'on voit dans toutes les villes de l'Afrique du Nord française. (al ʒe vu zɑ̃·ʃɑ̃·tra)

22. Je me réjouis de visiter ce grand port cosmopolite, surtout les quartiers‿arabes. Je me promets‿aussi d'aller à la plage tous les jours, et de nager quand‿il fera assez chaud. (ʒə m re ʒwi)

23. Vous‿irez ensuite à Tunis sans doute?

24. Oui. Nous pensons‿y rester deux jours avant de reprendre l'avion pour Marseille.

12. That's what [ce que] my friend was telling me. He very much admires the Port of Casablanca. I think that France has developed Morocco in a [d'une] splendid manner. Now commerce and agriculture are very prosperous there.

13. You are quite right [Vous‿avez tout‿à fait raison]. Marrakech will interest you particularly, especially [surtout] the marketplace where the famous "souks" are to be found [se trouvent]. Without a guide one may easily get lost there [s'y perdre].

14. It seems [Il paraît] that the "souks" are very curious-looking [curieux à voir] and that they have [sont] remained as [tels qu'] they were several centuries ago [il‿y a plusieurs siècles].

15. That is right [juste]. They have not changed. They sell there [On‿y vend] fruits, vegetables, meat and all kinds [toutes sortes] of leather articles, artistically decorated by [à la] hand.

16. I intend [Je compte] to buy several beautiful bill-folds [porte-feuilles] and purses [porte-monnaie] in Moroccan leather. I shall give [offrirai] them to my friends at Christmas.

17. Don't be afraid to [N'ayez pas peur de] bargain. It's the custom there [là-bas].

18. Thanks for the advice [conseil]. I shall follow it.

19. Will you stay a long time in Algiers?

20. About [Environ] a week, according to [d'après] what [ce que] my friend told me.

21. Algiers will delight you [vous‿enchantera]. There again you will find that curious and picturesque mixture [mélange] of the ancient and the modern which one sees in all the towns of French North Africa.

22. I rejoice at the thought [Je me réjouis] of visiting this great cosmopolitan port, especially the Arab districts [quartiers]. I intend (I promise myself, *je me promets*) also to go to the beach [la plage] every day [tous les jours] and to swim when it is warm enough [il fera assez chaud].

23. No doubt you will then [ensuite] go to Tunis?

24. Yes. We expect to stay there [Nous pensons y rester] two days before taking the plane again [avant de reprendre l'avion] for Marseilles.

25. Quels magnifiques pays vous‿allez voir! Vous‿avez de la chance! A propos, connaissez-vous Marseille?

26. Oui, j'y suis‿allé déjà une fois, en revenant d'une petite excursion en Corse que je n'oublierai pas de sitôt.

27. Que vous‿est-il donc[1] arrivé là-bas?

28. Tout d'abord, j'ai perdu une de mes valises en cours de route. Naturellement c'était celle qui contenait mes vêtements légers d'été. Ensuite, en retournant à Marseille j'ai eu le mal de mer pendant toute la traversée. (sɛl ki kɔ̃•t nɛ)

29. En‿effet le mal de mer est‿une chose qu'on ne peut pas‿oublier facilement! C'est peut-être pour cette raison que vous voyagez‿ en‿avion?

30. C'est juste. J'avoue que j'ai peur maintenant de prendre le bateau, même pour une petite traversée.

31. Allons, allons! Il vaut mieux ne plus[2] y penser. Que pensez-vous de Marseille?

32. C'est‿une ville très‿intéressante, surtout son vieux port. Malheureusement il a plu presque continuellement pendant mon séjour, et je n'ai pas pu me promener jusqu'au fameux sanctuaire de Notre-Dame de la Garde. (kɔ̃ ti nɥɛl mɑ̃—ʒys ko fa mø sɑ̃•k tɥɛːr də nɔ trə dam də la gard)

33. Espérons qu'il fera beau la prochaine fois que vous‿y serez! En‿attendant, je souhaite que vous fassiez un‿excellent voyage en‿Afrique du Nord.

34. Merci bien. Je ne manquerai pas de vous‿envoyer de temps‿en temps une carte postale.

35. Si vous n'êtes pas trop‿occupé! Ça me fera plaisir d'avoir de vos nouvelles.

---

[1] *donc* merely adds emphasis to the question.

[2] Note the use of *ne . . . plus*, no longer, not . . . any more.

25. What magnificent countries you are going to see! You are lucky [Vous‿avez de la chance]! By the way [A propos], do you know Marseilles?

26. Yes, I went there once [une fois] on my return [en revenant] from a short trip to Corsica which I shall not soon [de sitôt] forget.

27. What happened to you there?

28. In the first place [Tout d'abord], I lost one of my suitcases on the way [en cours de route]. Naturally it was the one which [celle qui] contained my light summer suits. Then, on the way back [en retournant] to Marseilles, I was seasick [j'ai eu le mal de mer] during the entire passage [la traversée].

29. Seasickness is indeed [en‿effet] a thing which one cannot easily forget! It is perhaps for this reason that you travel by [en] plane?

30. That's right [juste]. I confess [J'avoue] that I am afraid now to take the boat even for a short trip.

31. Come, come [Allons]! It is better [Il vaut mieux] not to think about it any more.[2] What do you think of Marseilles?

32. It is a very interesting city, especially its old port. Unfortunately it rained [il a plu] almost continually during my stay [mon séjour], and I was unable to [je n'ai pas pu] take a walk to the [jusqu'au] famous sanctuary of Notre-Dame de la Garde.

33. Let us hope that the weather will be fine [il fera beau] the next time (that) you are there [vous‿y serez]! In the meanwhile [En‿attendant], I wish that you may have [que vous fassiez] an excellent journey in North Africa.

34. Many thanks. I shall not fail [Je ne manquerai pas] to send you a post card [une carte postale] from time to time.

35. If you are not too busy [occupé]! It will be a pleasure to hear from you (It will give me pleasure to have news of you. *Ça me fera plaisir d'avoir de vos nouvelles.*).

1. Que le temps passe vite! Me voici déjà à la fin de mes vacances!

2. C'est vraiment dommage! Je m'étais‿habitué à vous, mon cher⁀ami. Je regrette de vous voir partir. (ʒə me tɛ za bi tɥe)

3. Moi aussi, je regrette de vous quitter, de quitter aussi ce beau pays de France. Peu à peu j'ai appris à bien connaître les Français et à comprendre leurs coutumes.

4. Vous‿avez fait beaucoup de progrès. Maintenant vous parlez français presque couramment.

5. C'est‿exact, et j'ai pu m'en servir partout en‿Europe. Dans tous les pays que j'ai visités; en Belgique, en Suisse, en‿Angleterre, en‿Espagne, en‿Italie et en‿Allemagne j'ai été très‿étonné de rencontrer toujours des personnes qui parlaient très bien le français.

6. Vous‿aurez‿encore l'occasion de parler français au Canada, avant de retourner chez vous aux‿États-Unis. A propos, partez-vous directement de Paris pour le Canada?

7. Non, pas du tout. Je prends l'avion de Paris à Dakar, et ensuite de Dakar⁀à Natal, au Brésil. De là je prends le bateau pour Haïti, où j'irai voir l'ami d'enfance dont je vous‿ai parlé. (da kar—na tal—bre zil—a i ti)

8. Ah, oui! Celui qui possède de vastes plantations de café et de canne à sucre aux‿environs de Port-au-Prince? (sə lɥi ki pɔ sɛ·d də vɑ·s tə plɑ̃ tɑ sjɔ̃·d ka fe ed kan⁀a sy:kr⁀o zɑ̃ vi rɔ̃ də pɔr o prɛ̃·s)

9. C'est juste. Il⁀a aussi d'immenses champs de coton où travaillent des centaines de nègres et, ce qui est surprenant, c'est que tous ces nègres parlent français. Ne trouvez-vous pas‿extraordinaire qu'on continue encore de parler français à Haïti, presque un siècle et demi après son‿indépendance? (di mɑ̃·s ʃɑ̃·d kɔ tɔ̃—a prɛ sɔ nɛ̃ de pɑ̃ dɑ̃·s)

1. How [Que] quickly time passes! Here I am [Me voici] already at the end of my vacation!

2. It's really a pity [C'est vraiment dommage]! I had become accustomed [Je m'étais‿habitué] to you, my dear friend. I regret to see you go [partir].

3. I, too, [Moi aussi, je] regret to leave you, also to leave this beautiful country of France. Little by little [Peu à peu] I have learned to know the French well and to understand their customs.

4. You have made much progress. Now you speak French almost fluently.

5. That is so [exact], and I have been able to make use of it [m'en servir] everywhere in Europe. In all the countries which I visited: in Belgium, in Switzerland, in England, in Spain, in Italy and in Germany I was much surprised [j'ai été très‿étonné de] always to meet people [des personnes] who spoke French very well.

6. You will still [encore] have the opportunity [l'occasion] of speaking French in Canada, before returning to your home [avant de retourner chez vous] in the United States. By the way, are you going [partez-vous] from Paris straight to [directement pour] Canada?

7. No, not at all. I take the plane from Paris to Dakar, then from Dakar to Natal, in [au] Brazil. From there I take the boat to [pour] Haiti where I shall call on [j'irai voir] the childhood friend I spoke to you about (of whom I spoke to you, *dont je vous‿ai parlé*).

8. Oh, yes. The one who owns [celui qui possède] vast coffee and sugar cane [canne à sucre] plantations in the neighborhood [aux‿ environs] of Port-au-Prince?

9. That's right. He has immense cotton fields also where hundreds [des centaines] of Negroes are working, and the surprising thing is that [ce qui est surprenant, c'est que] all these Negroes speak French. Don't you find it extraordinary that they [on] still continue to speak French in Haiti, almost a century and a half after its independence?

10. En‿effet, c'est vraiment remarquable. Cela prouve que les Haïtiens ont toujours préféré la langue et la culture françaises, et qu'ils n'ont jamais‿oublié que leurs‿ancêtres étaient français. (le a i sjɛ̃—lœːr zɑ̃ sɛːtr⁀e tɛ frɑ̃ sɛ)

11. Mon cousin attendra mon bateau à Montréal. Nous ferons plusieurs‿excursions en‿auto à Québec⁀et dans quelques‿endroits du vieux Canada français. Mon cousin m'a dit que les Canadiens français ont gardé la plupart des coutumes de leurs‿ancêtres. (ka na djɛ̃)

12. C'est tout‿à fait vrai. Ils sont restés français de cœur bien qu'ils soient Canadiens par la pensée. N'oubliez pas d'aller voir la maison de Montcalm quand vous serez‿à Québec.

13. Certainement pas. Je ne manquerai pas non plus[1] d'aller visiter la fameuse basilique de Sainte-Anne de Beaupré, à une petite distance de cette ville.

14. Le village de Sainte-Anne de Beaupré est devenu maintenant le lieu sacré de pèlerinage de tout le Canada catholique. Tous les‿ans d'innombrables malades et infirmes viennent implorer le secours miraculeux de Sainte-Anne. Vous voyez, les Français ont leur Sainte Bernadette à Lourdes et les Canadiens leur Sainte-Anne de Beaupré. (lə ljø sa kred pɛl ri naːʒ—di nɔ̃ bra blə ma lad⁀e ɛ̃firm vjɛn⁀ɛ̃ plɔ re lə skuːr mi ra ky lø)

---

[1] Note the use of *ne . . . pas . . . non plus*, not either. Other examples: *Il n'a pas d'argent non plus*, He hasn't any money either; *Ne parlez pas non plus*, Don't speak either; *Lui non plus*, Neither does he.

10. Indeed it really is remarkable. It proves that the Haitians have always preferred the French language and culture, and that they have never forgotten that their ancestors were French.

11. My cousin will meet [attendra] my boat at Montreal. We shall make several excursions by car [en‿auto] to Quebec and to a few spots [dans quelques‿endroits] of old French Canada. My cousin told me that the French Canadians have kept most [la plupart] of the customs of their ancestors.

12. That's quite [tout‿à fait] true. They have remained [sont restés] French in their heart [de cœur] although they are [bien qu'ils soient] Canadian in their [par la] thought. Don't forget to see [d'aller voir] Montcalm's house while you are [quand vous serez] in Quebec.

13. Certainly not. I shall not fail either [Je ne manquerai pas non plus] to visit the famous basilica of Sainte-Anne de Beaupré, at a short distance from that city.

14. The village of Sainte-Anne de Beaupré has now become [est devenu] the holy place [le lieu sacré] of pilgrimage of all Catholic Canada. Every year countless [d'innombrables] sick and crippled persons [infirmes] come to implore the miraculous help [le secours] of Sainte-Anne. You see, the French have their Sainte Bernadette at Lourdes and the Canadians their Sainte-Anne de Beaupré.

ANECDOTES FOR TRANSLATION EXERCISES

Le Banquier Anglais et l'Irlandais

Un banquier de Londres[1] avait besoin d'un domestique. Un‿ Irlandais vint[2] s'offrir pour⁀entrer à son service.

"De quel pays êtes-vous?" lui demanda[3] le banquier.

"Je suis‿Anglais," répondit[4] l'autre.

"De quel⁀endroit,[5] s'il vous plaît?"

"De Dublin."

---

[1] A banker of London.

[2] Irregular *Prétérit* of *venir,* to come. It has already been stated that the historical tense, the *Prétérit* or *Passé défini,* is used in narratives. The regular conjugation of the historical tense is given in the next note.

Prét: Je vins, tu vins, il vint, nous vînmes, vous vîntes, ils vinrent.

[3] The *Prétérit* or *Passé défini,* the historical tense, adds the following endings to the stem in the three regular conjugations, ending in *er, ir, re.* All verbs ending in *oir* are irregular. They form the 3rd conjugation.

1st	2nd	3rd	4th
——ai	——is	——us	——is
——as	——is	——us	——is
——a	——it	——ut	——it
——âmes	——îmes	——ûmes	——îmes
——âtes	——îtes	——ûtes	——îtes
——èrent	——irent	——urent	——irent

If, therefore, we take *parler,* to speak, *finir,* to finish, *vendre,* to sell, and *recevoir,* to receive, we form the

Prétérit

1st	2nd	3rd	4th
Je parl*ai*	Je fin*is*	Je reç*us*	Je vendis
tu parl*as*	tu fin*is*	tu reç*us*	tu vend*is*
il parl*a*	il fin*it*	it reç*ut*	il vend*it*
nous parl*âmes*	nous fin*îmes*	nous reç*ûmes*	nous vend*îmes*
vous parl*âtes*	vous fin*îtes*	vous reç*ûtes*	vous vend*îtes*
ils parl*èrent*	ils fin*irent*	ils reç*urent*	ils vend*irent*

[4] Replied, historical tense of répondre, to reply, to answer.

[5] From which place?

"Comment pouvez-vous dire que vous êtes Anglais, puisque[6] vous êtes né en Irlande?"

"Mais, monsieur, si j'étais né dans une écurie,[7] ce ne serait pas une raison, je crois, pour que je fusse[8] un cheval."

La Prévoyance[1]

Une bonne vieille,[2] après avoir fait ses prières devant l'image[3] de saint Michel, prit[4] deux petits cierges,[5] et en alluma un pour l'archange[6] et l'autre pour Satan, représenté sous ses pieds.

Le curé du village,[7] qui passait par là en ce moment, s'en aperçut.[8] Il s'écria:[9] "Eh! que faites-vous là? Est-ce que vous êtes folle?[10] Vous brûlez[11] un cierge au diable?"[12]

"Non, monsieur le curé, je ne suis pas folle. J'ai toujours entendu dire qu'il était prudent d'avoir des amis partout:[13] on ne sait pas où l'on ira."

Léon X et l'Alchimiste[1]

Un alchimiste qui se vantait[2] d'avoir trouvé le secret[3] de faire de l'or,[4] demandait une récompense[5] à Léon Dix.

[6] Since, as.
[7] *Une écurie,* a stable.
[8] Subjunctive (imparfait) of *être,* to be.

Imp. Subj. Que je fusse, que tu fusses, qu'il fût, que nous fussions, que vous fussiez, qu'ils fussent.

---

[1] Precaution, foresight.
[2] A good old woman. *Vieille* is the feminine form of *vieux,* old. (vjɛ:j)
[3] The image, statue.
[4] The historical tense of the irregular verb *prendre,* to take.

Prét: Je pris, tu pris, il prit, nous prîmes, vous prîtes, ils prirent.

[5] Candles.
[6] The archangel. (lar kɑ̃:ʒ)
[7] The village priest. (vi la:ʒ)
[8] Observed it.—*Apercevoir,* to perceive, is conjugated like *recevoir,* to receive. The historical tense is conjugated:

Prét: Je reçus, tu reçus, il reçut, nous reçûmes, vous reçûtes, ils reçurent.

[9] He cried out. Historical tense.
[10] *Folle,* feminine form of *fou,* crazy.
[11] You burn.
[12] *Le diable,* the devil.
[13] Everywhere.

---

[1] The *alchimiste.* (al ʃi mist)—[2] boasted.—[3] the secret.—[4] gold.—[5] a reward.

Le pape[6] parut[7]‿acquiescer à sa demande.

Le charlatan se flattait[8] déjà d'avoir fait fortune[9]; mais s'étant de nouveau[10] présenté à Leon X pour le même motif,[11] celui-ci lui fit[12] donner un grand sac[13] vide,‿en lui disant: "Puisque vous savez faire de l'or, tout ce qu'il vous faut c'est‿un sac pour le mettre."

Le Martyre de Saint Sébastien

Deux paysans[1] furent‿envoyés[2] par leur village dans‿une ville, pour choisir‿un peintre habile[3], qui devait faire‿un tableau[4] pour le maître-autel[5] de eur église. Il devait représenter le martyre de saint Sébastien.

Le peintre‿auquel‿ils s'adressèrent[6] leur demanda[7] s'il devait représenter le saint vivant ou mort.[8]

Cette question les mit[9] quelque temps dans l'embarras.[10]

Enfin[11] l'un d'eux dit:[12] "Le plus sûr[13] c'est de le représenter vivant: si on veut l'avoir mort,‿on pourra toujours bien le tuer.[14]"

Remède Contre Les Rats[1]

Un‿aubergiste[2] qui avait‿un peu écorché[3] un de ses‿hôtes,[4] se plaignait[5] devant lui de ce que les rats dévoraient[6] ou gâtaient[7] tout dans la maison.

L'étranger lui dit: "Il‿y a un bon moyen[8] de vous‿en débarrasser."[9]

---

[6] The Pope.—[7] Historical tense of paraître, to appear.

Prét: Je parus, tu parus, il parut, nous parûmes, vous parûtes, ils parurent.

[8] Flattered himself.—[9] To have already made his fortune.—[10] Again, anew. —[11] For the same purpose.—[12] Historical tense of *faire*, to make, to do.

Prét: Je fis, tu fis, il fit, nous fîmes, vous fîtes, ils firent.

[13] A large empty bag.

---

[1] Two peasants.—[2] Were sent.—[3] A skilful painter.—[4] A painting.—[5] The High-Altar.—[6] Historical tense of *s'addresser*, to apply.

[7] Historical tense of *demander*, to ask.—[8] Alive or dead.

[9] Historical tense of *mettre*, to put, to place.

Prét: Je mis, tu mis, il mit, nous mîmes, vous mîtes, ils mirent.

[10] *Embarrass, i. e.*, rather embarrassed them.—[11] At last, finally.—[12] Historical tense of *dire*, to say, to tell.

Prét: Je dis, tu dis, il dit, nous dîmes, vous dîtes, ils dirent.

[13] The surest, best way is (would be).—[14] To kill him.

---

[1] A remedy against rats.—[2] An innkeeper.—[3] To overcharge.—[4] Guest.—[5] Complained; Imperfect of plaindre, to complain (sə plɛ̃: dr) (conjugated like craindre, to fear).—[6] Devoured.—[7] Spoiled.—[8] Means, remedy. (mwa jɛ̃)—[9] To get rid of them.

—"Ah! Monsieur, vous me rendriez un grand service."

—"Rien n'est plus simple."

—"Et comment donc?"

—"Vous n'avez qu'à leur présenter une note aussi chère que la mienne, et le diable m'emporte[10] s'ils reviendront jamais."

L'Esprit de l'Enfance[1]

Un monsieur âgé,[2] se trouvant un soir dans la société de quelques personnes qui s'amusaient beaucoup des mots spirituels[3] d'un‿enfant, dit‿à quelqu'un près de lui que les‿enfants spirituels faisaient‿ordinairement[4] des‿hommes sots.[5]

L'enfant l'entendit et lui dit: "Monsieur, vous‿aviez sans doute beaucoup d'esprit quand vous‿étiez jeune."

Le Poète et le Pâtissier[1]

Un poète avait fait‿une chanson[2] à la louange[3] des pâtés[4] du meilleur pâtissier du pays. Celui-ci, pour lui montrer sa reconnaissance,[5] lui envoya[6] un des pâtés qu'il avait tant loués[7] dans la chanson.

Le poète fut‿extrêmement satisfait d'une pareille attention; mais quelle fut sa surprise! quelle fut sa douleur![8] En mangeant le dernier morceau du délicieux[9] pâté, il découvre[10] que le papier sur lequel le pâté a été mis[11] au four[12] c'est justement la copie[13] de la chanson qu'il avait‿envoyée au pâtissier. Il court[14] en fureur[15] chez lui et l'accuse[16] hautement du crime[17] très grave de lèse-poésie.[18]

---

[10] And may the devil take me.

---

[1] Childhood.—[2] Old.—[3] Witty.—[4] Generally.—[5] Stupid.

---

[1] The Poet and the Pastry cook.—[2] A song.—[3] In praise of.—[4] The patties. —[5] His gratitude.—[6] Historical tense of *envoyer*, to send.—[7] Praised.—[8] His grief. —[9] Delicious.—[10] Discovers.—[11] Part of mettre.—[12] *Le four*, the oven.—[13] The copy.

[14] *Courir*, to run; *courant*, running; *couru*, ran.

Pres: Je cours, tu cours, il court, nous courons, vous courez, ils courent.

Imp: Je courais, tu courais, il courait, nous courions, etc.

Prét: Je courus, tu courus, il courut, nous courûmes, vous courûtes, ils coururent.

Fut: Je courrai, tu courras, il courra, nous courrons, vous courrez, ils courront.

Cond: Je courrais, tu courrais, il courrait, nous courrions, etc.

Pres. Subj: Que je coure, que tu coures, qu'il coure, que nous courions, que vous couriez, qu'ils courent.

Imp. Subj: Que je courusse, que tu courusses, qu'il courût, que nous courussions, que vous courussiez, qu'ils courussent.

[15] In a fury, enraged.—[16] Accuses him.—[17] Le crime, the crime.—[18] High treason in regard to poetry. (*Lèse-majesté*, high treason).

"Mais, monsieur," répond l'autre sans s'émouvoir,[19] "pourquoi vous fâcher?[20] Vous‿avez fait une chanson sur mes pâtés, et moi, j'ai fait un pâté sur votre chanson."

Le Jeune Mathématicien

Un fermier,[1] qui ne savait ni[2] lire ni écrire, et qui avait quelques‿épargnes,[3] voulut[4] faire donner de l'instruction à son fils⁀unique[5] et l'envoya dans‿un pensionnat.[6]

Après‿y avoir passé deux‿années, le jeune homme revint[7] chez ses parents, et entra[8] dans la ferme[9] au moment où son père et sa mère se mettaient‿à table devant‿un plat de viande et un plat de légumes.[10]

Après les‿embrassements d'usage,[11] le fermier dit[12]‿à son fils, tandis que[13] la mère préparait‿un troisième couvert:[14] "Eh bien, mon garçon, as-tu bien‿employé ton temps? Es-tu devenu savant?"[15]

"Oh! oui, mon père," répondit l'écolier[16] avec suffisance.[17]

"Sais-tu compter, surtout, mon fils?"

"J'étais le plus fort en‿arithmétique," répondit‿encore le jeune drôle,[18] "et je puis vous donner la preuve[19] que je sais faire des comptes[20] que vous ne feriez pas vous-même."

"Je ne dis pas non . . . mais voyons la preuve de ton savoir."

"Voici: combien de plats croyez-vous‿avoir sur votre table?"

"Deux," répondit le père; "un plat de viande, un‿autre de légumes."

"Eh bien, vous vous trompez. Il⁀y a trois plats sur notre table."

"Parbleu![21] je serais bien‿aise d'entendre ton raisonnement[22] à l'appui[23] de ce compte-là."

"Rien de plus facile; nous disons: plat de viande, cela fait un; plat de légumes, cela fait deux; j'additionne[24] et je dis: un et deux font trois."

---

[19] Without becoming excited.—[20] Get angry.

---

[1] A farmer.—[2] *Ni—ni*—neither—nor.—[3] Savings.—[4] Historical tense of *vouloir*, to want, to desire.

Prét: Je voulus, tu voulus, il voulut, nous voulûmes, vous voulûtes, ils voulurent.

[5] Only.—[6] Boarding-school.—[7] Historical tense of *revenir*, to return.—[8] Historical tense of *entrer*, to enter.—[9] The farm.—[10] A dish of vegetables.—[11] The customary salutations.—[12] Historical tense of *dire*, to tell, to say.—[13] While.—[14] A third cover.—[15] A scholar.—[16] The pupil.—[17] With conceit, conceitedly.—[18] The young rogue.—[19] The proof.—[20] How to do computations.—[21] You don't say!—[22] Reasoning, argument.—[23] In support of.—[24] I add.

"C'est juste, c'est fort juste," dit le fermier. "Eh bien, je vais manger un plat, ta mère mangera le second, et toi, tu mangeras le troisième en récompense de ton savoir."

Le Meunier et Son Fils[1]

Un jour un meunier et son fils conduisirent[2] leur âne[3] à la ville pour le vendre au marché.

Chemin faisant, ils rencontrèrent[4] un homme à cheval qui leur dit en riant: "Vous‿êtes bien sots[5] de laisser aller l'âne sans charge,[6] et sans qu'aucun de vous songe à le monter."

Aussitôt le père dit‿à son fils d'enfourcher[7] l'âne.

Quelques moments après ils rencontrèrent un charretier.[8] Celui-ci cria au fils: "Un vigoureux[9] garçon comme toi devrait‿avoir honte de se faire porter par cette bête[10] et de laisser cheminer à côté de soi son vieux père."

En‿entendant ces paroles,[11] le fils sauta[12] lestement[13] à bas de l'âne et fit[14] monter le vieillard[15] à sa place.

Un peu plus loin ils rencontrèrent une paysanne[16] qui dit‿au meunier: "Vous‿êtes vraiment un père sans‿entrailles[17] de rester si commodément assis sur cet‿âne, tandis que votre pauvre enfant a de la peine[18] à vous suivre à pied sur ce chemin sablonneux.[19]"

Alors le père fit monter le fils derrière lui sur l'âne.

A quelque distance de là, ils rencontrèrent un berger[20] qui faisait paître[21] son troupeau[22] le long de la route.[23]

En voyant passer les deux‿hommes montés sur l'âne le berger s'écria:[24] "Oh! la pauvre bête! elle doit‿inévitablement succomber[25]

---

[1] The Miller and His Son.

[2] Historical tense of *conduire*, to conduct, to lead.

Prét: Je conduisis, tu conduisis, il conduisit, nous conduisîmes, vous conduisîtes, ils conduisirent.

[3] Their donkey.—[4] Historical tense of *rencontrer*, to meet.—[5] Stupid.—[6] Without any burden.—[7] To bestride.—[8] A wagoner.—[9] Vigorous.

[10] This beast.—[11] These words.—[12] Historical tense of *sauter*, to jump.—[13] Nimbly.—[14] Historical tense of *faire*, to make. (Conjugated before.)—[15] The old man.—[16] A peasant-woman. (yn pe i zan)—[17] *Les‿entrailles* (ã tra:j) (fem.), the entrails, bowels.—*Un père sans‿entrailles*, (ã tra:j) a heartless father.—[18] Trouble, difficulty.—[19] Sandy.

[20] A shepherd.—[21] Who was grazing.—[22] His flock.—[23] Roadside.—[24] Historical tense of *s'écrier*, to cry out.—[25] To succumb.

sous ce double fardeau.[26] Vous‿êtes vraiment les bourreaux[27] de cet‿animal."

Alors ils descendirent[28] de l'âne tous les deux,[29] et le fils dit‿au père: "Que faut-il faire maintenant de cet‿âne pour contenter tout le monde? Il ne nous reste plus qu'à lui lier[30] les jambes, le suspendre[31] à un bâton[32] et le porter sur nos‿épaules[33] au marché."

"Tu le vois maintenant, mon fils," répondit le père, "on ne peut jamais réussir[34] à contenter tout le monde, et la sagesse[35] nous conseille[36] de suivre cette maxime: "Fais ton devoir,[37] et ne t'inquiète nullement de ce que peut dire le monde."

Le Paysan au Ciel[1]

Il mourut[2]‿une fois un pauvre paysan qui vint[3]‿à la porte du paradis.[4]

En même temps il mourut‿un riche seigneur[5] qui monta aussi au ciel.

Saint Pierre[6] arriva avec ses clefs,[7] ouvrit[8] la porte et fit‿entrer le seigneur; mais, sans doute, il n'avait pas vu le paysan, car il le laissa[9] dehors[10] et ferma la porte.

---

[26] *Fardeau,* burden, load.—[27] The torturors.—[28] Historical tense of *descendre,* to descend, to get off.—[29] Both of them.—[30] To tie.—[31] To suspend, to hang.—[32] From a stick.—[33] On our shoulders.—[34] To succeed.—[35] Wisdom.—[36] Counsels us.—[37] Thy duty.

---

[1] In Heaven.

[2] Historical tense of *mourir,* to die.

Prét: Je mourus, tu mourus, il mourut, nous mourûmes, vous mourûtes, ils moururent.

[3] Historical tense of *venir,* to come.

[4] Paradise.—[5] Lord of the manor.—[6] St. Peter.—[7] With his keys.

[8] Historical tense of *Ouvrir,* to open, *ouvrant,* opening; *ouvert,* opened.

Pres: J'ouvre, tu ouvres, il ouvre, nous‿ouvrons, vous‿ouvrez, ils‿ouvrent.
Imp: J'ouvrais, tu ouvrais, il ouvrait, nous‿ouvrions, etc.
Prét: J'ouvris, tu ouvris, il ouvrit, nous‿ouvrîmes, vous‿ouvrîtes, ils‿ouvrirent.
Fut: J'ouvrirai, tu ouvriras, il ouvrira, nous‿ouvrirons, etc.
Cond: J'ouvrirais, tu ouvrirais, il‿ouvrirait, nous‿ouvririons, etc.
Pres. Subj: Que j'ouvre, que tu ouvres, qu'il ouvre, que nous‿ouvrions, que vous‿ouvriez, qu'ils‿ouvrent.
Imp. Subj: Que j'ouvrisse, que tu ouvrisses, qu'il ouvrît, que nous‿ouvrissions, que vous‿ouvrissiez, qu'ils‿ouvrissent.

[9] Historical tense of *laisser,* to leave.—[10] Outside.—

Le paysan entendit[11] la joyeuse[12] réception que le ciel faisait au richard[13] avec du chant[14] et de la musique.

Quand le bruit[15] se fut apaisé,[16] saint Pierre revint et fit entrer le pauvre homme.

Celui-ci s'attendait à ce qu'à son entrée le chant et la musique recommencent. Mais tout resta[17] tranquille. On le reçut de bon cœur, les anges[18] allèrent au-devant de lui, mais personne ne chanta.[19]

Il demanda à saint Pierre pourquoi on ne le recevait pas comme le riche, et si la partialité[20] régnait au ciel comme sur la terre.

"Non," lui répondit le saint, "tu nous es aussi cher qu'aucun autre, et tu goûteras[21] tout comme celui qui vient d'entrer, les joies[22] du paradis; mais, vois-tu, des pauvres paysans comme toi, il en entre ici tous les jours, tandis que des riches, il n'en vient pas un tous les cent ans."

Garrick

Le célèbre acteur[1] Garrick avait un merveilleux talent pour contrefaire[2] le langage,[3] les manières et jusqu'à l'extérieur[4] même des personnes qu'il ne voyait pas habituellement.[5]

Il rencontre un jour, dans une rue de Londres, un jeune homme qu'il avait vu plusieurs fois,[6] et qui paraissait accablé[7] d'une profonde douleur. Il s'arrête et lui en demande la cause.

"J'ai perdu mon père," répond le jeune homme, "il est mort dans cette auberge,[8] que vous apercevez[9] à l'extrémité de la rue, et le maître de l'hotel, profitant du désordre[10] où la douleur m'avait jeté[11] a pris dans la valise de mon père le portefeuille[12] qui contenait tout nos biens.[13]"

Garrick, touché[14] de ce récit,[15] conçoit[16] à l'instant l'idée de lui faire restituer ce larcin.[17] Il se rappelait parfaitement avoir vu le vieillard; il avait remarqué son costume bizarre,[18] la longue canne[19]

---

[11] Historical tense of *entendre*, to hear.—[12] Joyful, glad.—[13] Gave the rich man. [14] Singing.—[15] The sounds.—[16] Had subsided.—[17] Historical tense of *rester*, to remain.—[18] The angels.—[19] Historical tense of *chanter*, to sing.—[20] Partiality (la par sja li te).—[21] Goûter, to taste, to enjoy.—[22] The joys.

---

[1] Actor.—[2] To imitate —[3] The language, style, manner of voice.—[4] The exterior, appearance.—[5] Habitually.—[6] Several times.—[7] Overwhelmed, crushed.

[8] This inn.—[9] Perceive, see.—[10] The disorder.—[11] Plunged.—[12] The pocket-book.—[13] Our wealth.—[14] Touched —[15] The story.—[16] *Concevoir*, to conceive. —[17] The stolen goods.—[18] His queer costume.—[19] The long cane.

qu'il tenait à la main et je ne sais quoi d'original répandu[20] sur toute sa personne.

"Avez-vous," dit Garrick, "conservé[21] les habits que portait votre père au moment de sa mort?"

"Oui, sans doute."

"Envoyez-les moi, et je vous ferai rendre votre portefeuille."

Le jeune homme eut[22] bientôt porté chez Garrick le costume de son père; l'acteur, après s'en être revêtu,[23] alla frapper[24] à la porte de l'aubergiste.

Un voleur[25] est rarement un esprit fort:[26] celui-ci, depuis son vol,[27] s'imaginait[28] toujours voir le défunt[29] à ses côtés, et quand il ouvrit la porte, il crut[30] reconnaître réellement celui qu'il avait vu enterrer[31] deux jours auparavant;[32] il pâlit[33] et resta immobile.

Garrick, contrefaisant alors la voix[34] du vieillard: "Eh bien," lui dit-il, "mon cher hôte, me voici de retour[35] de mon petit voyage."

"Vous vous portez bien?" dit l'aubergiste sans oser le regarder en face.

"Parfaitement. Je vais maintenant partir pour Liverpool, où je m'embarque pour l'Irlande. Je viens vous faire mes adieux,[36] vous remercier de vos bons offices et vous demander ma valise."

"La . . . la . . . voici," dit le fripon,[37] qui s'était hâté[38] d'aller la chercher et d'y remettre furtivement[39] le portefeuille.

Le jeune homme, en revoyant sa fortune, n'en pouvait croire ses yeux[40] et ses larmes de reconnaissance[41] touchèrent Garrick plus que les applaudissements[42] du théâtre.

Un Pari[1]

Un monsieur à cheval s'arrêta un soir devant une auberge qui était remplie[2] de voyageurs. Il entra dans la cour, appela l'aubergiste d'une voix forte, et lui dit d'avoir soin de son cheval et de le mettre à l'écurie.[3]

---

[20] Spread.—[21] Preserved.—[22] Historical tense of *avoir*, to have.
Prét: J'eus, tu eus, il eut, nous eûmes, vous eûtes, ils eurent.

[23] After having dressed himself in it.—[24] To knock.—[25] A thief.—[26] A man of strong mind.—[27] His theft.—[28] Imagined —[29] The defunct, the dead man.

[30] Historical tense of *croire*, to believe.
Prét: Je crus, tu crus, il crut, nous crûmes, vous crûtes, ils crurent.

[31] To bury.—[32] Before —[33] He grew pale.—[34] The voice.—[35] Here I am back.—[36] I came to bid you good-bye.—[37] The rogue, rascal, knave, thief.—[38] Hastened.—[39] Furtively.—[40] His eyes.—[41] His tears of gratitude.—[42] The applause.

---

[1] A bet.—[2] Filled.—[3] The stable.

"Nous n'avons pas une seule place," dit l'aubergiste, "l'écurie est remplie de chevaux."

"Oui, oui," répondit le voyageur, qui paraissait ne pas entendre, "je penserai à vous demain."

"Mais je vous dis que nous n'avons pas une seule place."

"Donnez-lui de l'avoine[4] et tout le foin[5] qu'il voudra manger," dit le voyageur; et il entra sans façon[6] dans la maison.

"Il doit être fou," dit l'aubergiste.

"Je crois qu'il est sourd,[7]" répliqua[8] le garçon d'écurie, "mais en tout cas[9] nous devons avoir soin de son cheval, nous en sommes responsables.[10]"

Notre voyageur était entré dans la maison. L'hôtesse[11] lui répéta qu'il était impossible de le loger.

"Pas de compliments," cria-t-il si haut que l'hôtesse trembla,[12] "pas de façons,[13] je vous prie, tout va fort bien. Je me contente de peu, vos paroles sont entièrement inutiles,[14] car je suis si sourd que je n'entendrais pas un coup de canon.[15]"

Aussitôt il prit une chaise et s'assit[16] auprès du feu, comme s'il eût été chez lui. L'aubergiste et sa femme qui ne savaient pas comment s'en débarrasser, résolurent[17] de lui faire passer la nuit sur une chaise, car tous les lits étaient occupés.

---

[4] Oats.—[5] As much hay.—[6] Without ceremony, without further ado. —[7] Deaf.—[8] Historical tense of *répliquer*, to reply.—[9] At any rate, in any case.—[10] Responsible.—[11] The hostess.—[12] Historical tense of *trembler*, to tremble. —[13] No ceremonies.—[14] Useless.—[15] *Un coup de canon*, a cannon-shot.

[16] Historical tense of *s'asseoir*, to sit down.

Prét: Je m'assis, tu t'assis, il s'assit, nous nous assîmes, vous vous assîtes, ils s'assirent.

[17] *Résoudre*, to resolve; *résolvant*, resolving; *résolu*, resolved.

Pres: Je résous, tu résous, il résout, nous résolvons, vous résolvez, ils résolvent.

Imp: Je résolvais, tu résolvais, il résolvait, nous résolvions, etc.

Prét: Je résolus, tu résolus, il résolut, nous résolûmes, vous résolûtes, ils résolurent.

Fut: Je résoudrai, tu résoudras, il résoudra, etc.

Cond: Je résoudrais, tu résoudrais, il résoudrait, etc.

Pres. Subj: Que je résolve, que tu résolves, qu'il résolve, que nous résolvions, que vous résolviez, qu'ils résolvent.

Imp. Subj: Que je résolusse, que tu résolusses, qu'il résolût, que nous résolussions, que vous résolussiez, qu'ils résolussent.

Bientôt après, il vit[18] que le repas était servi dans une pièce voisine.[19] Il prit aussitôt une chaise et se mit à table. En vain[20] lui cria-t-on aussi fort que l'on put[21] à l'oreille[22] que c'était pour une société particulière[23] qui n'admettait aucun étranger. Il sembla croire qu'on voulait le placer au haut de la table, c'est-à-dire à la place d'honneur. Il les remercia de leur politesse,[24] en les assurant que sa place lui paraissait très convenable. On vit alors qu'on ne pouvait pas s'en faire comprendre, et on le laissa tranquille.

Après qu'il eut assez bien mangé, il mit sur la table un billet de cent francs pour payer son dîner, mais l'hôtesse le repoussa[25] dédaigneusement[26] en disant: "Quoi! vous croyez qu'un repas comme vous en avez absorbé[27] un se donne pour cent francs?"

"Je vous demande pardon, madame," répondit-il, "je veux payer moi-même mon dîner; je remercie ces messieurs de leur politesse, mais je ne souffrirai pas qu'ils payent pour moi."

Il regarda alors à sa montre, sortit de la pièce, en souhaitant[28] une bonne nuit à la société, et trouva bientôt le chemin d'une chambre à coucher.

Les autres voyageurs rirent[29] de bon cœur de son apparente stupidité[30] et envoyèrent un domestique pour voir où il était allé. Celui-ci revint bientôt et raconta[31] qu'il avait pris possession d'une de leurs chambres. On résolut alors de l'en chasser de force.[32]

Comme ils s'approchaient[33] de la porte, ils entendirent qu'il la barricadait[34] avec les meubles[35] et qu'il se parlait à lui-même à haute voix. Ils prêtèrent[36] l'oreille et l'entendirent qui disait:

"Que je suis donc malheureux! Quelqu'un pourrait briser[37] la porte sans que je l'entende; ces messieurs peuvent être des gens honnêtes,

---

[18] Historical tense of *voir*, to see.

Prét: Je vis, tu vis, il vit, nous vîmes, vous vîtes, ils virent.

[19] In an adjoining room.—[20] In vain.

[21] Historical tense of *pouvoir*, to be able.

Prét: Je pus, tu pus, il put, nous pûmes, vous pûtes, ils purent.

[22] The ear.—[23] Private company.—[24] Politeness.—[25] Pushed it back.—[26] Disdainfully.—[27] Eaten.

[28] Wishing.

[29] Historical tense of *rire*, to laugh.

Prét: Je ris, tu ris, il rit, nous rîmes, vous rîtes, ils rirent.

[30] His apparent stupidity.—[31] Historical tense of *raconter*, to tell.—[32] To drive him out by force.—[33] Approached.—[34] He was barricading it.—[35] The furniture.—[36] Historical tense of *prêter*, to lend.—[37] To break.

mais peut-être qu'ils ne le sont pas. Comme j'ai quelque argent, je ne veux pas m'exposer au danger.[38] Non, je ne me mets pas au lit et je n'éteins[39] pas la lumière; je reste debout[40] toute la nuit, je prends mes pistolets,[41] et si quelqu'un entre ici, je tire dessus immédiatement.[42]"

Quand ses auditeurs[43] entendirent cela, ils n'essayèrent plus de le déloger;[44] il se mit au lit, passa une nuit tranquille, et le monsieur dont il avait pris la chambre dût chercher un gîte[45] ailleurs.

Le lendemain matin, notre voyageur descendit, alla chercher son cheval, le conduisit devant la porte, où il trouva la société déjà réunie[46] et prête à se moquer de lui[47] encore une fois.

Quand il fut monté, il jeta[48] cinquante francs au valet d'écurie pour son cheval et de l'argent aussi pour l'aubergiste, et il dit alors d'un air tout différent:

"Messieurs, je vous remercie de la politesse que vous m'avez témoignée.[49] Je demande pardon à l'un de vous de lui avoir pris son lit. La nuit précédente[50] on avait refusé ici un logement à un de mes amis, et il a parié[51] vingt louis d'or que je n'en trouverais pas. C'est pour cela que j'ai fait le sourd. Je vous laisse à juger[52] si je l'ai bien fait."

Il donna de l'éperon à son cheval[53] et partit.

---

[38] *Le danger*, danger.—[39] *Éteindre*, to extinguish. (Conjugated like *craindre*, to fear.)—[40] I remain up, I shall stay up.—[41] My pistols.—[42] I shall at once fire on him.—[43] Listeners, hearers.—[44] To dislodge.—[45] A resting-place.—[46] Assembled.—[47] To make fun of him.—[48] Historical tense of *jeter*, to throw.—[49] Which you have shown me.—[50] Preceding.—[51] He bet.—[52] To judge.—[53] He gave the spur to his horse.

VOCABULAIRE *(Suite)*	**VOCABULARY** *(Continuation)*
Les bagages sont-ils examinés sur le navire, avant de débarquer, ou à terre après le débarquement? (na vi:r—de bar kə mɑ̃)	Will the baggage be examined on board before landing, or on shore after landing?
Où faut-il porter les bagages pour la visite de la douane?	Where must I take my baggage for the custom-house examination?
Qu'est-ce qui paie des droits?	What is liable to duty?
Je ne pense pas avoir quoi que ce soit à déclarer.	I do not think I have anything to declare.
Faut-il ouvrir les malles?	Have the trunks to be opened?
Faut-il sortir les effets?	Have the things to be taken out?
Nous voici à la frontière. Les officiers de la douane française viennent.	Here we are at the frontier. Here come the French custom-house officers.
Avez-vous des articles à déclarer?	Have you anything dutiable with you?
Sur quels articles y a-t-il des droits d'entrée?	On which articles do you collect duties?
Sur les cigares seulement.	On cigars only.
Je n'ai ni cigares ni cigarettes, je ne fume pas.	I have neither cigars nor cigarettes. I don't smoke.
Veuillez ouvir cette malle.	Please open this trunk.
Qu'y a-t-il dans cette malle?	What does this trunk contain?
Il n'y a que des vêtements, du linge et des effets à mon usage.	It contains nothing but clothing, linen and personal effects.
Avant d'Arriver	**Before Arriving**
A quelle heure arriverons-nous à Paris?	At what time shall we reach Paris?
Serons-nous bientôt arrivés à Paris?	Shall we soon arrive in Paris?
Sommes-nous encore loin de Paris?	Are we still far from Paris?

VOCABULAIRE	VOCABULARY
Combien de tunnels nous reste-t‿il encore‿à passer?	How many tunnels have we still to pass?
Avons-nous déjà passé la Seine?	Have we already crossed the Seine?
Quel‿est ce fleuve?	What is the name of this river?
Quelle‿est cette montagne (cette‿île)? (i:l)	What is the name of this mountain? (this island?)
Le train a dix minutes de retard.	The train is ten minutes late.
Je crains que nous ne soyons‿en retard.	I am afraid we shall be late.

L'arrivée	**The Arrival**
Porteur, vite, trouvez-moi un taxi. Voilà mon bulletin de bagage.	Porter, get a taxi for me, quick! Here is my baggage-check.
Où délivre-t‿on les bagages?	Where is the baggage delivered?
Il‿y a trois colis, porteur; cette malle, ce sac (de voyage) et ce carton à chapeaux.	There are three pieces, porter; this trunk, this traveling bag and this hat-box.
Portez-moi tout ceci au taxi numéro 227.	Take all these to taxi No. 227.
Chauffeur‿attendez mes bagages.	Chauffeur, wait for my baggage.
Chauffeur, donnez-moi votre numéro et restez pour‿attendre mes bagages.	Chauffeur, give me your number and wait for my baggage.
Placez la malle sur le siège du chauffeur.	Place the trunk on the chauffeur's seat.
Conduisez-moi à l'Hôtel Continental (kɔ̃ ti nɑ̃ tal)	Drive me to the Continental Hotel.

L'Hôtel — Les Chambres — Le Mobilier	**Hotel — Rooms — The Furniture**
L'hôtel	The hotel
Un hôtel de premier‿ordre	A first-class hotel
Un hôtel de second‿ordre	A second-class hotel

VOCABULAIRE	VOCABULARY
Pouvez-vous me recommander un‿hôtel⁀à Blois?	Can you recommend me a hotel in Blois?
Quel⁀est le meilleur hôtel⁀à Boulogne?	Which is the best hotel in Boulogne?
A quel hôtel descendez-vous?	At what hotel do you stop?
Faut‿il prendre un taxi?	Is it necessary to take a taxi?
Je vous recommande cet‿hôtel.	I recommend you this hotel.
La pension (pã sjõ)	The boarding-house
Le propriétaire	The proprietor
Le garçon	The waiter
La femme de chambre	The chamber-maid
Veuillez nettoyer ma chambre de suite.	Please arrange (clean) my room at once.
Faites mon lit, je vous prie.	Please fix my bed.
L'ascenseur (la sã sœ:r)	The elevator

La Chambre	The Room
Une chambre sur le devant Une chambre donnant sur la rue	A front room
Une chambre sur le derrière Une chambre donnant sur la cour	A back room
La chambre à coucher	The bed-room
Le salon	The drawing-room
Le petit salon	The sitting-room
Une chambre au rez-de-chaussée	A room on the ground floor
Une chambre au premier, au second, au troisième (étage)	A room on the second, third, fourth floor
Puis-je avoir⁀une chambre?	Can I have a room?
Y a-t‿il des chambres disponibles?	Have you any rooms vacant?
Je voudrais‿une chambre à un lit.	Let me have a single room.
Je voudrais‿un petit salon et une chambre à coucher à deux lits.	I would like a sitting-room and a bed-room with two beds.
A quel⁀étage?	On what floor?
Je ne voudrais pas‿être logé trop haut.	I would not like to be lodged too high up.
Y a-t‿il⁀un‿ascenseur?	Is there an elevator?

VOCABULAIRE	**VOCABULARY**
Pourrais-je avoir une chambre au rez-de-chaussée.	Could I have a room on the ground floor?
Je désirerais une chambre au premier avec vue sur le lac.	I should wish to have a room on the second floor overlooking the lake.
Cette chambre donne-t-elle sur la rue ou sur la cour?	Does this room look out on the street or the court?
La chambre ne me convient pas; faites-m'en voir une autre.	I do not like this room; show me another.
Je l'arrête.	I'll take it.
Je resterai quelques jours; quel est le prix de cette chambre par jour?	I shall stay a few days. What is the price of this room per day?
Le service compris?	Including tips?
C'est trop cher; pourrais-je en avoir une à meilleur marché?	That is too dear; couldn't I have one at a cheaper price?
Quel est le prix par jour pour la pension, la chambre et le service?	What is the charge for board, room and attendance per day?
La porte	The door
Cette porte ne ferme pas.	This door does not shut.
Où donne cette porte?	Where does this door lead to?
Cette porte communique avec le petit salon.	This door opens into the sitting-room.
La fenêtre La croisée (krwa ze)	The window
A une fenêtre; à deux fenêtres	With one window; with two windows.
Donnez-moi une chambre à deux fenêtres; les chambres à une fenêtre sont trop sombres.	Give me a room with two windows; the rooms with one window are too dark.
Le plancher (lə plɑ̃ ʃe)	The floor (of a room)
Le tapis (lə ta pi)	The carpet
Une descente de lit (yn dɛ sɑ̃:t)	A bedside carpet or rug
N'avez-vous pas de tapis sur le plancher?	Haven't you any carpets on the floor?

VOCABULAIRE	VOCABULARY
Nous‿avons seulement des descentes de lit.	We have only bedside rugs.
On trouve rarement des tapis couvrant‿entièrement le plancher en Belgique.	One rarely finds carpets covering the whole room in Belgium.
Le plafond (lə pla fɔ̃)	The ceiling

Le lit; les lits	The bed; the beds
Propre	Clean
Frais	Fresh
La couverture de laine	The blanket
Le traversin (tra vɛr sɛ̃)	The bolster
Un matelas (mat lɑ)	A mattress
Un sommier élastique	A spring-mattress
Un drap (de lit)	A sheet
Faites mettre des draps propres.	Have clean sheets put on.
Les draps de lit ne sont pas très propres.	The sheets are not very clean.
Cette couverture ne me suffit pas; donnez-m'en une autre.	This blanket is not enough for me; give me another one.
J'aime à avoir la tête haute; donnez-moi encore un‿oreiller. (ɔ rɛ je)	I like my head to be high; give me another pillow.
Dormir	To sleep
Vous‿êtes-vous bien reposé?	Did you rest well?
Ordinairement je dors très bien, mais la nuit dernière j'ai mal dormi.	I generally sleep very well, but last night I slept badly.
Faire le lit	To make the bed
Veuillez faire mon lit de suite.	Please make my bed at once.
Je suis très fatigué et je veux me retirer de suite.	I am very tired and wish to go to bed at once.
A quelle heure s'est-il couché?	At what time did he go to bed?
Il s'est couché à dix‿heures.	He went to bed at ten o'clock.
Je n'ai pas fermé l'œil de la nuit.	I have not slept a wink the whole night (I have not closed the eye during the night.)

VOCABULAIRE	VOCABULARY
Éveiller (e vɛ je)	To call[1]; to awaken
Éveillez-moi de bonne heure; je veux partir par le premier train.	Call me early; I want to leave by the first train.
Je veux faire la grasse matinée; que personne ne vienne me déranger demain matin.	I want to have a long night's rest; don't allow any one to disturb me to-morrow morning.
Qu'on ne me réveille pas‿avant neuf‿heures; je veux prendre une bonne nuit de repos. (nœ vœ:r)	I am not to be called before nine o'clock; I wish to have a good night's rest.

La Table	The Table
Le tapis de table	The table-cover
La chaise	The chair
La chaise à bascule	The rocking-chair
La garde-robe[2]	The wardrobe
Une armoire à glace	A wardrobe with mirrors
La commode	The chest of drawers
Une commode à trois tiroirs	A bureau with three drawers
Le miroir (mi rwa:r)	The mirror
Le sofa Le canapé	The sofa
La lampe[3] (lɑ̃:p)	The lamp
L'ampoule (lɑ̃ pu:l)	The bulb
La prise de courant (pri:z də ku rɑ̃)	The socket
Une lumière plus forte	A better (stronger) light
Un‿abat-jour[4]	A shade (for a lamp)

[1] To call, *appeler*, in phrases like these:

Comment cela s'appelle-t-il en français?	What do you call this in French?

But:

Voulez-vous venir me prendre?	Will you call for me?
Voulez-vous que j'aille vous prendre?	Shall I call for you?
Est-on venu le prendre?	Has it been called for?

[2] *Ma garde-robe*, my dresses, my clothes. [3] A street lamp, *un réverbère*.

[4] *L'ombre*, the shade, shadow.—*La nuance*, shade (of colors).

VOCABULAIRE	VOCABULARY
La cheminée	The chimney
La bougie (bu ʒi)	The candle
Le gaz (gɑ:z)	The gas
Allumer	To light
Éteindre (e tɛ̃:dr)	To put out
Ouvrez le robinet (rɔ bi nɛ)	Turn on (the gas).
Fermez le robinet.	Turn off (the gas).
Une allumette	A match
Des‿allumettes[1]	Matches
Apportez-moi de l'eau fraîche à boire.	Bring me fresh water to drink.
Apportez-moi de l'eau fraîche pour la toilette.	Bring me fresh water to wash with.
Remplissez la carafe (le pot‿à eau).	Fill the water bottle (the pitcher).
Où est la sonnette?	Where is the bell?
A quelle heure dîne-t-on à la table d'hôte?	At what hour is the table d'hôte dinner?
Nettoyez ces‿habits, garçon.	Clean these clothes, boy.
Mes‿habits et mes bottes sont mouillés; faites-les sécher. (mu je)	My clothes and boots are wet; please dry them.
Faites du feu (fø)	Light a fire.
Veuillez me procurer un commissionnaire parlant‿anglais, s'il est possible. (pɔ si bl)	Get me a messenger, one who speaks English, if possible.
Y a-t-il des lettres pour moi?	Are there any letters for me?
Est-on venu me demander?	Did anyone inquire for me?
Si l'on vient me demander, vous direz que je rentrerai à six‿heures.	If anyone asks for me, say that I shall be back at six o'clock.

VOCABULAIRE	VOCABULARY
Si l'on vient me demander, vous direz que je suis‿allé chez monsieur Quéry, où l'on me trouvera jusqu'à quatre heures.	If anyone inquires for me, say that I have gone to Mr. Quéry's, where I can be found till four o'clock.
Si le tailleur vient m'apporter mon‿habit, dites-lui de revenir demain matin.	If the tailor should bring me my coat, tell him to call again to-morrow morning.
S'il m'arrive des paquets, faites-es mettre dans ma chambre s'il vous plaît.	If any packages should come for me, have them put into my room, please.
Pourrais-je écrire quelques mots au bureau?	Could I write a few lines in the office?
Donnez-moi, s'il vous plaît, tout ce qu'il faut pour⁀écrire.	Please give me some writing material.
Je partirai demain par le train de six heures, gare de l'est. Pourrai-je prendre l'omnibus de l'hôtel?	I start to-morrow by the six o'clock train, East Station. Shall I be able to take the hotel omnibus?
Faites-moi appeler à temps.	Have me called in time.
Commandez-moi un taxi et faites descendre mes‿effets.	Get me a taxi in good time and have my baggage brought down.
Dites qu'on fasse ma note.	Have my bill made out.
Donnez-moi la note, je vous prie.	Please give me my bill.
Je n'ai pas‿eu cela.	I have not had this.
C'est déjà payé.	That has already been paid.
Je trouve ce prix trop‿élevé.	I find this charge too high.
Réveillez-moi demain matin à cinq‿heures; frappez vigoureusement à ma porte. (vi gu røz mɑ̃)	Call me at five to-morrow; knock loudly at my door.
Je serais désolé de manquer le train.	I should be sorry to miss the train.

VOCABULAIRE	VOCABULARY
Les‿habits (le za bi)	**Dress**
Le vêtement (vɛt mɑ̃)	The suit
Un complet (kɔ̃ plɛ)	A suit, a complete suit of clothes.
Le pardessus Le paletot	The overcoat
Un pardessus d'été	A summer overcoat
Un pardessus d'hiver	A winter overcoat
Un‿habit	A coat; a dress-coat
Un smoking	A tuxedo, evening jacket
La jaquette	The cut-away
Un gilet (ʒi lɛ)	A vest
Le gilet blanc	The white vest
Un pantalon Une paire de pantalons	Trousers
Les bretelles (brə tɛl)	Suspenders
La poche	The pocket
Le mouchoir (mu ʃwa:r)	The handkerchief
Le bouton (bu tɔ̃)	The button
Il manque‿un bouton.	A button is off here.
Faites-moi, je vous prie, mettre‿un bouton, mais bien solidement.	Please have a button put on, but strongly.
Boutonnez votre pardessus.	Button your overcoat.
Déboutonnez votre smoking.	Unbutton your tuxedo.
La boutonnière	The buttonhole
La boutonnière‿est déchirée; je vous prie de la refaire.	The buttonhole is torn; please mend it.
Le tire-bouton (tir bu tɔ̃)	The button-hook
La chemise (ʃmi:z)	The shirt
La chemise de nuit	The night-shirt
Changer de chemise	To put on a clean shirt
Le devant de chemise Le plastron	The shirt front
Le col	The (shirt) collar

VOCABULAIRE	**VOCABULARY**
Le faux-col	The collar (to button on)
Un col montant (or droit)	A stand-up collar
Un col rabattu	A turn-down collar
Les manchettes (mɑ̃ ʃɛt)	The cuffs
La cravate	The necktie
Lier; attacher (lje)	To tie
Faire un nœud (nø)	To tie a knot
Le gilet de flanelle	The flannel waistcoat
Les caleçons (kal sɔ̃)	The drawers
Les souliers	The shoes
Une paire de souliers	A pair of shoes
Une paire de bottes	A pair of boots
Des bottines	High shoes
Prenez-moi la mesure d'une paire de bottes.	Measure me for a pair of boots.
Les pantoufles	The slippers
La robe	The dress
Le peignoir	The dressing gown
Le jupon (ʒy pɔ̃)	The petticoat
Le linge (lɛ̃:ʒ)	The linen
Les gants	The gloves
Une paire de gants	A pair of gloves
Des gants de chevreau Des gants de peau	Kid-gloves
Le manteau (mɑ̃ to)	The cloak
La pelisse Le manteau de fourrure	The fur-cloak
Le manchon (mɑ̃ ʃɔ̃)	The muff

Chez‿un Tailleur	**At a Tailor's**
Pouvez-vous me recommander un bon tailleur?	Can you recommend me a good tailor?
Travaille-t-il bien?	Is his workmanship good?
Faites-moi voir vos‿échantillons. (vo zɛ ʃɑ̃ ti jɔ̃)	Show me your samples.

VOCABULAIRE	VOCABULARY
Je voudrais‿un pardessus.	I want an overcoat.
Prenez mes mesures pour‿un costume.	Measure me for a suit.
A la dernière mode	In the latest fashion
Pas trop serré	Not too tight
Pas trop large	Not too loose
Un peu plus long	A little longer
Pas tout‿à fait si long	Not quite so long
Avec‿un rang de boutons	Single breasted
Avec deux rangs de boutons	Double breasted
La doublure	The lining
Quand pouvez-vous me livrer ce pardessus?	When can I have this overcoat?
Pas‿avant?	Not before?
Je ne peux pas‿attendre‿aussi longtemps; il me le faut pour mardi.	I can not wait so long; I must have it by Tuesday.
Envoyez-le-moi contre remboursement.	Send it to me C. O. D.
Pouvez-vous me recommander une maison de confection près d'ici?	Can you recommend me a clothing store near here?
Montrez-moi un vêtement foncé (clair).	Show me a dark (light) colored garment.
Comment me va-t-il?	How does it fit?
Me va-t-il bien?	Does it fit well?
Il me serre trop la taille.	It is too tight around the waist.
Il me gêne sous les bras.	It is too tight under the arms.
Les manches ne sont‿elles pas trop grandes?	Are not the sleeves too large?
J'aime les pantalons collants.	I like my trousers to be close fitting.
Est-ce que vous vous chargez‿aussi de réparations?	Do you also undertake repairs?

VOCABULAIRE	VOCABULARY
Le pantalon est‿usé en bas; rentrez-le un peu.	The trousers are worn at the bottom; turn them in a little.
Rebordez mon pardessus et changez les boutons.	Re-hem my overcoat and put on new buttons.
Faites partir ces taches-là.	Remove those stains.

Une Couturière	A Dressmaker
Un tailleur pour dames	A ladies' tailor
Je voudrais me faire faire une robe.	I wish to have a dress made.
Montrez-moi des‿échantillons.	Show me some samples.
Faites-moi voir des gravures de mode. (gra vy:r)	Let me see some fashion-plates.
Faites-moi la robe sur ce modèle.	Make the dress from this design.
Prenez-moi mesure.	Take my measure.
Le devant	The front
Le derrière	The back
Le haut	The top
Le bas	The bottom
Le corps	The body
La jupe	The skirt
Je fournirai l'étoffe.	I shall supply my own materials.
Combien me faut‿il de mètres?	How many meters (yards) will it take?
A combien me reviendrait la robe, tout compris?	What would this dress cost inclusive of everything?
Cette coupe est‿elle encore à la mode?	Is this pattern still fashionable?
Je désire la robe courte (longue).	I wish to have a short (a long) dress.
Je ne la voudrais pas trop collante; j'aime à être très‿à l'aise.	I do not want it to fit too tightly; I like to feel very comfortable.
Une garniture (gar ni ty:r)	A trimming
Vous mettrez‿une garniture de passementerie.	Trim the dress with lace-work.

VOCABULAIRE	VOCABULARY
Une robe montante	A high-necked dress
Une robe décolletée	A low-necked dress
Montrez-moi des‿échantillons de rubans.	Show me some samples of ribbons
Mettez-moi sur ce manteau des boutons d'ivoire. (di vwa:r)	Put ivory-buttons on this cloak.
Je voudrais‿avoir ma robe pour samedi matin.	I should like to have my dress on Saturday morning.
Quand faudra-t‿il venir l'essayer?	When shall I call to try it on?
Me prend‿elle bien la taille?	Does it fit well in the waist?
Le corsage (kɔr sa:ʒ)	The waist
Veuillez‿essayer le corsage.	Please try on the waist.
Ce corsage vous va très bien.	This waist fits you very well.
Retoucher	To change, to alter
Retouchez ce corsage; il ne va pas.	Alter this waist; it doesn't fit.
L'épaule	The shoulder
La robe va mal‿aux‿épaules; veuillez la retoucher.	The dress fits badly in the shoulders; please alter it.
Les manches sont trop‿étroites (trop larges; trop longues; trop courtes).	The sleeves are too narrow (too wide; too long; too short).
Faire des plis (pli)	To wrinkle
La manche fait des pl s là; veuillez la retoucher.	The sleeve wrinkles right there; change it please.
Le col‿est trop bas.	The collar is too low.
Le col n'est pas‿assez haut.	The collar is not high enough.
Quand ma robe sera-t‿elle finie?	When will my dress be done?
Votre robe sera finie demain sans faute.	Your dress will be done to-morrow without fail.

La Toilette	Dressing
S'habiller (sa bi je) Faire sa toilette	To dress
Il s'habille.	He is dressing.
N'êtes-vous pas‿encore habillé?	Aren't you dressed yet?
N'êtes-vous pas‿encore prêt?	Aren't you ready yet?

VOCABULAIRE	VOCABULARY
Elle change de robe.	She is changing her dress.
Il se déshabille.	He is undressing.
Le goût (gu)	The taste
Elle s'habille avec beaucoup de goût.	She dresses with a great deal of taste.
Ce chapeau vous va très bien.	This bonnet is very becoming to you.
Croyez-vous que ce chapeau me va?	Do you think this hat is becoming to me?
Je trouve qu'il vous va très bien.	I think it very becoming to you.
La couleur (ku lœ:r)	The color
Cette couleur ne me va pas.	This color is not becoming to me.
La figure (fi gy:r)	The face
Le teint (tɛ̃)	The complexion
Délicat (de li kɑ)	Delicate
Rosé (ro ze)	Rosy
Elle a un teint délicat et rosé; elle ne peut pas porter une couleur aussi criarde (aussi voyante).	She has a delicate, rosy complexion; she cannot wear such a loud color.
Cette couleur est trop criarde; voici la bonne couleur.	This color is too loud; this is the right one.

Laver	To Wash
Je voudrais me laver les mains.	I should like to wash my hands.
Je voudrais faire ma toilette.	I should like a wash and brush-up.
Apportez-moi de l'eau, du savon et des serviettes.	Bring me some water, soap and towels.
Y a-t-il de l'eau dans ma chambre?	Is there any water in my room?
Il faut d'abord que je me lave.	First of all I must have a wash.
Le lavabo La cuvette	The wash-basin
Le pot à eau	The pitcher
Un morceau de savon	A cake of soap
L'éponge (le pɔ̃:ʒ)	The sponge
La serviette	The towel
Essuyer (ɛ sɥi je)	To dry; to wipe

VOCABULAIRE	VOCABULARY
Je m'essuie les mains.	I am drying my hands.
Essuyez vos mains avec cette serviette.	Dry your hands with this towel.
Se rincer la bouche (rɛ̃ se)	To rinse one's mouth
Je me rince la bouche.	I am rinsing my mouth.
La dent; les dents	The tooth; the teeth
La brosse à dents	The tooth-brush
Je me brosse les dents.	I am brushing my teeth.
La brosse à cheveux	The hair-brush
La brosse à ongles	The nail-brush
Il se brosse les cheveux.	He is brushing his hair.
Le peigne	The comb
Je me peigne.	I am combing my hair.
La raie	The parting
La raie est droite.	The parting is straight.
La raie est de travers.	The parting is crooked.
L'huile	The oil
La pommade	The ointment
La lime (li:m)	The file
Je lime mes‿ongles.	I am filing my nails.
La poudre	The powder
La poudre de riz	Toilet-powder
La poudre dentifrice (dɑ̃ ti fris)	Tooth-powder
La boîte à poudre	The powder-box
La houppe à poudre La houpette	The powder puff
Elle s'est poudré la figure.	She powdered her face.
Se baigner	To bathe
Prendre un bain.	To take a bath
Il se baigne; il prend‿un bain.	He is bathing; he takes a bath.
Se raser	To shave
Je me rase toujours moi-même.	I always shave myself.

Le Coiffeur (kwa fœ:r)	**The Barber**
Je voudrais me faire faire la barbe.	I wish to be shaved.

VOCABULAIRE	VOCABULARY
Faites-moi la barbe, s'il vous plaît.	Please shave me.
Rasez-moi toute la barbe.	Take off the whole of my beard.
Vous me laisserez seulement la moustache.	Leave the moustache only.
Les favoris	The side whiskers
La barbe	The beard (full beard)
Rasez-moi le menton. (mɑ̃ tɔ̃)	Shave the chin.
La peau sensible (sɑ̃ sibl)	Sensitive skin
Ma barbe est très raide; savonnez-la davantage. (da vɑ̃ ta:ʒ)	My beard is very stubborn, lather it more thoroughly.
Votre rasoir n'est pas‿assez tranchant. (trɑ̃ ʃɑ̃)	Your razor is not sharp enough.
Je voudrais me faire tailler les cheveux.	I wish to have my hair cut.
Court par derrière, un peu plus long sur le devant.	Short behind, a little longer in front.
Rafraîchissez seulement, mes cheveux tombent.	Take off only a little, I am losing my hair.
Je grisonne. (gri zɔn)	I am getting gray.
Donnez-moi un coup de peigne,[1] je vous prie.	Dress my hair, please.
Faites-moi la raie au milieu (sur le côté).	Part my hair in the middle (on the side).
Donnez-moi un coup de fer.	Curl my hair.
Donnez-moi un coup de brosse.	Brush my hair.
Les ciseaux (si zo)	The scissors

[1] Veuillez-donner un coup de fer à ce chapeau. Please iron this hat.

Le coup means literally the stroke, blow, knock, and is used very frequently in French. Thus we say:

Un coup de peigne, s'il vous plaît.	Please comb my hair.
Un coup de brosse, s'il vous plaît.	Please brush my hair.
Un coup de fer, s'il vous plaît.	Please curl my hair.
Donnez‿un coup de balai à cette chambre.	Please sweep the room.

VOCABULAIRE	VOCABULARY
Du linge blanc (propre)	**Clean Linen**
Du linge sale	Soiled linen
Faites porter ce linge chez la blanchisseuse. (blɑ̃ ʃi sø:z)	Send these clothes to the laundress.
La note y est.	The laundry list is there.
Quand pouvez-vous me le rendre?	When can you send it back?
Il me faut le linge pour jeudi.	I must have the laundry by Thursday.
N'oubliez pas de raccommoder les chemises.	Do not forget to mend the shirts.
L'amidon (la mi dɔ̃)	The starch
Amidonner (a mi dɔ ne)	To starch
Repasser; donner un coup de fer	To iron; to press
Ne repassez pas mes cols aussi raides (rɛ:d)	Do not ron my collars so stiff.
Articles de Parure (ar ti klə dpa ry:r)	**Articles of Ornament**
Des bijoux	Jewels
Des diamants (dja mɑ̃)	Diamonds
La perle; les perles	The pearl; the pearls
La bague (bag)	The ring
La bague de diamants	The diamond ring
Les boucles d'oreille	The ear-rings
Le bracelet (bras lɛ)	The bracelet
Le collier (kɔl je)	The necklace
La montre	The watch
La chaîne de montre	The watch-chain
Les boutons de chemise	The studs
Les boutons de manchettes	The cuff-buttons
Les lunettes (ly nɛt)	The spectacles
Le lorgnon (lɔr ɲɔ̃)	The eye-glass
Myope (mjɔp)	Near-sighted
Presbyte	Far-sighted
La lorgnette (de spectacle)	The opera-glass
La canne	The cane

VOCABULAIRE	VOCABULARY
L'ombrelle L'en-tout-cas	The parasol
Le parapluie	The umbrella
L'éventail (le vɑ̃ tɑ:j)	The fan

Le Temps / The Time

Le Temps	The Time
L'heure	The time; the hour
La mesure (lam zy:r)	The time; the measure
Battre la mesure	To beat time
Aller en mesure	To keep time
Perdre la mesure	To get out of time
Trois fois	Three times
Une autre fois	Another time
Alors	At that time
Aujourd'hui	At the present time
En même temps	At the same time
Pendant longtemps	For a long time
Il y a longtemps que je ne vous‿ai vu.	I have not seen you for a long time.
On peut faire cela en‿un rien de temps.	This can be done in no time.
De bonne heure; à temps	In good time
De mon temps	In my time
Pour quelque temps	For some time
De temps‿en temps	From time to time
Venir⁀à propos	To come at the right time
Cela vient fort‿à propos.	That comes just at the right time.
Arriverons-nous à temps?	Shall we be in time?
A quelle heure le train part-il pour⁀Orléans?	At what time does the train start for Orleans?
Combien de temps nous reste-t-il jusqu'au départ?	How much time have we before the train starts?
Sommes-nous à temps pour le train?	Are we in time for the train?
Où aurons-nous le temps de manger quelque chose?	Where shall we have time to eat something?

VOCABULAIRE	VOCABULARY
En‿aurons-nous le temps?	Have we time for it?
Avez-vous le temps de m'accompagner?	Have you time to accompany me?
Je n'ai pas le temps.	I have not the time.
Donnez-vous le temps.	Take your time.

L'Heure	The time; the hour; o'clock
Quelle heure avons-nous? Quelle heure est-il?	What is the time? What time is it?
Pourriez-vous me dire l'heure qu'il est?	Could you tell me the time?
Il est une heure et demie.	It is half-past one.
Vers les cinq‿heures	Towards five o'clock
Il n'est pas loin de quatre heures.	It is nearly four o'clock.
Il est quatre heures moins trois.	It is three minutes to four.
Six‿heures vont sonner. Il va être six‿heures.	It is about to strike six o'clock.
Six‿heures viennent de sonner.	It has just struck six.
La demie sonne.	The half hour is striking.
A sept heures précises A sept heures sonnantes	Punctually at seven
De huit heures du matin jusqu'à trois‿heures du soir	From 8 A.M. to 3 P.M.

La Division du Temps	Division of Time
Aujourd'hui	To-day
Demain	To-morrow
Après-demain	The day after to-morrow
Hier	Yesterday
Avant-hier	Day before yesterday
Ce matin	This morning
Demain matin	To-morrow morning
Demain à midi	To-morrow noon
Demain soir	To-morrow night
Hier soir	Last night
La veille	The day (night) before

VOCABULAIRE	VOCABULARY
Le lendemain	The day after
Cette semaine	This week
La semaine prochaine	Next week
La semaine passée	Last week
Huit jours	Eight days, a week
Après huit jours	After a week
Pendant huit jours	During a week
Pour huit jours	For a week
Dans huit jours	In a week
Plus de huit jours	More than a week
Demain en huit	To-morrow week
Dans la huitaine	In the week
Il y a huit jours	A week ago
Il y a eu hier huit jours	A week ago yesterday
Quinze jours Une quinzaine	A fortnight

Les Mois	The Months
Janvier (ʒɑ̃ vje)	January
Février (fe vri je)	February
Mars (mars)	March
Avril (a vr l)	April
Mai (me)	May
Juin (ʒɥɛ̃)	June
Juillet (ʒɥi jɛ)	July
Août (u)	August
Septembre (sɛp tɑ̃:br)	September
Octobre (ɔk tɔbr)	October
Novembre (nɔ vɑ̃:br)	November
Décembre (de sɑ̃:br)	December
Le premier décembre	On the first of December
Le trois janvier	On January third
Au commencement de mai Les premiers jours du mois de mai	At the beginning of May
A la fin de mai (fɛ̃)	The last of May
Ce mois de juin-ci	This June
Au mois de juin prochain	Next June

VOCABULAIRE	VOCABULARY
Au mois de juin dernier	Last June
Ce mois-ci	This month
Le mois prochain	Next month
Le mois dernier	Last month
Le premier du mois courant (ku rɑ̃)	The first inst.
A la fin du mois	At the end of this month
Trois mois Un trimestre	A quarter of a year
Six mois Un semestre	Half a year
Neuf mois	Three quarters of a year
Un‿an	A year
En dix-huit cent quatre-vingt-treize	In 1893
Le jour le plus long	The longest day
Le jour le plus court	The shortest day

Fêtes de l'Église	Religious Holidays
La Toussaint (tu sɛ̃)	All Saints' Day
La Fête des Morts	A'l Souls' Day
Le Mercredi des Cendres (sɑ̃:dr)	Ash Wednesday
Noël	Christmas
Pâques	Easter
Le Vendredi Saint	Good Friday
Le Carême	Lent
La Mi-Carême	Mid-Lent
Le Jour de l'An	New Year's Day
Le Dimanche des Rameaux	Palm Sunday
La Semaine Sainte	Holy Week
Le Mardi Gras	Shrove Tuesday
La Pentecôte	Whitsuntide

Le Médecin	The Physician
Je suis souffrant; faites venir‿un médecin.	I am not well, send for a doctor.
Voulez-vous que j'aille chercher un médecin?	Shall I go for a doctor?

VOCABULAIRE	VOCABULARY
Quel médecin me recommandez-vous?	What physician do you recommend to me?
Y a-t-il ici un médecin anglais?	Does an English physician live here?
Quels sont ses honoraires pour une consultation (pour une visite)?	What are his charges for a consultation (for a visit)?
Quelles sont les heures du docteur?	What are his office-hours?
Faudra-t-il attendre longtemps?	Shall I have long to wait?
Je souffre de.	I suffer from. . . . . .
J'ai la fièvre.	I feel feverish.
J'ai des chaleurs et des frissons.	I feel hot and cold.
Je ne sais pas trop ce que j'ai.	I don't exactly know what is the matter with me.
J'éprouve un malaise général.	I feel altogether uncomfortable.
J'ai mal à la tête (aux dents, à la gorge, à la poitrine, au ventre).	I have a head-ache (toothache, pain in the throat, in the chest, stomach-ache).
J'ai mal au cœur.	I feel sick. (Of nausea *only*).
Le pied me fait mal.	I have a pain in the foot.
Le bras me fait mal.	My arm pains me.
J'ai le foie malade.	I am suffering from my liver.
J'ai de la difficulté à respirer. J'ai peine à reprendre haleine.	I experience difficulty in breathing.
Je n'ai pas dormi de la nuit.	I have not slept all night long.
Je passe bien des nuits blanches.	I pass many sleepless nights.
Je crois que j'ai un embarras gastrique.	I think my stomach is out of order.
Je n'ai pas d'appétit.	I have no appetite at all.
Pouvez-vous me donner un remède contre . . . ?	Can you prescribe for me for . . . ?
Combien de fois par jour dois-je prendre ce remède?	How many times a day must I take this medicine?
Dois-je me mettre à la diète?	Have I to diet myself?
Que puis-je manger (boire)?	What may I eat (drink)?
Puis-je fumer?	Am I allowed to smoke?
J'ai été blessé dans une chute.	I have been injured through a fall.

VOCABULAIRE	VOCABULARY
Je me suis cassé le bras.	I broke my arm.
Je me suis foulé le pied. (fu le)	I have sprained my ankle.
Je me sens‿un peu mieux.	I feel a little better.
Je ne me sens pas‿encore mieux.	I don't feel any better yet.
Je suis‿enrhumé. (ã ry me)	I have a cold.
Je me suis‿enrhumé.	I took a cold.
J'ai attrapé un rhume.	I caught cold.
Vous‿allez vous‿enrhumer.	You are going to take cold.
Je me suis brûlé.	I burnt myself.
J'ai la figure enflée.	My face is swollen.
Est-ce qu'il y a quelque chose de sérieux à ma maladie?	Is my sickness serious?
Je puis vous‿assurer que cela ne sera rien.	Assuredly no.
Vous prendrez ces poudres.	You will take these powders.
Combien faudra-t-il en prendre par jour?	How many have I to take a day?
Prenez‿en trois.	Three.
Dites-moi, je vous prie, combien je vous dois.	Please tell me how much I owe you.

PART TEN

CONTENTS

The Verb

1. The conjugation of verbs in French, as in English, is made up of simple and compound forms.

2. The simple forms are expressed by a single word, as: J'ai, I have; je parle, I speak; je vendais, I sold, etc.

3. Simple tenses are made up of the stem and the termination, as **parl**-er, **fin**-ir, **vend**-re, **rec**-evoir. Parl-, fin-, vend-, rec- are stems, and, in regular verbs, remain always unchanged.

Er, ir, re and evoir are endings and vary to indicate various tenses and persons. As: Parl-er, **to speak**; je parl-e, **I speak**; nous parl-ons, **we speak**; nous parl-ions, **we spoke, we were speaking**; nous parl-erons, **we shall speak.**

4. Compound tenses are made up of one of the auxiliaries **avoir** and **être,** coupled with the past participle of the verb conjugated, as: J'ai parlé, **I have spoken**; j'ai fini, **I have finished**; j'aurais vendu, **I would have sold**; il avait reçu, **he had received.**

5. The auxiliary is usually **avoir, to have.** Verbs which are conjugated with **être, to be,** are given later.

Complete Conjugation of Avoir, To Have

The four forms are given: **affirmative, interrogative, negative** and **negative-interrogative.**

To have, **avoir**; having, **ayant**; had, **eu, eue, eus, eues**; to have had, **avoir eu**; having had, **ayant‿eu.**

Indicatif Présent

J'ai, I have	ai-je? have I?
tu as, thou hast	as-tu? hast thou?
il‿a, he has	a-t-il? has he?
nous‿avons, we have	avons-nous? have we?
vous‿avez, you have	avez-vous? have you?
ils‿ont, they have	ont-ils? have they?

NOTE.—Throughout these tables the pronouns of the third person may be changed. Instead of *il a*, he has, and *ils ont*, they have (*m.*), the pupil may recite *elle a*, she has, or *on a*, one has, and *elles ont*, they have (*f.*).

je n'ai pas, I have not	n'ai-je pas, have I not?
tu n'as pas etc.	n'as-tu pas? etc.
il n'a pas	n'a-t-il pas?
nous n'avons pas	n'avons-nous pas?
vous n'avez pas	n'avez-vous pas?
ils n'ont pas	n'ont-ils pas?

Imparfait

j'avais, I had	avais-je? had I?
tu avais etc.	avais-tu? etc.
il‿avait	avait-il?
nous avions	avions-nous?
vous aviez	aviez-vous?
ils‿avaient	avaient-ils?

je n'avais pas, I had not	n'avais-je pas? had I not?
tu n'avais pas etc.	n'avais-tu pas? etc.
il n'avait pas	n'avait-il pas?
nous n'avions pas	n'avions-nous pas?
vous n'aviez pas	n'aviez-vous pas?
ils n'avaient pas	n'avaient-ils pas?

Prétérit ou Passé Défini

j'eus, I had	eus-je? had I?
tu eus, etc.	eus-tu? etc.
il‿eut	eut-il?
nous‿eûmes	eûmes-nous?
vous‿eûtes	eûtes-vous?
ils‿eurent	eurent-ils?

je n'eus pas, I had not	n'eus-je pas? had I not?
tu n'eus pas, etc.	n'eus-tu pas? etc.
il n'eut pas	n'eut-il pas?
nous n'eûmes pas	n'eûmes-nous pas?
vous n'eûtes pas	n'eûtes-vous pas?
ils n'eurent pas	n'eurent-ils pas?

Passé Indéfini

j'ai eu, I have had, etc.	ai-je eu? have I had, etc.?
je n'ai pas‿eu, I have not had	n'ai-je pas‿eu? have I not had?

Plus-que-Parfait

j'avais‿eu, I had had, etc.	avais-je eu? had I had, etc.
je n'avais pas‿eu, I had not had	n'avais-je pas‿eu? had I not had?

Passé Antérieur

j'eus‿eu, I had had, etc.
je n'eus pas‿eu, I had not had

eus-je⁀eu? had I had? etc.
n'eus-je pas‿eu? had I not had?

Futur

j'aurai, I shall have
tu auras, etc.
il⁀aura
nous‿aurons
vous‿aurez
ils‿auront

aurai-je? shall I have?
auras-tu? etc.
aura-t‿il?
aurons-nous?
aurez-vous?
auront‿ils?

je n'aurai pas, I shall not have
tu n'auras pas, etc.
il n'aura pas
nous n'aurons pas
vous n'aurez pas
ils n'auront pas

n'aurai-je pas? shall I not have?
n'auras-tu pas? etc.
n'aura-t‿il pas?
n'aurons-nous pas?
n'aurez-vous pas?
n'auront‿ils pas?

Futur Antérieur

j'aurai eu, I shall have had, etc.
je n'aurai pas‿eu, etc., I shall not have had

aurai-je⁀eu, shall I have had, etc.
n'aurai-je pas‿eu? etc., shall I not have had?

Conditionnel Présent

j'aurais, I should have
tu aurais, etc.
il⁀aurait
nous‿aurions
vous‿auriez
ils‿auraient

aurais-je? should I have?
aurais-tu? etc.
aurait‿il?
aurions-nous?
auriez-vous?
auraient‿ils?

je n'aurais pas, I should not have
tu n'aurais pas, etc.
il n'aurait pas
nous n'aurions pas
vous n'auriez pas
ils n'auraient pas

n'aurais-je pas? should I not have?
n'aurais-tu pas? etc.
n'aurait‿il pas?
n'aurions-nous pas?
n'auriez-vous pas?
n'auraient‿ils pas?

Conditionnel Passé

j'aurais‿eu, I should have hade tc.	aurais-je‿eu? should I have had? etc.
je n'aurais pas‿eu, I should not have had etc.	n'aurais-je pas‿eu? Should I not have had? etc.

Impératif

aie, have (thou)	n'aie pas, do not have
ayons, let us have	n'ayons pas, do not let us have
ayez, have (you)	n'ayez pas, do not have

Subjonctif Présent

que j'aie, that I may have, etc.	que je n'aie pas, that I may not have, etc.
que tu aies	que tu n'aies pas
qu'il‿ait	qu'il n'ait pas
que nous‿ayons	que nous n'ayons pas
que vous‿ayez	que vous n'ayez pas
qu'ils‿aient	qu'ils n'aient pas

Imparfait

que j'eusse, that I might have	que je n'eusse pas, that I might not have
que tu eusses etc.	que tu n'eusses pas, etc.
qu'il‿eût	qu'il n'eût pas
que nous‿eussions	que nous n'eussions pas
que vous‿eussiez	que vous n'eussiez pas
qu'ils‿eussent	qu'ils n'eussent pas

Passé

que j'aie eu, that I may have had, etc.

Plus-que-parfait

que j'eusse eu, that I might have had, etc.

Idiomatic Uses of Avoir; To Have

1. **Avoir** is used idiomatically in the following connections:

Avoir besoin (de)	To need, to be in need of
" chaud	To be warm
" froid	" cold
" faim	" hungry
" soif	" thirsty
" sommeil	" sleepy
" peur (de)	" afraid (of)
" honte (de)	" ashamed (of)
" raison (de)	" right (in)
" tort (de)	" wrong (in)
" cours	" current
" coutume (de)	" accustomed (to)
" dessein (de)	To intend to
" envie (de)	To have a desire (to)
" lieu (de)	" cause (of)
" lieu	To happen
" mal	To have a pain
" bonne mine	To look well
" peine (à)	To have difficulty (in)
" pitié	To take pity
" soin	To take care
" sujet (de)	To have occasion (for)

2. The following expressions relating to one's **feelings, age, stature** and to **dimensions generally** are given with **avoir.**

a. Qu'avez-vous?	What is the matter with you? What ails you?
Avez-vous quelque chose?	Is anything the matter with you?
Je n'ai rien.	Nothing is the matter with me.
Qu'a votre frère?	What is the matter with your brother?
Je ne sais ce qu'il **a.**	I don't know what ails him.

In the absence of a personal subject, the impersonal verb **il y a** is used; as:

Qu'y a-t-il?	What is the matter?
Il n'y a rien.	Nothing is the matter.

b. J'ai faim et soif.	I am hungry and thirsty.
Il⁀a froid, chaud.	He is cold, warm.
Nous‿avons sommeil.	We are sleepy.
J'ai honte de le dire.	I am shamed to say so.
Vous‿avez raison.	You are right.
Ils‿ont tort.	They are wrong.
c. Quel⁀âge a-t-il?	How old is he?
Il⁀a vingt ans.	He is twenty years old.
Quelle⁀est sa taille?	What is his size?
Il⁀a cinq pieds, six pouces.	He is five feet six inches tall.

The expressions *He is twenty years old, He is five feet six inches tall,* may be rendered by the verb *être* and an adjective: *Il⁀est‿âgé de vingt ans, Il⁀est haut de cinq pieds, six pouces;* but the construction with *avoir* is preferable.

The verb **être** is used with an adjective in sentences like the following, expressing comparison:

Il⁀est plus‿âgé que moi.	He is older than I.
Il⁀est moins grand que moi.	He is not as tall as I.

d. When the difference between the two terms of a comparison is to be stated, either construction may be used.

With *avoir*, the term expressing the difference is the object of the verb; it is followed by the preposition *de* and a comparative adverb (*plus* or *moins*), expressing excess or deficiency.

Il⁀a deux ans de plus que moi.	He is two years older than I.
Il⁀a deux pouces de moins que moi.	He is two inches shorter than I.

With the verb *être* and an adjective, the adjective is in the comparative degree, and the term expressing the difference, preceded by the preposition *de*, follows the second term of the comparison:

Il⁀est plus‿âgé que moi de deux ans.	He is two years older than I.
Il⁀est moins grand que moi de deux pouces.	He is two inches shorter than I.

Dimensions

Dimensions may be stated in various ways:

1. By using the verb **avoir** with a noun[1] expressing dimension; as:

[1] Nouns expressing dimension are formed from adjectives of dimension, by adding *ur* to their feminine endings; as *haut, haute, hauteur, long, longue longueur,* etc. They are of the feminine gender.

Combien ce clocher a-t-il de hauteur?	How high is that steeple?
Ce clocher a deux cents pieds de hauteur (or de haut).	That steeple is two hundred feet high.

2. It can also be expressed:

Quelle est la hauteur de ce clocher?	What is the height of that steeple?
La hauteur de ce clocher est de deux cents pieds, or	The height of that steeple is two hundred feet.
Ce clocher est haut de deux cents pieds.	That steeple is two hundred feet high.
La façade de l'église est de deux cents pieds.	The front of the church is two hundred feet long?
Quelle est la grandeur de cette chambre?	What is the size[2] of this room?
Elle a seize pieds de longueur sur quinze de largeur.	It is sixteen feet long by fifteen wide.
Quelle est l'étendue de ce parc?	What is the size[2] of that park?
Il a trois milles de circonférence.	It is three miles in circumference.

3. When the dimension of a thing is stated without a verb, either the noun or the adjective may be used; as:

Une table longue de trois pieds; or, *Une table de trois pieds de longueur,* or, *de long.*	A table three feet long.

Note: Either form is correct; but the adjectives *épais,* thick, and *profond'* deep, are not used in such sentences. Thickness and depth are expressed by the nouns *épaisseur* and *profondeur.*

Complete Conjugation of Être — To be

To be, **être;** being, **étant;** been, **été;** to have been, **avoir été;** having been, **ayant‿été.**

---

[2] The word *size* is variously expressed, according to the adjective which the object requires: Une grande maison; la grandeur de la maison, *the size of the house.* Une grosse pierre; la grosseur de la pierre, *the size of the stone.* In speaking of a person, either taille or stature is used. Il est de petite taille, or de petite stature, he is of a small size. Taille means *cut, shape,* from tailler, *to cut, to shape.*

Indicatif Présent

je suis, I am	suis-je? am I?
tu es, thou art	es-tu? art thou?
il⁀est, he is	est-il? is he?
nous sommes, we are	sommes-nous? are we?
vous‿êtes, you are	êtes-vous? are you?
ils sont, they are	sont-ils? are they?
je ne suis pas, I am not	ne suis-je pas? am I not?
tu n'es pas, etc.	n'es-tu pas? etc.
il n'est pas	n'est-il pas?
nous ne sommes pas	ne sommes-nous pas?
vous n'êtes pas	n'êtes-vous pas?
ils ne sont pas	ne sont-ils pas?

Imparfait

j'étais, I was	étais-je? was I?
tu étais, etc.	étais-tu? etc.
il⁀était	était-il?
nous‿étions	étions-nous?
vous‿étiez	étiez-vous?
ils‿étaient	étaient-ils?
Je n'étais pas, I was not	n'étais-je pas? was I not?
tu n'étais pas, etc.	n'étais-tu pas? etc.
il n'était pas	n'était-il pas?
nous n'étions pas	n'étions-nous pas?
vous n'étiez pas	n'étiez-vous pas?
ils n'étaient pas	n'étaient-ils pas?

Prétérit ou Passé Défini

je fus, I was	fus-je? was I?
tu fus, etc.	fus-tu? etc.
il fut	fut-il?
nous fûmes	fûmes-nous?
vous fûtes	fûtes-vous?
ils furent	furent-ils?
je ne fus pas, I was not	ne fus-je pas? was I not?
tu ne fus pas, etc.	ne fus-tu pas? etc.
il ne fut pas	ne fut-il pas?
nous ne fûmes pas	ne fûmes-nous pas?
vous ne fûtes pas	ne fûtes-vous pas?
ils ne furent pas	ne furent-ils pas?

Passé Indéfini

j'ai été, I have been, etc.	ai-je été? have I been? etc.
je n'ai pas‿été, I have not been, etc.	n'ai-je pas‿été? have I not been? etc.

Plus-que-Parfait — Passé Antérieur

j'avais‿été, I had been, etc.	avais-je été? had I been?
j'eus‿été	eus-je été?
je n'avais pas‿été, I had not been	n'avais-je pas‿été? had I not been
je n'eus pas‿été	n'eus-je pas‿été?

Futur

je serai, I shall be	serai-je? shall I be?
tu seras, etc.	seras-tu, etc.
il sera	sera-t-il?
nous serons	serons-nous?
vous serez	serez-vous?
ils seront	seront-ils?
je ne serai pas, I shall not be	ne serai-je pas? shall I not be?
tu ne seras pas, etc.	ne seras-tu pas? etc.
il ne sera pas	ne sera-t-il pas?
nous ne serons pas	ne serons-nous pas?
vous ne serez pas	ne serez-vous pas?
ils ne seront pas	ne seront-ils pas?

Futur Antérieur

j'aurai été, I shall have been	aurai-je été? shall I have been?
je n'aurai pas été, I shall not have been	n'aurai-je pas‿été? shall I not have been?

Conditionnel Présent

je serais, I should be	serais-je? should I be?
tu serais, etc.	serais-tu? etc.
il serait	serait-il?
nous serions	serions-nous?
vous seriez	seriez-vous?
ils seraient	seraient-ils?
je ne serais pas, I should not be	ne serais-je pas? should I not be?
tu ne serais pas, etc.	ne serais-tu pas? etc.
il ne serait pas	ne serait-il pas?
nous ne serions pas	ne serions-nous pas?
vous ne seriez pas	ne seriez-vous pas?
ils ne seraient pas	ne seraient-ils pas?

Conditionnel Passé

j'aurais été, I should have been
je n'aurais pas été, I should not have been

aurais-je été? should I have been?
n'aurais-je pas été? should I not have been?

Impératif

sois, be (thou)
soyons, let us be
soyez, be (you)

ne sois pas, do not be
ne soyons pas, do not let us be
ne soyez pas, do not be

Subjonctif Présent

que je sois, that I may be
que tu sois, etc.
qu'il soit
que nous soyons
que vous soyez
qu'ils soient

que je ne sois pas, that I may not be
que tu ne sois pas, etc.
qu'il ne soit pas
que nous ne soyons pas
que vous ne soyez pas
qu'ils ne soient pas

Imparfait

que je fusse, that I might be
que tu fusses, etc.
qu'il fût
que nous fussions
que vous fussiez
qu'ils fussent

que je ne fusse pas, that I might not be
que tu ne fusses pas, etc.
qu'il ne fût pas
que nous ne fussions pas
que vous ne fussiez pas
qu'ils ne fussent pas

Passé

que j'aie été, That I may have been, etc.

que je n'aie pas été, That I may not have been, etc.

Plus-que-Parfait

que j'eusse été, That I might have been, etc.

que je n'eusse pas été, That I might not have been, etc.

Use of the Auxiliary Verbs

The verbs **avoir** and **être** are auxiliary verbs when they are used in the formation of compound tenses.

Avoir is used in the compound tenses of:

1. All active verbs;
2. Most neuter verbs;
3. All essentially impersonal verbs.

Être is used in the compound tenses of:

1. Certain neuter verbs;
2. All pronominal verbs;
3. In the formation of the passive voice.

Neuter Verbs Conjugated with Être

1. Neuter verbs whose past tenses express a change in the place or condition of the subject are conjugated, in the compound tenses, with the auxiliary verb **être**: Nous sommes venus, vous‿êtes arrivé, elle⁀est partie, je suis né, ils sont morts.

Some neuter verbs, which come within the above definition, are conjugated with *avoir;* such as *courir, marcher, paraître, périr, succéder, succomber, voyager,* etc.: *Nous avons couru, vous‿avez marché, elle⁀a paru, ils‿ont péri, il⁀a succédé, ils‿ont succombé à la fatigue, nous‿avons voyagé,* etc.

List of Neuter Verbs Conjugated with Etre, to be

Arriver, to arrive	Être arrivé, to have arrived
Aller, to go	" allé, to have gone
Décéder, to decease	" décédé, to have deceased
Entrer, to enter; to go or come in	" entré, to have entered
Rentrer, to re-enter; to come home	" rentré, to have come in
Retourner, to return; to go back	" retourné, to have returned
Rester, to remain, to stay	" resté, to have remained
Tomber, to fall	" tombé, to have fallen
Mourir, *irr.*, to die	" mort, to have died
Naître, *irr.*, to be born	" né, to have been born
Partir, *irr.*, to start	" parti, to have started
Sortir, *irr.*, to go out; to come out	" sorti, to have gone out
Venir, *irr.*, to come	" venu, to have come
Devenir, *irr.*, to become	" devenu, to have become
Parvenir, *irr.*, to reach; to succeed	" parvenu, to have attained
Revenir, *irr.*, to return; to come back	" revenu, to have returned

2. Some neuter verbs are occasionally used as active verbs, and are then conjugated with **avoir.**

Il⁀a monté la montagne.	He ascended the mountain.
Nous avons descendu la rue.	We descended the street.
Ils ont passé la rivière.	They crossed the river.
Il a sorti le cheval.	He took the horse out.

3. Some neuter verbs are conjugated with **avoir or être,** according to the sense in which they are used.

Convenir, to suit, takes *avoir* and *convenir*, to agree, takes *être*.

Cette maison nous aurait convenu.	That house would have suited us.
Ils sont convenus de revenir.	They agreed to come back.

Demeurer, to live, to reside, to inhabit, to stay at, to tarry, takes *avoir; demeurer*, to stay, or to remain behind, takes *être*.

Nous‿avons demeuré deux‿ans à Paris.	We lived two years in Paris.
Il⁀a demeuré longtemps à le faire.	He was a long time doing it.
Il⁀est demeuré à Paris quand nous sommes revenus.	He remained in Paris when we returned.

Expirer, to perish, takes *avoir; expirer*, to expire, to run out, takes *avoir* when the time is stated, and *être* when no time is given.

Tous deux ont‿expiré de misère.	Both perished of misery.
Son bail⁀a expiré à la Saint-Jean.	His lease expired at mid-summer.
Ces baux sont‿expirés.	Those leases have expired.

The verb *être* is used in all tenses of the passive voice: it is part of the passive verb; as *être⁀aimé*, to be loved. But the usual compound tenses of passive verbs have the auxiliary verb *avoir*, because *être* is conjugated with *avoir: J'ai été aimé*, I was loved.

Être or Aller

The past tenses of **être** are used to state that we have been somewhere whence we have returned, and the past tenses of **aller** are used when the action of going is to be expressed.

J'ai été à la banque ce matin.	I went to the bank this morning.
De là je suis‿allé à la poste.	From there I went to the post-office.

In the first of these two sentences, it is not the action of going which we intend to express. We might say just as well, "I was at the bank this morning." In the second sentence, the action of going is stated, and we could not substitute in English, "I was" for "I went."

THE CONJUGATIONS

There are four conjugations in French, which are distinguished by the termination of the infinitive mood. The termination is added to the root:

The first ends in *er;* as, *aimer*, to love: *aim* (root) *er*.
The second ends in *ir;* as, *finir*, to finish: *fin* (root) *ir*.
The third ends in *evoir;* as, *recevoir*, to receive: *rec* (root) *evoir*.
The fourth ends in *re*, as, *vendre*, to sell: *vend* (root) *re*.

Termination of every tense of all the verbs of the First Conjugation:

Indicatif Présent: e, es, e, ons, ez, ent (*ent* is mute).
Imparfait: ais, ais, ait, ions, iez, aient (*ais, ait, aient* are pronounced *é*).
Prétérit ou *Passé Défini: ai, as, a, âmes, âtes, èrent.*
Futur: erai, eras, era, erons, erez, eront.
Conditionnel: erais, erais, erait, erions, eriez, eraient (*rais, rait, raient* are pronounced *rè*).
Subjonctif Présent: e, es, e, ions, iez, ent (*ent* is mute).
Imparfait: asse, asses, ât, assions, assiez, assent.

Aimer — To love, to like, to be fond of

To love, aimer; loving, aimant; loved, aimé, aimée, aimés, aimées; to have loved, avoir aimé; having loved, ayant aimé.

Indicatif Présent

j'aime, I love	est-ce que j'aime? do I love?
tu aimes, thou lovest	aimes-tu? doest thou love?
il aime, he loves	aime-t-il? does he love?
nous aimons, we love	aimons-nous? do we love?
vous aimez, you love	aimez-vous? do you love?
ils aiment, they love	aiment-ils? do they love?
je n'aime pas, I do not love	est-ce que je n'aime pas? do I not love?
tu n'aimes pas, etc.	n'aimes-tu pas? etc.
il n'aime pas	n'aime-t-il pas?
nous n'aimons pas	n'aimons-nous pas?
vous n'aimez pas	n'aimez-vous pas?
ils n'aiment pas	n'aiment-ils pas?

Imparfait

j'aimais, I was loving	aimais-je? was I loving?
tu aimais, etc.	aimais-tu? etc.
il aimait	aimait-il?
nous aimions	aimions-nous?
vous aimiez	aimiez-vous?
ils aimaient	aimaient-ils?

je n'aimais pas, I was not loving, etc.	n'aimais-je pas? was I not loving? etc.
tu n'aimais pas	n'aimais-tu pas?
il n'aimait pas	n'aimait-il pas?
nous n'aimions pas	n'aimions-nous pas?
vous n'aimiez pas	n'aimiez-vous pas?
ils n'aimaient pas	n'aimaient-ils pas?

Prétérit

j'aimai, I loved	aimai-je? did I love?
tu aimas, etc.	aimas-tu? etc.
il aima	aima-t-il?
nous‿aimâmes	aimâmes-nous?
vous‿aimâtes	aimâtes-vous?
ils‿aimèrent	aimèrent-ils?
je n'aimai pas, I did not love	n'aimai-je pas? did I not love?
tu n'aimas pas, etc.	n'aimas-tu pas? etc.
il n'aima pas	n'aima-t-il pas?
nous n'aimâmes pas	n'aimâmes-nous pas?
vous n'aimâtes pas	n'aimâtes-vous pas?
ils n'aimèrent pas	n'aimèrent-ils pas?

Passé Indéfini

j'ai aimé, I have loved, etc.	ai-je aimé? have I loved? etc.
je n'ai pas‿aimé, I have not loved	n'ai-je pas‿aimé, have I not loved?

Plus-que-Parfait — Passé Antérieur

j'avais‿aimé, I had loved, etc.	avais-je aimé? had I loved, etc.
j'eus‿aimé	eus-je aimé?
je n'avais pas‿aimé, I had not loved	n'avais-je pas‿aimé? had I not loved?
je n'eus pas‿aimé	n'eus-je pas‿aimé?

Futur

j'aimerai, I shall love	aimerai-je? shall I love?
tu aimeras, etc.	aimeras-tu? etc.
il aimera	aimera-t-il?
nous‿aimerons	aimerons-nous?
vous‿aimerez	aimerez-vous?
ils‿aimeront	aimeront-ils?
je n'aimerai pas, I shall not love	n'aimerai-je pas? shall I not love?
tu n'aimeras pas, etc.	n'aimeras-tu pas? etc.
il n'aimera pas	n'aimera-t-il pas?
nous n'aimerons pas	n'aimerons-nous pas?
vous n'aimerez	n'aimerez-vous pas?
ils n'aimeront pas	n'aimeront-ils pas?

Futur Antérieur

j'aurai aimé, I shall have loved
je n'aurai pas‿aimé, I shall not have loved

aurai-je aimé? shall I have loved?
n'aurai-je pas‿aimé? shall I not have loved?

Conditionnel

j'aimerais, I should love
tu aimerais, etc.
il⁀aimerait
nous‿aimerions
vous‿aimeriez
ils‿aimeraient

aimerais-je? should I love?
aimerais-tu? etc.
aimerait‿-il?
aimerions-nous?
aimeriez-vous?
aimeraient‿-ils?

je n'aimerais pas, I should not love
tu n'aimerais pas, etc.
il n'aimerait pas
nous n'aimerions pas
vous n'aimeriez pas
ils n'aimeraient pas

n'aimerais-je pas? should I not love?
n'aimerais-tu pas? etc.
n'aimerait‿-il pas?
n'aimerions-nous pas?
n'aimeriez-vous pas?
n'aimeraient‿-ils pas?

Conditionnel Passé

j'aurais‿aimé, I should have loved
je n'aurais pas‿aimé, I should not have loved

aurais-je⁀aimé? should I have loved?
n'aurais-je pas‿aimé, should I not have loved?

Impératif

aime, love
aimons, let us love
aimez, love

n'aime pas, do not love
n'aimons pas, do not let us love
n'aimez pas, do not love

Subjonctif Présent

que j'aime, that I may love
que tu aimes, etc.
qu'il⁀aime
que nous‿aimions
que vous‿aimiez
qu'ils‿aiment

que je n'aime pas, that I may not love
que tu n'aimes pas, etc.
qu'il n'aime pas
que nous n'aimions pas
que vous n'aimiez pas
qu'ils n'aiment pas

Imparfait

que j'aimasse, that I might love
que tu aimasses, etc.
qu'il⁀aimât
que nous‿aimassions
que vous‿aimassiez
qu'ils‿aimassent

que je n'aimasse pas, that I might not love
que tu n'aimasses pas, etc.
qu'il n'aimât pas
que nous n'aimassions pas
que vous n'aimassiez pas
qu'ils n'aimassent pas

Passé

que j'aie aimé, that I may have loved, etc. | que je n'aie pas‿aimé, that I may not have loved, etc.

Plus-que-Parfait

que j'eusse‿aimé, that I might have loved, etc. | que je n'eusse pas‿aimé, that I might not have loved, etc.

There are about five thousand verbs in the first conjugation, nearly all of which are conjugated like *aimer*.

Orthographical Remarks on the Verbs of the First Conjugation (and also on the verbs in -*cevoir*)

ger.—Verbs ending in **ger** retain **e** before **a, o;** as, mangeant, mangeons, je mangeais, etc.

ç.—Verbs in which **c** has the sound of **s** in the infinitive, as, placer, effacer, recevoir, etc., take **c** cedilla (ç) before **a, o, u;** as, **I placed,** je plaçai, il plaça, nous plaçâmes; **I received,** je reçus, il reçut, etc.

y.—Verbs which have **y** preceding the termination **er** of the infinitive, as, envoyer, payer, essayer, etc., change **y** into **i** before **e** mute; as, **I send,** etc., j'envoie, tu envoies, ils envoient; **I pay,** etc., je paie, tu paies, ils paient; **I shall try,** etc., j'essaierai, tu essaieras, etc.

yer, ier.—Verbs ending in **yer, ier,** as, payer, se fier (**to trust**), etc., require **i** after **y** and **i** in the first and second persons plural:

1st, of the **imparfait de l'indicatif.** 2d, of the **subjonctif présent.**

Nous payions, vous payiez—que nous payions, que vous payiez. Nous nous fiions, vous vous fiiez—que nous nous fiions, que vous vous fiiez.

é, e.—Verbs which have **é** or **e** in the next to the last syllable of the infinitive, require a grave accent (è) on that **é** or **e** before a consonant followed by an **e** mute; as:

Répéter, **to repeat—je répète,** tu répètes; je répèterai, etc. Révéler, **to reveal**—je révèle, il révèle, je révèlerais, etc. Mener, **to lead**—je mène, il mène; je mènerai, etc. Peser, **to weigh**—je pèse, il pèse; je pèserais, etc.

eler, eter.—Verbs having **e** mute before the terminations **ler, ter,** double **l** and **t** when followed by **e** mute; as:

Appeler, **to call**—j'appelle, il appelle; j'appellerai, etc. Jeter, **to throw**—je jette, il jette; je jetterais, etc.

Except **geler,** to freeze; **peler,** to peel; **acheter,** to buy, etc., which follow the preceding rule: il gèle, je pèle, il achète, etc.

List of Some Regular Verbs ending in er

Accepter (de)	to accept	Gagner	to win; to earn
Ajouter	to add	Glisser	to slide
Allumer	to light	Gronder	to scold
Amener (à)	to bring	Jeter	to throw
Appeler (à)	to call	Jouer	to play
Avaler	to swallow	Manier	to handle
Avouer	to acknowledge	Manquer (de)	to fail to
Bâiller	to yawn	Manquer (de)	to lack (anything)
Balancer	to swing	Montrer (à)	to show
Blesser	to wound	Nager	to swim
Cacher	to hide	Oser	to dare
Casser	to break	Passer	to call; to pass
Causer	to chat	Peser	to weigh
Chatouiller	to tickle	Plier	to fold
Chercher (à)	to look for; to try	Plisser	to pleat
Chiffonner	to ruffle	Prêter	to lend
Commander (de)	to order	Pousser (à)	to push
Compter	to count	Quitter	to leave
Cracher	to spit	Réclamer	to claim
Demander (de)	to ask	Récompenser	to reward
Dépenser	to spend	Refuser (de)	to refuse
Dessiner	to draw	Regarder	to look
Éclairer	to light	Regarder (à)	to look at
Écouter	to listen	Renoncer (à)	to give up
Écraser	to crush	Répliquer	to reply
Effrayer	to frighten	Ressembler	to look like
Embrasser	to kiss	Retourner	to return
Emmener	to take (with one)	Sécher	to dry
Emporter	to take (away)	Siffler	to whistle
Emprunter	to borrow	Souffler	to blow
Enseigner (à)	to teach	Soupçonner (de)	to suspect
Épeler	to spell	Soupirer	to sigh
Épousseter	to dust	Tousser	to cough
Espérer	to hope	Traverser	to cross
Éviter (de)	to avoid	Trouver	to find
Frapper	to strike	Verser	to pour out
Frotter	to rub	Viser	to aim
Fumer	to smoke	Voler	to steal; to fly

Second Conjugation

Terminations of the Second Conjugation, added to the root

Indicatif Présent: is, is, it, issons, issez, issent
Imparfait: issais, issais, issait, issons, issiez, issaient
Prétérit ou *Passé Défini:* is, is, it, îmes, îtes, irent
Futur: irai, iras, ira, irons, irez, iront
Conditionnel: irais, irais, irait, irions, iriez, iraient
Subjonctif Présent: isse, isses, isse, issions, issiez, issent
Subjonctif Imparfait: isse, isses, ît, issions, issiez, issent

Finir — To finish, to conclude

To finish, **finir;** finishing, **finissant;** finished, **fini, finie, finis, finies;** to have finished, **avoir fini;** having finished, **ayant fini.**

Indicative Présent

je finis, I finish, I am finishing
tu finis, etc.
il finit
nous finissons
vous finissez
ils finissent

Imparfait

Je finissais, I was finishing
tu finissais, etc.
il finissait
nous finissions
vous finissiez
ils finissaient

Prétérit

je finis, I finished
tu finis, etc.
il finit
nous finîmes
vous finîtes
ils finirent

Futur

je finirai, I shall finish
tu finiras, etc.
il finira
nous finirons
vous finirez
ils finiront

Passé Indéfini

j'ai fini, I have finished
tu as fini, etc.
il⁀a fini
nous‿avons fini
vous‿avez fini
ils‿ont fini

Futur Antérieur

j'aurai fini, I shall have finished
tu auras fini, etc.
il⁀aura fini
nous‿aurons fini
vous‿aurez fini
ils‿auront fini

Plus-que-Parfait

j'avais fini, I had finished
tu avais fini, etc.
il⁀avait fini
nous‿avions fini
vous‿aviez fini
ils‿avaient fini

Conditionnel Présent

Je finirais, I should finish
tu finirais, etc.
il finirait
nous finirions
vous finiriez
ils finiraient

Passé Antérieur

j'eus fini, I had finished
tu eus fini, etc.
il‿eut fini
nous‿eûmes fini
vous‿eûtes fini
ils‿eurent fini

Conditionnel Passé

j'aurais fini, I should have finished
tu aurais fini, etc.
il‿aurait fini
nous‿aurions fini
vous‿auriez fini
ils‿auraient fini

Impératif

finis, finish (thou)
finissons, let us finish
finissez, finish (you)

Subjonctif Passé

que j'aie fini, that I may have finished
que tu aies fini, etc.

Subjonctif Présent

que je finisse, that I may finish

que tu finisses, etc.
qu'il finisse
que nous finissions
que vous finissiez
qu'ils finissent

Subj. Plus-que-Parfait

que j'eusse fini, that I might have finished
que tu eusses fini, etc.
qu'il‿eût fini
que nous‿eussions fini
que vous‿eussiez fini
qu'ils‿eussent fini

Subj. Imparfait

que je finisse, that I might finish
que tu finisses, etc.
qu'il finît
que nous finissions
que vous finissiez
qu'ils finissent

Every tense should be conjugated in the four usual forms.

est-ce que je finis? do I finish?
finis-tu? etc.
finit-il?
finissons-nous?
finissez-vous?
finissent-ils?

je ne finis pas, I do not finish
tu ne finis pas, etc.
il ne finit pas
nous ne finissons pas
vous ne finissez pas
ils ne finissent pas

est-ce que je ne finis pas? do I not finish?
ne finis-tu pas? etc.
ne finit-il pas?
ne finissons-nous pas?
ne finissez-vous pas?
ne finissent-ils pas?

The Second conjugation is divided into four classes:

First class, like **finir,** about 300 verbs.
Second class, like **sentir,** to feel.
Third class, like **ouvrir,** to open.
Fourth class, like **tenir,** to hold.

NOTE.—The second, third and fourth classes may be considered as irregular verbs.

First Class—Like FINIR

Aboutir	to end in	Enlaidir	to grow ugly
Accomplir	to accomplish	Établir	to establish
Adoucir	to soften	Fléchir	to bend
Affermir	to strengthen	Fleurir	to bloom, to blossom
Affranchir	to free	Fournir	to supply
Agir	to act	Franchir	to leap
Agrandir	to enlarge	Frémir (de)	to shudder (with)
Amoindrir	to lessen	Garnir	to trim, to adorn
Amortir	to deaden	Gémir	to groan
Aplanir	to level	Grandir	to grow tall
Aplatir	to flatten	Grossir	to grow larger
Appauvrir	to impoverish	Haïr	to hate
Applaudir	to applaud	Hennir	to neigh
Approfondir	to examine thoroughly	Jouir (de)	to enjoy
Asservir	to enslave	Munir	to provide
Assortir	to match	Noircir	to blacken
Avertir (de)	to inform (of)	Nourrir	to feed
Avilir	to debase	Pâlir	to grow pale
Bannir	to banish	Polir	to polish
Bâtir	to build	Pourrir	to rot
Bénir	to bless	Punir	to punish
Blanchir	to whiten	Réfléchir	to reflect
Bondir	to bound, to leap	Répartir	to distribute
Chérir	to cherish	Retentir	to resound
Choisir	to choose	Réussir (à)	to succeed
Définir	to define	Subir	to undergo
Durcir	to harden	Ternir	to tarnish
Éblouir	to dazzle	Trahir	to betray
Élargir	to widen	Unir	to unite
Endurcir	to harden	Vieillir	to grow old

Second Class

Comprising verbs conjugated like *sentir*, to feel, ending in *tir*, *mir*, *vir:* *Sent-ir*, *sentant*, *senti*.

I feel, etc. je sens, tu sens, il sent, nous sentons, vous sentez, ils sentent
I felt, je sentais, etc.—je sentis, nous sentîmes, etc.—j'ai senti—j'avais senti—j'eus senti
I shall feel, je sentirai—nous sentirons
I should feel, je sentirais—nous sentirions
sens, sentons, sentez—que je sente—que je sentisse—qu'il sentît

The following verbs are conjugated like **sentir:**

Consentir, to consent
Démentir, to belie
Départir, to distribute
Desservir, to clear the table
Dormir, to sleep
Endormir, to lull asleep
Mentir, to lie
Partir (être), to depart
Pressentir, to anticipate
Redormir, to sleep again
Repartir (être), to set out again
Ressentir, to resent
Ressortir (être), to go out again
S'endormir (refl.), to fall asleep
Se rendormir, to fall asleep again
Servir, to serve
Sentir, to smell
Sortir (être), to go out

Third Class

Ending in *vrir* and *frir*, as *ouvrir* (*ouvr-ir*); to open; *ouvrant*, opening; *ouvert*, *e*, opened.

I open, etc. j'ouvre, tu ouvres, il⁀ouvre, nous‿ouvrons, vous‿ouvrez, ils‿ouvrent
I opened, j'ouvrais, etc.—j'ouvris—nous‿ouvrîmes—j'ai ouvert—j'avais‿ouvert—j'eus‿ouvert
I shall open, j'ouvrirai, etc.
I should open, j'ouvrirais, etc.
ouvre, ouvrons, ouvrez—que j'ouvre—que nous‿ouvrions—que j'ouvrisse—qu'il⁀ouvrît

The following verbs are conjugated like **ouvrir:**

Rouvrir, to open again
Entr'ouvrir, to half open
Couvrir, to cover
Recouvrir, to cover again
Souffrir, to suffer
Offrir, to offer
Découvrir, to discover

Fourth Class

Tenir (*ten-ir*), to hold; *tenant*, holding; *tenu, e, s, es*, held

I hold, etc., je tiens, tu tiens, il tient, nous tenons, vous tenez, ils tiennent
I held, je tenais, etc.—je tins—nous tînmes, vous tîntes, ils tinrent—j'ai tenu, j'avais tenu, j'eus tenu
I shall hold, je tiendrai—nous tiendrons
I should hold, je tiendrais, etc.
tiens, tenons, tenez—que je tienne—que nous tenions, que vous teniez, qu'ils tiennent—que je tinse, que tu tinsses, qu'il tînt, que nous tinssions, etc.

Conjugate the following verbs like **tenir**:

S'abstenir (refl.), to abstain
Appartenir (à), to belong to
Contenir, to contain
Détenir, to detain
Entretenir, to entertain
Maintenir, to maintain
Obtenir, to obtain
Retenir, to retain
Soutenir, to uphold
Venir (être), to come
Contrevenir, to contravene
Convenir (être), to agree

Devenir (être), to become
Disconvenir (être), to deny
Intervenir (être), to intervene
Parvenir (être), to attain
Prévenir, to warn
Provenir (être), to proceed from
Revenir (être), to come again, come back
Survenir (être), to befall
Subvenir, to relieve, provide
Se souvenir (refl.), to remember
Se ressouvenir (refl.), to recollect

Third Conjugation

Terminations of the Third Conjugation

Indicatif Présent:	ois, ois, oit, evons, evez, oivent
Imparfait:	evais, evais, evait, evions, eviez, evaient
Prétérit or *Passé Défini:*	us, us, ut, ûmes, ûtes, urent
Futur:	evrai, evras, evra, evrons, evrez, evront
Conditionnel:	evrais, evrais, evrait, evrions, evriez, evraient
Subjonctif Présent:	oive, oives, oive, evions, eviez, oivent
Imparfait:	usse, usses, ût, ussions, ussiez, ussent

Recevoir — To receive

To receive, **recevoir**; receiving, **recevant**; received, **reçu**; to have received, **avoir reçu**; having received, **ayant reçu.**

Indicatif Présent

je reçois, I receive
tu reçois, etc.
il reçoit
nous recevons
vous recevez
ils reçoivent

Imparfait

je recevais, I was receiving
tu recevais, etc.
il recevait
nous recevions
vous receviez
ils recevaient

Prétérit

je reçus, I received
tu reçus, etc.
il reçut
nous reçûmes
vous reçûtes
ils reçurent

Passé Indéfini

j'ai reçu, I have received
tu as reçu
il⁀a reçu
nous‿avons reçu
vous‿avez reçu
ils‿ont reçu

Plus-que-Parfait

j'avais reçu, I had received
tu avais reçu, etc.
il⁀avait reçu
nous‿avions reçu
vous‿aviez reçu
ils‿avaient reçu

Impératif

reçois, receive (thou)
recevons, let us receive
recevez, receive (you)

Passé Antérieur

j'eus reçu, I have received
tu eus reçu, etc.
il⁀eut reçu
nous‿eûmes reçu
vous‿eûtes reçu
ils‿eurent reçu

Futur

je recevrai, I shall receive
tu recevras, etc.
il recevra
nous recevrons
vous recevrez
ils recevront

Futur Antérieur

j'aurai reçu, I shall have received
tu auras reçu, etc.
il⁀aura reçu
nous‿aurons reçu
vous‿aurez reçu
ils‿auront reçu

Conditionnel

je recevrais, I should receive
tu recevrais, etc.
il recevrait
nous recevrions
vous recevriez
ils recevraient

Conditionnel Passé

j'aurais reçu, I should have received
tu aurais reçu, etc.
il⁀aurait reçu
nous‿aurions reçu
vous‿auriez reçu
ils‿auraient reçu

Subjonctif Présent

que je reçoive, that I may receive
que tu reçoives, etc.
qu'il reçoive
que nous recevions
que vous receviez
qu'ils reçoivent

Subj. Imparfait

que je reçusse, that I might receive
que tu reçusses, etc.
qu'il reçût
que nous reçussions
que vous reçussiez
qu'ils reçussent

Subj. Plus-que-Parfait

que j'eusse reçu, that I might have received
que tu eusses reçu, etc.
qu'il‿eût reçu
que nous‿eussions reçu
que vous‿eussiez reçu
qu'ils‿eussent reçu

Subjonctif Passé

que j'aie reçu, that I may have received
que tu aies reçu, etc.
qu'il‿ait reçu
que nous‿ayons reçu
que vous‿ayez reçu
qu'ils‿aient reçu

Infinitif présent: recevoir
passé: avoir reçu
Participe présent: recevant
passé: reçu

Je ne reçois pas, etc., I do not receive

Do I receive?
est-ce que je reçois? etc.

Do I not receive?
est-ce que je ne reçois pas? etc.

The Third Conjugation has only seven regular verbs, namely:

To perceive, apercevoir; the cedilla (ç) is used before o and u
To conceive, concevoir (conc-evoir)
To deceive, décevoir (déc-evoir)
To owe, to have to (do something), devoir (d-evoir), participle dû (a circumflex accent is placed on û in the masculine singular)
To still owe, redevoir (red-evoir), redû
To collect, percevoir (perc-evoir)
To receive, recevoir (rec-evoir)
For other verbs ending in *oir* see irregular verbs

Fourth Conjugation

The Fourth Conjugation may be divided into four classes, namely:

First ending in	**andre, endre, ondre, erdre, ordre;**	conjugated like	**vendre,** to sell.
Second "	**aître, oître;**	"	**paraître,** to appear.
Third "	**uire;**	"	**réduire,** to reduce.
Fourth "	**aindre, eindre, oindre;**	conjugated like	**plaindre,** to pity.

First Class

vendre (vend-re), to sell; *vendant*, selling; *vendu, e*, sold

Terminations to be added to the Root

Indicatif Présent:	s, s, —, ons, ez, ent.
Imparfait:	ais, ais, ait, ions, iez, aient.
Prétérit:	is, is, it, îmes, îtes, irent.
Futur:	rai, ras, ra, rons, rez, ront.
Conditionnel:	rais, rais, rait, rions, riez, raient.
Subjonctif Présent:	e, es, e, ions, iez, ent.
Imparfait:	isse, isses, ît, issions, issiez, issent.

Indicatif Présent

je vends, I sell
tu vends, etc.
il vend
nous vendons
vous vendez
ils vendent

Prétérit

je vendis, I sold
tu vendis, etc.
il vendit
nous vendîmes
vous vendîtes
ils vendirent

Imparfait

je vendais, I was selling
tu vendais, etc.
il vendait
nous vendions
vous vendiez
ils vendaient

Passé Indéfini

j'ai vendu, I have sold
tu as vendu, etc.
il͡ a vendu
nous‿avons vendu
vous‿avez vendu
ils‿ont vendu

Plus-que-Parfait

j'avais vendu, I had sold
tu avais vendu, etc.
il͡ avait vendu
nous‿avions vendu
vous‿aviez vendu
ils‿avaient vendu

Conditionnel Passé

J'aurais vendu, I should have sold
tu aurais vendu, etc.
il͡ aurait vendu
nous‿aurions vendu
vous‿auriez vendu
ils‿auraient vendu

Passé Antérieur

j'eus vendu, I had sold
tu eus vendu, etc.
il͡ eut vendu
nous‿eûmes vendu
vous‿eûtes vendu
ils‿eurent vendu

Futur

je vendrai, I shall sell
tu vendras, etc.
il vendra
nous vendrons
vous vendrez
ils vendront

Futur Antérieur

j'aurai vendu, I shall have sold
tu auras vendu, etc.
il aura vendu
nous aurons vendu
vous aurez vendu
ils auront vendu

Conditionnel

je vendrais, I should sell
tu vendrais, etc.
il vendrait
nous vendrions
vous vendriez
ils vendraient

Subjonctif Passé

que j'aie vendu, that I may have sold
que tu aies vendu, etc.
qu'il ait vendu
que nous ayons vendu
que vous ayez vendu
qu'ils aient vendu

Subj. Plus-que-Parfait

que j'eusse vendu, that I might have sold
que tu eusses vendu
qu'il eût vendu
que nous eussions vendu
que vous eussiez vendu
qu'ils eussent vendu

Infinitif

Présent: vendre, to sell
Passé: avoir vendu, to have sold

Impératif

vends, sell (thou)
vendons, let us sell
vendez sell (you)

Subjonctif Présent

que je vende, that I may sell
que tu vendes, etc.
qu'il vende
que nous vendions
que vous vendiez
qu'ils vendent

Subjonctif Imparfait

que je vendisse, that I might sell
que tu vendisses, etc.
qu'il vendît
que nous vendissions
que vous vendissiez
qu'ils vendissent

Participe

Présent: vendant, selling
Passé: vendu, vendue, vendus, ayant vendu, having sold

Other forms:

est-ce que je vends? do I sell?
vends-tu? etc.
je ne vends pas, I do not sell.
est-ce que je ne vends pas? do I not sell? etc.
ne vends-tu pas?
vendais-je? did I sell?
je ne vendais pas, I did not sell
ne vendais-je pas? did I not sell?

The following verbs are conjugated like **vendre:**

Attendre, to wait for
Confondre, to confound
Condescendre, to comply
Correspondre, to correspond
Descendre, to go down
Défendre, to forbid
Détendre, to unbend
Entendre, to hear
Étendre, to stretch out
Fendre, to split
Fondre, to melt
Mordre, to bite
Pendre, to hang
Perdre, to lose
Pondre, to lay eggs
Prétendre, to pretend
Refondre, to melt again
Répondre, to answer
Répandre, to spill
Rendre, to render, to restore
Suspendre, to suspend
Tendre, to hold out
Tondre, to shear
Tordre, to twist

Second Class

Conjugated like **paraître** (par-aître), to appear; **paraissant,** appearing; **paru,** appeared.

I appear, etc., je parais, tu parais, il paraît, nous paraissons, vous paraissez, ils paraissent
I appeared, je paraissais, tu paraissais, etc.—je parus, nous parûmes—j'ai paru, etc.
I shall appear, je paraîtrai, tu paraîtras, etc.
I should appear, je paraîtrais, etc.
parais, paraissons, paraissez—que je paraisse, etc.—que je parusse, que tu parusses, qu'il parût, que nous parussions, etc.

The usual verbs of this class are:

Apparaître, to appear
Accroître, to increase
Comparaître, to appear
Connaître, to know
Croître, to grow
Méconnaître, not to recognize
Décroître, to decrease
Disparaître, to disappear
Reconnaître, to recognize

The circumflex accent is always placed on **i** (**î**) before **t.** Moreover, in the verb **croître** and its derivatives the circumflex is also placed on **i** and **u** (**î, û**) before **s** ending the word; as: **je croîs, je crûs, tu crûs.**

Third Class

Conjugated like **réduire** (réd-uire), to reduce; **réduisant,** reducing; **réduit, e,** reduced.

I reduce, etc., je réduis, tu réduis, il réduit, nous réduisons, vous réduisez, ils réduisent
I reduced, je réduisais, etc.—je réduisis, tu réduisis, nous réduisîmes, etc.—j'ai réduit, etc.
I shall reduce, je réduirai, etc.
I should reduce, je réduirais—ils réduiraient
réduis, réduisons, réduisez—que je réduise—que je réduisisse—qu'il réduisît

The following are conjugated like **réduire.**

Conduire, to conduct
Construire, to construct
Cuire, to cook, to bake
Déduire, to deduct
Détruire, to destroy
Enduire, to plaster
Instruire, to instruct
Introduire, to introduce
Induire, to induce
Produire, to produce
Recuire, to cook again
Séduire, to seduce
Traduire, to translate

Fourth Class

Conjugated like **plaindre** (pl-aindre), to pity; **plaignant,** pitying; **plaint, e,** pitied.

I pity, je plains, tu plains, il plaint, nous plaignons, vous plaignez, ils plaignent
I pitied, je plaignais, etc.—je plaignis—nous plaignîmes, etc.—j'ai plaint, etc.
I shall, should pity, je plaindrai, etc.—je plaindrais, etc.
Pity, plains, plaignons, plaignez
Subjonctif: que je plaigne—que je plaignisse—qu'il plaignît, etc.

The following verbs are conjugated like **plaindre:**

Adjoindre, to adjoin
Astreindre, to confine to
Atteindre, to reach
Ceindre, to gird
Contraindre, to compel
Craindre, to fear
Déteindre, to take out the color
Empreindre, to imprint
Enfreindre, to infringe
Enjoindre, to enjoin
Enceindre, to enclose
Éteindre, to extinguish
Feindre, to feign
Joindre, to join
Oindre, to anoint
Peindre, to paint
Restreindre, to limit
Teindre, to dye

Verbes Réfléchis. — Reflexive Verbs

Modèle: Se Dépêcher.

Reflexive verbs are those in which the action is reflected upon the subject, as: To flatter oneself, I wash myself, etc. Many verbs, however, are reflexive in French, which are not so in English. For instance, **Se dépêcher,** to hasten.

Se Dépêcher, to make haste[1]

Indicatif Présent

Je me dépêche, I am hurrying, etc.
Tu te dépêches
Il se dépêche
Nous nous dépêchons
Vous vous dépêchez
Ils se dépêchent

Imparfait

Je me dépêchais, I was hurrying, etc.
Tu te dépêchais
Il se dépêchait
Nous nous dépêchions
Vous vous dépêchiez
Ils se dépêchaient

Prétérit

Je me dépêchai, I hastened, etc.

Futur

Je ne me dépêcherai pas
Tu ne te dépêcheras pas
Il ne se dépêchera pas
Nous ne nous dépêcherons pas
Vous ne vous dépêcherez pas
Ils ne se dépêcheront pas

} I shall not hurry, etc.

Conditionnel Présent

Me dépêcherais-je? Would I hurry? etc.
Te dépêcherais-tu?
Se dépêcherait-il?
Nous dépêcherions-nous?
Vous dépêcheriez-vous?
Se dépêcheraient-ils?

Impératif

Affirm. { Dépêche-toi, Hurry (thou)
Dépêchons-nous, Let us hurry
Dépêchez-vous, Hurry (you)

Neg. { Ne te dépêche pas, Do not hurry, etc.
Ne nous dépêchons pas
Ne vous dépêchez pas

Subjonctif Présent

Que je me dépêche, That I may hurry, etc.
Que tu te dépêches
Qu'il se dépêche
Que nous nous dépêchions
Que vous vous dépêchiez
Qu'ils se dépêchent

Imparfait

Que je me dépêchasse, That I might hurry, etc.

[1] Do I hasten, *Est-ce que je me dépêche? Te dépêches-tu? Se dépêche-t-il?* etc. I do not hasten. etc., *Je ne me dépêche pas. Tu ne te dépêches pas,* etc. Do I not hasten? etc. *Est-ce que je ne me dépêche pas? Ne te dépêches-tu pas?* etc. Would I not hurry? etc. *Ne me dépêcherais-je pas? Ne te dépêcherais-tu pas?* etc.—*Se dépêchant, me dépêchant,* etc., making haste.

Temps Composés

Passé Indéfini

Je me suis dépêché, I hurried, have hurried, did hurry, etc.
Tu t'es dépêché
Il s'est dépêché
Nous nous sommes dépêchés
Vous vous‿êtes dépêchés
Ils se sont dépêchés

Negative Form

Je ne me suis pas dépêché
Tu ne t'es pas dépêché, etc.

Passé Indéfini

Me suis-je dépêché? Did I hurry, etc.
T'es-tu dépêché?
S'est‿il dépêché?
Nous sommes-nous dépêchés?
Vous‿êtes-vous dépêchés?
Se sont‿ils dépêchés?

Negative-Interrogative

Ne me suis-je pas dépêché?
Ne t'es-tu pas dépêché? etc.

Conjugate the following three tenses in the same manner:

Plus-que-Parfait

Je m'étais dépêché, I had hurried, etc. — M'étais-je dépêché? etc.

Je ne m'étais pas dépêché, I had not hurried, etc. — Ne m'étais-je pas dépêché? etc.

Futur

Je me serai dépêché, etc.

Conditionnel

Je me serais dépêché, etc.

Subjonctif (Passé et Plus-que-Parfait)

Que je me sois dépêché, that I (may) have hurried. — Que je me fusse dépêché.

The reflexive pronouns (*me*, myself or to myself; *te*, thyself, or to thyself; *se*, himself, herself, oneself; also, to himself, etc.; *nous*, ourselves, or to ourselves; *vous*, yourself, or to yourself; *se*, themselves, or to themselves) are really pronoun-objects, and as such, are always placed immediately before the verb (except with the imperative-affirmative; see above). But the pronoun-subjects (*je, tu, il, nous, vous, ils, elles*) change their place in interrogative forms and come after the verb (see Conditionnel above, and the Passé Indéfini).

In the negative forms of these verbs, *ne* comes in its usual place, just before the pronoun-objects (that is, just before *me*, *te*, etc.).

Agreement of Past Participle of Reflexive Verbs

Although conjugated with **être,** the past participles of these verbs agree with the direct object, if that object precedes the verb.

This will appear logical, if it is remembered that **être** with these verbs has really the force of **avoir.** Ex.:

Elle s'est promenée, She (herself) took a walk.
Ils se sont dépêchés, They (themselves) hurried.
Elles se sont dépêchées, They (themselves) hurried.

If the past participle of reflexive verbs appears often to agree with the subject, it is only when the subject and direct object actually refer to the same person or thing. Ex.:

Elle s'est coupée, She has cut herself.
But:
Elle s'est coupé la main, She cut her hand.

Coupé is made feminine in the first, because agreeing with the direct-object herself (s'). It remains invariable in the second, because the direct-object, **la main,** does not precede it.

Reciprocal Use of Reflexive Verbs

Sometimes, the reflexive pronouns **se, nous, vous,** have the meaning of each other, one another: Ils s'aiment, They like each other; Ils se font mal, They hurt one another.

List of Reflexive Verbs Conjugated According to Their Respective Conjugations

S'abonner à, to subscribe to
S'accorder, agree
S'adoucir, soften
S'adresser, address one's self
S'affaiblir, become weak
S'affermir, strengthen
S'aimer, love each other
S'amuser, amuse one's self
S'appeler, be named
S'apprivoiser, become tame
S'approcher, approach
S'arrêter, stop
S'assoupir, grow drowsy
Se baisser, stoop
Se blesser, wound one's self
Se brouiller, disagree
Se cacher, conceal one's self
Se chauffer, warm one's self
Se convenir, suit each other
Se coucher, go to bed
Se défier, distrust
Se dépêcher, make haste
Se déshabiller, undress one's self
S'endurcir, harden
S'empresser, be eager
S'endormir, to fall asleep
S'enfermer, shut up
S'enrhumer, take cold
S'enrichir, grow rich
S'envoler, fly away
S'étonner, wonder
S'évanouir, faint away
S'éveiller, awake
S'exprimer, express one's self
Se fâcher, get angry
Se fier, trust
Se lever, get up, rise
Se marier, get married

Se méfier, mistrust
Se mêler, mix, meddle
Se moquer, laugh at
Se noyer, drown one's self
Se peigner, comb one's self
Se pencher, bend

Se plaindre, complain
Se promener, take a walk
Se rapprocher, to come nearer
Se reculer, move back
Se rendre à, go to
Se retirer, withdraw

Passive Verbs. — Verbes Passifs

The only passive forms in French are those made up of the past participle of any active verb (aimer; flatter; estimer; haïr; etc.), and the various tenses of the verb **être**. Thus:

Etre aimé, to be loved.

Indic. Présent

I am loved, etc.
Je suis‿aimé
Tu es‿aimé
Il est‿aimé
N. sommes‿aimés
V. êtes‿aimés
Ils sont‿aimés

Imparfait

I was loved, etc.
J'étais‿aimé
Tu étais‿aimé
Il était‿aimé
N. étions‿aimés
V. étiez‿aimés
Ils étaient‿aimés

Prétérit

I was loved, etc.
Je fus‿aimé
Tu fus‿aimé, etc.

Futur

I shall be loved, etc.
Je serai aimé
Tu seras aimé, etc.

Conditionnel

I would be loved, etc.
Je serais‿aimé
Tu serais‿aimé
Il serait‿aimé
N. serions‿aimés
V. seriez‿aimés
Ils seraient‿aimés

Impératif

Be thou loved, etc.
Sois‿aimé
Soyons‿aimés
Soyez‿aimés[1]

Subjonc. Présent

That I (may) be loved, etc.
Que je sois‿aimé
Que tu sois‿aimé
Qu'il soit‿aimé
Que n. soyons‿aimés
Que v. soyez‿aimés
Qu'ils soient‿aimés

Imparfait du Subj.

That I (might) be loved, etc.
Que je fusse⁀aimé

Temps Composés

Infinitif

To have been loved
Avoir⁀été aimé

Participe

Having been loved
Ayant‿été aimé

Plus-que-Parfait

I had been loved, etc.
J'avais‿été aimé, etc.

Passé Antérieur

I had been loved, etc.
J'eus‿été aimé, etc.

Conditionnel Passé

I would have been loved, etc.
J'aurais‿été aimé, etc.

Subjonctif Passé

That I (may) have been loved, etc.
Que j'aie été aimé, etc.

[1] If *vous* refers to one person, the past participle takes no *s*.

Passé Indéfini	Futur Antérieur	Subj. Plus-que-Parfait
I was or have been loved.	I shall have been loved.	I (might) have been loved.
J'ai été aimé.	J'aurai été aimé, etc.	Que j'eusse été aimé, etc.

Complement of Passive Verbs

Passive verbs (generally) take **de** for their complement, if they express a sentiment or passion. They take **par,** if expressing an action of the body or mind. Ex.: **Cet homme est estimé de tout le monde.** But: **Carthage fut détruite par les Romains: Ce livre a été écrit par cet auteur.**

Use of the Active and Passive Verbs Contrasted

The French omit the use of the passive voice wherever the active form (with **on** or **ils**) can as well be used. Ex.:

It is said we shall have war, **On dit que nous aurons la guerre.**
The eclipse can be seen, **On pourra voir l'éclipse.**

Unipersonal Verbs — Verbes Unipersonnels

To snow, **neiger**

Conjugated like **aimer** in the third person singular.

It snows	il neige
It was snowing	il neigeait
It snowed	il neigea
It has snowed	il a neigé
It had snowed	il avait, or, il eut neigé
It will snow	il neigera
It will have snowed	il aura neigé
It would snow	il neigerait
It would have snowed	il aurait neigé
That it may snow	qu'il neige
That it might snow	qu'il neigeât
That it may have snowed	qu'il ait neigé
That it might have snowed?	qu'il eût neigé

Does it snow? neige-t-il? it does not snow, il ne neige pas; does it not snow? ne neige-t-il pas?

Each tense should be conjugated in the usual interrogative and negative forms.

A list of unipersonal verbs conjugated like the third person singular of the model verb:

Dégeler, to thaw
Faire (irreg.) des‿éclairs, to lighten
Falloir (irreg.), to be necessary
Geler, to freeze
Grêler, to hail
Pleuvoir (irreg.), to rain
Tonner, to thunder

Many verbs can be used unipersonally; as:

Il⁀importe, it matters
Il suffit, it is enough
Il s'agit de, it is a question of
Il convient, it becomes
Il paraît, it appears
Il semble, it seems
Il⁀arrive, it happens
Il s'entend, it is a matter of course

Verbs conjugated with être in their Compound Tenses

1. Reflexive verbs, in which **être** is employed for **avoir.**

2. Passive verbs.

3. Unipersonal verbs take **avoir;** but those that are accidentally unipersonal, as, **il est arrivé un malheur, a misfortune has happened** may take **être.**

4. Some neuter verbs, as:

Aller, to go
Arriver, to arrive
Décéder, to die
Entrer, to enter
Intervenir, to intervene
Mourir, to die
Naître, to be born
Parvenir, to attain, to succeed
Revenir, to come again
Sortir (persons), to go out
Venir, to come
Rester, to remain, to stay

Also the following:

Convenir, to agree
Devenir, to become
Survenir, to occur
Tomber, to fall

Irregular Verbs of the Four Conjugations

Abattre, to pull down (avoir); like battre.

Absoudre, to absolve; absolvant, absous, absoute (*f.*)—j'absous, tu absous, il⁀absout, nous‿absolvons, vous‿absolvez, ils‿absolvent—j'absolvais (no past definite). j'absoudrai, j'absoudrais—absous, absolvons, absolvez, que j'absolve (no imp. subj.).

Abstraire, to abstract; like traire. We prefer **faire abstraction de.**

Accourir, to run to (avoir and être), like courir.

Accroire is only used with faire; as, il s'en fait accroire, he makes himself believe, etc.

Accueillir, to welcome; conjugated like cueillir.

Acquérir, to acquire (avoir), acquérant, acquis, e—j'acquiers, tu acquiers, il acquiert, nous acquérons, vous acquérez, ils acquièrent —j'acquérais, j'acquis, j'acquerrai, j'acquerrais—acquiers, acquérons, acquérez—que j'acquière, que j'acquisse, qu'il acquît.

Admettre, to admit (avoir); like mettre.

Aller, to go (être); allant, allé, e—je vais, tu vas, il va, nous allons, vous allez, ils vont—j'allais, j'allai, j'irai, j'irais—va, allons, allez—que j'aille, que nous allions, que vous alliez, qu'ils aillent—que j'allasse, qu'il allât.

S'en aller, to go away; s'en allant, allé, e—je m'en vais, tu t'en vas, il s'en va, nous nous en allons, vous vous en allez, ils s'en vont —je m'en allais, je m'en allai, je m'en suis allé, je m'en étais allé, je m'en fus allé, je m'en irai, je m'en serai allé, je m'en irais, je m'en serais allé—va-t'en, allons-nous-en, allez-vous-en—que je m'en aille, que je m'en allasse.

Apprendre, to learn (avoir); like prendre.

Assaillir, to assault (avoir), assaillant, assailli, e—j'assaille, nous assaillons, ils assaillent—j'assaillais, j'assaillis, j'assaillirai, j'assaillirais—assaille, que j'assaille, que j'assaillisse.

S'asseoir, to sit down; s'asseyant, assis, e—je m'assieds, tu t'assieds, il s'assied, nous nous asseyons, vous vous asseyez, ils s'asseient—je m'asseyais, je m'assis, je me suis assis, je m'étais assis, je me fus assis, je m'assiérai, je me serai assis, je m'assiérais, je me serais **or** fusse assis—assieds-toi, asseyons-nous, asseyez-vous—que je m'asseie, que nous nous asseyions, que vous vous asseyiez, qu'ils s'asseient—que je m'assisse, que je me sois assis, que je me fusse assis.

Battre, to beat; battant, battu, e (avoir) je bats, tu bats, il bat, nous battons, vous battez, ils battent—je battais, je battis, je battrai, je battrais—bats—que je batte, que je battisse.

Bénir, to bless, is regular, except the past participle béni, e, which is written bénit, e, when speaking of things consecrated by the church, as, pain bénit, eau bénite.

Boire, to drink; buvant, bu, e (avoir)—je bois, tu bois, il boit, nous buvons, vous buvez, ils boivent—je buvais, je bus, je boirai, je boirais—bois, buvons, buvez—que je boive, que nous buvions, que vous buviez, qu'ils boivent, que je busse, qu'il bût.

Bouillir, to boil; bouillant, bouilli, e (avoir)—je bous, tu bous, il bout, nous bouillons, vous bouillez, ils bouillent—je bouillais, je bouillis, je bouillirai—bous, bouillons, bouillez—que je bouille, que je bouillisse.

Taken in an active sense, it is used with faire, faire bouillir; as a neuter verb, it is used figuratively; as, je bous d'impatience, etc.

Braire, to bray (asses); generally used in the following expressions only: il brait, ils braient—il braira, ils brairont—il brairait, ils brairaient—qu'il braie, qu'ils braient.

Bruire (a defective verb), to roar, to rustle; bruyant—ils bruissent, il bruyait, ils bruyaient, ils bruissaient—qu'il bruisse.

Choir, to fall; used only in the infinitive; as, il s'est laissé choir.

Circoncire, to circumcise; circoncisant, circoncis—je circoncis, je circoncisais, je circoncis, je circoncirai, je circoncirais—circoncis—que je circoncise, que je circoncisse.

Circonscrire, to circumscribe; like écrire.

Clore, to close; closant, clos, e (avoir)—je clos, tu clos, il clôt—(no plural, no imperfect, no past definite)—je clorai, je clorais—clos (no plural)—que je close—(no imperfect).

Combattre, to fight; combattant, etc., like battre.

Commettre, to commit; like mettre.

Complaire, to please; like plaire.

Comprendre, to comprehend, to understand; like prendre.

Compromettre, to compromise; like mettre.

Conclure, to conclude; concluant, conclu—je conclus, tu conclus, il conclut, nous concluons, vous concluez, ils concluent—je concluais, nous concluions, vous concluiez—je conclus, je conclurai, je conclurais—conclus—que je conclue, que nous concluions, que vous concluiez, qu'ils concluent—que je conclusse.

Concourir, to concur, to compete; like courir.

Confire, to preserve (fruit, etc.); confisant, confit, e—je confis, nous confisons—je confisais, je confis, je confirai, je confirais—confis—que je confise, que nous confisions, que je confisse.

Conquérir, to conquer; like acquérir, but it is used only in the following tenses: infinitive, participle, past definite, imperfect subjunctive, and compound tenses.

Contredire, to contradict; like dire, **except** in the second person plural of the present indicative and imperative, vous contredisez, contredisez.

Contrefaire, to counterfeit; like faire.

Convaincre, to convince; like vaincre.

Corrompre, to corrupt; like rompre.

Coudre, to sew; cousant, cousu, e (avoir)—je couds, tu couds, il coud, nous cousons, vous cousez, ils cousent—je cousais, je cousis, je coudrai, je coudrais—couds, cousons, cousez—que je couse, que je cousisse, qu'il cousît.

Courir, to run; courant, couru (avoir)—je cours, tu cours, il court, nous courons, vous courez, ils courent—je courais, je courus, je courrai, je courrais—cours, courons, courez—que je coure, que je courusse.

Croire, to believe; croyant, cru, e (avoir)—je crois, tu crois, il croit, nous croyons, vous croyez, ils croient—je croyais, nous croyions, vous croyiez—je crus, je croirai, je croirais—crois—que je croie, que nous croyions, que vous croyiez, que je crusse.

Cueillir, to gather; cueillant, cueilli, e—je cueille, nous cueillons—je cueillais, je cueillis, je cueillerai, je cueillerais—cueille—que je cueille, que je cueillisse, qu'il cueillît.

Débattre, to debate; like battre.

Déchoir, to decay; (no present participle), déchu, e, je déchois, tu déchois, il déchoit, nous déchoyons, vous déchoyez, ils déchoient—(no imperfect)—je déchus, je décherrai, je décherrais—que je déchoie, que nous déchoyions—que je déchusse.

Découdre, to rip; like coudre.

Décrire, to describe; like écrire.

Dédire, to disown; like dire, **except** vous dédisez.

Défaire, to undo; like faire.

Se défaire, to get rid of; like faire.

Démettre, to remove; like mettre.

Se démettre, to resign; like mettre.

Déplaire, to displease; like plaire.

Dépourvoir, to take away what is wanted or necessary; used in the infinitive and compound tenses.

Désapprendre, to forget; like prendre.

Dire, to say, to tell; disant, dit, e—je dis, tu dis, il dit, nous disons, vous dites, ils disent—je disais, je dis, nous dîmes, je dirai, je dirais—dis, disons, dites—que je dise, que je disse, qu'il dît.

Discourir, to discourse; like courir.

Dissoudre, to dissolve; like absoudre.

Distraire, to divert; like traire.

S'ébattre, to sport, to be merry; like battre.

Échoir, to be due, to expire; échéant, échu, e—il⁀échoit, ils‿échoient —(no imperfect)—il⁀échut, ils‿échurent, il⁀écherra, ils‿écherront, il⁀écherrait, ils‿écherraient—(no present subjunctive)—qu'il⁀échût, qu'ils‿échussent.

Éclore, to blow, to hatch; used only in the following cases: éclos, e—il⁀éclôt, ils‿éclosent, il⁀éclôra, ils‿éclôront, il⁀éclôrait, ils‿éclôraient—qu'il⁀éclose, qu'ils‿éclosent—il⁀est‿éclos, etc.

Écrire, to write; écrivant, écrit, e—j'écris, tu écris, il⁀écrit, nous‿écrivons, vous‿écrivez, ils‿écrivent—j'écrivais, j'écrivis, j'écrirai, j'écrirais—écris, écrivons, écrivez—que j'écrive, que j'écrivisse, qu'il⁀écrivît.

Élire, to elect; like lire.

Émouvoir, to stir; like mouvoir.

Enclore, to enclose; like clore.

Encourir, to incur; like courir.

S'enfuir, to flee, to run away; like fuir.

S'enquérir, to inquire; like acquérir.

S'ensuivre, to follow (unipersonal); s'ensuivant, ensuivi—il s'ensuit, il s'ensuivait, il s'ensuivit, il s'ensuivra, il s'ensuivrait—qu'il s'ensuive, qu'il s'ensuivît.

S'entremettre, to mediate; like mettre.

S'entre-nuire, to injure one another; like nuire.

Entreprendre, to undertake; like prendre.

Entrevoir, to have a glimpse of; like voir.

Envoyer, to send; envoyant, envoyé, e (avoir)—j'envoie, tu envoies, il⁀envoie, nous‿envoyons, vous‿envoyez, ils‿envoient—j'envoyais, tu envoyais, il⁀envoyait, nous‿envoyions, vous‿envoyiez, ils‿envoyaient—j'envoyai, j'enverrai, j'enverrais—envoie, envoyons, envoyez—que j'envoie, que nous‿envoyions, que vous‿envoyiez, qu'ils‿envoient, que j'envoyasse, qu'il⁀envoyât.

S'éprendre, to be smitten; like prendre.

Équivaloir, to be equivalent; like valoir.

Exclure, to exclude; excluant, exclu; like conclure.

Extraire, to extract; like traire.

Faillir, to fail; faillant, failli, used only in the past definite and compound tenses of the indicative mood, je faillis, nous faillîmes, j'ai failli, j'avais failli.

Faire, to do, to make; faisant, fait, e—je fais, tu fais, il fait, nous faisons, vous faites, ils font—je faisais, je fis, nous fîmes, je ferai, je ferais—fais, faisons, faites—que je fasse, que je fisse, qu'il fît.

Falloir (a unipersonal verb), to be necessary, must; fallu, been necessary; il faut, il fallait, il fallut, il faudra, il faudrait—qu'il faille, qu'il fallût.

Férir, to strike; used only in *sans coup férir*, without striking a blow.

Fleurir, to blossom, regular except in speaking of the arts, sciences and empires. Its part. pres. is florissant, flourishing; and the third persons of the imperf. indic. are florissait, florissaient.

Forfaire, to forfeit; like faire.

Frire, to fry; (no part. pres.)—frit—je fris, tu fris, il frit, nous faisons frire, vous faites frire, ils font frire—je faisais frire, je fis frire, je frirai, je frirais—fais frire—que je fasse frire, que je fisse frire.

Fuir, to fly, to flee; fuyant, fui—je fuis, nous fuyons—je fuyais, nous fuyions—je fuis, je fuirai, je fuirais—fuis—que je fuie, que nous fuyions, que je fuisse.

Gésir, to lie; gisant—il gît, nous gisons, vous gisez, ils gisent—je gisais, etc.—ci-gît, here lies; ci-gisent, here lie.

Haïr, to hate; haïssant, haï, e—je hais, tu hais, il hait, nous haïssons, vous haïssez, ils haïssent—je haïssais, je haïs, nous haïmes, vous haïtes, ils haïrent—je haïrai, je haïrais—hais, haïssons, haïssez—que je haïsse, que je haïsse, qu'il haït.

Honnir, to dishonor; past part. honni. Motto of the Order of the Garter: "Honni soit qui mal y pense."

Importer, to be of consequence (a unipersonal verb) il⁀importe, il⁀importait; and also to import, conjugated like aimer.

Inscrire, to inscribe; like écrire.

Interdire, to forbid; like dire.

Interrompre, to interrupt; like rompre.

Lire, to read, lisant, lu, e—je lis, tu lis, il lit, nous lisons, vous lisez, ils lisent—je lisais, je lus, je lirai, je lirais—lis—que je lise, que je lusse, qu'il lût.

Luire, to shine, luisant, lui—je luis, tu luis, il luit, nous luisons, vous luisez, ils luisent—je luisais—(no past definite)—je luirai, je luirais—luis—que je luise—(no imperfect).

Malfaire, to do wrong; used only in the infinitive.

Maudire, to curse; maudissant, maudit, e—je maudis, nous maudissons—je maudissais, je maudis, je maudirai, je maudirais—maudis —que je maudisse.

Médire, to slander; like dire, except vous médisez—médisez.

Se méprendre, to mistake; like prendre.

Mettre, to put; mettant, mis, e—je mets, tu mets, il met, nous mettons, vous mettez, ils mettent—je mettais, je mis, je mettrai, je mettrais—mets—que je mette, que je misse, qu'il mît.

Moudre, to grind; moulant, moulu, e—je mouds, tu mouds, il moud, nous moulons, vous moulez, ils moulent—je moulais, je moulus, je moudrai, je moudrais—que je moule, que je moulusse, qu'il moulût.

Mourir, to die; mourant, mort, e (être)—je meurs, tu meurs, il meurt, nous mourons, vous mourez, ils meurent—je mourais, je mourus, je mourrai, je mourrais—meurs, mourons, mourez—que je meure, que je mourusse.

Naître, to be born; naissant, né, e (être)—je nais, tu nais, il naît, nous naissons—je naissais, je naquis, je naitrai, je naitrais—nais, naissons, naissez—que je naisse, que je naquisse, qu'il naquît.

Nuire, to hurt; past part., nui. The rest like réduire.

Omettre, to omit; like mettre.

Ouïr, to hear; ouï—j'ouïs, I heard—ils ouïrent—j'ai ouï, etc.—que j'ouïsse, qu'il ouït.

Paître, to graze; paissant, etc.—say: je fais paître, je faisais paître, je fis paître, je ferai paître, etc.

Parcourir, to go through; like courir.

Parfaire, to complete; like faire (obsolete).

Permettre, to permit; like mettre.

Plaire, to please; plaisant, plu—je plais, tu plais, il plaît, nous plaisons, vous plaisez, ils plaisent—je plaisais, je plus, je plairai, je plairais—plais, plaisons, plaisez—que je plaise, que je plusse.

Pleuvoir, to rain (unipersonal); plu—il pleut, il pleuvait, il plut, il pleuvra, il pleuvrait—qu'il pleuve, qu'il plût.

Poindre, to dawn; only used in il poindra.

Poursuivre, to pursue; like suivre.

Pourvoir, to provide; pourvoyant, pourvu, e—je pourvois, tu pourvois, il pourvoit, nous pourvoyons, vous pourvoyez, ils pourvoient—je pourvoyais, tu pourvoyais, il pourvoyait, nous pour-voyions, vous pourvoyiez, ils pourvoyaient—je pourvus, je pourvoirai, je pourvoirais—pourvois, pourvoyons, pourvoyez—que je pourvoie, que vous pourvoyiez, qu'ils pourvoient—que je pourvusse, qu'il pourvût.

Pouvoir, to be able; pouvant, pu—je puis or je peux, tu peux, il peut, nous pouvons, vous pouvez, ils peuvent—je pouvais—je pus, tu pus, il put, nous pûmes, vous pûtes, ils purent—je pourrai, je pourrais,—(no imperative)—que je puisse, que je pusse, qu'il pût.

Prédire, to foretell; like dire, except vous prédisez—prédisez, impératif.

Prendre, to take; prenant, pris, e—je prends, tu prends, il prend, nous prenons, vous prenez, ils prennent—je prenais, je pris, je prendrai, je prendrais—prends, prenons, prenez—que je prenne, que nous prenions, que vous preniez, qu'ils prennent—que je prisse.

Prescrire, to prescribe; like écrire.

Prévaloir, to prevail; like valoir, except the pres. subj. que je prévale, que tu prévales, qu'il prévale, que nous prévalions, que vous prévaliez, qu'ils prévalent.

Prévoir, to foresee; like voir, except the future and conditional; je prévoirai, tu prévoiras, il prévoira, nous prévoirons, vous prévoirez, ils prévoiront—je prévoirais, tu prévoirais, il prévoirait, nous prévoirions, vous prévoiriez, ils prévoiraient.

Promettre, to promise; like mettre.

Proscrire, to proscribe; like écrire.

Quérir, to fetch; used (seldom) in the infinitive, after aller, envoyer, venir; as: allez me quérir . . .; envoyez quérir cet homme; il m'est venu quérir, etc.

Rabattre, to abate; like battre.

Rapprendre, to learn again; like prendre.

Se rasseoir, to sit down again; like s'asseoir.

Ravoir, to have again; used only in the infinitive.

Rebattre, to beat again; like battre.

Reboire, to drink again; like boire.

Reclure, to shut up; only in the infinitive and compound tenses.

Reconquérir, to conquer again; like acquérir.

Recoudre, to sew again; like coudre.

Recourir, to have recourse, to run again; like courir.

Récrire, to write again; like écrire.

Recueillir, to gather; like cueillir.

Redéfaire, to undo again; like faire.

Relire, to read again; like lire.

Reluire, to shine; like luire.

Remettre, to put again, to deliver; like mettre.

Remoudre, to grind again; like moudre.

Renaître, to be born again, to spring up again, to revive; like naître. No past part., no compound tenses.

Renvoyer, to send back; like envoyer.

Reprendre, to take again; like prendre.

Requérir, to require; like acquérir.

Résoudre, to resolve; résolvant, résolu, e—je résous, tu résous, il résout, nous résolvons, vous résolvez, ils résolvent—je résolvais, je résolus, je résoudrai, je résoudrais—résous, résolvons, résolvez—que je résolve, que je résolusse, qu'il résolût.

Revaloir, to return like for like; like valoir.

Revêtir, to invest; like vêtir.

Revivre, to revive; like vivre.

Revoir, to review, to see again; like voir.

Rire, to laugh; riant, ri—je ris, tu ris, il rit, nous rions, vous riez, ils rient—je riais, tu riais, il riait, nous riions, vous riiez, ils riaient—je ris, nous rîmes—je rirai, je rirais—ris, rions, riez—que je rie, que tu ries, qu'il rie, que nous riions, que vous riiez, qu'ils rient—que je risse, qu'il rît.

Rompre, to break; rompant, rompu, e—je romps, tu romps, il rompt, nous rompons, vous rompez, ils rompent—je rompais, je rompis, je romprai, je romprais—romps, rompons, rompez—que je rompe, que je rompisse.

Saillir, to gush out (is regular, and conjugated like finir), to project; saillant, sailli—il saille, ils saillent, il saillait, ils saillaient—(no past definite)—il saillera, ils sailleront, il saillerait, ils sailleraient—qu'il saille, qu'ils saillent, qu'il saillît, qu'ils saillisent.

Satisfaire, to satisfy; like faire.

Savoir, to know; sachant, su, e—je sais, tu sais, il sait, nous savons, vous savez, ils savent—je savais, je sus, nous sûmes—je saurai, je saurais—sache, sachons, sachez—que je sache, que je susse.

Secourir, to help; like courir.

Seoir, to become, to fit; seyant—il sied, ils siéent—il seyait, ils seyaient—il siéra, ils siéront—il siérait, ils siéraient—only are in use. To sit, only in séant; sis, e, situated.

Soumettre, to submit; like mettre.

Sourire, to smile; like rire.

Souscrire, to subscribe; like écrire.

Soustraire, to subtract; like traire.

Suffire, to suffice; suffisant, suffi—je suffis, tu suffis, il suffit, nous suffisons, vous suffisez, ils suffisent—je suffisais, je suffis, nous suffîmes, je suffirai, je suffirais—suffis, suffisons, suffisez—que je suffise, que je suffisse.

Suivre, to follow; suivant, suivi, e—je suis, tu suis, il suit, nous suivons, vous suivez, ils suivent—je suivais, je suivis, je suivrai, je suivrais—suis, suivons, suivez—que je suive, que je suivisse.

Surfaire, to exact, to overcharge; like faire.

Surgir, to issue, to rise; used figuratively; as, il surgira des difficultés, difficulties will arise, etc.

Surprendre, to surprise; like prendre.

Surseoir, to put off (a law term; sursoyant, sursis—je sursois, tu sursois, il sursoit, nous sursoyons, vous sursoyez, ils sursoient—je sursoyais, tu sursoyais, il sursoyait, nous sursoyions, vous sursoyiez, ils sursoyaient—je sursis, je sursoirai, je sursoirais—sursois—que je sursoie, que tu sursoies, qu'il sursoie, que nous sursoyions, que vous sursoyiez, qu'ils sursoient—que je sursisse.

Survivre, to outlive; like vivre.

Taire, to conceal; taisant, tu—je tais, tu tais, il tait, nous taisons, vous taisez, ils taisent—je taisais, je tus, je tairai, je tairais—tais, taisons, taisez—que je taise, que je tusse, qu'il tût—avoir tu, ayant tu.

Se taire, to be silent; like taire.

Traire, to milk; trayant, trait, e—je trais, tu trais, il trait, nous trayons, vous trayez, ils traient—je trayais, tu trayais, il trayait, nous trayions, vous trayiez, ils trayaient—(no past definite)—je trairai, tu trairas, etc.—je trairais—trais, trayons, trayez—que je traie, que tu traies, qu'il traie, que nous trayions, que vous trayiez, qu'ils traient—(no imperfect subjunctive).

Transcrire, to transcribe; like écrire.

Transmettre, to convey; like mettre.

Tressaillir, to start; tressaillant, tressailli—je tressaille, je tressaillais, je tressaillis, je tressaillirai, je tressaillirais—tressaille—que je tressaille, que je tressaillisse.

Vaincre, to vanquish; vainquant, vaincu, e—je vaincs, tu vaincs, il vainc, nous vainquons, vous vainquez, ils vainquent—je vainquais, je vainquis, je vaincrai, je vaincrais—vaincs, vainquons, vainquez—que je vainque, que je vainquisse.

Valoir, to be worth; valant, valu, e—je vaux, tu vaux, il vaut, nous valons, vous valez, ils valent—je valais, je valus, je vaudrai, je vaudrais—que je vaille, que tu vailles, qu'il vaille, que nous valions, que vous valiez, qu'ils vaillent, que je valusse, qu'il valût.

Vêtir, to dress; vêtant, vêtu, e—je vêts, tu vêts, il vêt, nous vêtons, vous vêtez, ils vêtent—je vêtais, je vêtis, je vêtirai, je vêtirais—vêts, vêtons, vêtez—que je vête, que je vêtisse, etc.

Vivre, to live; vivant, vécu—je vis, tu vis, il vit, nous vivons, vous vivez, ils vivent—je vivais, je vécus, je vivrai, je vivrais—vis,—vivons, vivez—que je vive, que je vécusse.

Voir, to see; voyant, vu, e—je vois, tu vois, il voit, nous voyons, vous voyez, ils voient—je voyais, tu voyais, il voyait, nous voyions, vous voyiez, ils voyaient—je vis, nous vîmes—je verrai, je verrais—vois, voyons, voyez—que je voie, que tu voies, qu'il voie, que nous voyions, que vous voyiez, qu'ils voient—que je visse, etc.

Vouloir, to be willing; voulant, voulu—je veux, tu veux, il veut, nous voulons, vous voulez, ils veulent—je voulais, je voulus, je voudrai, je voudrais—veuille, veuillez—que je veuille, que tu veuilles, qu'il veuille, que nous voulions, que vous vouliez, qu'ils veuillent, que je voulusse, etc.

Objective Case after Verbs

Some verbs have two objects, a direct and an indirect; as:

I gave a watch to my son.	J'ai donné une montre à mon fils.
I gave it to him.	Je la lui ai donnée.
I bought it for him.	Je l'ai achetée pour lui.
I paid the watch-maker for it.	Je l'ai payée à l'horloger.

The objective case after passive verbs is preceded by **de** or **par.** By **de,** to express a **feeling,** a **passion,** an operation of the **soul;** by **par,** to express an action in which the **body** or the **mind** alone is concerned.

Examples

We are loved by our children.	Nous sommes‿aimés de nos‿enfants.
That girl is beloved by her aunt.	Cette fille‿est chérie de sa tante.
Wicked persons are detested by everybody.	Les méchants sont détestés de tout le monde.
This novel was written by Alexander Dumas.	Ce roman a été écrit par Alexandre Dumas.
That boy has been chastised by his father.	Ce garçon a été corrigé par son père.
This parcel has been brought by John.	Ce paquet a été apporté par Jean.

The following verbs have for their object another verb in the infinitive:

Aimer mieux, to like better	Oser, to dare
Compter, to intend	Penser, to think
Croire, to believe	Pouvoir, to be able
Daigner, to deign	Prétendre, to pretend, claim
Devoir, ought	Savoir, to know
Entendre, to hear	Sembler, to seem
Espérer, to hope	Valoir mieux, to be better
Faire, to make	Venir, to come
Falloir, must, to be necessary	Voir, to see
S'imaginer, to imagine	Vouloir, to be willing
Laisser, to let	

Examples

She prefers to stay in rather than to go out.	Elle aime mieux rester que de sortir.
I intend to buy a new hat.	Je compte‿acheter un chapeau neuf.
I believe I can remember that.	Je crois pouvoir me rappeler cela.
Deign to listen to what I tell you.	Daignez écouter ce que je vous dis.
We are to dine out.	Nous devons dîner en ville.
I have had my trousers mended.	J'ai fait raccommoder mon pantalon.
I must give him forty francs.	Il me faut lui donner quarante francs.
He imagines he is learned.	Il s'imagine‿être savant.
I dare not say that.	Je n'ose pas dire cela.
We cannot explain that to you.	Nous ne pouvons pas vous‿expliquer cela.
He pretends to learn that easily.	Il prétend apprendre cela facilement.
I know how to skate.	Je sais patiner.
It is better not to play at all.	Il vaut mieux ne pas jouer du tout.
Come and dine with us.	Venez dîner avec nous.

The following verbs require the preposition **à** before another verb in the infinitive:

S'abaisser, to humble oneself
S'abandonner, yield oneself
Aboutir, to result
S'accoutumer, accustom oneself
S'acharner, be excited
Aider, help
Aimer, like to
S'animer, get animated
S'appliquer, apply to
Apprendre, learn to
S'apprêter, prepare oneself
Aspirer, aspire to
S'assujétir, subject oneself
S'attacher, attach to
S'attendre, expect a thing
Autoriser, authorize
S'avilir, demean oneself

Avoir, have to
Balancer, hesitate
Se borner, limit oneself
Chercher, seek, look for
Se complaire, take delight in
Concourir, cooperate
Condamner, condemn
Consentir, consent
Consister, consist
Conspirer, conspire
Se consumer, be consumed
Contribuer, contribute
Convier, invite
Coûter, cost
Décider, determine to
Désapprendre, to unlearn
Se déterminer, resolve to
Dévouer, devote

Disposer, dispose
Donner, give
Dresser, train to
Tarder, delay, to tarry
Tendre, tend
Employer, employ in
Encourager, encourage
Engager, engage
S'enhardir, make bold
Enseigner, teach
S'entendre, understand
S'étudier, make it one's study
Exceller (à faire), excel in
Exciter, excite to
Exhorter, exhort to
Se fatiguer, fatigue oneself
Former, form to
Habituer, accustom to
Hésiter, hesitate
Inciter, incite to
Instruire, teach
Inviter, to invite
Se mettre, begin to

Montrer, show to
S'offrir, offer
Parvenir, succeed in
Pencher, incline to
Penser, think of
Persévérer, persevere
Persister, persist
Se plaire, be pleased
Se plier, be folded
Porter, induce
Se préparer, get ready
Provoquer, provoke
Réduire, reduce
Renoncer, renounce
Répugner, be repugnant to
Se résigner, submit oneself
Se résoudre, resolve
Réussir, succeed in
Servir, be of use to
Songer, think of
Travailler, work, to labor
Viser, aim to
Vouer, to vow

The following verbs take the preposition **de** before another verb in the infinitive:

S'abstenir, to abstain from
Achever, complete
Accuser, charge
Affecter, affect
S'affliger, afflict oneself
S'agir (*impers*), to be in question
Ambitionner, to aspire
S'applaudir, praise oneself
Appréhender, apprehend
Avertir, warn
S'aviser, think of
Blâmer, blame
Brûler, burn with
Cesser, to cease
Charger (se), charge
Commander, order
Conjurer, entreat
Conseiller, to advise
Convenir, agree
Craindre, fear
Dédaigner, disdain to
Défendre, forbid
Défier, defy
Délibérer, deliberate
Désespérer, despair
Détester, detest
Différer, to defer; to delay
Dire, say, to tell
Disconvenir, disown, to deny

Dispenser, exempt from
Éluder, evade
Empêcher, prevent from
Enjoindre, enjoin
S'enorgueillir, get proud of
Entreprendre, undertake
S'étonner, be astonished at
Éviter, avoid
S'excuser, excuse oneself for
Feindre, feign
Féliciter, congratulate
Se flatter, flatter oneself
Frémir, shudder
Gagner, gain, to have advantage
Gémir, groan
Se glorifier, glory in
Hâter, hasten
S'indigner, be indignant
Inspirer, inspire
Interdire, forbid
Jurer, swear
Languir, languish
Mander, inform
Manquer, miss, to fail
Méditer, meditate
Menacer, threaten
Parler, speak of
Permettre, allow
Persuader, persuade
Avoir peur, be afraid
Préférer, prefer
Prendre garde, take care not to
Préserver, preserve
Prier, beseech
Projeter, form projects
Promettre, promise
Se proposer, propose
Protester, protest
Punir, punish
Recommander, recommend
Refuser, refuse
Regretter, regret
Se réjouir, rejoice at
Se repentir, repent
Reprocher, reproach
Retarder, delay
Rire, laugh
Risquer, risk
Rougir, blush
Sommer, summon
Souffrir, suffer
Souhaiter, wish

Mériter, deserve
Négliger, neglect
Obtenir, obtain
Offrir, offer
Ordonner, give order
Oublier, to forget
Soupçonner, suspect
Suggérer, suggest
Supplier, beseech
Tenter, be tempted
Trembler, tremble
S'approcher, approach
Se vanter, boast
Se fâcher, to grow angry at something

Tenses of the Verb

The Indicative Mood

1. The Present Tense in French has no variety of expression corresponding to the English **I give, I do give, I am giving,** etc.; all alike are rendered by the simple present **je donne,** etc.

2. As in English, the Present is often used instead of the Past in lively narration.

Thus, **La nuit approche, l'instant arrive; César se présente.** Night draws nigh, the moment comes; Caesar presents himself.

And in French, present and past are mixed and interchanged in the same sentence.

3. The Present not infrequently stands where the Future would be more logically correct.

Thus, **Dès que je pourrai, je reviens.** As soon as I shall be able, I (shall) come back. **Je pars demain.** I set out to-morrow.

4. The Present is regularly used (instead of the Present Perfect, as in English) for past action continued into the present, or for what has been and still is.

Thus, **Il est ici depuis une semaine.** He has been here for a week. **Je l'ai déjà depuis deux ans.** I have had it two years already.

We similarly use the Imperfect for the English Pluperfect.

The Imperfect

1. The Imperfect expresses past action viewed as **continuous,** as a lasting condition or quality, or as a habitual and repeated action.

The distinction, when the Imperfect is employed in French can be easily made. Whenever in English, **I was giving,** or **I kept giving,** or **I used to give,** or **I gave repeatedly,** or the like could be used, in French the Imperfect is employed.

2. The Imperfect is used either in conversation or narration to express:

a. A past action which was already going on, when the one expressed by either the Past Indefinite or Prétérit takes place. Ex.:

When I came in, he was writing.
Quand je suis‿entré, il⁀écrivait;

or, Quand j'entrai (prétérit; narrative style) il⁀écrivait.

I saw her yesterday. She was walking about.
Je l'ai vue hier. Elle se promenait.

b. A continued action:

While I spoke, he wrote, Tandis que je parlais, il⁀écrivait.
Where were you yesterday? Où étiez-vous hier?

c. A repeated or habitual action:

1. Every time I spoke, he interrupted me,
Chaque fois que je parlais, il m'interrompait.
2. Last summer I took a walk every morning,
L'été passé, je faisais une promenade tous les matins.
I used to read a good deal, then, Je lisais beaucoup, alors.

The Prétérit and Past Indefinite Tenses

The Past Indefinite and Prétérit represent a past action as single or momentary.

Practically, the Past Indefinite or Conversational Tense alone of these two, is used in conversation:

I saw him yesterday, Je l'ai vu hier.

While the Prétérit or Historical Tense fills in narration the same office as the Past Indefinite in conversation:

Cæsar saw him and said . . . César le vit, et dit . . .

The Pluperfect and the Past Anterior

The Pluperfect and the Past Anterior both answer to the English Pluperfect, but the French Pluperfect is its ordinary equivalent, and much the more commonly used of the two tense forms.

a. In general, the Past Anterior is used only after certain particles, which give a special definiteness to the action expressed, in its relation to another past action. These particles are quand and lorsque, **when;** après que, **after;** dès que and aussitôt que, **as soon as;** à peine, **hardly;** and the like: thus, Lorsqu'il eut fini, je sortis. **When he had finished, I went out.**

b. Only the Pluperfect can be used after si, **if.**

The Future

The Future in French corresponds to the English Future.

a. The French, however, often use the Future in compound sentences where it is logically more correct, but where in English the Present is used instead: thus, Vous direz ce qu'il vous plaira. You will say what you (shall) please. Tant qu'il vivra. As long as he lives (or shall live).

b. The Future is used after si only in the sense of whether: thus, Je ne sais s'il viendra. I know not whether he will come.

c. As in English, the Future is sometimes used in an imperative sense: thus, Tu ne tueras pas. Thous shalt not kill; or to express a probability: thus, Ce sera quelque grand‿homme. He is doubtless some great man.

The Future Perfect

The Future Perfect is used like the corresponding tense in English.

a. Its peculiarities of use are closely analogous to those of the simple Future: thus, Tu recueilleras ce que tu auras semé. Thou wilt reap what thou hast (shalt have) sown. Il aura rendu quelques services. He has doubtless rendered some services.

The Conditional

The Conditional agrees in its general use with the English Conditional, or verb-phrase made with the auxiliaries **would** and **should.**

a. The Conditional answers to a past tense as a future to a present: thus, J'espère qu'il viendra, j'espérais qu'il viendrait. I hope he will come, I hoped he would come. Je ne sais s'il viendra; je ne savais s'il viendrait. I don't know whether he will come; I did not know whether he would come, and so on.

b. In a hypothetical sentence, the Conditional is used in the conclusion: thus, Si je l'avais, je serais content, If I had it, I should be satisfied. If quand is used instead of si, the Conditional may stand also in the other clause: thus, quand je l'aurais, if I had it; also after que, in an idiomatically inverted sentence: thus, Je l'aurais, que je n'en serais pas content. I might have it, and yet not be satisfied.

c. As in English, the Conditional is used to soften a request or statement: thus, auriez-vous la bonté . . . would you have the kindness . . . je voudrais que . . . I should like to have . . . Saurais (Conditional of **savoir,** to know), is idiomatically used in the sense of the Present can.

The Conditional Perfect

The Conditional Perfect corresponds to the same tense in English, and is related to the simple Conditional precisely as the Future Perfect to the Future.

Syntax of the Verb

1. The verb agrees in number and person with its **subject,** whether that subject precedes or follows, as:

They run too fast.	Ils courent trop vite.
The women and children came afterward.	Vinrent‿ensuite les femmes et les enfants.

2. A verb is put in the plural when it has two or more singular subjects, as:

My father and mother are out.	Mon père⁀et ma mère sont sortis.
Liberty, Equality, Fraternity, are famous words.	Liberté, Égalité, Fraternité, sont des mots fameux.

3. When the subjects are of different persons, the verb is put in the plural, and agrees with the subject pronoun which would represent the group.

Henry and I will go to Europe.	Henri et moi nous‿irons en Europe.
You and your sister are late.	Vous et votre sœur⁀êtes, or vous‿êtes,‿en retard.
Peter, you and I are friends.	Pierre, vous et moi sommes, or nous sommes,‿amis.

The Subjunctive Mood

The Subjunctive Mood is so called because it always depends upon another verb, to which it is usually united by a conjunction; or, rather upon a main clause expressing **doubt, wish, fear, command, necessity, indecision, supposition, surprise,** etc.; in one word, all that which is not positive.

Rule I.—The Subjunctive is used after impersonal and other verbs, expressing **doubt, wish,** etc.

I desire that he should write.	Je désire	qu'il⁀écrive.
It is important that he should write.	Il⁀est‿important	
I intend that he shall write.	Je prétends	
It is necessary for him to write.	Il⁀est nécessaire	
It will be necessary for us to leave.	Il faudra	que nous partions.
It will be best that we should leave.	Il sera utile	

RULE II.—The Subjunctive is used after most interrogative and negative clauses, unless we have a positive act to express.

Do you believe—think, suspect, imagine—that there are robbers here?	Croyez-vous—pensez-vous, soupçonnez-vous, vous‿imaginez-vous—qu'il⁀y ait des voleurs⁀ici?
I will never believe—I do not suppose—that there can be any.	Je ne croirai jamais—je ne suppose pas—qu'il puisse⁀y en‿avoir.

But with a positive fact, the Indicative Mood is used:

Does that man believe there is a God?	Cet‿homme croit‿il qu'il⁀y a un Dieu?
He does not believe that there is a God.	Il ne croit pas qu'il⁀y a un Dieu.

RULE III.—The following compound conjunctions require the Subjunctive after them:

Afin que, in order that	Pour que, in order that
A moins que (ne), unless	Pourvu que, provided
Au cas que, in case that	Non pas que, not that
Avant que, before	Pour peu que, however little
Bien que, though	Quoique, though
De crainte que } for fear that	Sans que, without
De peur que } for fear that	Si tant‿est que, if it is true that
En cas que, in case that	Soit que, whether
Encore que, although	Jusqu'à ce que, till
Loin que, far from	Non que, not that
Malgré que, notwithstanding	De ce que requires the Indicative
Afin que vous sachiez.	In order that you may know.
A moins que vous ne lui écriviez.	Unless you write to her.

The negative *ne* is used after the following without implying negation: à moins que, de peur que, de crainte que; and after the verbs craindre, avoir peur, trembler, appréhender, empêcher.

J'ai peur que Madame S. ne vienne pas,	I fear Mrs. S. will not come.
J'ai peur que Madame S. ne vienne,	I fear Mrs. S. will come.
Je crains qu'il n'écrive pas,	I fear he will not write.
Je crains qu'il n'écrive,	I fear he will write.

RULE IV.—Use the Subjunctive after the following expressions:

Quel que, quoi que, whatever
Quelque, quelque . . . que, si . . . que, however
Qui que, qui que ce soit, whoever

Whatever may be your opinion	Quelle que soit votre opinion
Whatever may be his feelings	Quels que soient ses sentiments
Whatever you may say	Quoique vous disiez
However rich you may be	Quelque riche que vous soyez
However tall he may be	Si grand qu'il soit
Whoever says so is in the wrong.	Qui que ce soit qui le dise, a tort.

Tout . . . que, though, requires the Indicative; as:

Though you are learned, you may be mistaken.	Tout savant que vous‿êtes, vous pouvez vous tromper.

Rule V.—The Subjunctive generally comes after il n'y a, il n'y a pas, il n'y a que, il n'est, il n'est pas, il n'est que, followed by a noun or a pronoun.

There is nobody who knows that.	Il n'y a personne qui sache cela.
There are none who know that.	Il n'y a pas d'hommes qui sachent cela.
There are but few / There are few } who know that.	Il n'en‿est guère / Il en‿est peu } qui sachent cela.

Rule VI.—Unless it is intended to affirm the thing positively the Subjunctive is used after relative pronouns when they are preceded by a superlative or by an equivalent; as, le seul, **the only one**; l'unique, **the sole**; le premier, le dernier, etc.; as:

That is the finest house I know.	Voilà la plus belle maison que je connaisse.
It is, perhaps, the only book I can lend you.	C'est peut‿être le seul livre que je puisse vous prêter.
Do you know the last who came?	Connaissez-vous le dernier qui est venu?
He lent me the only book he had.	Il m'a prêté le seul livre qu'il avait.

Sometimes not only the verb which requires the Subjunctive is understood, but even the **que** which precedes that verb is not expressed. This takes place in certain exclamations; as:

May heaven! Would to God!	Fasse le ciel! Plût‿à Dieu!
Whatsoever may happen!	Advienne que pourra!
France forever!	Vive la France!

The Subjunctive must be used in some particular expressions, as:

Who goes there?	Qui vive?
He has taken nothing, so far as I know.	Il n'a rien pris, que je sache.
We said nothing bad, to my knowledge.	Nous n'avons rien dit de mal, que je sache.

The Concord of the Tenses in the Subjunctive, with Reference to the Verb in the first Proposition of the Sentence

TWO IMPORTANT RULES.—I. After the présent de l'indicatif and the futur, come the présent or the passé composé of the Subjunctive.

You must come immediately.	Il faut que vous veniez tout de suite.
You will be obliged to come to-morrow.	Il faudra que vous veniez demain.
It is sufficient for you to have neglected nothing.	Il suffit que vous n'ayez rien négligé.
It will be sufficient for you to be back before Sunday.	Il suffira que vous soyez de retour avant dimanche.

II. After the imparfait, prétérit, passé indéfini, plus-que-parfait, passé antérieur, and conditionnel, come the imparfait or the plus-que-parfait of the Subjunctive.

It was necessary that you should come.	Il fallait que vous vinssiez.
It has been necessary, etc.	Il fallut que vous vinssiez. Il a fallu que vous vinssiez.
It had been necessary, etc.	Il avait fallu, que vous vinssiez.
It would be necessary, etc.	Il faudrait que vous vinssiez.
It would have been necessary, etc.	Il aurait fallu que vous vinssiez.

EXAMPLES

I do not believe that he will succeed.	Je ne crois pas qu'il réussisse.
It will be necessary for you to buy it.	Il faudra que vous l'achetiez.
What shall I say?	Que voulez-vous que je dise?
Is it not a pity that your son has torn his coat?	N'est-ce pas dommage que votre fils‿ait déchiré son‿habit?
Is it certain that you have lost your purse?	Est‿il certain que vous‿ayez perdu votre porte-monnaie?
Do you think he has sold his house?	Pensez-vous qu'il‿ait vendu sa maison?
Where would it be necessary for me to go?	Où faudrait‿il que j'allasse?
What would you have me do?	Que voudriez-vous que je fisse?
What did you wish me to say?	Que vouliez-vous que je disse?
I wished you to write to me.	Je désirais que vous m'écrivissiez.
You ought to have come earlier.	Il aurait fallu que vous fussiez venu plus tôt.

REMARKS.—1. Sometimes, although the first verb is in the present or future, the second is in the imperfect or pluperfect of the Subjunctive; this takes place when the second verb depends on a conditional expression which is itself in the imperfect or pluperfect of the Indicative, as:

I doubt whether you would do that if I told you to do it.	Je doute que vous fissiez cela si je vous disais de le faire.
I doubt whether he would have succeeded if . . .	Je doute qu'il‿eût réussi, si . . .

2. Sometimes, also, although the first verb is in one of the past tenses, the second is in the present or prétérit of the Subjunctive.

a. When a thing is referred to which is true at the moment we are speaking, as:

It was the will of God that we should be mortal.	Dieu a voulu que nous soyons mortels.

b. When it is wished to express a future after afin que, bien que, de crainte que, etc., as:

You have been so careless that I cannot believe you capable of doing much.	Vous‿avez‿été‿trop‿insouciant pour que je vous croie capable de grand'chose.

The Participle

There are two Participles, the present and the past. The Present Participle ends in **ant,** and is always invariable.

It must not be confounded with the verbal adjective ending in **ant,** which is variable, and expresses a state. The Present Participle generally has an objective case; the verbal adjective has none, and may be placed before the noun.

Present Participles

Children obeying their parents	Des‿enfants obéissant à leurs parents
A mother loving her daughter	Une mère‿aimant sa fille
Children caressing their mother	Des‿enfants caressant leur mère
A rain fertilizing the soil	Une pluie fécondant le sol
Words offending decency	Des paroles offensant la pudeur

Verbal Adjectives

They have obedient children.	Ils‿ont des‿enfants‿obéissants.
I have a loving mother.	J'ai une mère‿aimante.
We have caressing children.	Nous‿avons des‿enfants caressants.
It is a fertilizing rain.	C'est‿une pluie fécondante.
Those are offensive words.	Ce sont des paroles‿offensantes.

The following verbal adjectives end in **ent,** instead of **ant:** adhérent, affluent, coïncident, différent, divergent, équivalent, excellent, expédient, négligent, précédent, violent.

There are three principal rules for the Past Participle.

RULE I.—Employed **without an auxiliary,** the past participle is a qualifier which takes the gender and number of the noun which it qualifies.

Except: attendu, considering; excepté, except; ouï, heard; supposé, supposing; vu, considering; non compris, not including; y compris, including, etc., which are invariable when they are placed before the nouns, because they take the place of prepositions; as, attendu que **for** en considération de, etc.

RULE II.—The Past Participle conjugated with être, or any other verb but avoir, is a true adjective, and agrees with the subject in gender and number.

The subject stands sometimes before, sometimes after the verb, as:

Noble souls gain by being known.	Les‿âmes nobles gagnent à être connues.
Blessed be those charitable ladies.	Bénies soient ces dames charitables.
Mr. and Mrs. B. are going to Rouen.	M. et Mme. B. sont partis pour, or sont‿allés à Rouen.
The letters are all written.	Les lettres sont toutes écrites.
Your lesson is not known.	Votre leçon n'est pas sue.
She appeared afflicted.	Elle paraissait‿affligée.

RULE III.—The Past Participle of an active verb, conjugated with **avoir,** is variable, if it is preceded by the direct object of the verb; then it agrees in gender and number with that object.

Invariable.—1st. If there is no direct object; 2nd. If the direct object is after the Participle.

This Rule III is the most important and the principal one.

The letters I have written	Les lettres que j'ai écrites
I have sent them (*f.*) to the post-office.	Je les‿ai envoyées à la poste.
Here are the books she gave me.	Voici les livres qu'elle m'a donnés.
She sent them to me yesterday.	Elle me les‿a envoyés hier.
I have written my two letters.	J'ai écrit mes deux lettres.
She has written nothing.	Elle n'a rien écrit.

Remarks

I. **Participle followed by an Infinitive.**—The Past Participle of an active verb, preceded by a direct object pronoun, and followed by an infinitive with or without a preposition before it, is **variable,** if the preceding pronoun is the direct object of the principal verb; as:

The ladies I heard singing	Les dames que j'ai entendues chanter
The children I saw playing	Les‿enfants que j'ai vus jouer

The Participle is **invariable,** if the preceding pronoun is the object of the infinitive; as:

The robbers I saw condemned	Les voleurs que j'ai vu condamner
The children I saw punished	Les‿enfants que j'ai vu punir

The participle *fait,* done, made, is always invariable before an infinitive, as:

I have had them mended.	Je les‿ai fait raccommoder.

II. **Past Participle of Reflexive Verbs.**—In reflexive verbs, the auxiliary **être** always takes the place of **avoir**; as, je me suis habillé, etc.; the Participle of these verbs follows the third rule (p. 323).

1. If the verb is essentially reflective [reflexive], the Participle agrees always with the reflexive pronoun, which is the direct object of the verb; as:

They laughed at your threats.	Ils se sont moqués de vos menaces.
They (*f.*) did not remember your promises.	Elles ne se sont pas souvenues de vos promesses.

2. If the verb is accidentally reflective, the Participle is variable, and follows the third rule, when the reflective is derived from an active verb; and invariable, if the verb by itself is a neuter verb; as, se plaire, se rire, se parler, se succéder, se nuire, etc.

What hard words they said to each other.	Quelles dures paroles ils se sont dites (direct object, paroles, *f.*).
They said hard words to each other.	Ils se sont dit de dures paroles (direct object after, third rule).
They were pleased with each other.	Ils se sont plu (a neuter verb).
They spoke to each other this morning.	Ils se sont parlé ce matin (se is an indirect pronoun: *to* each other).
They (*f.*) applied to me.	Elles se sont‿adressées à moi (se for elles-mêmes).
She gave herself much trouble.	Elle s'est donné beaucoup de peine (direct object after).

Essentially reflective verbs are: s'emparer, s'abstenir, se moquer, se souvenir, etc. See list of reflective verbs.

III.—1. The Past Participle of an impersonal verb is always invariable; as:

Great misfortunes have happened.	Il est arrivé de grands malheurs.
The snow we have had this winter	La neige qu'il y a eu cet hiver

2. The participle preceded and followed by **que** is invariable; as:

The persons I thought you knew.	Les personnes que j'ai cru que vous connaissiez.

3. The participle is invariable when it has for an object **l'** representing a whole clause; as:

The news is better than we had believed.	La nouvelle est meilleure que nous ne l'avions cru.

4. The participle preceded by **le peu de** is variable when **le peu** is taken in a positive sense, and means a little quantity, amount; as:

He robbed me of the few francs I had won.	Il m'a volé le peu de francs que j'avais gagnés.

The participle is invariable, when **le peu** is taken in a negative sense, and means the **want**; as:

The little security he gave me.	Le peu de sécurité qu'il m'a donné.

When variable, the participle agrees with the direct object which precedes it; when invariable, the participle agrees with **le peu,** which is masculine singular.

5. The participle preceded by an adverb of quantity agrees with the noun following the adverb; as:

Was there ever so much beauty crowned?	Jamais tant de beauté fut-elle couronnée?

Negation

1. A verb is made negative in a simple tense by putting **ne** before and **pas** after it; in a compound tense, before and after the auxiliary.

a. It must always be borne in mind that in any compound form the auxiliary is the real verb, the added participle being only a verbal adjective. All rules, therefore, as to the place of negative words, subject and object pronouns, and so on, given with reference to the verb, apply to the auxiliary, and not to the participle in compound forms.

b. The **ne** comes after the subject, but precedes a pronoun object. It is abbreviated always to **n'** before a vowel or **h** mute.

2. Examples of tenses inflected negatively are:

je ne suis pas, I am not	je n'avais pas‿eu, I had not had
tu n'es pas, thou art not	tu n'avais pas‿eu, thou hadst not had
il n'est pas, he is not	il n'avait pas‿eu, he had not had
nous ne sommes pas, we are not	nous n'avions pas‿eu, we had not had
vous n'êtes pas, you are not	vous n'aviez pas‿eu, you had not had
il ne sont pas, they are not	ils n'avaient pas‿eu, they had not had

Point is sometimes used instead of **pas**, which makes a stronger or more emphatic negative; thus:

il n'est point fou.	He certainly is not crazy.

3. For never, nobody, and nothing, the French say ne . . . jamais (literally: not ever), ne . . . personne (literally: not a person), and ne . . . rien (literally: not a thing), respectively, the two words being separated, and the **ne** put always before the verb (or auxiliary); thus:

Je ne suis jamais malade.	I am never ill.
Il n'avait jamais‿été chez nous.	He had never been at our house.
Je n'ai vu personne.	I have seen nobody.
Personne n'a eu mon livre.	No one has had my book.
N'avez-vous rien?	Have you nothing?
Rien ne serait plus cruel.	Nothing would be more cruel.

4. With the verbs **savoir, pouvoir, oser,** and **cesser, pas** is usually omitted, especially when an infinitive follows, and when the negation is not emphatic.

Thus, je ne sais ce que c'est, I don't know what it is, il ne peut tarder, he cannot delay, elle n'oserait revenir, she would not dare to come back, vous ne cessez de rire, you do not stop laughing. Saurais in the sense of **can** has **ne** only; thus, je ne saurais le dire, I cannot say; also usually **puis**: thus, je ne puis, I cannot (but je ne peux pas).

5. **Ne** is often used alone after **si,** after rhetorical questions introduced by **qui,** after **que** in the sense of **why?** or **unless,** with a perfect tense, after **depuis que** and **il y a . . . que,** and in a negative clause depending on one that is negative or impliedly so. Thus: Si ce n'est vous? if it is not you? Qui de nous n'a ses défauts? who of us has not his faults? Que ne se corrige-t-il? why does he not correct himself? Il y a trois mois que je ne l'ai vu, I have not seen him these three months. Vous n'avez pas‿un ami qui ne soit‿aussi le mien, you have not a friend who is not also mine, and Avez-vous‿un ami qui ne soit‿aussi le mien, have you (*i. e.*, surely you have not) a friend who is not also mine?

6. **Ne** is used without **pas** in certain special phrases; thus, n'importe, no matter, n'avoir garde de, take care not to, n'avoir que faire, not have anything to do, ne plaise or ne déplaise, may it not please or displease, and a few others. Thus: à Dieu ne plaise, God forbid, je n'ai garde de désavouer ma faute, I take care not to disavow my fault.

7. Of **ne . . . que,** meaning **only,** the **que** (but, except) stands before the word upon which it bears; thus, je ne verrai qu'elle, I shall see only her, je ne la verrai que demain, I shall see her only to-morrow, je ne la verrai demain qu'après le dîner, I shall see her only after the dinner to-morrow. If the **only** qualifies the verb itself, a paraphrase is made with **faire,** thus, elle ne fait que pleurer, she merely cries.

8. The negative **ne** belongs strictly to the verb, and can never be used except with a verb expressed. If the verb, then, is omitted (for example, in answers), the **ne** is also omitted, and the second part of the negation (pas, rien, jamais, etc.) has by itself a negative sense, thus:

Avez-vous des livres? have you any books?	Pas‿un, not one.
Qu'avez-vous? what have you?	Rien, nothing.
Qui est‿ici? who is here?	Personne, nobody.

9. After a negative verb, the partitive sense of a noun is expressed by **de** alone, without the article, thus:

Je n'ai pas de pain.	I have no bread.
Nous n'avions guère de vin.	We had scarcely any wine.
Vous n'aurez plus de patience.	You will no longer have patience.

a. After **ni . . . ni,** both preposition and article are omitted and the partitive sense is left unexpressed as in English; thus:

Je n'ai ni pain ni beurre,	I have neither bread nor butter.

b. On the other hand, after **ne . . . que, only,** both preposition and article are used; thus:

Nous ne voyons que des‿ennemis,	We see only enemies.

10. The negative word, **non,** is especially used as direct answer to a question, meaning **no**; thus: voulez-vous le faire? non, will you do it? no.

a. It also stands in incomplete expressions, for an omitted negative verb or clause; thus: je gage que non, I wager that it is not so; si l'on souffre ou non, whether one suffers or not; non que je le croie, not that I believe it.

b. It is used to negative a particular member of a sentence which is not a verb; thus: il demeure à la campagne, non loin d'ici; he lives in the country, not far from here; il périt, non sans gloire, he perished, not without glory. Especially, with a negative alternative opposed to a positive; thus: nous voulons un maître et non (**or** non pas) une maîtresse, we want a master, and not a mistress; je le ferai non seulement pour lui, mais aussi pour ses enfants, I shall do it not only for him, but also for his children.

c. **Non plus, not any more, not any sooner,** standing after a negative verb or after **ni, nor,** is often best rendred by **either;** thus: je ne le ferai pas non plus, I shall not do it either; ni moi non plus, nor I either.

11. In dependent clauses, **ne** is often used after certain verbs when no negation is really implied:

a. After verbs of fear or apprehension, of hindering, of doubt or denial; also, after nouns and adjectives of like meaning; thus: je crains qu'il ne vienne, I fear he may come; empêchez qu'il ne vienne, prevent his coming; évitez qu'il ne vous parle, avoid his speaking to you; de peur qu'il ne vienne, for fear that he is coming; point de doute que cela ne soit, no doubt that is so; il est dangereux que la vanité n'étouffe la reconnaissance, it is to be feared that vanity might stifle gratitude.

In such cases, the verb of the dependent clause is always subjunctive; and the **que** with following **ne** may often be best rendered in English by **lest:** Je crains qu'il ne vienne, I fear lest he may come, and so on.

But there are also many exceptions; thus: **ne** is not inserted after an expression of fear or apprehension that is negative or implies a negation; nor, in modern style, after **défendre, forbid;** nor unless the expression of doubt or denial is negative or implies negation; nor, generally, before an infinitive—and other more irregular cases occur.

b. After the expressions of time **il y a . . . que, depuis que,** and **avant que,** a superfluous **ne** is sometimes inserted; thus: je serai sorti avant qu'il n'entre, I shall have gone out before he comes in.

c. A **ne** is inserted before a verb following and depending on a comparative; thus: c'est plus vrai que vous ne le croyez, it is truer than you think.

d. A **ne** is inserted before the subjunctive after **à moins que, unless;** thus: à moins que vous ne veniez, unless you come; also often after **sans que, without;** thus: sans que cela ne paraisse, without its appearing.

The Definite Article

There are two genders in the French language, viz.: the masculine and feminine.

This distinction applies not only to persons, but also to inanimate objects.

In order to indicate this distinction of gender, the definite article is prefixed to substantives.

There are two forms for the Definite Article, viz.: **le** for the masculine, and **la** for the feminine form.

EXAMPLES

MASCULINE	FEMININE
le père, the father	la mère, the mother
le fils, the son	la fille, the daughter
le frère, the brother	la sœur, the sister
le cousin, the cousin	la cousine, the cousin
le beau-frère, the brother-in-law	la belle-sœur, the sister-in-law
le beau-père, the father-in-law	la belle-mère, the mother-in-law
le neveu, the nephew	la nièce, the niece
le grand-père, the grandfather	la grand'mère, the grandmother
le petit-fils, the grandson	la petite-fille, the granddaughter

RULE.—Before nouns beginning with a vowel or an unaspirated (*i. e.*, mute) **h, le** and **la** are changed into **l',** thus forming but one word with the noun.

EXAMPLES

MASCULINE	FEMININE
l'oncle, the uncle	l'amie, the friend
l'ami, the friend	l'assiette, the plate
l'homme, the man	l'habitude, the custom, habit
l'état, the state	

The article must be used in French not only before nouns used in a **definite** sense, but also before nouns employed in a **general** sense; as:

Men are subject to error.	Les hommes sont sujets à l'erreur.
Children like games.	Les enfants aiment le jeu.
Little girls like dolls.	Les petites filles aiment les poupées.
Virtue is the reverse of vice.	La vertu est l'opposé du vice.
Wine is common in France.	Le vin est commun en France.

Before the names of countries, provinces, rivers, winds, mountains, etc., the Definite Article is used; as:

I have visited France, Italy and Germany.	J'ai visité la France, l'Italie, et l'Allemagne.
The Pyrenees, the ocean, the north, the south, the east, the west	Les Pyrénées, l'océan, le nord, le sud, l'est, l'ouest

Before titles prefixed to names, before the names of dignitaries, of systems of doctrine, of certain bodies, of seasons, etc., we use the Definite Article; as:

Marshal Foch	Le Maréchal Foch
General Pershing	Le Général Pershing
President Lincoln	Le Président Lincoln
Christianity; at school	Le christianisme, à l'école
Spring, summer, autumn, winter	Le printemps, l'été, l'automne, l'hiver

The Article is not used in French:

1. Before nouns taken adjectively; as:

I am an American by birth.	Je suis Américain de naissance.
He is a merchant.	Il est marchand, *or*, négociant.
His father is a physician.	Son père est médecin.

2. When there is a relation of qualification between the two nouns by means of **de**; as:

The Queen of England	La reine d'Angleterre
The King of Denmark	Le roi de Danemark

3. When **en** is employed; as:

I will go to France.	J'irai en France.
He lives in Belgium.	Il demeure en Belgique.

4. In proverbs; as:

Poverty is not a vice.	Pauvreté n'est pas vice.

5. Before nouns preceded by **sans, avec, ni, entre,** etc., as:

A man without merit	Un homme sans mérite
I have neither pens nor paper.	Je n'ai ni plumes ni papier.

6. The article is frequently omitted in enumerations; as:

Men, women, children, all perished!	Hommes, femmes, enfants, tout périt!
Glory, honor, fortune, all is lost.	Gloire, honneur, fortune, tout‿est perdu!

7. Before a substantive employed to particularize another which precedes; as:

Mary, the daughter of Mrs. B.	Marie, fille de Mme. B.

Repetition of the Article and other Determinatives

When the article is used, it must be repeated before all the substantives, subjects, or objects. **Ce, cet, cette, ces, mon, ton, son, ma, leur, de,** etc., must also be repeated before every substantive; as:

Painting, poetry and music are sisters.	La peinture, la poésie, et la musique sont sœurs.
My father, mother and sisters	Mon père, ma mère, et mes sœurs
These large and these small rooms	Ces petites et ces grandes chambres

However, if several adjectives qualify the same noun, we do not repeat the determinative; as:

The young and kind Mrs. S.	La jeune et bonne Madame S.

Usage allows the article to be omitted in several forms, as in the following:

Fathers and mothers	Les pères‿et mères
The officers and soldiers	Les‿officiers‿et soldats
Ancient and modern history	L'histoire ancienne et moderne

Articles and Contractions of the Articles

Singular

Masculine	Feminine	With the Apostrophe	
le	la	l'	the
du	de la	de l'	of the
au	à la	à l'	to the
le	la	l'	the

Plural

les	the	Only one form both for the masculine, feminine and apostrophe.
des	of the	
aux	to the	
les	the	

The Partitive Article

Such expressions as "Give me some wine." "Have you any books?" "Bring me some eggs," etc., are rendered in French by the so-called Partitive Article. "Donnez-moi du vin." "Avez-vous des livres?" "Apportez-moi des‿œufs."

The Partitive Article is really the preposition **de** contracted with the Definite Article, as for instance: du vin, some win; de l'eau, some water; de la bière, some beer; des magasins, some stores (**or** simply stores).[1]

In questions, **any** is used in English instead of some, but in French this must always be rendred by the Partitive Article, as: Have you any bread? Avez-vous du pain? Has he bought any handkerchiefs? A-t‿il acheté des mouchoirs? Has he made any purchases? A-t‿il fait des emplettes?

Use of the Partitive Article

1. Sometimes (but not often) the adjective precedes the French noun. In such cases the Partitive Article is expressed by **de**; as:

Beautiful flowers (*or* some [any] fine flowers), de belles fleurs.[2]

2. In the same manner **de** is used when a negative occurs in a French sentence.

I do not drink wine.	Je ne bois pas de vin.
I drink no water.	Je ne bois pas d'eau.
I have no change.	Je n'ai pas de monnaie.
I have no money.	Je n'ai pas d'argent.

3. **De** is used after nouns expressing measure, weight, quantity or number where **of** is used in English.

a bottle of wine	une bouteille de vin
a cup of coffee	une tasse de café
a pair of stockings	une paire de bas

[1] *Some* is not always used in English, but in French the Partitive Article must be employed whenever some part or parts of a totality are meant.

[2] In French the adjective is usually placed after the noun, so that the above rule holds good in a few cases only.

This rule is no longer followed very strictly.

4. **De** must be employed after the following adverbs of quantity:

Assez, enough	rien, nothing
beaucoup, much, many, a great many, a great deal	quelque chose, something
combien, how much, how many	trop, too much, too many
peu, little, few	trop peu, too little, too few
plus, more	tant, so much, so many
moins, less	autant, as much, as many

EXAMPLES

Je n'ai pas‿assez d'argent sur moi.	I have not money enough with me.
J'ai vu beaucoup de personnes.	I have seen a great many persons.
Combien d'échantillons avez-vous reçus?	How many samples have you received?
Il a lu peu de livres.	He has read few books.
Vous‿avez fait trop de fautes.	You have made too many mistakes.
Apportez-moi plus d'eau chaude, garçon.	Waiter, bring me more hot water.

5. **De** + noun is used in the place of an English adjective describing a material, as:

a gold ring	une bague d'or
a silver spoon	une cuiller d'argent
a silk dress	une robe de soie
a velvet hat	un chapeau de velours
a wooden table	une table de bois

The Indefinite Article

Besides the Definite Article, there is also an indefinite one for the singular, answering to the English **a** or **an,** viz.: **un** for the masculine, and **une** for the feminine. Ex.: un oncle, an uncle; un gilet, a vest; une lettre, a letter.

The Indefinite Article does not contract.

Singular

MASCULINE	FEMININE
un	une, a
d'un	d'une, of a
à un	à une, to a
un	une, a

The Indefinite Article is omitted in exclamations; also before names of nationality:

What a beautiful landscape!	Quel beau paysage!
He is French.	Il‿est français.

The Indefinite Article is not used before nouns of weight or measure; but **le, la, l'** instead; as:

Ten francs a pound	Dix francs la livre
How much a metre?	Combien le mètre?

The Noun

No Adjective Use of Nouns

A noun is the name of a living creature or a thing. The French cannot say, a gold pen, a dining-room, the water pitcher, the steam engine (thus using one noun as an adjective to the other) but, only, a pen of gold, a room for[1] dining, the pitcher for[1] water, the engine with[1] steam.

Une plume d'or; une salle à manger.
Le pot‿à eau; la machine à vapeur.

No Possessive Case in French

In French one cannot say, **my father's coat, my brother's clerk,** but:

The coat of my father	L'habit de mon père
The clerk of my brother	Le commis de mon frère

Plural of Nouns

The plural of nouns is formed by adding a silent **s** to the singular:

L'homme, les‿hommes; l'ami, les‿amis

Nouns ending in **s, x** or **z,** in the singular, remain unchanged in the plural.

Le bras, the arm	Les bras, the arms
La voix, the voice	Les voix, the voices
Le nez, the nose	Les nez, the noses

Nouns in **au** or **eu** add **x** to the singular:

Le couteau, les couteaux; un cheveu, des cheveux

[1] *For* and *with* in this connection, are both rendered by *à*.

Nouns in **al,**[1] and a few nouns in **ail,** change **al** and **ail** into **aux:**

Le cheval, les chevaux; le corail, les coraux[2]

Seven nouns in **ou** take **x** in the plural. They are:

Bijou, jewel; *caillou,* pebble; *chou,* cabbage; *genou,* knee; *hibou,* owl; *joujou,* plaything, toy; *pou,* louse

Plural: Bijoux, cailloux, etc.

Irregular Plurals

Le ciel, the sky	Les cieux, the skies
L'œil, the eye	Les‿yeux, the eyes
L'aïeul, the ancestor	Les‿aïeux
Le bétail, cattle	Les bestiaux

The Feminine of Nouns

Nouns which have both a masculine and a feminine form generally add **e** to the masculine form:

Le marchand, storekeeper	La marchande, storekeeper

Substantives Derived from Verbs

Several nouns are derived from verbs; as **fin,** end, from **finir; don,** gift, from **donner,** etc. They are formed as follows:

1. By removing the termination of the verb; as:

Finir, fin, an end	Aviser, avis, a counsel
Bondir, bond, a bound	Chanter, chant, a song
Sauter, saut, a jump	Refuser, refus, a refusal
Dessiner, dessin, a drawing	Appeler, appel, an appeal

2. By removing, together with the termination of the verb, the second of the double consonants preceding the termination; as:

Donner, don, a gift	Réveiller, réveil, the awakening
Conseiller, conseil, advice	Rançonner, rançon, a ransom
Amasser, amas, a heap	Bannir, ban, exile
Bourdonner, bourdon, a drone-fly, a great bell	Recuellir, recueil, a selection
Travailler, travail, work	Babiller, babil, prattle
Fusiller, fusil, a gun	Pardonner, pardon, a pardon
	Fracasser, fracas, a noise

---

[1] The following nouns in *al* take *s: Bal,* ball; *carnaval,* carnival; *chacal,* jackal; *régal,* a treat; *pal,* a pale.

[2] But, *éventail,* a fan, *éventails.*

3. In the verbs ending in **yer** in the infinitive, **y** being equal to **ii**, the noun is formed by removing **ier**; as:

Employer, emploi, a place
Envoyer, envoi, a message
Ennuyer, ennui, boredom
Appuyer, appui, a support
Balayer, balai, a broom
Renvoyer, renvoi, a discharge
Essayer, essai, a trial
Remblayer, remblai, an embankment

Some nouns are derived more indirectly from verbs: sometimes by removing only the last letter of the infinitive; sometimes three or more letters; as:

Disputer, dispute, a dispute
Ruiner, ruine, ruin
Caresser, caresse, a caress
Forcer, force, strength
Congédier, congé, leave
Retourner, retour, the return
Contourner, contour, outline
Sommeiller, somme, a nap

The Adjective

All adjectives agree in gender and number with the substantive or pronoun to which they relate, as: Le bon enfant, the good child; la bonne femme, the good woman; elle est heureuse, she is happy.

Adjectives are divided into two classes, viz.: **Qualifying** and **determining adjectives.**

Qualifying Adjectives

Formation of the Feminine Form

The feminine of adjectives and participles is generally formed by the addition of the letter **e.**

Masc.	Fem.	
vrai	vraie	true
joli	jolie	pretty
connu	connue	known
général	générale	general
charmant	charmante	charming

Exceptions

Adjectives ending in **e** mute remain unchanged in the feminine; as:

Masc.	Fem.	
sage	sage	wise
aimable	aimable	amiable

Adjectives ending in **f** change **f** into **ve** in the feminine as:

MASC.	FEM.	
actif	active	active
bref	brève	short
neuf	neuve	new
vif	vive	quick

Adjectives ending in **l** double it in the feminine; as:

MASC.	FEM.	
cruel	cruelle	cruel
pareil	pareille	similar
nul	nulle	no, none
éternel	éternelle	eternal
gentil	gentille	nice
tel	telle	such
vermeil	vermeille	vermilion

In the same manner monosyllables in **s, n** and **t** are formed; viz., doubling **s, n** and **t** in the feminine; as:

MASC.	FEM.	
bon	bonne	good
gros	grosse	big
sot	sotte	stupid

To these belong also the following:

MASC.	FEM.	
épais	épaisse	thick
exprès	expresse	express
muet	muette	dumb
sujet	sujette	subject

Adjectives ending in **x** change the same into **se**:

MASC.	FEM.	
heureux	heureuse	happy
jaloux	jalouse	jealous
paresseux	paresseuse	lazy

But **faux,** false, makes its feminine **fausse.**

Adjectives ending in **er** and **et** take in the feminine the **grave accent.**

MASC.	FEM.	
léger	légère	light
complet	complète	complete

Of the adjectives ending in **c** the following three change this **c** into **che**:

MASC.	FEM.	
blanc	blanche	white
franc	franche	frank
sec	sèche	dry

The others ending in **c** take **que**:

MASC.	FEM.	
public	publique	public
turc	turque	Turkish
caduc	caduque	decrepit
grec	grecque	Greek

The following adjectives do not follow any of the above rules:

MASC.	FEM.	
long	longue	long
aigu	aiguë	acute
frais	fraîche	fresh
doux	douce	sweet, soft
malin	maligne	wicked
bénin	bénigne	benign

The following are more irregular in the formation of their feminine:

MASC.	FEM.	
beau (bel)	belle	beautiful
nouveau (nouvel)	nouvelle	new
mou (mol)	molle	soft
fou (fol)	folle	foolish
vieux (vieil)	vieille	old

The above words in parentheses, **bel, nouvel,** etc., are used before masculine nouns beginning with a vowel or h mute, as: un bel‿arbre, a fine tree; un nouvel‿ordre, a new order; un fol‿espoir, a foolish hope, etc.

The Plural of Adjectives

The rules given for the plural of substantives apply also to adjectives. Ex.:

SINGULAR	PLURAL
Grand, *f.* grande; great	grands, *f.* grandes
gras, *f.* grasse; fat	gras, *f.* grasses
royal, *f.* royale; royal	royaux, *f.* royales
beau, *f.* belle; beautiful	beaux, *f.* belles
vieux, *f.* vieille; old	vieux, *f.* vieilles

Fou, mou and **bleu** (blue) make in the plural **fous, mous** and **bleus.**

Position of Adjectives in a Sentence

Adjectives are generally placed after the nouns which they qualify; as, for instance:

le tailleur français	the French tailor
l'homme heureux	the happy man
de l'eau fraîche	some fresh water

But the following, in their common acceptation, are generally placed before their nouns:

autre	other	grand	great
beau	fine	gros	large
bon	good	jeune	young
cher	dear	joli	pretty
méchant	wicked	petit	small
mauvais	bad	saint	holy
meilleur	better	tout	all
moindre	least	vieux	old
nouveau	new	vrai	true
demi	half		

Many of these, however, may be constantly found in French books placed **after,** and many of the others may be found **before** their nouns. The safe rule is to place the adjective **after** its noun.

The following adjectives have a different meaning, according as they stand before or after their noun:

Un bon homme, a simple man	Un homme bon, a kind man
Un brave homme, a nice man	Un homme brave, a brave man
Mon cher ami, my dear friend	Une robe chère, a costly dress
Un certain conte, a certain story	Une nouvelle certaine, sure news
Différentes / Diverses } choses } sundry things	Des objets { différents / divers } different or dissimilar objects

La dernière année, the last year (of a series)	L'année dernière, last year (the preceding year)
Une fausse clef, a skeleton key	Une clef fausse, a wrong key (in music)
Un galant homme, a gentleman	Un homme galant, a courteous man
Un grand homme, a great man	Un homme grand, a tall man
Une grande dame, a great lady	Une dame grande, a tall lady
Un malhonnête homme, a dishonest man	Un homme malhonnête, a rude man
Un maigre dîner, a poor dinner	Un dîner maigre, a fish dinner
Un pauvre homme, a man to be pitied	Un homme pauvre, a poor man
Un petit homme, a small man	Un homme petit, a mean man
Ma propre main, my own hands	Les mains propres, clean hands
Une sage femme, a midwife	Une femme sage, a wise woman
Un seul enfant, a single child	Un enfant seul, a child alone
Un simple soldat, a common soldier	Un soldat simple, a silly soldier
Un unique tableau, a single picture	Un tableau unique, a matchless picture
Un vrai conte, a downright story	Un conte vrai, a true story

Degrees of Comparison

The Comparative is formed by placing the adverb **plus,** more, before the adjective, while **le plus** or **la plus** (fem.) is prefixed to denote the Superlative.

POSITIVE		COMPARATIVE	
haut (*m.*) haute (*f.*)	high	plus haut plus haute	higher
beau (*m.*) belle (*f.*)	beautiful	plus beau plus belle	more beautiful

SUPERLATIVE	
le plus haut la plus haute	the highest
le plus beau la plus belle	the most beautiful

There is in French also a lower and lowest degree which is formed by the words **moins,** less, for the Comparative, and **le (la) moins,** the least, for the Superlative.

POSITIVE		COMPARATIVE	
cher (*m.*)	dear	moins cher	less dear, *i. e.*, cheaper
chère (*f.*)		moins chère	

SUPERLATIVE

le moins cher	the least dear, *i. e.*, the cheapest
la moins chère	

The following three adjectives have an irregular comparison.

Bon, *f.* bonne, *good;* meilleur, e, better; le meilleur, la meilleure, the best
Mauvais, e, meaning *bad;* pire, worse; le pire, *f.* la pire, the worst
Petit, e, *small;* moindre, less; le moindre, *f.* la moindre, the least

As before an adjective is rendered by **aussi; as** after it and **than,** are both translated by **que.** Ex.:

Il‿est‿aussi bon que moi, he is as good as I am.
Elle est plus belle que sa cousine, she is handsomer than her cousin.

Complement of Adjectives

The complement of an adjective is either a noun or a verb preceded by a preposition, **de, à, en,** etc.

Adjectives expressive of feeling, also denoting plenty, scarcity, or want, and those generally which are followed, in English, by **of, with,** or **from,** require the preposition **de** before the dependent noun or infinitive.

Je suis content de ce travail.	I am satisfied with this work.
Je suis heureux de vous le dire.	I am happy to tell you so.
Êtes-vous fâché de l'apprendre?	Are you sorry to hear it?
Il‿est‿à court d'argent.	He is short of money.
La vie est pleine de misère.	Life is full of misery.
Comblé de faveurs; libre de blâme.	Loaded with favors; free from blame.

Adjectives which denote fitness, disposition, inclination, advantage, likeness and the opposite qualities, require the preposition **à** before the dependent noun, and also before the dependent infinitive, provided they are not construed with the impersonal verb **il est,** it is.

Il‿est propre à tout.	He is fit for anything.
Il‿est disposé à vous rendre service.	He is disposed to oblige you.
Ces circonstances sont favorables à notre projet.	These circumstances are favorable to our project.
C'est‿une chose difficile à faire.	That is a difficult thing to do.
La religion est nécessaire à l'homme.	Religion is necessary to man.

But these, and all other adjectives, when they are construed with the impersonal verb **il est,** it is, require the preposition **de** before the dependent infinitive.

Il est utile de savoir cela.	It is useful to know that.
Il est difficile de contenter tout le monde.	It is difficult to please everybody.
Il est nécessaire de lui en parler.	It is necessary to speak to him about it.

A few adjectives are followed by **à** in French and by **for** in English; as:

Je suis sensible à votre bonté.	I am grateful for your kindness.

A few others are followed in French by **à,** and in English by **in**; as:

Il est exact à remplir ses devoirs.	He is punctual in fulfilling his duties.

Government of Adjectives

The following is a list of adjectives with the prepositions which they require when they qualify a definite subject:

Adroit à, dexterous in
Affable envers, affable to
Alarmant pour, alarming to
Antérieur à, prior to
Apre à, eager for
Ardent à, ardent for
Assidu à, auprès de, assiduous in, to
Attentif à, attentive to, mindful of
Aveugle sur, blind to
Avide de, eager for, greedy of
Capable de, capable of
Célèbre par, pour, famous for
Chéri de, cherished by
Civil envers, à l'égard de, civil to
Commun à, avec, common to
Comparable à, avec, comparable to
Complice de, accessory to
Connu de, known to
Consolant pour, consolatory to
Constant dans, en, constant to
Cruel à, envers, cruel to
Dangereux pour, à, dangerous to
Endurci à, contre, dans, hardened, inured to
Esclave de, slave to
Fâché de, contre, sorry for, angry with
Faible de, en, deficient in
Fameux par, dans, en, famous for, renowned in
Fort en, de, strong by—en, sur, à, skilled in, on
Fou de, mad for, doting on
Furieux de, enraged at
Gros de, big with
Habile à, dans, en, skilful, clever in
Heureux à, dans, en, lucky in—de, happy to
Ignorant en, sur, de, ignorant of, in
Impatient de, impatient for, at
Incapable de, incapable of, unable to
Indulgent à, pour, envers, indulgent to
Inébranlable à, contre, dans, steadfast in
Ingrat envers, ungrateful to
Inquiet de, sur, uneasy for, about
Insolent avec, insolent to

Invisible à, pour, invisible to
Ivre de, intoxicated with
Justiciable de, amenable to
Las de, weary of, to
Lent dans, à, slow in, to
Libre de, free from, at liberty to
Libéral de, envers, liberal of, towards
Nécessaire à, pour, necessary to
Offensé de, offended at
Officieux envers, officious to
Patient à, dans, à l'égard de, patient to
Prêt à, ready to
Prodigue de, en, envers, prodigal of, to
Reconnaissant de, grateful, thankful for
Responsable de, envers, accountable for, to
Sensible à, sensible of
Sévère pour, envers, à l'égard de, severe to
Voisin de, neighboring to

The Determining Adjectives

Possessive

SING. MASC.	SING. FEM.	PLURAL	
Mon	Ma	Mes	My
Ton	Ta	Tes	Thy
Son	Sa	Ses	His, Her or Its
Notre	Notre	Nos	Our
Votre	Votre	Vos	Your
Leur	Leur	Leurs	Their

NOTE.—The possessive adjectives agree in gender and number with the possessed object; not with the possessor, as in English.

Thus, a man and a woman will say alike:

Ma mère; mon père; mon livre; ma lettre

1. The possessive adjectives are not used with parts of the body, but **le, la, les** instead, whenever there is no danger of confusion of meaning thereby. Thus:

J'ai les yeux fatigués.	My eyes are tired.
Vous avez les mains enflées.	Your hands are swollen.

2. The possessive adjectives, however, are used:

a. When we wish to emphasize the part spoken of, as:

Il‿arrêta ses‿yeux sur l'inconnu, et dit: C'est lui.	He fixed his eyes upon the stranger, and said: It is he.

b. To express something that is habitual and special, as:

J'ai ma migraine.	I have my (usual) sick headache.
Ma jambe me fait mal.	My leg (the particular one) hurts.

c. When the use of the article would render the sense ambiguous; as:

Je vois que ma main s'enfle.	I see that my hand is swelling.

If **la** were substituted for **ma,** the sense would be ambiguous, for it would not be clear whose hand was meant.

3. The noun preceded by the possessive adjective **leur** is put in the singular when it is applied in a general sense, and in the plural when it has an individual or distributive application; as:

Bien des hommes passent leur vie à amasser des richesses dont‿ils ne jouissent pas.	Many men spend their lives in amassing wealth which they do not enjoy.
Ils‿ont sacrifié leurs vies à la patrie.	They sacrificed their lives to their country.

4. **Mon, ton, son** are used instead of ma, ta, sa, before feminine nouns beginning with a vowel or silent **h**:

Mon‿encre, my ink (instead of ma encre)
Mon‿amie, my friend (instead of ma amie)

5. With **mal, froid,** and **chaud** the article is used instead of the possessive adjective:

J'ai mal‿au bras; *not,* à mon bras.
J'ai froid aux mains; *not,* à mes mains.

6. The possessive adjectives are repeated before each noun, as:

Son père, sa mère‿et ses sœurs‿ont quitté la ville hier.	His (or Her) father, mother and sisters left the city yesterday.

Demonstrative Adjectives

The demonstrative adjective is rendered:

SINGULAR		PLURAL	
Masc. ce, cet	this *or* that	*Masc.*	ces, these *or* those
Fem. cette		*Fem.*	

The demonstrative adjective agrees with its noun in gender and number; as:

ce cheval	this horse
cette maison	this house
ces‿enfants	these children

The form cet is employed for the masculine instead of ce, when preceding a noun beginning with a vowel or mute **h**; as:

cet‿homme	this man
cet‿arbre	this tree
cet‿agent	this agent

The demonstrative adjective, **ce, cet, cette, ces,** does not point out persons or things by their relative position, as **this** and **that** do in English. The adverbs **ci** and **là** are used for that purpose. The use of these adverbial adjuncts is, however, only resorted to when this distinction is necessary, or when stress is laid on the demonstrative.

Thus, without emphasis:

Ce livre ne m'appartient pas.	This book does not belong to me.
Cette fleur sent bon.	That flower smells good.

But, with emphasis:

Cette⁀année-ci finira bientôt.	The year will soon end.
Ce jour-là sera à jamais mémorable dans l'histoire de notre pays.	That day will forever be memorable in the history of our country.

The demonstrative adjective is repeated before each noun; as:

Ces messieurs et ces dames	These gentlemen and ladies

Numeral Adjectives

1. The numeral adjectives are given in Books I and II.

2. The numeral adjective **un, une,** is used in French when no equivalent is used for it in English, in cases like the following: Il a un grand talent pour la musique, he has great talent for music. We say. Il a du talent pour la musique, with the noun in the partitive sense: But the partitive sense is changed into the indefinite sense by the use of the adjunct **grand,** which gives individuality to the noun. The following are examples.

Il m'a reçu avec bonté.	He received me with kindness.
Il m'a reçu avec⁀une bonté marquée.	He received me with marked kindness.
Il⁀a montré du courage.	He showed courage.
Il⁀a montré un courage⁀étonnant.	He showed astonishing courage.
Ils sont‿animés d'ardeur.	They are animated with ardor.
Ils sont‿animés d'une⁀ardeur⁀extraordinaire.	They are animated with extraordinary ardor.

3. The numeral adjectives **un, vingt** and **cent** are the only cardinal numbers which can take the plural form.

But **vingt** and **cent** are invariable when they are used for the ordinal numbers **vingtième** and **centième**; as: page quatre-vingt, page eightieth; l'an mil huit cent, in the year one thousand eight hundred.

4. The adjective **mille** is written **mil,** only when used to express the Christian era; as mil huit cent soixante-dix-sept. In all other cases the form **mille** is used; as: l'an deux mille de la création.

5. **Cent** and **mille,** as limiting adjectives, are not preceded by the numeral **un.** But limiting adjectives, when used as nouns, may be preceded by a limiting word; as:

Un cent d'huitres	One hundred oysters

6. The ordinal numeral adjectives take the gender and number of the noun which they limit; as:

Les premiers livres	The first books
Les premières leçons	The first lessons

The ordinal number **unième, first** and not **premier,** is used in connection with other numbers; as: vingt‿et unième, cent‿unième, etc. **Unième** is never used alone.

7. **Second** and **deuxième** should not be used indiscriminately. **Second** indicates order, **deuxième** denotes one of a series, and is correctly used only when a third, a fourth, etc., are supposed to exist: Le second tome, the second volume; la deuxième leçon, the second lesson.

8. The cardinal numbers are used instead of the ordinal:

a. For the days of the month, except the first.

Le premier janvier	The first of January.
Le deux février.	The second of February.
Le trois mars.	The third of March.
Nous partirons le quinze avril.	We shall start on the 15th of April.

The preposition **de** before the names of the months is generally omitted, and no preposition is used before the date.

b. After the names of sovereigns, and in quoting chapters, paragraphs and pages of books, except for the first of the series.

François premier	Francis the First
Henri quatre	Henry the Fourth
Chapitre deux, page huit	Chapter two, page eight

The Pronoun — Le Pronom

General Remarks

A pronoun stands in the place of a noun, with which it agrees in gender and number. But all pronouns do not represent nouns.

Some pronouns are used absolutely, that is, they do not refer to an antecedent noun; such are the interrogative pronouns, **qui, que, quoi,** and the indefinite pronouns, **un, chacun, quelqu'un,** etc.

Pronouns used absolutely are of the masculine gender and singular number.

1. The invariable pronoun **le** represents an adjective, a sentence, or a verb; as:

Êtes-vous malade? Je le suis.[1]	Are you sick? I am (so).
Vous ne travaillez pas comme vous le faisiez autrefois.	You do not work as you used to.

2. The pronouns **en** and **y** sometimes represent sentences; as:

Vous ne m'en avez pas parlé.	You did not speak to me about it.
Je n'y ai pas pensé.	I did not think of it.

3. The demonstrative pronouns **ce, ceci, cela** may also represent sentences.

Ce que je dis est vrai.	What I say is true.
C'est‿étonnant.	That is astonishing.
Qui vous‿a dit cela?	Who told you that?

Personal Pronouns — Conjunctive

The personal conjunctive pronouns have been explained. [Part VIII, p. 194-202.]

1. The pronoun **vous** may represent the second person singular or plural. The verb agrees with it in the plural.

Vous (sing.) n'êtes pas capable de faire cela vous-même.	You are not able to do that yourself.
Vous (plur.) n'êtes pas capables de faire cela vous-mêmes.	You are not able to do that yourselves.

2. The ellipsis of a part of a sentence, so common in English, particularly in answering questions, when the subject and the verb, often only an auxiliary verb, are given, and the remaining part of the

[1] When the attribute is a noun, the personal pronoun representing it agrees with the noun in gender and number: Êtes-vous la malade? Je la suis. Ces dames sont‿elles mariées? (*adj.*) Elles le sont (le invariable).

predicate is understood, is not admissible in French. All the parts of the sentence must be represented in French.

Il‿est studieux; vous ne l'êtes pas.	He is studious; you are not (so).
Il‿a de la patience; vous n'en‿avez pas.	He has patience; you have not (any).
Nous‿étions‿amis autrefois; nous ne le sommes plus.	We used to be friends; we are not now (so).
Avez-vous dit cela? Oui, je l'ai dit.	Have you said so? Yes, I have (said so). Did you say so? Yes, I did (say so).

3. **En** and **y.** The pronouns **en** and **y** are always indirect objects; **en** represents the relation of the preposition **de,** and **y** the relation of the preposition **à.** They are used with reference to things, for both genders and both numbers.

Laissez ce livre; j'en‿ai besoin.	Leave the book; I need it.
Voilà du papier; prenez‿en.	There is paper; take some.
Allez; j'y consens.	Go; I consent to it.

4. **En** is used with reference to persons when the sense is indeterminate; as:

Vous‿avez‿un frère; je n'en‿ai pas.	You have a brother; I have not (any).

5. **Y** is used with reference to persons when the sense of the noun is not precise and definite; as:

Plus‿on connaît le peuple, plus‿on s'y attache.	The better we know the common people, the more we become attached to them.

Disjunctive Personal Pronouns

The disjunctive personal pronouns are:

SINGULAR	PLURAL
Moi, I, *or* me	Nous, we, *or* us
Toi, thou, *or* thee	Vous, you
Lui, he, *or* him	Eux, they *or* them (*m.*)
Elle, she, *or* her	Elles, they, *or* them (*f.*)

The disjunctive personal pronouns are used:

1. When the verb is not expressed; as:

Qui m'appelle?—Moi.	Who calls me?—I.
Qui appelle-t‿il?—Moi.	Whom does he call?—Me.
Vous‿êtes plus grand que moi.	You are taller than I.

2. In apposition with other pronouns, for the sake of emphasis, also to state separately the persons forming a compound subject or object:

Toi, tu es l'homme.	Thou art the man.
Lui et moi, nous sommes‿amis.	He and I are friends.

3. After the verb être, to be, when it is preceded by **ce.**

C'est moi. C'est lui.	It is I. It is he.

4. After prepositions:

Il parle de moi.	He speaks of me.
Je vais chez[1] lui.	I am going to his house.

Compound Personal Pronouns

The adjective **même,** self, added with a hyphen to the disjunctive personal pronouns, forms a class of pronouns called compound personal pronouns; as:

Moi-même, myself	Nous-mêmes, ourselves
Toi-même, thyself	Vous-mêmes, yourselves
Vous-même, yourself	Eux-mêmes, themselves
Lui-même, himself	Elles-mêmes, themselves
Elle-même, herself	Soi-même, oneself

These pronouns are used for the sake of emphasis; as:

Je l'ai vu moi-même.	I have seen it myself.
Elle se blâme elle-même.	She blames herself.

Demonstrative Pronouns

These are:

	Masc.	Fem.
	Celui	celle, that
Pl.	ceux	celles, those
	celui-ci	celle-ci, this or the latter
Pl.	ceux-ci	celles-ci, these
	celui-là	celle-là, that (one) or the former
Pl.	ceux-là	celles-là, those

Neuter

ce and cela (abridged ça), that; ceci, this

1. **Ce** has only one form for both genders and numbers. Ex.: Ce fut mon ami; ce fut mon amie; ce furent mes amis; ce furent mes amies.

---

[1] The preposition *chez,* before the name of a person, and before a pronoun, is equivalent to the English expressions, *at the house of, to the house of.*

2. **Ce** is frequently used before the third person singular or plural with the auxiliary verb **être,** and means either this or that. C'est quelque chose que je ne connais pas. That is something (which) I do not know.— Est-ce là votre malle? Oui, c'est ma malle. Is that your trunk? Yes, that is my trunk.—Sont-ce là vos bas? Oui, ce sont mes bas. Are these your stockings? Yes, these are my stockings.

3. Celui-ci, celle-ci, ceux-ci, celles-ci, are translated this, these, or this one, etc. These pronouns are used in speaking either of persons or things, when it is necessary to indicate clearly which person or thing is spoken of: This is my hat, celui-ci est mon chapeau.

Celui-là, celle-là, ceux-là, celles-là, are used in the same manner, and must be translated by that, those, that one, etc.

4. Celui-ci, celle-ci, ceci, point out objects nearest to the speaker, while celui-là, celle-là, cela signify those farthest from him, as: Voici deux livres; prenez celui-ci, Charles gardera celui-là, **here are two books; you take this one and Charles will keep that one.**

5. Celui, celle, etc., must be used instead of celui-ci, celle-ci, celui-là, celle-là, ceux-là, etc., before a relative pronoun or preposition. They are then translated very frequently by **the one who,** or **he who, she who, they who.**

It is my father's (that of my father),	C'est celui de mon père.
This horse is the one of which I spoke to you.	Ce cheval‿est celui dont je vous‿ai parlé.

Possessive Pronouns

1. The possessive pronouns are formed from the possessive adjectives **mon, ton, son,** etc. They are:

le mien	la mienne, mine (my own)
le tien	la tienne, thine
le sien	la sienne, his, hers, its own
le nôtre	la nôtre, ours
le vôtre	la vôtre, yours
le leur	la leur, theirs

Pl. les miens, *f.* les miennes;—les nôtres, les vôtres, etc.

2. They agree in gender and number with the object possessed: Avez-vous votre billet? Oui, j'ai le mien. **Have you your ticket? Yes, I have mine.** Votre sœur est plus âgée que la mienne. **Your sister is older than mine.** Mon intention est aussi bonne que la vôtre. **My intention is as good as yours.**

The article (**le, la, les**) of these pronouns combines with the prepositions **de** and **à** in the usual way:

Du mien, de la mienne, des miens, des miennes, of mine.
Du sien, de la sienne, des siens, des siennes, of his, etc.
Au mien, à la mienne, aux miens, aux miennes, to mine.
Au leur, à la leur, aux leurs, aux leurs, to theirs.

3. Mine, his, hers, etc., are also rendered by à moi, à lui, à elle, à nous, à vous, à eux, à elles. For instance, in answer to the question: Whose book is this? à qui est ce livre? It's mine; or, it's his; or, it's hers, the answer may be either:

Ce livre est le mien; *or*, Ce livre est *à* moi.
" " " le sien; " " " " " lui.
" " " le sien; " " " " " elle.

Interrogative Pronouns

Lequel? Laquelle?

Singular		Plural	
MASC.	FEM.	MASC.	FEM.
lequel?	laquelle?	lesquels?	lesquelles?
duquel?	de laquelle?	desquels?	desquelles?
auquel?	à laquelle?	auxquels?	auxquelles?

This pronoun is used either without a noun, or is separated from it by **de**; but it agrees with the noun it refers to in gender and number. When the pronoun which (of) is used interrogatively, it is always expressed by **lequel, laquelle,** etc., as:

Lequel de ses fils est malade?	Which of his sons is ill?
Laquelle de vos sœurs est mariée?	Which of your sisters is married?
Voici plusieurs appartements. Lequel choisirez-vous?	Here are several apartments. Which will you choose?
Auquel de ces messieurs avez-vous donné ma lettre?	To which of these gentlemen have you given my letter?

Qui? Quoi? Que?

MASC. and FEM.	NEUTER
Qui, who?	Que, quoi, what?
de qui, whose, of whom? from whom?	de quoi { of what? from what?
à qui, to whom, whom?	à quoi, to what, at what?
qui, whom?	que, quoi, what?

Remarks

1. The interrogative pronoun **qui?** is only used of persons. Examples:

Qui est‿arrivé?	Who has arrived?
Qui est là?	Who is there?
De qui parlez-vous?	Of whom are you speaking?
A qui est cette malle?	To whom does this trunk belong?
Qui cherchez-vous?	Whom are you looking for?

2. Whose, when used interrogatively, must be rendered in French by **à qui.** Examples:

Whose book is this?	A qui est ce livre?
Whose trunk is this?	A qui est cette malle?

3. **Quoi,** what, is disjunctive, and is used either by itself, or after a preposition, as:

De quoi parlez-vous?	Of what are you speaking?
Quoi! vous‿êtes marié!	What! you are married!
Quoi! il ne veut pas le faire?	What! he will not do it?

4. **Que,** what, is conjunctive, and is only used before verbs, as:

Que voulez-vous?	What do you want?
Que demandez-vous?	What do you desire?
Qu'avez-vous vu?	What have you seen?
Qu'avez-vous?	What is the matter with you?

Que as an interrogative means what, **never** whom.

5. Instead of the simple form **qui?** the form **qui est-ce qui,** who? is very frequently used as subject, and **qui est-ce que,** whom? as direct object.

Qui est-ce qui rit?	Who is laughing?
Qui est-ce que vous cherchez?	Whom are you looking for?
Qui est-ce qui l'a fait?	Who has done it?
Qui est-ce que vous avez vu?	Whom have you seen?

6. Instead of the simple form **que?** what? the form **qu'est-ce que?** or even **qu'est-ce que c'est que?** is frequently used, but only as object.

Qu'est-ce que vous voulez?	What do you want?
Qu'est-ce que vous faites là?	What are you doing there?

7. What—subject—may be rendered by **qu'est-ce qui?** It must, however, be always the subject of the sentence and the pupil should not confound **qui est-ce qui?** who? with **qu'est-ce qui?** what?

Qu'est-ce qui vous‿afflige?	What afflicts you?
Qu'est-ce qui vous‿étonne?	What astonishes you?
Qu'est-ce qui vous manque?	What are you missing?

8. Observe the following idiomatic phrases:

Qu'est-ce que cela? Qu'est-ce que c'est que cela?	what is that?
Qu'est-ce que la vie? Qu'est-ce que c'est que la vie?	what is life?
Qu'y a-t-il de nouveau? Qu'est-ce qu'il‿y a de nouveau?	what is the news?

Relative Pronouns

The pronouns **qui, quoi,** and **lequel** serve also as relative pronouns. The declension of quoi and lequel has been given. That of qui, when relative, differs from the interrogative qui.

SINGULAR and PLURAL — MASCULINE and FEMININE

qui, who, which, that
de qui and *dont,* whose, of (from) whom, of which
à qui, to whom
que, whom, which, that

1. **Who, which,** and **that** are rendered by **qui,** when they are used as subjects of the next verb, whether they refer to persons or things, both for the singular and plural.

L'employé qui a écrit cette lettre n'est pas‿ici.	The clerk who wrote this letter is not here.
Passez-moi le plat qui est sur la table.	Hand me the dish which is on the table.
Les hommes qui l'ont dit sont partis hier soir.	The men who said it left last night.

The interrogative adjective *what,* joined to a noun, is always expressed by *quel,* fem. *quelle.*—Ex.: Quelle‿est la difficulté qui vous arrête, *what is the difficulty that detains you?*

2. The same pronouns, **whom, which, that,** when they are used as direct objects of the next verb, are rendered by **que.**

Est-ce là le chapeau neuf que vous‿avez‿acheté?	Is that the new hat which you have bought?
La leçon que vous m'avez donnée est très difficile.	The lesson which you have given me is very difficult.

Observe that the French must always express the relative pronoun, though it is frequently omitted in English.

3. Dont, **whose, of which,** is used for persons and things of both genders and numbers.

Voici la dame dont je vous‿ai parlé.	Here is the lady of whom I spoke to you.
C'est le monsieur dont‿il⁀a acheté le cheval.	That is the gentleman whose horse he bought.
C'est‿une maladie dont on ne connaît point la cause.	That is an illness the cause of which is unknown.
Est-ce là le jardin dont vous m'avez parlé?	Is that the garden of which you spoke to me?

4. **De qui** (both singular and plural) and **à qui,** to whom, are used only when referring to persons.[1]

Le négociant de qui j'ai reçu ces‿échantillons vient de faire banqueroute.	The merchant from whom I received these samples has just become bankrupt.
Voilà le monsieur à qui j'ai donné votre lettre.	There is the gentleman to whom I gave your letter.

When, however, animals or inanimate objects are spoken of, auquel, à laquelle, auxquels, or auxquelles, must be used.

Tel⁀est le bonheur auquel j'aspire.	Such is the good fortune to which I aspire.
C'est le chien auquel j'ai donné à manger.	That is the dog which I fed (to which I gave to eat).
C'est‿une occasion à laquelle je ne pensais pas.	That is an occasion I did not think of.

[1] *Qui* is mostly used after prepositions when persons are referred to; but after *entre*, between, and *parmi*, among, we must always write *lesquels* or *lesquelles*, whether persons or things are spoken of.

5. Difference between **dont, de qui** and **duquel, de laquelle,** etc.

Dont is used when it is governed by a noun which in the English sentence, is either subject or direct object; as:

Voilà une fleur dont la forme est très curieuse.	There is a flower whose form is very strange.
La dame dont vous voyez le portrait est‿à présent à Paris.	The lady whose portrait you see is at present in Paris.
Le monsieur dont j'instruis les‿enfants est très riche.	The gentleman whose children I instruct is very rich.

But **de qui,** or **duquel, de laquelle,** etc., must be employed when the noun which follows **whose** is governed by a preposition. (**De qui** refers only to persons, while duquel, de laquelle, etc., may be used both for persons and for things); as:

C'est‿un homme à la discrétion de qui vous pouvez vous fier.	He is a man to whose discretion you may trust.
J'honore cet homme aux bontés duquel (or de qui) je dois ma fortune.	I honor this man, to whose kindness I owe my fortune.
C'est‿un régiment à la valeur duquel l'ennemi n'a pu résister.	That's a regiment whose valor the enemy has been unable to resist.
C'est‿un jeune homme sur la parole de qui (or duquel) on ne peut pas compter.	That is a young man upon whose word one cannot rely.

6. **Lequel, laquelle, etc.,** are used after prepositions when reference is made to things, while **qui** is usually employed when persons are referred to; as:

Voilà le banc sur lequel je me suis‿assis.	Here is the bench on which I sat.
C'est‿une condition sans laquelle il ne veut rien faire.	That is a condition without which he will do nothing.

But:

Le marchand avec qui[1] j'ai voyagé est mort.	The merchant with whom I traveled is dead.

7. **Lequel, laquelle,** etc., must be used instead of **qui** or **que,** when by the use of the latter pronouns an ambiguity might arise; as:

---

[1] *Qui* always remains unchanged, even before a vowel or h silent, as: L'homme qui arrive;—à qui il parle—à qui elle pense;—de qui on se plaint

La tante de mon ami laquelle demeure à Londres.	My friend's aunt who lives in London.

(**qui demeure à Londres,** would mean: The aunt of my friend who is living in London, and would signify that the friend lives in London.)

J'ai vu le chauffeur de votre cousine, lequel viendra vous voir.	I have seen your cousin's chauffeur, who will call on you.

8. Such expressions as **he who, she who, they who, those who,** must be rendered by celui qui, celle qui (*fem.*); ceux qui (*pl. m.*); celles qui (*pl. f.*); as:

Celui qui est content, est riche.	He who is contended is rich.
Je l'enverrai à celle qui m'aime le mieux.	I will send it to her who loves me best.
Je parle de celui qui m'a vu chez le médecin américain.	I speak of the one who saw me at the American physician's.
J'ai donné le livre à celle qui a trouvé la clef avec laquelle votre sœur a ouvert la porte.	I gave the book to that one who found the key with which your sister opened the door.

9. That which **or** what, meaning really "that thing which," is rendered by **ce qui** when subject, and **ce que** when direct object. All that is rendered by **tout ce qui** when subject, and **tout ce que** when direct object; as:

Aimez tout ce qui est bon et beau.	Love all that (or everything which) is good and beautiful.
Faites ce que je vous dis.	Do what I tell you.
Ce qui est beau n'est pas toujours bon.	What is beautiful is not always good.

10. Proverbs and general statements often commence with **qui,** whoever; as:

Qui sert les malheureux sert la divinité.	Whoever helps unhappy persons helps Providence.
Qui casse les verres, les paie.	Who breaks the glasses pays for them.

11. **Quoi, what,** is a neuter pronoun, often without an antecedent, or may refer to a whole sentence.

Voilà de quoi il m'a entretenu.	That is what he entertained me with.
Je sais à quoi vous pensez.	I know what you are thinking of.
C'est‿à quoi je pense le moins.	This is a thing of which I think least.
De quoi s'agit-il là?	What is the matter there?
A quoi s'occupe-t-il?	What is he occupied with?
Il faut qu'il signe le contrat; sans quoi il sera nul.	He must sign the contract; otherwise it will be void.
Avez-vous de quoi payer ces factures?	Have you enough to pay these bills?
Il n'a pas de quoi vivre.	He has not wherewith to live.

Indefinite Pronouns

The indefinite pronouns are:

Autrui, others	On, one, someone, people, they
Chacun, everyone; each	Personne (ne), nobody
L'un l'autre, each other	Quelqu'un, somebody
L'un et l'autre, both	Quelques-uns, some; a few
L'un ou l'autre, either	Quiconque, whoever
Ni l'un ni l'autre (ne), neither	Un de, one of

The following indefinite adjectives are also used as pronouns:

Aucun (ne)	no one; none	Plusieurs, several; many
Nul (ne)		Tel, such a one
Pas‿un (ne)		Tout, all; everything

1. **Autrui, others,** is used with reference to persons only, after a preposition.

Ne riez pas des défauts d'autrui.	Do not laugh at other people's faults.

2. **Chacun, everyone,** used absolutely, is invariable and applies to persons only.

Chacun pense à soi.	Everyone thinks of himself.

3. **Chacun,** limited by a complement, may refer to either persons or things, and agrees with the noun in gender.

Chacun de ces messieurs.	Each of those gentlemen.
Chacune de ces maisons.	Each of those houses.

4. **L'un l'autre, each other,** is used with pronomial verbs to distinguish reciprocal from reflective action, as:

Ils s'aiment l'un l'autre.	They love each other.

5. When **l'un l'autre** refers to several persons, it is put in the plural; as:

Les hommes se trompent les‿uns les‿autres.	Men deceive one another.

6. **L'un** may be subject, and **l'autre** object; the latter being then preceded by a preposition; as:

Ils sont contents l'un de l'autre.	They are pleased with one another.

7. **L'un—l'autre,** used separately, mean **the former—the latter, some—some, some—others.**

L'un instruit, l'autre amuse.	The former, instructs, the latter amuses.
Les‿uns rient, les‿autres pleurent.	Some laugh, some weep.
Les‿uns chantent, d'autres dansent.	Some sing, others dance.

8. **L'un et l'autre, both; l'un ou l'autre, either; ni l'un ni l'autre, neither;** refer to antecedent nouns, with which they agree in gender and number.

L'un et l'autre, à mon sens, ont le cerveau troublé.	Both, in my opinion, are unsettled in their minds.

When **l'un et l'autre** is the object of a verb, a personal pronoun is used to represent the object before the verb.

Je les‿ai vus l'un et l'autre.	I saw them both.
Je veux leur parler à l'un et à l'autre.	I wish to speak to both.

9. **L'un ou l'autre, either the one or the other.** The verb is singular.

L'un ou l'autre viendra.	Either the one or the other will come.

10. **On.** This pronoun represents indefinitely the subject of the verb; we, you, they, one, people, someone, anyone.

On is often used in French with the active form of the verb, when in English the passive form is used; as:

On‿a apporté ce paquet pour vous.	This packet was brought for you.
On peut le voir à son bureau.	He may be seen at his office.
On le fait tous les jours.	It is done every day.

11. **On** is repeated before each verb that refers to the same subject which the first **on** represents.

On n'est pas heureux quand‿on‿est malade.	One is not happy when sick.
On vient et l'on va.	People come and go.

12. **Quelqu'un.** This pronoun used absolutely is masculine. When it is followed by a complement, it takes the gender of the limiting noun.

Il y a quelqu'un qui vous demande.	There is somebody inquiring for you.
Si quelqu'une de ces dames vous prie de chanter, faites-le	If any one of these ladies should ask you to sing, do it.

Quelqu'un requires **de** before the past participle which refers to it.

Y a-t-il quelqu'un de blessé?	Is there anybody hurt?

13. **Personne, nobody,** an indefinite pronoun, is masculine. **Personne, a person,** is a feminine noun.

Personne n'a été oublié.	No one has been forgotten.
Une personne a été oubliée.	One person has been forgotten.

Personne, nobody, like **quelqu'un,** requires **de** before the past participle which refers to it; as:

Il n'y a personne de blessé.	There is nobody hurt.

14. **Personne,** and not **quelqu'un,** is used in sentences implying doubt, or containing some other negative word; also after a comparative adverb.

Y a-t-il personne qui en doute?	Is there anyone who doubts it?
Il est parti sans payer personne.	He left without paying anybody.
Tu sais cela mieux que personne.	Thou knowest that better than anyone.

15. **Quelques-uns,** a few, agrees in gender and number with the noun to which it refers.

Prenez quelques-unes de ces poires.	Take a few of these pears.
J'en prendrai quelques-unes.	I shall take a few of them.

16. **Quiconque, whoever,** used absolutely, is masculine.

Quiconque est capable de mentir est indigne d'être compté au nombre des hommes.	Whoever is capable of telling a falsehood is unworthy of being considered a man.

17. Some of the indefinite adjectives are also used as indefinite pronouns: pas un, aucun, nul, autre, plusieurs, tel, and tout; as:

Pas‿une de ces demoiselles n'a su répondre à mes questions.	Not one of these young ladies was able to answer my questions.
Aucune ne mérite une récompense.	Not one deserves a reward.
Nul ne sait cela mieux que lui.	No one knows that better than he.
Plusieurs ont traité ce sujet différemment.	Several have treated this subject differently.
Il a tout‿appris.	He has learned everything.
Tel rit aujourd'hui qui pleurera demain.	Many a one laughs to-day who will weep to-morrow.

The Adverb — L'Adverbe

Adverbs may express manner, place, time, order, quantity, comparison, negation, doubt, etc.

List of Simple Adverbs

Ailleurs, elsewhere
Ainsi, thus; so
Alentour, around
Alors, then; at that time
Assez, enough
Aucunement, by no means
Aujourd'hui, to-day
Auparavant, before
Aussi, also; as
Aussitôt, immediately
Autant, as much
Autrefois, formerly
Autrement, otherwise
Beaucoup, much
Bien, well
Bientôt, soon
Certes, certainly
Céans, within; here within
Cependant, meanwhile
Ci, here
Combien, how much
Comme, as; like
Comment, how
Davantage, more
Dedans, within
Dehors, outside
Déjà, already
Demain, to-morrow
Derrière, behind
Désormais, henceforth
Dessous, under; below
Dessus, over; above
Devant, before
Dorénavant, henceforth
Encore, still
Enfin, in short; in fine
Ensemble, together
Ensuite, then; afterwards
Environ, about
Exprès, purposely
Fort, very; very much
Gratis, gratuitously
Guère, but little
Hier, yesterday
Ici, here
Incessamment, incessantly
Jadis, once; in former times
Jamais, ever; never
Jusque, till; until
Là, there
Loin, far
Longtemps, long
Lors, then
Maintenant, now
Mal, badly
Même, even; also

List of Simple Adverbs—Continued

Mieux, better
Moins, less
Naguère, not long since
Ne, not
Néanmoins, notwithstanding
Non, no
Notamment, specially
Nuitamment, by night
Nullement, by no means
Où, where
Oui, yes
Parfois, at times
Partout, everywhere
Pas, not
Peu, little
Pis, worse
Plus, more
Plutôt, rather
Pourtant, however
Près, close, nearly
Presque, almost
Puis, then
Quand, when
Quant‿à, with regard to; as to
Quasi, almost
Que (for combien), how
Quelquefois, sometimes
Sciemment, knowingly
Si, so
Si, yes
Soudain, suddenly
Souvent, often
Surtout, especially
Tant, so much
Tantôt, by and by; a little while ago
Tard, late
Tôt, soon
Toujours, always
Toutefois, however
Très, very
Trop, too; too much
Vite, quickly
Volontiers, willingly
Y (là), there

List of Compound Adverbs

A jamais, forever
A la fois, at a time; at once
A l'envi, in emulation of
A part, aside
Après-demain, the day after to-morrow
A présent, at present
A regret, with regret
Au moins, at least
Au reste, besides
Avant‿hier, the day before yesterday
Çà et là, here and there
Ci-après, hereafter
Ci-contre, on the other side
Ci-inclus, enclosed
Ci-joint, annexed
D'abord, at first
D'accord, agreed
D'ailleurs, moreover
De là, hence
De même, likewise
De plus, besides
De suite, in succession
Dès lors, since then
D'ici, from here
D'ordinaire, usually
D'où, whence
Du moins, at least
Du reste, however
En‿avant, forward
En sus, over and above
Jusque là, so far
Là-dessus, upon that, thereupon
Ni plus ni moins, neither more nor less
Non plus, not either

List of Compound Adverbs—Continued

Nulle part, nowhere
Par hasard, by chance
Pêle-mêle, pell-mell
Peut-être, perhaps
Plus tôt, sooner
Quelque part, somewhere
Sans doute, undoubtedly
Tôt‿ou tard, sooner or later
Tour⁀à tour, in turn
Tout‿à l'heure, presently; just now
Tout de suite, immediately
Une fois, once
Tout‿à coup, suddenly
Tout d'un coup, in one stroke

Formation of Adverbs in *ment*

1. Many adverbs are formed from adjectives by the addition of the syllable **ment.** When the adjective ends with a vowel, **ment** is added to the masculine form; when it ends with a consonant, to the feminine form, as:

Poli, polite	*adv.*, poliment, politely
Ordinaire, usual	" ordinairement, usually
Seul, *f.*, seule, alone	" seulement, only
Doux, *f.*, douce, soft	" doucement, softly; gently

Beau, beautiful; **nouveau,** new; **fou,** foolish; **mou,** soft, though ending in a vowel, add **ment** to the feminine forms: **bellement,** finely; **nouvellement,** newly; **follement,** foolishly; **mollement,** softly.

2. Adjectives ending in **nt,** change **nt** into **mment,** as:

Prudent, prudent	*adv.*, prudemment, prudently

Except,

Lent, slow	*adv.*, lentement, slowly
Présent, present	présentement, presently

Adjectives used as Adverbs

Many adjectives are used as adverbs, in which case they are invariable, as:

Adjective		Adverb	Adjective		Adverb
Cher,	dear,	dearly	Bas.,	low,	in a low voice
Faux,	false,	out of tune	Juste,	just,	correctly
Haut,	high,	loudly	Fort,	strong,	very; very much

Il vend cher.	He sells dear.
Elle chante faux.	She sings out of tune.
Vous parlez trop haut.	You speak too loud.
Parlez bas.	Speak in a low voice.
Elle joue juste.	She plays correctly.
Il gèle fort.	It freezes hard.

Comparison of Adverbs

1. Adverbs are compared in the same manner as adjectives:

Tard, late	plus tard, later	le plus tard, latest
Souvent, often	aussi souvent, as often	moins souvent, less often

2. The following are irregularly compared:

Bien, well	mieux, better	le mieux, best
Beaucoup, much	plus, more	le plus, most
Mal, badly	pis, worse	le pis, worst
Peu, little	moins, less	le moins, least

Adverbs Modifying Adverbs and Adjectives

Certain adverbs, when used to modify adjectives or other adverbs, assume in this connection a different meaning.

Bien fort, *or* très fort	Very strong
Fort bien, *or* très bien	Very well
Assez bien	Pretty well
Assez joli	Rather pretty
Un peu tard	Rather late
Trop tard	Too late
Si aimable	So amiable
Tout doucement	Quite gently

Adverbs of Negation

1. The adverbs of negation are:

Ne, not	Aucunement (ne), by no means
Pas (ne), not	Nullement (ne), by no means
Point (ne), not (with emphasis)	Que (ne), only, but; nothing but
Plus (ne), no longer	Guère (ne), but little; but few
Jamais (ne), never	Non, no

Adverbs of negation accompanying a verb, require **ne** before the verb.

The negative **pas** is generally omitted in the negative conjugation of the verbs **cesser,** to cease; **oser,** to dare; **pouvoir,** to be able; **savoir,** to know.

Elle ne cesse de pleurer.	She does not cease weeping.
Je n'ose parler de cela.	I dare not speak of that.
Je ne puis le faire.	I can not do it.
Je ne le puis.	I can not.
Je ne sais où il est.	I don't know where he is.

2. The adverbial phrase **du tout,** at all, is often added to negative adverbs to strengthen their sense, as, **pas du tout, point du tout. Du tout** is also used alone with the force of a negative.

Adverbs with a Regimen

The adverb, being equivalent to a preposition and its object, can have no regimen; its sense is complete without it. A few adverbs, however, retain the regimen of the adjectives from which they are formed; as, **conformément,** conformably; **antérieurement,** previously, etc.

Conformément à la loi	Conformably to law
Antérieurement au déluge	Previously to the deluge

Adverbs of Quantity

Adverbs of quantity are used with verbs and with nouns. When they are used with nouns they require the preposition **de** before the noun, and when the noun is not expressed, it is represented in the sentence by the pronoun **en**; as:

J'ai peu d'amis et vous‿en‿avez trop.	I have few friends, and you have too many.

The adverbs of quantity are:

Assez, enough
Autant, as much; as many
Beaucoup, bien, much; many
Combien, how much; how many
Davantage, more
Guère (ne), but little; but few
Moins, less; plus, more
Peu, little; few
Tant, so much; so many
Trop, too much; too many

The Preposition — La Préposition

Simple Prepositions

Après, after
A travers, through; across
Avant, before
Avec, with
Chez, at
Contre, against
Dans, in
Depuis, since
Derrière, behind
Dès, from
Devant, before
Durant, during
En, in
Entre, between
Envers, towards
Environ, about
Excepté, except
Hormis; except; but
Jusque, till; until
Malgré, in spite of
Moyennant, by means of
Nonobstant, notwithstanding

Simple Prepositions—Continued

Outre, besides	Sauf, safe
Par, by	Selon, according to
Parmi, among	Sous, under
Pendant, during	Suivant, according to
Pour, for	Sur, on; upon
Proche, near	Touchant, concerning
Sans, without	Vers, towards

Compound Prepositions

A cause de, on account of	Au lieu de, instead of
A côté de, by; next to	Au milieu de, in the middle of
A couvert de, secure from	Au moyen de, by means of
Avant de, before	Au niveau de, even with
A force de, by dint of	Au péril de, at the peril of
A l'abri de, sheltered from	Auprès de, near; by
A la faveur de, by means of	Au prix de, at the expense of
A la manière de, after the fashion	Au risque de, at the risk of
A la réserve de, excepting that	Au travers de, through; across
A l'égard de, with regard to	Aux dépens de, at the expense of
A l'exception de, excepted	En deçà de, on this side
A l'exclusion de, excepting	En dépit de, in spite of
De peur de, for fear of	En présense de, in presence of
A moins de, unless	Ensuite de, after
A raison de, at the rate of	Faute de, for want of
Au dedans de, within	Hors de, out of
Au dehors de, without	Le long de, along
Au delà de, on that side	Loin de, far from
Au-dessous de, under	Près de, near
Au-dessus de, upon	Quant‿à, as for; as to
Au-devant de, before	Vis-à-vis de, opposite to
Autour de, around	

Certain Prepositions

A, **at, in, to,** is used with reference to place and time.

A Boston comme à Paris	In Boston as in Paris
D'ici à Rome	From here to Rome
D'ici à quelques jours	A few days hence
Remettons cela à demain	Let us put that off until to-morrow
A temps; A l'heure	In time (not too late) On time (right time)

The preposition **à** expresses many relations; it denotes:

1. Direction towards an object; as:

Face à face; Vis‿à vis	Face to face; Opposite
Exposé au soleil	Exposed to the sun

2. Tendency in action; as:

Une disposition à se plaindre	A disposition to complain
La promptitude à agir	The readiness to act
Je commence à vous comprendre.	I begin to understand you.
Il aime à se faire valoir.	He likes to put himself forward.

3. That something is to be, or should be, done; as:

C'est‿une chose à faire.	It is a thing to be done.
L'avis n'est pas‿à mépriser.	The advice is not to be despised.
Terre à vendre ou à louer.	An estate for sale or to let.

4. That an action is in progress; as:

Ils sont‿à discuter l'affaire.	They are discussing the business.

5. Possession, and succession in turn:

Ce mouchoir est‿à moi.	This handkerchief belongs to me.
A qui est-ce à faire?	Whose deal is it?

6. À is used before the noun expressing the measure by which a thing is sold, and the manner in which, or the instrument by which a thing is accomplished; as:

Cela se vend au poids.	That is sold by weight.
Travailler à la journée, à l'aiguille.	To work by the day with the needle.
A la main	By hand

7. It is likewise used before the names of games after **jouer,** to play.

Jouer au trictrac, au billard	To play backgammon, billiards

Avant, devant, before. **Avant** denotes priority; **devant,** position; as:

Il est venu avant moi.	He came before I did.
Il s'est placé devant moi.	He placed himself before me.

Before the infinitive, **avant de** is used instead of **avant.**

Je vous verrai avant de sortir.	I shall see you before I go out.

Chez, with, among, at the house of. **Chez** may refer to one's home, office, store, or to one's country.

Chez nous, c'est bien différent.	With us, it is very different.
Chez les Romains, c'était la coutume.	Among the Romans, it was the custom.
Chacun est maître chez soi.	Everyone is master in his own house.
J'ai dîné chez lui; il était‿absent.	I dined at his house; he was absent.

De, of, from, is used with reference to place, time, cause, manner, etc.

De loin et de près	Far and near
De ce côté-ci et de ce côté-là	On this side and on that side
De tous côtés	From all sides
De porte⁀en porte	From door to door
De temps‿en temps	From time to time
De tout temps	At all times
De ma vie	In my life
De jour⁀et de nuit	By day and by night
De toute la nuit	All night long
De quelle manière?	In what manner?
De cette manière-ci	In this manner
De soi-même	Of one's own accord
De ma part	On my part; from me
Il est blâmé de sa négligence	He is blamed for his carelessness
De quoi s'agit-il?	What is it about?
De quoi se mêle-t-il?	What does he meddle with?

De expresses a variety of relations. It is used:

1. Before a past participle or adjective which refers to a preceding numeral adjective, a collective noun, or to the words **quelqu'un, personne,** and **rien,**

Y a-t-il quelqu'un de tué?	Is there anybody killed?
Il n'y a personne de tué.	There is nobody killed.
Combien y en‿a-t-il de blessés?	How many are wounded?
Il⁀y en‿a un grand nombre de blessés.	There are a great many wounded.

2. Before an adjective which refers to quelque chose, rien, que (interrogative), quoi; as:

Y a-t-il quelque chose de nouveau?	Is there anything new?
Il n'y a rien de nouveau.	There is nothing new.
Qu'y a-t-il de nouveau?	What is the news?
Quoi de plus beau!	What is more beautiful!

3. Before the name of a musical instrument, after the verb **jouer.**

Jouer du violon, de la harpe	To play on the violin, on the harp

4. To denote, cause, means, manner, result; as:

Frapper la terre du pied	To strike the earth with the foot
Se couvrir de gloire	To cover one's self with glory
Trembler de froid	To tremble with cold
Mourir de faim	To starve
Se mêler de quelque chose	To meddle with something
Que voulez-vous faire de cette lettre?	What will you do with that letter?

5. Between two nouns.

6. Before nouns taken in the partitive sense.

7. With adverbs of quantity.

8. Before the infinitive, after impersonal verbs, and after verbs expressing result.

9. Before the complement of certain adjectives.

10. After **plus** and **moins** before numeral adjectives.

11. Before the agent of a passive verb.

En, à, dans, in. À directs the mind to the locality; **dans** points to the inside of a place; **en** has a vague sense, and often forms with the noun which it precedes a kind of adverbial phrase:

Il est‿au magasin.	He is in (at) the store.
Il est dans le magasin.	He is in the store.
Le café est‿en magasin.	The coffee is stored.
A la campagne	In the country (not in town)
En campagne	In the field (military phrase)
Dans la dernière guerre	In the last war
En temps de guerre	In times of war

En is seldom used before a noun which is taken in the definite sense; the exceptions occur chiefly before nouns beginning with a vowel; as:

En l'honneur des dieux	In honor of the gods
En ce cas, *or* dans ce cas	In that case
En ce moment, *or* dans ce moment	At this moment

A la ville, en ville, dans la ville, **in town.** A la ville is used in opposition to à la campagne; en ville, **in town,** not at home; dans la ville, in the city. A la campagne comme à la ville, je me couche toujours tard. Mon père dîne‿en ville aujourd'hui. Il n'y a pas un homme dans la ville qui le sache.

En is used before the names of countries of the feminine gender, **à** and the articles before the names of countries of the masculine gender.

En France. En Angleterre	In *or* to France. In *or* to Eng.
Au Mexique. Au Canada	In *or* to Mex. In *or* to Can.
La France, l'Angleterre, *feminine*	le Mexique, le Canada, *masculine*

En is used before the names of three of the seasons: en été, in summer; en automne, in autumn; en hiver, in winter. A and the article are used before printemps: au printemps, in spring. We may also use dans and the article, and always do so when the names of the seasons are taken in a definite sense: Dans l'hiver de 1893, in the winter of 1893.

En, dans. When used with reference to time, **dans** precedes the epoch **at which,** and **en** the period **in which** anything has been, is to be, or can be done.

Je pars dans deux heures.	I leave in two hours (from now).
J'ai fait le trajet en deux heures.	I crossed over in two hours.

Par, by, through. Par la ville, through the city; par où, which way; par ici, this way; par là, that way; par amitié, through friendship.

Par is used before the unit of time by which anything is counted: par jour, a day; par mois, a month; par an, a year.

Six pour cent par an est l'intérêt légal dans l'État de New York.	Six per cent a year is the legal interest in the State of New York.

Par is used before the agent of a passive verb when the verb expresses action; but before **Dieu,** the preposition **de** is used.

Par is used after the verbs **commencer** and **finir** before the noun or verb which expresses the action with which we begin or finish.

Pour, afin de, in order to. **Pour** is used when the accomplishment of our purpose is within our reach; **afin de,** when the success of our effort is not sure.

Je suis venu pour vous dire cela.	I have come to tell you that.
Je lui ai montré la lettre afin de le décider à partir.	I showed him the letter in order to persuade him to leave.

The Conjunction — La Conjonction

List of Conjunctions

Afin que,[1] in order that
Ainsi, thus
Ainsi que / Aussi bien que } as well as
A moins que,[1] unless
Aussitôt que, as soon as
Avant que,[1] before
Bien que,[1] although
Car, for
Cependant, however
Depuis que, since (temporal)
Dès que, as soon as
Donc, then; therefore
Et, and
Jusqu'à ce que,[1] until
Lorsque, when
Mais, but
Néanmoins, nevertheless
Ni, neither; nor
Ou, or
Parce que, because
Pendant que, while
Pourquoi, why
Pourtant, however
Pour que,[1] in order that
Pourvu que,[1] provided
Puisque, since (casual)
Quand, when
Que, that
Quoique,[1] although
Sans que,[1] unless; without
Si, if; whether
Tant que, as soon as
Tandis que, while

Certain Conjunctions

Et, and, may, for emphasis, be repeated, but is generally used only between the last two of a succession of words.

Et le riche‿et le pauvre, etc.	Both the rich and the poor, etc.
Les plaintes, les regrets‿et les pleurs sont superflus.	Complaints, regrets, and tears are superfluous.

Ni, nor, is used to join similar parts of a negative proposition, or different propositions that express negation, as:

Il ne cultive ni les lettres ni les sciences.	He cultivates neither letters nor the sciences.
Il ne ressemble pas‿à son frère, ni de visage ni de caractère.	He does not resemble his brother, either in face or disposition.

Ni requires **ne** before a verb in a finite mood, but not before the infinitive, nor when it precedes **que** introducing a subordinate proposition.

Je ne vous loue ni ne vous blâme.	I neither praise nor blame you.
Je ne veux ni le louer ni le blâmer.	I will neither praise nor blame him.
Je ne veux ni qu'il lise ni qu'il‿écrive.	I will not allow him either to read or write.

---

[1] These conjunctions require the verb in the subjunctive mood.

Non plus is used with **ni** in the sense of either; as:

Ni moi non plus, ni mon frère non plus.	Nor I either, nor my brother either.

Parce que, because; **car,** for. **Car** is used when the speaker alleges his own reason for what precedes; **parce que,** when the cause lies in the thing itself; as:

Je n'achète pas de ce papier, car j'en‿ai assez.	I do not buy any of that paper, for I have enough.
Je n'achète pas de ce papier, parce qu'il boit.	I do not buy any of that paper, because it blots.

Parce que, par ce que. The first means because; the second, from what, by that which.

Je le veux, parce que cela est juste.	I will have it, because it is right.
Je le sais par ce qu'il m'a dit.	I know it from what he told me.

Parce que, because; **puisque,** since. The first introduces the cause for the action which precedes, the second refers to it as a consequence.

Je le veux, parce que cela est juste.	I will have it, because it is right.
Je le veux, puisque cela est juste.	I will have it, since it is right.

Quoique, although; **quoi que,** anything that, whatever.

Quoiqu'il soit riche, il n'est pas‿heureux.	Though he is rich, he is not happy.
Quoi que vous fassiez, faites le bien.	Whatever you may do, do it well.

Que used for Other Conjunctions

The conjunction **que** may take the place of many other conjunctions. It is used:

1. For **comme** after an adjective and after adverbs of time, in sentences like the following:

Malade qu'il‿est, il veut sortir.	Sick as he is, he wants to go out

2. For **combien,** in exclamatory sentences; as:

Que vous‿êtes bon!	How good you are!
Que de bonté vous‿avez pour moi!	How much kindness you show me!
Que de peine vous vous donnez!	How much trouble you take!

3. For **depuis,** after **il y a**; as:

Combien de temps y a-t-il que votre frère‿est parti?	How long is it since your brother started?

4. For **lorsque,** or **quand,** after **à peine,** and after adverbial expressions denoting time; as:

A peine fus-je arrivé qu'il vint me voir.	Scarcely had I arrived when he called on me.

It would be incorrect to use **lorsque** or **quand** in those sentences.

5. For **parce que,** after c'est; as:

S'il ne vient pas, c'est qu'il est malade.	If he does not come, it is because he is sick.

6. For **pourquoi,** at the head of an interrogative negative sentence; and then **pas** is suppressed; as:

Que ne puis-je vous aider?	Why can I not assist you?
Que ne vient-il?	Why does he not come?

This mode of questioning denotes regret or impatience.

7. For the conjunctions **afin que, jusqu'à ce que, à moins que, sans que,** etc.

8. To avoid the repetition of other conjunctions.

Que used Redundantly

Que is used redundantly:

1. Before the noun-subject, when the attribute introduced by **c'est** precedes the subject; as:

C'est un beau séjour que Paris.	Paris is a fine place to live in.
C'est une belle chose que la discrétion.	Discretion is a good thing.

When the subject is an infinitive, it is preceded by **que de.**

C'est un acte de charité que de dire la vérité.	It is an act of charity to tell the truth.

In such cases as the last, **que** may be omitted.

2. In exclamatory sentences, when the exclamative attribute precedes the subject; the verb is then omitted.

Quelle abnégation que la sienne!	What a self-denial his is *or* was.
Quel beau pays que la France!	What a beautiful country France is!
Quel homme que César!	What a man Cæsar was!

3. After **c'est-à-dire,** to introduce an explanatory sentence.

Nous sommes quittes maintenant, c'est-à-dire que je ne vous dois plus rien.	We are even now, that is to say, I do not owe you anything.

4. In connection with oui, si, non: oh que oui; oh que non; oh que si; je dis que oui; je crois que non, etc.

5. In elliptical expressions like the following:

Il aurait tout l'or du monde qu'il ne serait pas content.	He might have all the gold in the world, yet he would not be satisfied.

Which means, Il aurait tout l'or du monde (son caractère est tel) qu'il ne serait pas content.

Si, if; whether. **Si** elides the vowel only before **il** and **ils;** as: s'il, s'ils.

Si, if, is never followed by the future tense or the conditional mood. **Si** may be replaced by **que. Si** may be followed by the pluperfect tense of the subjunctive mood.

FINAL VOCABULARY

À, to, at, in, into
Abîmer, to ruin, to spoil
Accrocher, to hook, to hang upon a hook
Acier, *m.* steel
Actuellement, at present
Addition, *f.* addition, check (restaurant's)
Affaire, *f.* business, matter, lawsuit
Affiche, *f.* poster
Agir, to act
Agréable, pleasant, agreeable
Aider, to help, to assist
Aiguille, *f.* needle
Aimer, to love, to be fond of
Ainsi, so, thus
Ajouter, to add
Aller, to go, to be becoming
S'en aller, to go away, to leave
Allumer, to light, to kindle
Allumette, *f.* match
Alors, then, so
Ami, *m.* friend (male)
Amie, *f.* friend (female)
Amitié, *f.* friendship
Amour, *m.* love
Ananas, *m.* pineapple
Ane, *m.* ass, donkey
Apercevoir, to perceive, to notice
S'apercevoir, to notice, to find out
Apparaître, to appear
Appartenir, to belong
Appeler, to call, to send for
Apporter, to bring
Apprendre, to learn
S'appuyer, to lean, to rest
Après, after
Après-demain, the day after tomorrow
Arbre, *m.* tree
Argent, *m.* silver, money
Arracher, to tear, to pull away
Arrêt, *m.* stop, arrest
Arrêter, to stop, to arrest
Ascenseur, *m.* elevator
S'asseoir, to sit down
Assez, enough
Assiette, *f.* plate
Attendre, to wait for, to expect
Attraper, to catch
Aucun, none, not any
Aujourd'hui, to-day
Aussi, also
Autant, as much, as many
Auto, *f.* [short for automobile]
Autour, around
Autre, other
Avant, before, prior to
Avec, with
Avion, *m.* airplane
Avis, *m.* opinion, notice
Avoir, to have

Bague, *f.* ring
Baiser, *m.* kiss
Baisser, to let down, to lower
Balance, *f.* scales, balance
Balle, *f.* ball, bullet
Banc, *m.* bench
Banque, *f.* bank

Bas, *m.* stocking
Bas, low
Bateau, *m.* boat
Bâtiment, *m.* building
Battre, to beat, to defeat
Beau, beautiful, handsome
Beaucoup, much, many
Besoin, *m.* need
Bête, *f.* beast, animal
Beurre, *m.* butter
Bibliothèque, *f.* library
Bien, well
Bientôt, soon
Billet, *m.* note, ticket, billet
Blanc, white
Bleu, blue
Bœuf, *m.* ox, beef
Boire, to drink
Bois, *m.* wood
Boîte, *f.* box, case
Bon, good, kind
Bonheur, *m.* happiness
Bonjour, good day, good morning
Bonsoir, good evening, good night
Bonté, *f.* goodness, kindness
Bouche, *f.* mouth
Bougie, *f.* candle
Bras, *m.* arm
Brosse, *f.* brush
Bruit, *m.* noise
Brûler, to burn
Brun, brown
Bureau, *m.* desk, office, bureau

Cacher, to hide, to conceal
Cadeau, *m.* present, gift
Café, *m.* coffee, café
Calcul, *m.* calculation, arithmetic
Calendrier, *m.* calendar
Campagne, *f.* country, campaign
Canard, *m.* duck
Carte, *f.* card, map
Casser, to break
Ce, this, that
Cela (ça), that
Celui, that, the one
Cent, one hundred
Cerise, *f.* cherry
Chacun, each one
Chaise, *f.* chair
Chambre, *f.* room, bedroom
Champ, *m.* field
Chanter, to sing
Chapeau, *m.* hat
Chaque, each, every
Chat, *m.* cat
Chaud, warm, hot
Chemin, *m.* way, road
Cher, dear, expensive
Chercher, to look for
Cheval, *m.* horse
Cheveu, *m.* hair
Chez, at (to) one's house
Chien, *m.* dog
Chiffre, *m.* figure, number
Choisir, to choose, to select
Chose, *f.* thing
Ciel, *m.* sky, heaven
Cinq, five
Cinquante, fifty
Ciseaux, *m. pl.* scissors
Citron, *m.* lemon
Clair, clear, light
Clef, *f.* key
Cœur, *m.* heart
Coffre, *m.* trunk, chest, box
Comme, as, like
Comment, how
Commode, *f.* chest of drawers
Commode, convenient

Compter, to count, to consider
Conduire, to lead, to drive
Congé, *m.* leave, day-off
Connaître, to know, to be acquainted
Contre, against
Coq, *m.* cock, rooster
Corps, *m.* body, corps
Côté, *m.* side, direction
Se coucher, to go to bed, to lie down
Coudre, to sew
Couler, to flow, to run
Coup, *m.* blow, stroke
Couper, to cut
Cour, *f.* yard, court
Courir, to run
Coûter, to cost
Couverture, *f.* covering, blanket
Couvrir, to cover
Craindre, to fear
Crayon, *m.* pencil
Crier, to cry out, to shout, to scream
Croire, to believe, to think
Croix, *f.* cross
Cueillir, to pick, to pluck
Cuillère, *f.* spoon
Cuire, to cook
Cuisine, *f.* kitchen, cookery
Cuisinière, *f.* cook (female)

Dame, *f.* married lady
Dans, in, within, into
Davantage, more
De, of, out of, from
Debout, upright
Déchirer, to tear
Décider, to decide
Se décider, to make up one's mind
Dedans, inside, within
Dehors, outside, without
Déjà, already
Déjeuner, *m.* breakfast
Demander, to ask, to request
Demeurer, to live, to reside
Demi, half
Demoiselle, *f.* young girl, young lady
Dent, *f.* tooth
Dépense, *f.* expense
Dépenser, to spend
Depuis, since
Dernier, last
Derrière, behind
Des, some
Désormais, henceforth
Dessous, under, below
Dessus, on, above
Deux, two
Devant, before, in front of
Devenir, to become
Devoir, to have to, to owe
Devoir, *m.* duty, homework
Dieu, *m.* God
Difficile, difficult
Dimanche, *m.* Sunday
Dîner, *m.* dinner
Dire, to say
Dix, ten
Doigt, *m.* finger
Domestique, *m.* & *f.* servant
Donc, therefore, accordingly
Donner, to give
Dont, whose, of which
Dormir, to sleep
Dos, *m.* back
Doux, sweet, soft

Douze, twelve
Droit, straight, right
Dur, hard, tough
Durer, to last

Échapper, to escape
Éclairer, to light, to illuminate
École, *f.* school
Écouter, to listen
Écrire, to write
Effacer, to erase, to eclipse
Égal, equal, alike
Égarer, to mislead, to mislay
Église, *f.* church
Élève, *m. & f.* pupil, student
Élever, to bring up, to rear, to erect
Elle, she
Empêcher, to prevent
Emporter, to take away
En, in, any, of him (her, it, them)
Encore, yet, still, more
Encre, *f.* ink
S'endormir, to fall asleep
Enfant, *m. & f.* child
Enlever, to take off, to carry away
Ensemble, together
Entendre, to hear
Entre, between
Entrée, *f.* entrance, entering
Entretien, *m.* talk, maintenance
Envoyer, to send
Épaule, *f.* shoulder
Épingle, *f.* pin
Escalier, *m.* stairs
Espoir, *m.* hope
Essuie-mains, *m.* towel
Essuyer, to wipe, to dry
Et, and
Étage, *m.* story, floor
État, *m.* state, condition
Été, *m.* summer
Éteindre, to put out, to extinguish
Étranger, foreign
Être, to be
Étroit, narrow
Étudier, to study
S'éveiller, to wake up
Exiger, to require, to demand
Exprimer, to express

Fabrique, *f.* factory
Facile, easy
Façon, *f.* manner, way, shaped
Faim, *f.* hunger
Faire, to make, to do
Faute, *f.* fault, error, mistake
Femme, *f.* woman, wife
Fenêtre, *f.* window
Fer, *m.* iron
Fermer, to shut, to close
Feu, *m.* fire
Fier, proud
Fil, *m.* thread
Fille, *f.* girl, daughter
Fils, *m.* son
Fin, *f.* end
Fin, thin
Finir, to finish, to end
Fleur, *f.* flower
Fond, *m.* bottom
Force, *f.* strength, force
Fort, strong
Fourchette, *f.* fork
Frais, cool, fresh
Frapper, to strike, to hit
Frère, *m.* brother
Froid, cold

Front, *m.* forehead
Fumer, to smoke

Gant, *m.* glove
Garçon, *m.* boy, bachelor, waiter
Gare, *f.* railroad-station
Gauche, left, awkward
Genou, *m.* knee
Gens, *m.* & *f. pl.* people, folk
Glace, *f.* ice, mirror
Gorge, *f.* throat
Goût, *m.* taste
Goûter, to taste, to appreciate
Goutte, *f.* drop
Grand, great, large
Grand'mère, *f.* grandmother
Grand-père, *m.* grandfather
Gras, fat, greasy, rich
Gros, big, stout, thick
Guère, not much, scarcely

Habile, skilful, clever, able
Habiller, to dress
Habit, *m.* clothes, dress-coat
Habiter, to inhabit, to live in
Habitude, *f.* habit
Se hâter, to hurry
Haut, high
Heure, *f.* hour
Heureux, happy
Hier, yesterday
Hiver, *m.* winter
Homme, *m.* man
Hôte, *m.* host; guest
Huile, *f.* oil
Huit, eight
Humide, damp

Ici, here
Ignorer, to be unaware of
Île, *f.* island
Incendie, *m.* fire, conflagration
Infirme, invalid, disabled
Ingénieur, *m.* engineer
Inquiétude, *f.* anxiety, uneasiness
Inutile, useless
Ivre, drunk.

Jamais, never, forever
Jambe, *f.* leg
Jardin, *m.* garden
Jaune, yellow
Jeter, to throw, to hurl
Jeu, *m.* play, game
Jeudi, *m.* Thursday
Jeune, young
Joie, *f.* joy
Joli, pretty, nice
Jouer, to play
Jour, *m.* day

Là, there
Laine, *f.* wool
Laisser, to leave behind, to let alone
Lait, *m.* milk
Langue, *f.* tongue, language
Lapin, *m.* rabbit
Large, broad, wide
Laver, to wash
Le, the
Leur, their, to them
Se lever, to rise, to get up
Libre, free
Ligne, *f.* line
Lire, to read
Lit, *m.* bed
Livre, *m.* book

Loi, *f.* law
Loin, far
Lorsque, when
Lumière, *f.* light
Lundi, *m.* Monday
Lune, *f.* moon
Lunettes, *f. pl.* eye-glasses

Madame, *f.* Madam, Mrs.
Magasin, *m.* store
Main, *f.* hand
Maintenant, now
Mais, but
Maison, *f.* house
Maître, *m.* master, owner, teacher
Mal, *m.* evil, harm, pain, ache
Mal, badly, poorly
Malade, sick, ill
Malgré, in spite of
Malheur, *m.* misfortune, accident
Manger, to eat
Manteau, *m.* cloak, overcoat
Marché, *m.* market
Marcher, to walk
Mardi, *m.* Tuesday
Mari, *m.* husband
Matin, *m.* morning
Mauvais, bad, ill
Médecin, *m.* physician, doctor
Meilleur, better, best
Même, same, even (*adv.*)
Mener, to take (to a place), to lead
Menton, *m.* chin
Mer, *f.* sea
Merci, thanks
Mercredi, *m.* Wednesday
Mère, *f.* mother
Mettre, to put, to place, to put on
Midi, *m.* noon, south
Mien, mine
Mieux, better
Mille, thousand; mile
Minuit, *m.* midnight
Moi, I, me
Moins, less
Mois, *m.* month
Moitié, *f.* half
Mon, my
Monsieur, *m.* gentleman, Mr.
Morceau, *m.* piece
Mort, dead
Mot, *m.* word
Mouchoir, *m.* handkerchief
Mourir, to die
Mur, *m.* wall

Nager, to swim
Nappe, *f.* table-cloth
Né, born
Neuf, nine
Neuf, new
Nez, *m.* nose
Ni . . . ni . . ., neither . . . nor . . .
Noir, black
Nom, *m.* name
Non, no
Notre, our
Nôtre, ours
Nous, we
Nouveau, new, recent
Nuit, *f.* night

Oeil, *m.* eye
Oeuf, *m.* egg
On, one, they, we
Onze, eleven
Or, *m.* gold
Oreille, *f.* ear
Ôter, to take off, to remove

Ou, or
Où, where
Oui, yes
Ouvrir, to open

Pain, *m.* bread
Papier, *m.* paper
Par, by, through
Parce que, because
Parent, *m.* relative
Parents, *m. pl.* parents
Parler, to speak, to talk
Partie, *f.* part, party, game
Partir, to leave, to depart
Pas, *m.* step, pace
Patrie, *f.* fatherland
Pauvre, poor
Payer, to pay
Pays, *m.* country, land
Pendant, during
Pendule, *f.* clock
Perdre, to lose
Père, *m.* father
Personne, nobody
Petit, small, little
Peu, few, little
Peut-être, perhaps, maybe
Pied, *m.* foot
Pire, worse, worst
Plat, *m.* dish
Plein, full
Pleurer, to cry, to weep
Plume, *f.* feather, pen
Plus, more
Poche, *f.* pocket
Poire, *f.* pear
Pomme, *f.* apple
Porte, *f.* door
Porter, to carry, to wear
Pour, for
Pourquoi, why, what for
Pouvoir, to be able
Premier, first
Prendre, to take
Près de, near, next to
Presque, almost
Prier, to pray, to beg
Prix, *m.* price
Se promener, to take a walk
Prune, *f.* plum
Puis, then, after that
Punir, to punish

Quand, when
Quarante, forty
Quatorze, fourteen
Quatre, four
Que, that, than, whom, which, what
Quel, what, what sort of
Quelque, some
Quelqu'un, somebody
Qui, who, that, whom, which
Quinze, fifteen
Quoi, what
Quoique, although

Rarement, seldom
Règle, *f.* rule, ruler
Remplir, to fill, to fill up
Rencontrer, to meet
Rendre, to return, to give back
Répondre, to reply, to answer
Rester, to remain, to stay

Revenir, to come again, to come back
Rire, to laugh
Rond, round
Rouge, red

Sable, *m.* sand
Sac, *m.* bag
Saisir, to seize
Saison, *f.* season
Sale, dirty
Saluer, to greet
Samedi, *m.* Saturday
Sans, without
Sauter, to jump, to leap
Savoir, to know
Savon, *m.* soap
Seize, sixteen
Selon, according to
Semaine, *f.* week
Sentir, to feel, to smell
Sept, seven
Seul, alone, only
Si, if, whether, yes, so
Six, six
Soie, *f.* silk
Soif, *f.* thirst
Soir, *m.* evening
Soleil, *m.* sun
Son, his, her, its
Sortie, *f.* exit
Soulier, *m.* shoe
Sous, under
Souvent, often
Sucre, *m.* sugar
Sud, *m.* south
Sur, on, upon
Sûr, sure

Tableau, *m.* painting, picture
Tâcher, to try, to endeavor
Tant, so much, so many
Tante, *f.* aunt
Tard, late
Tasse, *f.* cup
Temps, *m.* time, weather
Tenir, to hold
Terre, *f.* earth, land, soil
Tête, *f.* head
Tirer, to pull, to shoot, to fire
Toit, *m.* roof
Tomber, to fall
Travail, *m.* work
Treize, thirteen
Trente, thirty
Très, very
Trois, three
Trop, too, too much, too many
Trouver, to find
Tu, thou, you
Tuer, to kill

Un, a, one
Utile, useful

Vache, *f.* cow
Vendredi, *m.* Friday
Venir, to come
Vent, *m.* wind
Verre, *m.* glass
Vers, toward, to, about
Verser, to pour
Vert, green
Viande, *f.* meat
Vide, empty

Vie, *f.* life
Vieux, old, aged
Vin, *m.* wine
Vingt, twenty
Visage, *m.* face
Vivant, alive
Vivre, to live
Voici, here is, here are
Voilà, there is, there are
Voir, to see
Voisin, *m.* neighbor
Voix, *f.* voice
Volonté, *f.* will
Votre, your
Vôtre, yours
Vouloir, to want, to wish
Vous, you
Vrai, true

Zéro, *m.* zero, naught

INDEX